COMMUNITY, HOME, AND IDENTITY

Law, Property and Society

Series Editor:
Robin Paul Malloy

The Law, Property and Society series examines property in terms of its ability to foster democratic forms of governance, and to advance social justice. The series explores the legal infrastructure of property in broad terms, encompassing concerns for real, personal, intangible, intellectual and cultural property, as well as looking at property related financial markets. The series is edited by Robin Paul Malloy, and book proposals are welcome from all interested authors.

Robin Paul Malloy is E.I. White Chair and Distinguished Professor of Law, and the Kauffman Professor of Entrepreneurship and Innovation at Syracuse University College of Law, USA. He is Director of the Center on Property, Citizenship, and Social Entrepreneurism. He is also Professor of Economics (by courtesy appointment) in the Maxwell School of Citizenship and Public Affairs, Syracuse University. Professor Malloy writes extensively on law and market theory and on real estate transactions and development. He has authored eight books (one now in its third edition and another in its second edition), and edited seven additional books. He has also written more than 30 scholarly articles, and contributed to 12 other books. His recent books include: LAW AND MARKET ECONOMY (2000, in English and translated into Spanish and Chinese); LAW IN A MARKET CONTEXT (2004); and REAL ESTATE TRANSACTIONS 3RD EDITION (with James C. Smith, 2007).

Community, Home, and Identity

Edited by

MICHAEL DIAMOND
Georgetown University Law Center, USA

TERRY L. TURNIPSEED
Syracuse University, USA

Routledge
Taylor & Francis Group
LONDON AND NEW YORK

First published 2012 by Ashgate Publishing

2 Park Square, Milton Park, Abingdon, Oxon OX14 4RN
711 Third Avenue, New York, NY 10017, USA

Routledge is an imprint of the Taylor & Francis Group, an informa business

First issued in paperback 2016

British Library Cataloguing in Publication Data
Community, home, and identity. -- (Law, property and society)
1. Property. 2. Home ownership--Law and legislation.
3. Identity (Philosophical concept) 4. Sociological
jurisprudence.
I. Series II. Diamond, Michael R. III. Turnipseed, Terry L.
346'.04-dc23

Library of Congress Cataloging-in-Publication Data
Community, home, and identity / [edited] by Michael Diamond and Terry L.Turnipseed.
p. cm. -- (Law, property and society)
Includes bibliographical references and index.
ISBN 978-1-4094-3854-0 (hardback)
1. Real property--United States. 2. Home ownership--Law and legislation--United States. 3. Real property--England. 4. Home ownership--Law and legislation--England. 5. Identity (Philosophical concept) 6. Sociological jurisprudence. I. Diamond, Michael R. II. Turnipseed, Terry L.

K736.C65 2012
343.42'025--dc23

ISBN 978-1-4094-3854-0 (hbk)
ISBN 978-1-138-25021-5 (pbk)

Contents

List of Contributors

Susan Bright is a Professor of Land Law at New College, Oxford University and Part-time Chair of the Residential Property Tribunal Service. In addition to writing in the broad area of landlord and tenant law, she has a particular interest in the way that property law interacts with the use of home.

Michael Diamond is a Professor of Law at the Georgetown University Law Center and is Director of Georgetown's Harrison Institute for Housing and Community Development. His research focuses on the intersection of law and poverty.

Vincent Di Lorenzo is a Professor of Law at St John's University School of Law and Senior Fellow at the Vincentian Center, St John's University.

Andrew Hayward is a Lecturer in Law at Durham Law School. He specializes in family property law and, specifically, the judicial application of trust principles to ownership disputes over the family home.

Nicholas Hopkins is a Professor of Law at the University of Southampton. He specializes in family property law and, specifically, the judicial application of trust principles to ownership disputes over the family home.

Antonia Layard is Professor of Law and Geography at Birmingham Law School, University of Birmingham. Her research interests are in law and geography, in particular investigating the construction of "the local" and place-making in law and society.

David Reiss is a Professor of Law at Brooklyn Law School. His research focuses on the secondary mortgage market.

Allison Brownell Tirres is an Assistant Professor at DePaul University College of Law where she teaches and writes in the areas of property, immigration, and legal history.

Terry L. Turnipseed is an Associate Professor of Law and an Associate Professor of Engineering and Computer Science (by courtesy appointment) at Syracuse University. His research focuses on Article I constitutional law, eminent domain, sexuality and the law, spousal property rights upon death, trust fiduciary law, transfer taxation, and the separation of church and state.

Sarah Waldek is a Professor of Law and the Robert Diab Scholar at Seton Hall University School of Law where she teaches estates and trusts and property. Her scholarship focuses on how the law influences behavior and shapes social and familial norms.

Preface

Michael Diamond

Community. Home. Identity. These words evoke ideas that are central to any society. As such, they have concerned scholars from a variety of fields for some time. Legal scholars, sociologists, anthropologists, psychologists, and economists, among others, have studied the impacts of home and community on one's identity and how one's identity is manifested in one's home and in one's community. How does the law affect these essential societal issues? More fundamentally, how *should* the law, if at all, help to shape them? There are varying legal and public policy implications depending on the answers to these questions and on how the terms community, home, and identity, are interpreted.

In this book we present a compilation of several papers that were presented during a two-day conference at the Georgetown University Law Center. The conference, the first annual meeting of the Association for Law, Property, and Society, drew more than 140 scholars from around the world. The chapters in this volume have been updated and revised and present the work of some of the leading thinkers about the connections between community, home, and identity. Several chapters address how the law, and lawyers, contribute (or detract) from the creation and maintenance of community and, in some cases, to the conscious destruction of communities. Others examine the degree of protection offered to individual and group identities through rules related to the title of property and use of such concepts as "home" and "identity property."

The book begins with a look at how, upon the advent, in late nineteenth century, of technological modernization that would affect local growth and property values, lawyers used the law to reshape a longstanding community. In her historical essay, Allison Brownell Tirres takes us through the transformation of El Paso, after the coming of the railroad to southwest Texas. From its beginnings as a town with a mixed and integrated culture and politics, comprised of Anglo- and Mexican-American residents sharing space and power, Tirres points to the fact that "in the span of only twenty years, El Paso changed from a close-knit, multicultural frontier community to a burgeoning, increasingly racially-segregated border metropolis." This, according to Tirres, was the result not merely of demographic changes, but rather of a planned and carefully implemented transformation using the law, particularly property law, as the catalyst. As such, her narrative illustrates the pattern of much of the racial and ethnic separation that followed.

This theme is continued, in slightly different fashion and in modern times, in Antonia Layard's chapter concerning community autonomy in the United

Kingdom and the resulting "right to exclude." Layard suggests that there is a current "vogue" in the UK for localism, as a result of a "rare cross-party consensus over devolving more power to town and county halls." This vogue, designed to give localities greater authority in planning and in shaping their own communities, has, on the one hand, a decidedly communitarian aspect; the devolving of power from a distant, somewhat anonymous, central national or regional authority to locals to shape and preserve their neighborhoods. This same localism, however, also has the seeds of a more pernicious separatism—Layard's right to exclude. She points out that "land use regulations can mean that 'outsiders' and 'others' find it difficult to live where they would otherwise choose," and asks how the balance between exclusion and preservation ought to be struck in society today.

Michael Diamond approaches this theme from another perspective. He addresses the destruction of community, in his case, communities of highly concentrated poverty. The destruction takes place, at least nominally, in the service of assisting the poor residents of such communities by creating mixed-income communities on the sites of formerly high-concentration, low-income neighborhoods or by relocating low-income residents to existing mixed-income communities. After discussing the social problems associated with high concentrations of poor residents in a geographic area, Diamond looks at several federal programs designed to alleviate these problems and assesses their effectiveness. He points out "a certain irony" in the governmental efforts to de-concentrate poverty since he claims it was governmental policies that, at least in part, created the concentrations in the first instance. Diamond critiques the de-concentration programs on both practical and conceptual grounds, but is primarily concerned with "the social, cultural, and political ramifications of destroying existing communities." After discussing the problems with the de-concentration policies currently in place, he offers alternatives to the destruction of high-concentration poor communities.

The next chapter examines affordable home-ownership in England. In doing so, Susan Bright and Nicholas Hopkins explore the methods and effects of subsidized homeownership under England's "Right to Buy" regime that offers council tenants (the rough equivalent of public housing tenants in the United States) the opportunity to purchase their dwelling unit. Bright and Hopkins are concerned with "the twin policy objectives of delivering the benefits of homeownership to the individual whilst creating sustainable mixed communities." They review the mechanics of providing subsidies, before turning to benefits of homeownership. In the case of individuals, they look not only at the possibility of wealth creation, but also at the sense of the new owner as having "arrived" and of having the "security of place." They then expand their view to the community benefits of homeownership. They cite a government report pointing out that filling the "aspirations gap" of those who wish to own homes is not sufficient reason for the public subsidy. There must also be a benefit to society. The programs that result from benefit trade-offs between individual and society requires, according to Bright and Hopkins, a re-examination of the meaning of homeownership.

David Reiss returns the discussion of governmental housing policy to the United States where he attempts to make sense of a "bewildering array" of federal housing programs. He, too, points out a lack of clarity and contradiction in government housing policy. Reiss seeks to identify "first principles" in US housing policy, "because our muddled housing agenda has left debates surrounding housing policy confused and unproductive." To do this, he has created a taxonomy of housing "ethics" and first principles, with a "goal of developing a more systematic approach to the evaluation of housing policy." In this way, he believes, one can determine whether individual programs are consistent with the first principles and whether programs, in the aggregate, are coherent or working at cross purposes.

Ethics is used in a different sense by Vincent Di Lorenzo. His chapter focuses on the issue of consumer protection in mortgage lending. Di Lorenzo states that a nation's "ethical viewpoint embraced by a society is frequently reflected in its laws." Given this premise, he asks "whether U.S. society sanctions business practices involving residential property which extract profits from individuals who are unable to protect themselves?" He answers this question in the negative and points to a long history of consumer protection for what he calls "an essential public good," one's home. Nevertheless, Di Lorenzo points out a "schism" between Congress and the federal agencies that regulate banks, with Congress recognizing the need for governmental intervention while the agencies rely on "market discipline" to address abusive lending practices. While it is possible that the agencies have failed to effectuate Congressional intent, Di Lorenzo believes that "the actions and viewpoints of Congress ... are a reflection of the ethical standards accepted by U. S. society, namely that business entities should not profit by inflicting significant financial injury on vulnerable individuals."

In our penultimate chapter, Sarah Waldeck introduces her concept of "identity property" which, she says, "is personhood property ratcheted down." Identity property is property that is "linked to one's sense of self and family" and is valued for that reason rather than its economic worth. Waldeck is concerned when property of high economic value is left to several persons who value it also as identity property. She uses a family cottage as an example. While the traditional legal remedy for co-owners of property who cannot agree on its use or disposition has been partition, Waldeck criticizes this remedy as being far too blunt. She believes the law is an inadequate discipline for the resolution of disputes between co-owners of identity property. She seeks ways for the law to foster cooperation between disputing co-owners of identity property and asks us to consider, for example, "what might unfold between co-tenants if partition actions involving identity property had three potential remedies instead of just two: a partition in kind, a partition by sale *and* temporal partition."

Andrew Hayward continues the theme of relational property by providing an English perspective on issues concerning the family home. His chapter revolves around the meaning society attaches to the concept of "home." The problem arises for Hayward in the context of "joint legal title disputes arising between cohabitants or platonic home-shares." How should the property be allocated when such relationships end acrimoniously? Or, if the relationship ends in death, who, between the former cohabitant who had no legal title or the heirs of the title-holding decedent, ought to have a stronger claim? Should, and if so, how ought, society distinguish between a home and a commercial enterprise? In attempting to answer these questions, Hayward analyzes the House of Lords' decision in *Stack v Dowden* in which Baroness Hale makes the home versus commercial enterprise distinction and claims that "in law 'context is everything.'" While Hayward praises the *Stack* opinion for "highlighting the need for reform … of this notoriously complex area," he nevertheless criticizes the majority opinion for its "potential to confuse rather than clarify" the law.

As can be seen, the relationship between community, home, and identity is both broad and multilayered. The chapters in this book have carved out several areas of this fascinating inquiry and dug quite deeply into them. We hope the work will spur debate and further thought in the field.

Acknowledgements

I would like to acknowledge the extraordinary research assistance of Jared Lamb and Thomas Davison. Without their tireless and exceptional efforts, this volume would not have been possible. I would also like to thank the Georgetown University Law Center for supporting the first annual conference of the Association for Law, Property, and Society, and Georgetown's Department of Academic Conferences and Continuing Legal Education for its efforts in making the conference a success.

MD

I would like to thank my mother, Dr. Jorja Turnipseed for her steadfast love and support, and my wonderful research assistant, Sherry Conaway, for her tireless efforts on this book.

TT

Chapter 1

Bordered Lands: Land Use, Legal Culture, and Community Development in the Nineteenth-Century Southwest

Allison Brownell Tirres

The county of El Paso, Texas, in the year 1870 was a quintessential frontier community. Located in the far western tip of Texas, it was difficult to reach from any major metropolis. Although officially a part of Texas, the lack of any railroad connection and the presence of hostile Indian tribes in this period made for a long, dangerous journey to and from other population centers in the region. El Paso was also a community on the borderline, bordered to the west by New Mexico, and to the south by Mexico.[1] The population of only 4,000 was predominantly of Mexican descent.[2] Many of its residents had lived in the region since before the Mexican-American War, when the US gained the El Paso area (and more than one-third of Mexico's northern territories) in the Treaty of Guadalupe-Hidalgo.[3] Due in large part to its isolation and its preexisting Mexican legal and cultural traditions, El Paso in 1870 was a hybrid place, where American law was present but practiced

---

1 While we are accustomed to considering the Rio Grande a north-south divide between the United States and Mexico, in the El Paso region it is actually more accurately described as an east-west divide. What we today call El Paso County, Texas, developed out of the Spanish colonial town of El Paso del Norte (today's Ciudad Juárez, Chihuahua, Mexico) and its surrounding settlements. The primary settlement up until the 1880s was El Paso del Norte, on the west bank of the Rio Grande. Land on the east bank, where the city of El Paso, Texas, is now located, was, during the Spanish colonial period, only sparsely inhabited and used mostly as a source of firewood and pasture lands for residents on the other side of the river. The terminology becomes clearer after 1888, when El Paso del Norte was renamed Ciudad Juárez, after the Mexican President Benito Juárez, who lived for some time in the city that now bears his name. For the geography and development of the sister cities of Juárez and El Paso, *see* Milo Kearney & Anthony Knopp, Border Cuates: A History of the US-Mexican Twin Cities (1995).

2 J. Lawrence McConville, A History of Population in the El Paso-Ciudad Juárez Area, 76, 80 (1966) (unpublished master's thesis, The University of New Mexico) (on file with author).

3 Treaty of Guadalupe Hidalgo, Feb. 2, 1848, US-Mex., art. VIII, 9 Stat. 922. *See* Richard Griswold del Castillo, The Treaty of Guadalupe Hidalgo: A Legacy of Conflict (1990).

in Spanish, where those of Mexican and American descent served side-by-side in the institutions that governed the county, and residents still celebrated Mexican Independence Day along with the Fourth of July.[4]

El Paso, Texas, in the year 1890 was a very different place. The population of the county had quadrupled, to more than 15,000. The city of El Paso saw even greater population growth, from a few hundred residents in 1870 to more than 10,000 in 1890.[5] The majority was still of Mexican descent, but now the population of those of Anglo-American descent was growing steadily.[6] Travelers could now reach El Paso by not one, but four different major railway lines, which connected the county not only to other parts of Texas, but also to San Francisco, St Louis, and Mexico City. These demographic changes had ramifications for legal culture. The old adobe courthouse, where those of Mexican and American descent had sat side-by-side to administer justice, was now replaced by an imposing brick edifice in a European style, where those who spoke only Spanish were no longer allowed to serve on juries as they had for decades before. By the end of the decade, juries were no longer a Mexican-American majority, trials were no longer conducted largely in Spanish, and residents were chastised for celebrating Mexican holidays. The balance of power had shifted from one racial/ethnic group to another. In the span of only 20 years, El Paso changed from a close-knit, multicultural frontier community to a burgeoning, increasingly racially segregated border metropolis.

El Paso County was not the only community to undergo dramatic change after the arrival of the railroads.[7] This is a familiar story in nineteenth-century history, of the ways that the railroads altered the character of the cities and towns they passed through, creating boom towns out of previously isolated enclaves.[8] The

---

4 *See* W.H. Timmons, El Paso: A Borderlands History 135–168, 175 (1990); Allison Brownell Tirres, American Law Comes to the Border: Law and Colonization on the US/ Mexico Divide, 1848–1890, 1–20, 116–162 (2008) (unpublished Ph.D dissertation, Harvard University) (on file with author).

5 US Bureau of the Census, Report on the Population of the United States, Eleventh Census, 1890 (1895), 31, 41–42, 241, 332.

6 Oscar J. Martinez, Border Boom Town: Ciudad Juarez Since 1848, 159 (1978); McConville, *supra* note 2, at 76, 80.

7 *See* David Hamer, New Towns in the New World: Images and Perceptions of the Nineteenth-Century Urban Frontier 113–138 (1990); Richard White, "It's Your Misfortune and None of My Own": A New History of the American West 298–327 (1991); Carol A. O'Conner, *A Region of Cities*, *in* The Oxford Encyclopedia of the American West 535–563 (Clyde A. Milner, II, Carol A. O'Connor & Martha A. Sandweiss, eds, 1994).

8 *See, e.g.*, William G. Thomas, Lawyering for the Railroad: Business, Law, and Power in the New South (1999) (noting the transformation in southern towns once the railroads ended their isolation). There is an extensive historical literature on the development of the railroads in the nineteenth and twentieth centuries and their effects on urban growth. *See, e.g.*, William Cronon, Nature's Metropolis: Chicago and the Great West (1994); Robert Reigel, The Story of the Western Railroads (1926); White, *supra* note 7, at 246–258. It is also important to note that the railroads did not just encourage the growth of small

scholarship tends to portray these things as inevitably linked: the railroads brought greater settlement, which changed the nature of formerly small towns, contributing to their modernization and urbanization. While there is truth to this general characterization, it is also clearly deficient.[9] We must go beyond demographic determinism if we are to understand the ways that communities change over time. It was not merely the arrival of more people that changed El Paso. These changes were the product of specific moves by local residents to reshape the area, particularly to whitewash its Mexican past while also promoting its transnational future as a cross-border trade hub.[10] Law and lawyers were key elements in the transformation of El Paso from an isolated, frontier community to a burgeoning border metropolis. The legal profession paved the way for the railroads' arrival by altering patterns of land use. As local politicians and merchants then sought to attract more settlers to the area, they targeted the area's unique legal culture as a problem, seeking to change not just the way land was used and owned—from communally to individually—but also to change the way law was practiced and enforced. This involved moving the county seat from a Mexican-American town to a predominantly Anglo-American one and tearing down the old adobe courthouse. These moves shifted the balance of power in the county, leading to greater segregation not just in the courthouse, but also in neighborhoods, schools, and social venues. Land ownership and patterns of land use were both reflections of and contributors to the creation of greater inequality in the community.

In many respects, this is a distinctly nineteenth-century story. It portrays community development in a particular era, when western land was still cheap and plentiful, the railroads were a major innovation, and racial hierarchies were firmly entrenched, if sometimes more fluid than we might expect. Yet there are remarkable overlaps with contemporary society. We continue to live in a world in

---

towns and cities, but also supported the growth of major urban areas. As historian Keith L. Bryant, Jr, notes, "[T]he urbanization of the West reflected the coming of the railways, with cities as diverse as Dallas, Los Angeles, Tacoma, Spokane, and Denver largely owing their existence, and their growth, to the presence of railways tapping their hinterlands." Keith L. Bryant, Jr, *Entering the Global Economy, in* The Oxford Encyclopedia of the American West (Clyde A. Milner, II, Carol O'Connor & Martha A. Sandweiss, eds, 1994), at 224.

9 *See, e.g.*, Davíd Montejano, Anglos and Mexicans in the Making of Texas, 1836–1986 76 (1987) ("Facilitated by an expanding railroad network, the new settlements basically Americanized the old Spanish-Mexican towns of the region"); Patricia Nelson Limerick, The Legacy of Conquest: The Unbroken Past of the American West 62 (1988) ("In a variety of ways—huge grants to subsidize railroad construction, grants to states, the distribution of land warrants to veterans, the sale of tracts made available by further reductions of Indian reservations—much desirable land was taken from the reach of homesteaders"). I would argue that the passive voice in these examples is not just a stylistic choice, but also an indicator of how much more there is to understand about the people behind these processes of colonization in the west.

10 *See* William Deverell, Whitewashed Adobe: The Rise of Los Angeles and the Remaking of Its Mexican Past (2005).

which technological change can spark shifts in wealth, equality and opportunity. We are not, despite some recent assertions to the contrary, in a post-racial era: *de facto* residential and educational segregation continues in many towns and cities in this country, El Paso included.[11] Urbanization and modernization—which today might be referred to as "gentrification"—bring decidedly mixed blessings, as they did in the 1880s and 1890s.[12] On the one hand, such changes in a community can bring greater prosperity and stability. On the other, they can bring greater racial stratification and socioeconomic inequality. As in the nineteenth century, law and lawyers continue to play a powerful role in these processes of change. The legal profession can be instrumental either in ensuring more egalitarian communities or in undermining them. The historical portrait discussed in this essay, of one community's experience with rapid development, thus has things to tell us not only about the nineteenth-century borderlands, but also about pitfalls in urban planning and development today.

The chapter begins by tracing the involvement of local attorneys in shifting land-ownership patterns in the county, in anticipation of the arrival of the railroads. Lawyers played key roles in making sure the railroad would come through their particular locale. Transforming the community was not only about attracting the railroads, however, but also about encouraging greater settlement. The second part of this chapter describes how lawyers, politicians, and others sought to recreate the area's legal culture, in the interest of attracting settlers as well as facilitating Anglo-American legal and political dominance. This change in legal culture was part of a broader shift towards Americanization and segregation. The third part of the chapter describes the ways that the built environment of the county changed, as well as the racial/ethnic make-up of its neighborhoods and public spaces. The railroads may have provided a catalyst for these dramatic changes, but it took individual actors to make such change actually happen in the community.

Lawyers and Land

By 1884, not just one but four railroad lines met in El Paso, connecting the county to both coasts and to the interior of Mexico.[13] The arrival of these transcontinental

11 *See, e.g.*, Hua Hsu, *The End of White America?*, *in* The Atlantic, Jan–Feb. 2009 (available at http://www.theatlantic.com/magazine/archive/2009/01/the-end-of-white-america/7208/) (last visited Aug. 19, 2011); Lydia Lum, *The Obama Era: A Post-racial Society?*, *in* 25 Diverse: Issues in Higher Education 14–16 (2009). On the persistence of racial disparities, *see* William Julius Wilson, More Than Just Race: Being Black and Poor in the Inner City (2009) (exploring the persistence of racial inequality in education, housing, employment, and other areas, and the interactions of race and poverty).

12 *See, e.g.*, Gentrification, Displacement, and Neighborhood Revitalization (J. John Palen & Bruce London, eds, 1984) (discussing various possible causes of gentrification).

13 Edward A. Leonard, *Rails to the Pass of the North*, 48 Password 11, 20–25 (2003).

railroads in the El Paso area—running east to west and north to south—was understandably met with great excitement on the part of most residents of El Paso, for a whole host of reasons. For merchants, it promised a method of shipping and receiving goods as well as a new clientele to buy their goods. For farmers, it meant the opening of bigger and better markets for their crops. For ranchers, it provided a faster and more efficient method of shipping beef cattle. For all residents who had traveled between El Paso and other parts of Texas or the rest of the country, the railroads promised a safer, faster means of transport. Beyond the functional advantages, the railroad also had symbolic power, as a potent sign of progress and civilization. The tracks connected a once isolated frontier to the major centers of population in the nation.

The railroads did not arrive in El Paso due to chance or luck. Their arrival was the product of more than three decades of speculation and planning on the part of the area's legal elite. Importantly, lawyers' efforts to ensure a path through the county had a profound impact on land ownership, even before the tracks themselves were laid down. As land ownership changed, so did the political and economic fortunes of El Paso's population.[14]

There were three primary ways in which local attorneys altered patterns of land ownership in the county: securing land titles, purchasing land for eventual development, and using town incorporation to place more land in the market, doing away in the process with communally held lands. Each of these processes guaranteed the railroads one of their most important assets: land. Land was an essential precondition for railroad development. While railroads were granted the rights of eminent domain, exercising this power could prove expensive and time-consuming. Many railroad corporations preferred either to accept donations of land, at no cost to them, or to buy land outright.[15] In El Paso, the railroads did not need to exercise eminent domain. Thanks to the local legal profession, El Paso delivered the land they needed, either for free or for a nominal fee. By 1886, railroad corporations owned or controlled almost one-third of all land in El Paso County.[16]

Addressing the land needs of the railroad met with particular challenges in this part of the country, due the insecurity of land titles after the US/Mexico War.

---

14 Part of the goal of this project is to situate economic development in its local legal context. Here I am aided by an observation by Duncan Kennedy, who writes: "[E]conomic activity can't be understood as something autonomous in relation to a set of passive institutional and legal conceptual constraints … Legal institutions and ideas have a dynamic, or dialectical, or constitutive relationship to economic activity." Duncan Kennedy, *Three Globalizations of Law and Legal Thought: 1850–2000*, *in* The New Law and Economic Development: A Critical Appraisal 19–73, 19 (David M. Trubek & Alvaro Santos, eds, 2006).

15 *See* James W. Ely, Jr, Railroads and American Law 38 (2001).

16 El Paso Bureau of Information, The City and County of El Paso, Texas, Containing Useful and Reliable Information Concerning the Future Great Metropolis of the Southwest, Its Resources and Advantages for the Agriculturalist, Artisan, and Capitalist 62 (1886).

When the US government received more than 500,000 square miles of Mexican territory after the war, it pledged to recognize all preexisting (Mexican) land rights.[17] Attempting to ascertain the status of land in the Southwest proved difficult, however, for many reasons. First of all, much of the land throughout the new southwestern portion of the US was under the control of Indian nations and tribes, either by custom (in the case of nomadic tribes such as the Apache) or by actual longstanding land grants from the Spanish Crown (in the case of settled tribes such as the Tigua Indians of El Paso). Those portions occupied by Mexican settlers were often also owned under grants of either the Spanish Crown or the Mexican government, which declared independence after 1821. Some of these grants had been to private individuals, while others were given in common to multiple families.[18] While there was a tradition in Anglo-American law of recognizing communal land grants, by the mid-nineteenth century this had fallen out of favor.[19] Hence, many of the instruments of land ownership under Spanish and Mexican law were not immediately translatable into Anglo-American legal terms. Furthermore, many Anglo-American dominated state and local governments in the Southwest were loathe to acknowledge the land claims of their Mexican-American and Indian fellow citizens, especially given the land needs of the increasing number of Anglo-American settlers to the Southwest. Through a combination of outright fraud, subtle deception, and costly litigation, states and municipalities managed to divest a great number of Mexican and Indian landholders.[20]

The push for railroad development was part of this overall story of land ownership in the Southwest in the nineteenth century.[21] Railroads needed land, but not just any land: they sought secure titles in order to ensure their investment was sound. Titles to land along the border—thanks to this occupation by the US and the shifts in policy—were uncertain, to say the least. One of the first lawyers to tackle the challenge of unclear titles in the El Paso area was Josiah Crosby. Crosby arrived in El Paso in 1852 and served as the area's district attorney. He

---

17 Treaty of Guadalupe Hidalgo, *supra* note 3.

18 For traditions of land ownership in Mexico and their interpretation in the southwestern United States, *see* María E. Montoya, Translating Property: The Maxwell Land Grant and the Conflict over Land in the American West, 1840–1900 (2002).

19 On Anglo-American law and communal property, *see* Edward T. Price, Dividing the Land, Early American Beginnings of Our Private Property Mosaic 29–48 (1995); Carol Rose, *Comedy of the Commons: Custom, Commerce, and Inherently Public Property*, 53 U. Chi. L. Rev. 711, 720 (1986).

20 *See* Guadalupe T. Luna, Chicana/Chicano Land Tenure in the Agrarian Domain: On the Edge of a "Naked Knife," 4 Mich. J. Race & L. 39, 78–133 (1998).

21 John Coatsworth has demonstrated the ways that railroads contributed directly to the concentration of land ownership in Mexico in the nineteenth century, by making agriculture more profitable and thus raising land prices as a result. He notes that the railroads "provid[ed] a powerful and unexpected incentive for legal and illegal expropriation of rural properties by men of wealth and political influence." John H. Coatsworth, Growth Against Development: The Economic Impact of Railroads in Porfirian Mexico 149–174 (1981).

had high hopes for the eventual settlement and expansion of the area. As district attorney, private counsel, and later state representative, Crosby made many efforts to make sure the lands within the county had secure titles, in order to foster such development as well as to enhance his own financial standing. One of his primary contributions as a state representative was convincing the Texas legislature to create a special land commission to decide the fate of land grants in the El Paso area.[22] Land commissions were a common way throughout the Southwest to address the titles to former Mexican lands. Landholders were required to bring documentation of their ownership before the members of the commissions, who would decide on their authenticity. In most of the Southwest, failure to appear before the commissions to quiet title resulted in the land being forfeited to the federal government. Texas, unlike other states, retained ownership of its public lands upon joining the Union. It therefore created a state commission to handle disputed titles. Until Crosby came to the legislature, however, this commission had not ventured as far as El Paso, which left landholdings in west Texas in a precarious position. Crosby knew that the development of the El Paso area depended, in part, on whether titles to land were secure. In addition to creating this new commission, Crosby also invested himself in the lands that would eventually become downtown El Paso, with an eye specifically to plotting out a path for the transcontinental railroad. He acquired land not only through purchase, but also as payment for his work representing landholders. Without ready cash at hand, land became an easier form of payment. It also, not unsurprisingly, functioned over time to shift ownership from a predominantly Mexican-American landholding elite to Anglo-American attorneys.

After the Civil War, it was another El Paso lawyer, Albert J. Fountain, who laid new ground work for the railroads' arrival. Fountain had arrived in the area during the Civil War, while serving as an officer with the Union Army. Under the army's command, he pursued Mescalero Apaches, who were thought to be providing support to Confederate forces. After the war, thanks to the influence of the local Republican Party leadership, he became deputy collector of customs, and then was elected a member of the state senate in 1868.[23] On 3 March 1871, the Congress of the United States authorized the Texas & Pacific Railroad Company to build a transcontinental line through the El Paso area.[24] It was a move that El Paso residents had long anticipated, and politicians from El Paso were quick to act. Just one month later, Fountain, in his capacity as state senator, introduced

---

22 Allison Brownell Tirres, The View from the Border: Law and Community in the Nineteenth Century, in 2 Transformations in American Legal History: Essays in Honor of Morton J. Horwitz 222–224 (Daniel W. Hamilton & Alfred L. Brophy, Harvard Law Sch., eds 2011).

23 *See* A.M. Gibson, The Life and Death of Colonel Albert Jennings Fountain 22–23 (1956).

24 *United States Statutes at Large*, 16: 673–679 (1871).

laws to incorporate the towns of San Elizario, Socorro and Ysleta.[25] Each of these settlements had been founded by Spanish settlers in the seventeenth century and were the primary centers of population on the northern side of the Rio Grande. Prior to this, they had been unincorporated towns, meaning that there was no municipal government to oversee town land or to levy taxes.

The laws established a town council for each of the settlements, composed of a mayor and nine aldermen, all of whom would be elected by the residents of the town. Each town would also have a constable, secretary, treasurer, assessor and collector, and "alcalde of acequias," as the laws stated (the *alcalde* was similar to a justice of the peace under the Mexican legal system).[26] The town government would be able to tax its residents and would be given the power to regulate all manner of industries and activities, including licensing disorderly houses, regulating the running of sheep, swine, horses, and dogs, and overseeing the maintenance of the *acequias* (irrigation ditches).[27] Most significantly, the town council was given the power to "grant or sell portions of real estate" within the town limits. The acts in essence provided a vehicle for the town government to tax and sell the "unoccupied" lands in the settlements, as well as allowing residents to perfect title to occupied lands.

In San Elizario and Socorro, no action was taken to fulfill the incorporation statutes until the late 1870s.[28] In Ysleta, however, the incorporation law had an immediate impact. Over the course of four years, the town council approved hundreds of land conveyances.[29] By the mid-1870s, the land of Ysleta was consolidated in far fewer hands, since a few investors were able to buy up plots of land while poor farmers were forced to sell due to inability to pay the taxes now levied.

Ysleta provided a good target for men seeking to capitalize on land in the El Paso area. Unlike San Elizario and Socorro, Ysleta still had a large population of native Indians, the Tigua. The Tigua Indian community had been resident in the

25 *An Act to Incorporate the Town of San Eleceario* [sic] *in El Paso County, April 5, 1871*, 6 *The Laws of Texas, 1822-1897*, 1221–27 (H.P.N. Gammel ed., 1898); *An Act to Incorporate the Town of Socorro in El Paso County, April 26, 1871, in id.* at 1314–21; *An Act to Incorporate the Town of Ysleta in El Paso County, May 9, 1871, in id.* at 1435–41. The Laws of Texas can be found online at http://texinfo.library.unt.edu/ lawsoftexas/ (last visited Sept. 5, 2008).

26 On the *alcalde*, *see* Charles Cutter, The Legal Culture of Northern New Spain, 1700–1810 (1995).

27 *Acts to Incorporate the Towns of San Elceario, Socorro, and Ysleta*, *supra* note 25.

28 J.J. Bowden, Spanish and Mexican Land Grants in the Chihuahuan Acquisition, 58–59, 153 (1971); Rick Hendricks & W.H. Timmons, San Elizario: Spanish Presidio to Texas County Seat 86 (1998).

29 Deed Records, Book B, El Paso County Records, MS 132, C.L. Sonnichsen Special Collections Department, University of Texas at El Paso.

El Paso area since the Pueblo Revolt in 1680.[30] Their rights to the land within the Tigua settlement had actually been certified by the state of Texas in 1854, but by the 1870s such Indian land rights were increasingly challenged all across the state. Communal land, in particular, was in an ambiguous position at this time: all such property that was once recognized in Mexico was supposed to be respected under the terms of the Treaty of Guadalupe Hidalgo, but American property law at that time rarely recognized communal rights to land. The Tigua themselves were in an ambiguous position as American citizens as well. Under the Treaty of Guadalupe-Hidalgo, all Indians should have been made citizens of the United States, since they were by that time full citizens of Mexico. Under American policy, however, many Indians were still considered wards of the state, thereby lacking significant rights such as the right to vote and to alienate their lands.[31] Thus, it is hard to define exactly what the Tigua's rights of citizenship were by the 1860s and 1870s. Under the original Spanish grant of 1751, they were not allowed to sell or will to their heirs any of the communal property granted to them. Yet we have clear proof that they did so after the Ysleta Incorporation. As wards of the state, they were not granted the franchise, yet there is clear evidence that some of the Tigua did vote in county and state elections and hold office in the 1860s and 1870s.[32]

The Tigua themselves lost the most in the incorporation, since their communal lands were divided up into lots by the council and put up for sale. The Tigua were able to petition for these lots, but many quickly sold them, apparently because they could not afford the taxes or were seeking quick cash to supplement their meager incomes as farming families.[33]

One of the primary purchasers of land granted by this petition process was Ward Blanchard. Although the historical record is not clear, it appears that Blanchard was an agent for the railroads, charged with purchasing lands for their eventual passage through the area. The El Paso County deed records contain a gift of 640 acres near Ysleta from the San Antonio & Mexican Gulf Railway Company to Blanchard in 1860, which he filed with the county clerk in 1874.[34] It is possible that this deed was in payment for Blanchard's services as a land agent in the El

30 On the Tigua of Texas generally, *see* Nicholas P. Houser, *The Ysleta Grant (to the Place of Beginning), in* Ysleta Del Sur Pueblo Archives (2000); Thomas A. Green, *Folk History and Cultural Reorganization: A Tigua Example*, 89 The Journal of American Folklore (1976); Mark Edwin Miller, Forgotten Tribes: Unrecognized Indians and the Federal Acknowledgment Process 209–255 (2004).

31 *Lipan Apache Tribe v. United States*, 180 Ct. Cl. 487 (1967).

32 The voting activity of Tigua Indians is gleaned from a comparison of the 1867 Voter's Registration List for Ysleta with a list compiled by Nicholas Houser of known Indian landholders in the 1871 Tays Survey of Ysleta. *See* 1867 Voter Registration Records, Texas State Library and Archives Commission, MF Reel VR-4; Houser, *supra* note 30.

33 Deed Records, Book E, El Paso County Records, MS 132, C.L. Sonnichsen Special Collections Department, University of Texas at El Paso; *Id.* 100–08.

34 *See* Deed Records, Book E, at 375, El Paso County Records, MS 132, C.L. Sonnichsen Special Collections Department, University of Texas at El Paso.

Paso area. Whether he was acting on his own auspices or at the bequest of outside investors, it is clear that Blanchard bought up most of the land that was sold by petitioners after they had acquired their deed from the town council.[35]

The same year that Ysleta became incorporated, another lawyer arrived in town. James Hague was born in Missouri, studied law in Jefferson, Texas, and was admitted to the Texas Bar when he was 21 years old. He was serving as a clerk in the Texas senate when the governor, E.J. Davis, appointed him to be the district attorney for El Paso County. Hague arrived in El Paso via stagecoach in 1871.[36]

Initially, Hague made strong ties with Ysleta. He served as their counsel in a lawsuit against Senecú, a neighboring town across the Rio Grande in Mexico. For his services, he was awarded land from the Ysleta town council as well.[37] But his hopes for the future were pinned on the small town of Franklin, where he resided along with most of the county's small Anglo-American population.[38] On July 4, 1871, he wrote prophetically, "The growth of El Paso depends upon the Southern Pacific coming to this exact spot, which will make El Paso a great town in a few years."[39]

In June of 1873, Hague was one of the cofounders of the El Paso Real Estate and Immigration Company. His fellow founders, Joseph Magoffin and Simeon Hart, had lived in El Paso much longer than he, but shared his vision of a burgeoning and modernized county.[40] In addition to acquiring land in Ysleta, Hague had also either purchased or been given, in exchange for legal services, a portion of the one of the oldest Spanish land grants in the area, known as the Ponce de León grant. On 9 April 1881, he deeded his portion of this land to the Galveston, Harrisburg and San Antonio Railway Company. Six other El Paso residents did the same, providing in total a 21.4 acre parcel upon which the Southern Pacific, the owner of the Galveston railway, was able to build freight and passenger depots as well as machine shops and residence quarters for employees.[41] It is unclear whether Hague himself first approached the Southern Pacific or if they came to him; his

35 Houser, *supra* note 30, at 106.

36 J. Morgan Broaddus, The Legal Heritage of El Paso 113–14 (1963).

37 Deed Records, Book E, 284, 287–288, 541–542, El Paso County Records, MS 132, C.L. Sonnichsen Special Collections Department, University of Texas at El Paso.

38 Hague and his family initially rented a house from Louis Cardis, who was killed by Charles Howard in 1877. *See* Interview by Jo Ann Hovious with Aileen Hague Hill, (April 10, 1973) Interview 79, at 1–2, Oral History Institution, University of Texas at El Paso; Lillian Hague Corcoran, *He Brought the Railroads to El Paso—the Story of Judge James P. Hague*, 1 Password (1956).

39 Letter from James P. Hague to Flora Brinck Hague (Sept. 4, 1871), *in* Corcoran, *supra* note 38, at 47.

40 Univ. Tex., *Handbook of Texas Online*, s.v. "James Price Hague," Available at http://www.tsha.utexas.edu/handbook/online/articles/HH/fhaff.html (accessed November 9, 2006).

41 *Stevens v. Galveston*, Harrisburg & San Antonio Ry. Co., 169 S.W. 644, 648 (1914 Tex. App.).

daughter later recalled that Hague had planned carefully to attract the railroad. "[I]n order to bring [the Southern Pacific] in," she noted, "my father donated land right through the center of town. He donated that land as a special gift with the understanding that if it stopped being used as railroad property it would revert back to the heirs."[42]

The consideration given by the Galveston railway for the property was nominal: only one dollar in most cases. In Hague's case, the land was given as a gift. It was clear that the real benefit to be gained by Hague and the other sellers was the proximity of their businesses and other properties to the land in question. As the Texas Court of Appeals found in a later lawsuit over the parcel, the "real consideration" was the "probability that [sellers'] other land would be enhanced in value" by the railway's location there, thereby allowing Hague and others "to derive a profit therefrom."[43]

Less than a year after Hague granted land to the railway, he was in court representing the Southern Pacific in its suit against the Texas & Pacific Railroad.[44] One year later, in 1882, a local paper noted that Hague was employed not just by one, but two railroad companies.[45] His fellow lawyer and judge, Allen Blacker, was also employed by a railroad company. Hague's law practice was in part responsible for his ability to attract the railroads to El Paso, since he was able to afford to purchase and donate land because of his business dealings. Like other lawyers practicing in El Paso during this period, Hague was sometimes paid by his clients in land rather than cash, either because cash was not at hand or because the cases themselves involved land and he was able to negotiate a portion of this land as his payment upon a successful verdict. In turn, Hague was then able to profit from the railroad's presence, since he became one of their primary attorneys in the area. One of his heirs noted proudly that Hague left "a large estate," being one of the wealthiest men in El Paso before his untimely death from tuberculosis in 1895.[46]

The stories of these three lawyers—Crosby, Fountain, and Hague—demonstrate the ways that lawyers were able to use the law to reshape the community. In the 1850s, Josiah Crosby laid the groundwork for the railroads to pass through El Paso by introducing and passing legislation regarding titles to land, purchasing such land himself, and having it surveyed in preparation for the new populations the railroads could bring. In the late 1860s and early 1870s, Albert Fountain introduced into the state legislature incorporation statutes which profoundly altered patterns of land ownership in the county. And in the 1870s and early 1880s, James Hague managed to entice the railroads to pass through Franklin with grants of land,

42 Interview by Jo Ann Hovious with Aileen Hague Hill (Apr. 10, 1973) Interview 79, at 11, Oral History Institute, University of Texas at El Paso.

43 *Stevens v. Galveston*, Harrisburg & San Antonio Ry. Co., 169 S.W. 644, 646 (1914).

44 *See* The Lone Star, November 2, 1881, at 3.

45 The Lone Star, March 4, 1882, at 2.

46 Corcoran, *supra* note 38, at 54.

becoming counsel for the railroads in the process. Hague's actions also managed to ensure that the Anglo-American-dominated part of the county—which by the 1880s was known not as Franklin, but as the city of El Paso—would receive the benefits of railroad business. The lines bypassed the other settlements of Socorro and San Elizario, and had only a spur route to Ysleta.

With these three methods—clearing titles, incorporating towns, and investing in land—local attorneys managed to make the area attractive to railroads, which could secure the area's future as an important crossroads and trade hub. The interest in attracting the railroads changed the landscape of land ownership. Once the railroads arrived, lawyers and politicians turned their attention towards transforming the area's local legal culture, from a hybrid of Mexican and American legal traditions to one that was fully Anglo-American, excluding much of the population in the process.

Transforming Legal Culture

Up until the 1870s, Anglos and *mexicanos* in El Paso had cooperated in local law and governance, bringing together customs and concepts from Anglo-American, Spanish, and Mexican legal systems in the local legal regime. During the 1870s, however, those of Mexican descent began to lose political and legal power, due in part to the landmark Texas Supreme Court case, *Lyles v. State*,[47] which barred non-English speakers from juries, and to a violent uprising over the possession of local salt beds, known as the El Paso Salt War.[48] These two events had already taken their toll on the county's Mexican-American population, removing them from traditional positions of power and increasing animosity and suspicion between Anglo-Americans and their *mexicano* neighbors. In the 1880s, the coming of the railroads exacerbated this downward slide, triggering further changes in El Paso's legal culture and political leadership. The 1880s witnessed a profound shift in El Paso, not just in population growth, but also in the transfer of power from the county's majority *mexicano* population to the still-minority Anglo-American community. By the 1890s, those of Mexican descent occupied a far different space in the county of El Paso, both literally and figuratively.

One of the most important aspects of the shifts in the political organization of the county occurred several years after the first railroad, when men like Hague and Blacker successfully worked to shift the seat of justice in the county from Ysleta to the city of El Paso. The key component of this change was the transfer of the county seat from Ysleta to El Paso. The county seat transfer had more than just geographical significance: as we will see, it was a move that significantly changed

47 *Lyles v. State*, 41 Tex. 172 (1874).

48 On the Salt War, *see generally* Paul Cool, Salt Warriors: Insurgency on the Rio Grande (2008); *Law, Race, and the Border: The El Paso Salt War of 1877*, 117 Harv. L. Rev. 941 (2002); Tirres, *supra* note 4, at 163–210.

the legal culture of the county and further disenfranchised Mexican Americans. The transfer was both a result of and a further catalyst for increasing legal, social, and economic segregation within the county of El Paso.

On 15 February 1886—just five years after the first railroad train arrived in El Paso—residents gathered for yet another civic celebration: the dedication of a new county courthouse. The courthouse was unlike anything yet built in the county: it was a three-story brick structure with wooden verandas, fifteen-foot ceilings, pine and maple walls and trim, and walnut staircases. It was topped with an imposing cupola and clock tower; a short time later, two alabaster statues of "Blind Justice," the classic pose of a woman wearing a blindfold and holding the scales of justice, were added.[49] Shortly after its completion, the *Dallas Morning News* called it "one of the largest and best structures of the kind in the Southwest," and "first class in every way."[50] A later article noted that the city of Marfa, in the neighboring county of Presidio, would be modeling its new courthouse after the one in El Paso.[51] El Pasoans celebrated that February night with a dinner, formal presentations, and dance, all held in the district courtroom, which could accommodate such functions once the chairs were moved.

Two years in the making, the courthouse was not just a symbol of the city's growth and prosperity, but also its new clout as the county seat, a status it captured from Ysleta with a countywide vote in 1883. In style and size, it was a remarkable contrast to the surrounding buildings, which were still primarily made of adobe and in a Spanish style. The new county courthouse was not only a symbol of the new wealth that the railroads brought in, but also of the ascendance of an American-dominated legal and political future. It was a key element of a larger cultural transformation, which altered not only the balance of power in the county itself—placing "American" El Paso over the "Mexican" settlements of Ysleta, San Elizario, and Socorro—but also the spaces that El Paso's residents of Mexican descent could occupy.

The location of the county seat was important for many reasons. As the center of government activity, it was central to the local life of the county. Particularly when the district court was in session, the county courthouse became not only a legal site, but also a social and cultural one, as residents traveled from across the county to serve as jurors, defendants, plaintiffs, witnesses, or simply to watch the trials and inquire about their outcome.[52] Ysleta, reports historian J. Morgan

---

49 Herb Marsh, Jr & Robert Dinsmoor, *El Paso Courthouses: Past and Present*, 40 PASSWORD 80–81 (1995).

50 "Courthouse Accepted," DALLAS MORNING NEWS, Jan. 21, 1886, at 3.

51 "Struggle for the Postoffice—New Courthouse at Marfa—Postal Matters," DALLAS MORNING NEWS, Feb. 10, 1886, at 3.

52 Historians writing about southern courtrooms have noted the close connections between the local courthouse and the larger community. *See generally* Laura F. Edwards, *Status without Rights: African Americans and the Tangled History of Law and Governance in the Nineteenth-Century US South*, 112 AM. HIST. REV. 365 (2007); ARIELA J. GROSS,

Broaddus, was "overpopulated with visitors" when the district court was in session.[53] This benefited merchants and farmers in and near Ysleta, who had a larger crowd to buy their goods while the court was in session. "The district court has dragged its slow length along into the seventh week of the session," one local paper reported in 1882, noting that this state of affairs "is all very well for Ysleta, but not so for litigants."[54]

The desire of some El Paso residents to move the county seat to their own town grew not only out of practicalities, but also out of a perception of Ysleta's identity as a "Mexican" town. For the growing Anglo-American population of El Paso, Ysleta was not just too far away or too difficult to reach, it was also too Mexican. This critique against Ysleta had begun even before the railroads arrived. In 1879, a newspaper editor in the nearby town of Mesilla, New Mexico, wrote disapprovingly of the population's failure to celebrate the Fourth of July. "There was not a flag hoisted or a single shot fired in Ysleta to greet the coming of the greatest of our National Holidays," he wrote. "Business has been conducted throughout the day as usual and to the shame of Ysleta there has been no display of patriotism by anyone."[55] In 1881, the same paper reported with dismay that "of the twelve grand jurors now in session in Ysleta, ten of them cannot speak English," a fact which is interesting not only for the critique, but also because, if true, it indicates that officials in Ysleta were not abiding by the Texas Supreme Court decision in *Lyles v. State*, which had declared English-only juries in 1874.[56] In 1882, another newspaper editor complained that the justice of the peace in Ysleta was unable to speak English and had to have an interpreter present in order to explain his rulings to some members of the jury, who did not speak Spanish.[57]

There was no doubt that Ysleta was primarily governed, at this time in its history, by those of Mexican descent. In the election of 1882, the town's mayor, three out of four aldermen, and the town marshal all had Spanish surnames.[58] County government was also almost completely comprised of men with Spanish surnames. The slate of the justices of the peace was similarly composed. This was not at all a novel situation in El Paso County, since most legal and commercial business had been conducted in Spanish ever since the Anglo-American occupation began in 1848. The fact that it would draw such attention and disapprobation in

---

Double Character: Slavery and Mastery in the Antebellum Southern Courtroom (2000).

53 Broaddus, *supra* note 36, at 130.

54 The Lone Star, Nov. 22, 1882.

55 Mesilla Valley Independent, July 12, 1879, cited in Rex E. Gerald, *Aboriginal Use and Occupation by Tigua, Manso, and Suma Indians*, *in* Apache Indians, at 176 (David Agee Horr ed., New York and London: Garland Publishing, 1974).

56 The Lone Star, Oct. 29, 1881.

57 The Lone Star, Feb. 1, 1882.

58 The Lone Star, April 8, 1882, 3 ("A. Guerra, Mayor; Candelario, T. Provencio, T. Yrigoyen, J.V. Piarote, and Frank Mayer, aldermen; C. Benavidez, marshall").

the late 1870s and early 1880s was a foreshadowing of further isolation of Spanish and Mexican culture to come.

Under Texas law, a vote to move the county seat could not take place unless residents submitted a petition with at least 100 signatures requesting a vote. In addition, a county seat vote could only take place once every five years.[59] In the fall of 1882, two El Paso residents—A.M. Loomis and Joseph Sweeney—began circulating a petition to support the holding of a vote.[60] "Judge" Loomis, as the local paper referred to him, had served as sheriff and tax collector in the 1870s. He was likely hopeful that his sponsorship of such a petition would earn him more votes in the next election, when he was planning to run for the position of county judge.[61] Despite the general dissatisfaction among Anglo-Americans with the location of the county seat, El Paso's petition failed to achieve the requisite number of signatures. There are indications that some residents failed to sign not because they did not want the county seat to move, but rather because they thought that they did not have enough votes yet to succeed, and they preferred to wait another year or two to attempt the process rather than failing at the polls and having to wait five years before trying again.[62]

It was Ysletans themselves who filed a successful petition, apparently assuming that their chances were better sooner rather than later, and that they would easily win a vote, due to their larger size, and be able to retain the seat for at least another five years. After receiving the successful petition in November of 1883, county judge Marshall Rogers declared that the vote would take place on 3 December 1883. In one month, El Paso's boosters worked hard to gain as many votes in their favor as possible. Texas law stated that in order to move the county seat more than five miles from the geographical center, the winners would require a two-thirds majority.[63] With at least 1,000 registered voters in the county, this would mean more than 600 would have to vote in El Paso's favor. Community leaders not only encouraged current voters to vote through bribery, but also sought to register new voters as quickly as possible. They were shameless about their push. *The Lone Star* encouraged as many votes as possible: "There is no registration required nor any vexatious preliminaries … the large body of Mexicans … has but to go before the clerk of the district court and declare their intention to become citizens of the

59 *See* Act approved March 28, 1881, *in* 9 The Laws of Texas, *1822–1897*, 159 (H.P.N. Gammel ed., 1898).

60 The Lone Star, Nov. 7, 1883.

61 Loomis lost the election to J.A. Buckler. *See* The Lone Star, Nov. 12, 1884; Broaddus, *supra* note 36, at 142; Nancy Lee Hammons, A History of El Paso County Texas, to 1900, 81 (1983). Joseph Sweeney's identity is harder to confirm. This may have been the father of a practicing lawyer and founding member of the bar association, also named Joseph Sweeney, who was born in San Antonio in 1875 and came to El Paso as a small child. Sweeney served two terms as mayor of El Paso. *See* Broaddus at 227.

62 The Lone Star, Nov. 7, 1883.

63 Broaddus, *supra* note 36, at 141.

United States and then, if they lived in the legal period in the state and county, they are entitled to vote ... every ballot counts ..."[64]

News of the upcoming vote went as far as San Francisco. A local paper there reported on the eve of the vote: "In anticipation of the election for a change of county seat on tomorrow, many Mexican citizens were naturalized by the Deputy County Clerk in the Council rooms. About one hundred qualified before Saturday night. The merchants of El Paso will close their stores on election day and work at the polls."[65] El Paso's merchants did, indeed, do their part to encourage voting. One paper reported that area merchants were "remaining on the streets all day and hurrying back and forth, on foot and in carriages, buggies, and wagons, hunting up and bringing in the voters." Not only the merchants but also railroad employees helped on election day, running special trains for residents around the county to reach their polling places. As the *Lone Star* wrote approvingly, "The Santa Fe railroad men did nobly yesterday. They not only voted solidly for El Paso but they worked like beavers to bring in the vote along the line of the road between this city and the state line."[66]

El Paso won the vote easily: 2,252 for El Paso versus 476 for Ysleta, for a total of 2,728.[67] Given that there were only 1,000 officially registered voters in the county, Ysletans immediately noted the outright fraud and sought indictments against those responsible. Where such calls for legal action had been heard in the past, such as the granting of an injunction by the district judge when Ysleta attempted to gain the seat from San Elizario in 1874, this time there was no response. It was not helpful that the district attorney, who would have been responsible for pursuing such indictments, was James Hague.

The ironies of the transfer of the county seat are clear. In an effort to distance El Paso from its Mexican past, as represented by Ysleta and its sandstone courthouse, leaders in El Paso had to enlist the help of a Mexican-American and Mexican electorate. They sought quickly to make new citizens of such men in order to further their immediate purposes. The paramount goal—to have "justice" take its seat in its proper place as part of Anglo-American culture—was attained through injustice.

The movement of the county seat was not just a geographical switch, but also a cultural one, one that had the power to alter the racial/ethnic balance that had prevailed to date in the county. Up until the transfer of the county seat from Ysleta, men of Mexican descent had dominated county government. In 1876, 1880, and 1884, for example, the county judge and three out of four county commissioners had Spanish surnames.[68] After the county seat transfer was completed in late 1884,

---

64 *Id.*

65 *County Seat Election*, San Francisco Bulletin, Dec. 3, 1883, at 3.

66 The Lone Star, Dec. 5, 1883.

67 Broaddus, *supra* note 36, at 141.

68 For 1876, the county judge was Joseph Magoffin and the county commissioners M.C. Alderete, Guadalupe Lucero, Julian Arias, and J.N. Garcia; in 1880, the county judge

far fewer men of Mexican descent served as county officials. By 1886, in fact, the proportions had been reversed: the county judge and all but one commissioner had non-Spanish surnames.

The transfer effected jury composition as well. The composition of petit and grand juries in El Paso had already been changed irreparably by the *Lyles* case, which prohibited the participation of any citizens who could not speak English. The county seat transfer also had a lasting effect on jury composition, but through informal practice rather than formal adjudication. It was common practice in many late nineteenth-century towns for the sheriff to round up jurors on the streets of the county seat when the formal jury summons had failed.[69] In 1881, for example, a local paper reported that only half of the 36 jurors summoned to serve in the fall term of the district court in Ysleta had appeared, and only 8 of these were qualified jurors. In order to find more candidates, reported the paper, "[t]he sheriff was ordered to summon a sufficient number of talesmen to fill out the panel. He was in town yesterday carrying out his instructions."[70] The make-up of these "talesmen" (a word describing jury members who had been summoned through this informal procedure) depended upon who happened to be in town on the day that court had convened.[71] In El Paso, those hanging around the courthouse were far more likely to be of Anglo-American descent than of Mexican descent, due to the general demographic differences between the two settlements. As a result, the juries called in the county of El Paso after the seat moved were far less likely to contain those of Mexican descent than they had been before 1884, when the seat was in Ysleta.

Overall, jury selection depended on both the sheriff and the court clerk, who was charged with creating the list of eligible jurors from which the *venire* would be drawn each court term. After 1884, both the sheriff and the clerk (who served as both county and district clerk) were far more likely themselves to be of Anglo-American descent. In fact, Manuel E. Flores, who had been clerk since 1880, was

---

was José Baca and the commissioners were Pablo Romero, B.S. Dowell, Demetrio Urtiaga, and Gregorio Garcia; in 1884, the county judge was J.A. Buckler and the commissioners were J. Cobos, J.M. Gonzales, R.F. Campbell, and J. Armendariz. *See* HAMMONS, *supra* note 61, at 83–84.

69 As Ariela Gross describes, in the antebellum South "it was permissible to convene bystander juries composed of qualified men who happened to be at court that day, if there were not enough jurors from the regular *venire*." ARIELA J. GROSS, DOUBLE CHARACTER: SLAVERY AND MASTERY IN THE ANTEBELLUM SOUTHERN COURTROOM 37 (2000).

70 THE LONE STAR, October 26, 1881. The article does not directly state why so few of those reporting were qualified, but a related article in the same issue reported that "it is said that quite a number of the jurors on the *venire* summoned for last Monday were residents of Mexico, which is, to say the least, somewhat peculiar."

71 *Black's Law Dictionary* defines a "talesman" as "A person summoned to act as a juror from among the by-standers in the court." HENRY CAMPBELL BLACK, BLACK'S LAW DICTIONARY 1014 (1991).

defeated in the first election after the removal of the county seat: his opponent, Frank P. Clark, won by 407 votes, 1186 to 779.[72]

Whether due to the change in location or to outright discrimination, the participation of those with Spanish surnames decreased precipitously after 1884. In 1885, El Paso gained a federal district court. Citizens had sent a lengthy petition in 1885 declaring their dire need for a federal court close by. In the first jury panel drawn for the federal court, only one out of the 32 jurors had a Spanish surname.[73] This was a far cry from the composition of district juries just ten years before, which would have been composed of a majority of those with Spanish surnames. It also was not an accurate reflection of the county's demographics, since those of Mexican descent still represented more than 50 per cent of the population.[74]

Some of the changes in county government and jury composition can be attributed to the massive influx of Anglo-Americans to El Paso during the 1880s, which no doubt swelled the ranks of those voting for Anglo-American candidates for city, county, and statewide office. But such demographic change cannot account for the drastic nature of the change, since men with Spanish surnames still represented a majority of those on the voter registration lists for the county as a whole. A larger cultural shift was at hand, one that shunned the prior influence of Mexican-Americans on the legal culture as a whole.

With the county courthouse and the county government in the hands primarily of Anglo-Americans, complaints about the remaining Mexican-American legal officials and their style of "Mexican justice" in the surrounding towns increased.[75] In 1885, a grand jury investigated the state of the justice courts in El Paso County. "We find the justices-of-peace [sic] at Ysleta, Concordia, Cuadrilla, and Socorro incompetent and their dockets are found in unsatisfactory condition. In most cases, we find them kept in the Spanish language, and not in proper form, as required by Law. The constables in most precincts do not speak English."[76]

Triumphant residents of the city of El Paso lost little time in sealing their victory. They promptly began plans for the new courthouse, which would serve as both a literal and symbolic marker of the changes they had won. Promoting the future of El Paso as a great metropolitan center meant divorcing it not only from its Mexican past, but also its Mexican present. The new brick courthouse would

---

72 The Lone Star, Nov. 12, 1884. *See also* Hammons, *supra* note 11, at 83.

73 Doris Wallingford Busalacchi, History of the Federal Judiciary District of Western Texas, 6–7 (1950) (unpublished seminar paper, University of Texas at El Paso) (on file with author). The man in question was J.D. Ochoa, who was one of the few elite *mexicanos* still included in positions of power in El Paso. He had also been the lone *mexicano* member of the official welcoming party for the Southern Pacific railroad in 1881. El Paso Herald, June 1, 1881.

74 *See* McConville, *supra* note 2, at 76, 80.

75 The Lone Star, October 29, 1881 (discussing "an amusing illustration of Mexican justice" in the case of a cattle rustler who, the paper claimed, was improperly exonerated by a *mexicano* justice of the peace).

76 Report of the Grand Jury, *reprinted in* El Paso Times, Nov. 24, 1885.

be a clear sign of this break from the past. It would also indicate the ascendance of the city of El Paso to the leadership of the county as a whole. As one resident concluded triumphantly after the vote transferring the county seat to El Paso, "Nobody now doubts that this city rules El Paso county."[77]

New Boundaries: Americanization and Segregation

The changes in El Paso's legal culture, hastened by the arrival of the railroads, both reflected and contributed to a broader shift in the county's spatial organization and built environment. In the mid- to late 1880s, the predominant adobe buildings were razed and replaced by brick and wooden ones. One newspaper article, entitled "El Paso's Bright Future: Indeed the Marvel of the Far West," reported approvingly that "the ancient adobes that lined the commercial thoroughfares and fulfilled the demands of trade before the railroads, and when the city was but a straggling and unknown frontier village, are being torn down to make room for massive and lofty edifices for business and office purposes."[78] In a similar vein, El Paso boosters claimed in 1886 that "[t]he old adobe buildings are fast giving way to business blocks as substantial and elegant as can be found in Texas; while of residence property there has been erected, on all sides of the business center, properties which have transformed an open common into a beautiful city of comfortable and elegant homes."[79]

The writers may have celebrated the demise of the "open common" as an aesthetic matter, but it was of much greater significance than this. The open commons in the heart of the town had been a key feature not just in El Paso, but in most Spanish and Mexican settlements throughout the borderlands.[80] In colonial times, the commons allowed settlers shared pasturage for their animals. Residents literally owned the land in common, and no one family or individual was able to claim the space as their own. It also provided a key gathering place for residents. Its transformation from common space to private homes, which the above article recounts, was part of the overall shift away not only from Spanish architectural style, but also from El Paso's Spanish and Mexican legal heritage, since it favored privatization over common resources. In this way it was similar to the process of town incorporation in the 1870s, which also shifted commonly owned lands to private hands.

The transfer of the county seat was part and parcel of an attempt to erase the county's Mexican past and ensure its commercial future. Attempts to "Americanize" did not stop with the county courthouse. In the newly ascendant city, lawyers and politicians—who were sometimes one and the same—in the late 1880s and 1890s

77 The Lone Star, Dec. 5, 1883, 3.

78 "El Paso's Bright Future," *Dallas Morning News*, Feb. 8, 1886.

79 El Paso Bureau of Information, *supra* note 16, at 9.

80 *See* David J. Weber, The Spanish Frontier in North America 60–91 (1992).

institutionalized inequality in schools, neighborhoods, the police department, and other public services. This was a marked departure from how things had been for the first 40 years after the Treaty of Guadalupe Hidalgo. Their actions resulted, hence, not just in the segregation of the county as a whole—with the centers of Mexican-American political power now in the outlying settlements—but also with the segregation of the city itself.

To be sure, residential segregation was not only the result of intentional action, but also the outcome of preexisting economic inequality between the populations, as well as from the desire of new migrant populations—of both Anglo-American and Mexican-American descent—to settle in neighborhoods with people of similar ethnic, religious, and national backgrounds. But city leaders actively accommodated and fostered the divisions within the city through municipal regulation.

The city had been divided into justice precincts, called "wards," when first incorporated in 1873.[81] These wards, each of which had its own justice of the peace, became increasingly segregated by nationality or racial or ethnic background after 1881. By 1900, the vast majority of the city's *mexicano* population was living in segregated neighborhoods in southeastern El Paso.[82] Not coincidentally, these communities, known as "Chihuahuita," "Segundo Barrio," and East El Paso, were also the closest to the Rio Grande, which would periodically flood and destroy all the surrounding homes. A fourth settlement of *mexicanos* was established after such a flood, when residents of Chihuahuita attempted to move further north to rebuild on safer ground.

The railroad tracks proved a strong and lasting border not only between "Mexican" and "American" El Paso, but also between "white" El Pasoans and all others. Not coincidentally, El Paso's burgeoning Chinese-American community also lived almost completely "south of the tracks."[83] One resident later recalled that the Chinese residents, many of whom had worked on the railroads that led into

---

81 *See* "An Act to incorporate the City of El Paso," May 17, 1873, *in* 7 *The Laws of Texas, 1822–1897*, 1138–71 (H.P.N. Gammel ed. 1898).

82 Monica Perales, Smeltertown: A Biography of a Mexican-American Community, 1880–1973, 42 (2004) (unpublished Ph.D dissertation, Stanford University) (on file with the author).

83 On Chinese-American communities in El Paso and the southwest generally, *see* Leo M. Jacques, *Have More Quick Money Than Mandarins: The Chinese in Sonora*, 17 Journal of Arizona History 201 (1976); Erika Lee, *Enforcing the Borders: Chinese Exclusion Along the US Borders with Canada and Mexico, 1882–1924*, 89 Journal of American History 54 (2002); Clifford A. Perkins, *Reminiscences of a Chinese Inspector*, 17 Journal of Arizona History 181 (1976); Anna Louise Fahy, Chinese Borderland Community Development: A Case Study of El Paso, 1881–1909 (2001) (unpublished master's thesis, University of Texas at El Paso) (on file with author).

the city, "all lived down in south El Paso. That's where the Mexicans, most people who were not Anglo-Saxons, lived."[84]

Historian Mario García notes that the barrier proved strong enough to prevent the growth of these non-white neighborhoods any further north. He writes that, "the rigidity of this boundary forced the Mexican district to grow in an eastward direction but still south of the tracks and along the border."[85] Proximity to the border meant not only the risk of repeat flooding by the Rio Grande, but also the threat of land dispossession, since a large portion of this southeastern land, called the "Chamizal," was still contested by the US and Mexico.[86] Many of these communities were also, not coincidentally, located near various industrial operations that employed the increasingly large numbers of Mexican immigrants at the turn of the century.[87] A sizable community grew next to the smelter plant, known as Smeltertown, as well. Even this industrial town was segregated. Historian Monica Perales notes that "a high wooden fence" separated the wood and brick homes of the Anglo-American management from the adobe tenements of the Mexican and Mexican-American workers.[88]

The city of El Paso's first school district was established in 1882, but made no provision for the schooling of children who did not speak English. In fact, the school board declared that only English-speaking students could attend the district schools. At the same time, however, they took notice of the continuing prominence of Spanish in the county, adding Spanish language instruction to their elementary education program.[89] While English-speaking students would learn Spanish, Spanish-speaking students had no similar opportunities to learn English. As a result, few, if any, students of Mexican descent enrolled in the first public elementary school in El Paso.[90]

---

84 Interview by Leon Metz and Robin Fuller with Mrs. Hugh White, June 3, 1968, Interview 48, transcript, at 11, Oral History Institute, University of Texas at El Paso.

85 Mario T. Garcia, Desert Immigrants: The Mexicans of El Paso, 1880–1920, 131 (1981).

86 *See* Sheldon B. Liss, A Century of Disagreement: The Chamizal Conflict, 1864–1964 (1965); Luis Torres, Chamizal National Memorial (1994).

87 García, *supra* note 85.

88 Perales, *supra* note 82, at 58. For residential segregation in El Paso, *see also* David Dorado Romo, Ringside Seat to a Revolution: An Underground Cultural History of El Paso and Juárez, 1893–1923, 193–244 (2005).

89 While the school board did not want to educate Spanish-speaking students, they did offer Spanish instruction to English-speaking students, at least during the mid-1880s. *See* Jo Ann Platt Hovious, Social Change in Western Towns: El Paso, Texas, 1881–1889, 123 (1972) (unpublished master's thesis, University of Texas at El Paso) (on file with author).

90 Conrey Bryson, *A Man Named Aoy*, 35 Password 95 (1990) ("The rolls of the first public school, opened March 5, 1883, show an enrollment of 94 pupils, and not a Spanish surname in the list").

In 1887, a local resident, Olivius V. Aoy, created a private elementary school expressly for Spanish-speaking students.[91] Five years later, the school was incorporated by the school district and named the "Mexican Preparatory School." In 1899, the district opened a second school for Spanish-speaking students, since overcrowding at the Mexican Preparatory School had become extreme. By this time, the initial rationale for segregating the schools by language ability had morphed into general race- and nationality-based segregation, in part because the schools grew out of and were located in racially segregated neighborhoods.[92] By the 1920s, school officials were referring to the elementary schools located "south of the tracks" as being part of "the Mexican District," while referring to those schools "north of the tracks" as part of "the American district."[93] Throughout the early twentieth century, the "Mexican district" schools were typically overcrowded, underfunded, and placed the greatest emphasis on vocational training, rather than general education or preparation for high school and college.[94]

The process of segregating Spanish-speaking ("Mexican") and English-speaking ("American") children was not foreordained or automatic. Up until the early 1880s, children of both Anglo-American and Mexican descent had been educated together, although typically it was only the children of elite families who could afford to send their children to school. Mary Dowell, for example, who was the daughter of Ben Dowell, the one-time mayor of Franklin, and Juana Márquez Dowell, a Tigua Indian, received instruction in 1866 alongside the son of José María Flores and the children of the Gillett brothers, who had fought for the Confederacy in the Civil War.[95] In 1868, the wife of Judge Gaylord Clarke taught school in the El Paso area, attracting as pupils both Anglo-American and Mexican-American children. After she left the area in 1870, Joseph Tays replaced her, continuing to teach classes that included children with both Spanish and non-Spanish surnames.[96] The division within schools of "Mexican" and "American" children was thus a historical process, not an automatic practice.

By the end of the 1890s, new borders crisscrossed the space of El Paso County. Although the railroads did not, themselves, create the borders, they came to represent them, marking off the difference between "American" and "Mexican,"

91 Aoy was born in Spain and had been ordained a Catholic priest. After traveling to the US, he left the priesthood and converted to the Mormon faith. He assisted in the first translation of the *Book of Mormon* into Spanish in the 1880s. *See id.*

92 As Ariela Gross explains, lawmakers used this equation between language and race repeatedly throughout the early twentieth century to discriminate against those of Mexican descent. Ariela J. Gross, *The "Caucasian Cloak": Mexican Americans and the Politics of Whiteness in the 20th-Century Southwest*, 95 Georgetown Law Journal 95 (2006).

93 *See* report cited in *Alvarado v. El Paso Independent School District*, 426 F. Supp. 575, 579 (1976).

94 *See* García, *supra* note 85, at 110–114; Bryson, *supra* note 90; *Alvarado v. El Paso Independent School District*, 426 F. Supp 575, 578–579 (1976).

95 Nancy Hamilton, Ben Dowell: El Paso's First Mayor 43 (1976).

96 *Id.* at 44.

between white and other. When we look closely at these lines of division, we see that these internal borders shaped the lives of El Paso's residents to an equal or even greater extent than did the international line dividing them from Mexico. As new economic relationships and connections formed across the borderline, the borders within the county—between different racialized groups and between El Paso and the "Mexican" towns of Ysleta, San Elizario, and Socorro—hardened.

Epilogue

For the county of El Paso, the railroads spelled both the beginning and the end: the beginning of its modern incarnation as a transborder trade hub; and the end of a particular form of hybrid culture and shared power between Anglo-Americans and Mexican-Americans—in other words, the marginalization of its Mexican cultural, legal, and political heritage. This shift, though fairly sudden, was not merely the outcome of demographic change. Instead, it was a product of years of speculation and planning, including the deployment of specific legal devices that made the spatial and political reorganization of the county possible. Most damaging in the long-term were the changes in property ownership—as land passed from Mexican and American-Indian hands to Anglo-American ones—and in the county's geography, as power became consolidated in the city of El Paso, and city leaders, in turn, redrew municipal boundaries along racially segregated lines.

The Mexican past did not disappear, however. In the older settlements of Socorro, San Elizario, and Ysleta, Mexican-Americans and Tigua Indians continued to hold most positions of power, and town council minutes continued to appear in a mix of Spanish and English.[97] These historic settlements returned to small, close-knit, self-sufficient communities centered on agriculture. The distance, both literal and figurative, from the burgeoning industrial city of El Paso allowed residents of these towns to retain customs and procedures from an earlier era and also allowed political presence for those of Mexican descent.

This relegation of *mexicano* cultural and political power to the small towns was not without costs. The settlements never regained their place of importance in the county. Today, these towns do not enjoy the political, economic, or cultural prominence that is enjoyed by the city of El Paso. Poverty rates in both San Elizario and Socorro are higher and the median household income is significantly lower than in El Paso.[98] But to look merely at economic indicators would be to miss the cultural contributions of these towns today. Residents have managed to preserve the historic mission churches and chapels, first constructed during the Spanish

97 Oral Histories in Socorro and San Elizario, Texas (Center for Anthropological Research, New Mexico State University) (unpublished paper) (on file with author).

98 US Census, 2000. In El Paso in 1999, 22.2% of the population was below the poverty level, compared with 32.6% in Socorro and 39.5% in San Elizario. The median household income in El Paso is $32,124, compared with $24,087 in Socorro.

colonial era. These buildings are located on a linked "Mission Trail," along the former *Camino Real* from Mexico City to Santa Fe, and they draw tourists from around the country. The towns host various cultural festivals throughout the year, including a commemoration of the First Thanksgiving, which occurred in San Elizario in April of 1598.[99]

In the past few decades, the city of El Paso itself has witnessed a resurgence of Mexican-American political power and cultural presence. It is visible in El Paso's schools, neighborhoods, city council meetings, and halls of justice. One can again hear Spanish in the courtroom and jury box. The newly constructed federal courthouse is named for a well-known Mexican-American civil rights activist, Albert Armendariz, Sr., something that would no doubt surprise those who labored to fund and build the county courthouse of 1886.[100] The city prides itself on its Mexican heritage, using connections to Mexico to draw both tourists and capital.

The late nineteenth century set a precedent of segregation and stratification that lasted for close to a century. This division was fostered by a particular social vision of modernization, which attempted to disconnect the area from its Mexican past. The county still struggles with the remnants of this past; El Paso's population is more than 82 per cent percent of Latino or Hispanic origin, but a higher percentage of Latinos in El Paso are below the poverty line, and Latinos are still underrepresented in city and county government.[101] While the county still struggles with economic inequality and racial stratification, it does so from the point of view of a new social vision, which sees strength in the area's diverse population and unique historical legacy.

Acknowledgement

For their helpful comments, I wish to thank Michael Diamond, Daniel Hamilton, Anadelia Romo, Christopher Schmidt, Stephen Siegel, and the attendees of a workshop at the first annual meeting of the Association for Law, Property, and Society. Portions of this chapter are drawn from Allison Brownell Tirres, *Lawyers and Legal Borderlands*, 50 Am. J. of Legal Hist. 157 (2010).

99 *The El Paso Mission Trail, available at* http://www.epcounty.com/history/missiontrail.htm (last visited Aug. 15, 2011).

100 Newspaper Tree, *Judge Albert Armendariz Federal Courthouse "a fitting tribute to a hometown hero,"* (Sept. 9, 2010), http://newspapertree.com/news/4239-judge-albert-armendariz-federal-courthouse-a-fitting-tribute-to-a-hometown-hero (last visited Aug. 15, 2011).

101 US Census, 2000 and 2010.

Chapter 2
'Shaping the Place' and the Ability to Exclude: Housing and Localism in England

Antonia Layard

Localism is currently *en vogue* in the United Kingdom. There is presently a 'rare cross-party consensus over devolving more power to town and county halls'[1] building on existing initiatives towards a 'new localism'[2] with political support for market alternatives to bureaucratic organisation, service provision, economic entrepreneurship and regulatory innovation. Much of this new devolved focus adds an explicitly legal, sub-local government dimension, epitomised by the provisions in the Localism Act 2011, which aims to radically alter the ability of local communities to shape their neighbourhoods through planning law.[3] Launching their 'Big Society' project, the current coalition government has land use high in their sights, promising to 'radically reform the planning system to give neighbourhoods far more ability to determine the shape of the places in which their inhabitants live'.[4]

Yet while localism and empowering communities to 'shape the place' may have much to recommend them, these empowering and even inclusionary policies can also exclude and restrict, particularly in the residential context. Land use regulations can mean that 'outsiders' and 'others' find it difficult to live where they would otherwise choose. This analysis of three localist, residential land-use interventions will explore these exclusionary tensions within such micro-localism. It will consider the building of affordable housing for 'locals' in rural areas, imposing restrictions on housing in multiple occupation and attempts to limit the use of properties in national parks as second or holiday homes. The analysis will

1 Peter Hetherington, *Tory Localism Isn't Totally Convincing*, Guardian Newspaper, March 31, 2010.

2 Gerry Stoker, *New Localism, Progressive Politics and Democracy*, *in* Restating the State?, 1–25 (A. Gamble & T. Wright eds, 2004); Nick Clark, *In What Sense 'Spaces of Neoliberalism'? The New Localism, the New Politics of Scale, and Town Twinning* 28 Political Geography 496 (2009); Jeff Bishop, *From Parish Plans to Localism in England: Straight Track or Long and Winding Road?* 25 Planning Practice & Research 611 (2010).

3 For a comparison between US and UK processes and approaches to land use, *see* Sarah Elwood, *Partnerships and Participation: Reconfiguring Urban Governance in Different State Context*, 25 Urban Geography 755–770 (2004).

4 *Building the Big Society* (2010), *available at* www.cabinetoffice.gov.uk/media/407789/building-big-society.pdf *(last visited Jan. 31, 2011).*

suggest that while localism may have much to recommend it, place-shaping land-use laws require careful and transparent evaluation to ensure that localism serves progressive, rather than regressive, policy ends.

To suggest that localist land-use practices might be restrictive will come as little surprise to analysts of exclusionary zoning, epitomised in ordinances that 'exclude classes of persons from a specified area'.[5] By investigating the relationship between land use and identity, critics have outlined how, for example, local decisions to require large lot sizes for new construction, minimum floor areas or single family housing exclude potential residents from localities where they might otherwise wish to live. Poorer individuals and families are priced out not simply by the market, but also by the locally imposed ordinances that have required housing to be built in prescribed forms, prohibiting the construction of smaller and cheaper residential units instead. In extreme cases, as Schragger notes: 'One might want to live in Beverly Hills (or, more important, one may desperately want not to live in Compton), but one may literally have no choice'.[6]

While exclusionary zoning is an unfamiliar concept in the United Kingdom, these regulatory restrictions are still as much about people as places as the 'anti-snob' laws introduced in some states acknowledge. Localist restrictions on residential land use are motivated at least in part by differences in lifestyle, encapsulating a desire by local communities to protect that which they deem valuable from dissipation by incomers who have different interests and needs and who may use land in different ways. Whether entirely exclusionary or merely restrictive, these types of centrally facilitated local interventions shape residential geographies in subtle and dynamic ways.

This tension between localism and exclusion or restriction acknowledges the fact that however much exclusionary zoning is critiqued in academic and policy circles, it is undeniably popular on the ground. Indeed, localism is currently advocated throughout the United Kingdom with little consideration for its possible exclusionary effects in land-use planning, particularly at the 'micro-local' or neighbourhood scale. Restrictive effects are, however, evident in a concerted campaign by local neighbourhood groups to restrict the number of houses in multiple occupation to prevent 'unbalanced' or 'unsustainable' neighbourhoods.

---

5 L.G. Sager, Tight Little Islands: Exclusionary Zoning, Equal Protection, and the Indigent, 21 Stanford L. Rev. 767 (1969); Henry A. Span, How the Courts Should Fight Exclusionary Zoning 32 Seton Hall L. Rev. 1 (2003); Norman Williams, The Background and Significance of Mount Laurel II, 26 Wash. U.J. Urb. & Contemp. L. 3 (1984); Norman Williams &Tatyana Doughty, Studies in Legal Realism: Belle Terre, Mount Laurel and Berman, 29 Rutgers L. Rev. 73 (1976); Mandara Meyers, (Un)equal Protection for the Poor: Exclusionary Zoning and the Need for Stricter Scrutiny, 6 U. Pa. J. Const. L. 349 (2004).

6 Richard C. Schragger, The Limits of Localism, 100 Mich. L. Rev. 371, 416 (2002).

They are also the consequence of measures to promote affordable housing that prioritise 'locals' to live within newly built properties in rural locations.[7]

The balance between localism and exclusionary zoning is a nuanced one, and as a technique, restrictive land-use planning can have either progressive or regressive ends. Proposed rules to exclude or restrict holiday homes in rural and coastal communities could, for instance, protect rural and coastal communities from unrestricted purchases of properties as second homes, maintaining a 'year round' culture that full-time residents would prefer. Similarly, prioritising affordable housing for 'locals' in rural locations might maintain distinctive and rooted ways of life, while restrictions on multiple occupation could prevent rent-seeking landlords from transforming predominantly family, owner-occupier communities with well-maintained properties and gardens into portfolios of rental properties.

To explore this balance between local place shaping and restriction, this analysis will begin with an overview of the philosophy of localism and its relationship with land use, suggesting that despite its popularity, it retains key uncertainties, particularly in the way in which localities can separate themselves from the world beyond, the justifications for localism and the overlap between local identity, local autonomy and local democracy. The analysis will suggest that given these uncertainties, localist land-use philosophies should not proceed without restraint, and that critical land-use lawyers should evaluate them for potentially regressive effects. It may well be that exclusion or restriction may be deemed politically desirable but these effects should, this chapter suggests, be transparently assessed. In particular, the analysis will caution that a comparison of different restrictive, localist residential land-use rules suggests that critical evaluation is required to ensure that the role played by politics, power and influence is clearly understood.

Localism and Land Use

Philosophies of land-use localism aim to empower local residents to shape the place where they live, contributing to a regulatory framework for determining residential geographies in their area: there is long-standing political and philosophical support for local land-use regulation and the belief that a 'bottom up' approach is beneficial to both people and place. The nineteenth century American 'home rule' movement, for example, was underpinned by a belief that localities were best equipped to govern themselves[8] with advocates of localism continuing to state the

7 These differ from those noted by Robert C. Ellickson, *The Irony of 'Inclusionary' Zoning*, 54 S. Cal. L. Rev. 1167 (1981).

8 Terrance Sandalow, The Limits of Municipal Power Under Home Rule – A Role for the Courts, 48 Minn. L. Rev. 643, 709 (1964); Richard Briffault, Home Rule and Local Political Innovation, 22 J.L. & POL. 1, 31 (2006); Matthew J. Parlow, Progressive Policy-

advantages today.[9] Similarly, in the United Kingdom, the current government have introduced a legislative proposal for a 'general power of competence', which will give local authorities 'an explicit freedom to act in the best interest of their voters unhindered by the absence of specific legislation supporting their actions for all local authorities'.[10] This builds on an existing but currently underused 'power of first resort'[11] in the Local Government Act 2000 that gives local authorities a power to do (almost[12]) anything that they consider likely to promote or improve the economic, social or environmental well-being of any part of their area.[13]

In the United Kingdom, the current Conservative-Liberal Democrat government now aims to implement an 'open source planning system' in order to give neighbourhoods more ability to shape their place,[14] increasing community control of land use. Such developments build on deep-set devolution within the United Kingdom, with devolved planning powers meaning that the four home nations of England, Scotland, Wales and Northern Ireland are already developing increasingly distinctive land-use policies. Self-determination is embedded in many aspects of land-use law and is, according to the rhetoric of central government, set to trickle down to the neighbourhood scale expanding on existing localist initiatives. As regulators explore 'how low can you go',[15] the focus has moved increasingly to neighbourhoods and parishes (both urban and rural), even though the current 9,000 neighbourhood, community, parish and town councils in England cover only a third of the population, with many gaps in large cities.[16] Supplementing these practical concerns about capacity are fundamental difficulties with the way localism is currently understood, and the implications this has for separation, definition and justification.

---

making on the Local Level: Rethinking Traditional Notions of Federalism, 17 Temp. Pol. & Civ. Rts. L. Rev. 371 (2008).

9 David J. Baron & Gerald E. Frug, Defensive Localism: A View of the Field from the Field, 21 J.L. & Pol. 261 (2005); Richard Briffault, Home Rule for the Twenty-First Century, 36 Urb. Law. 253 (2004).

10 For an Irish general power of competence, *see* Victoria Jenkins, Local Government Reform and Sustainable Development in Wales and Ireland, Envtl. L. Rev. 21, 25 (2009).

11 DCLG, Formative Evaluation of the Take-Up and Implementation of the Well Being Power – Annual Report 2006 (2006); ODPM, Formative Evaluation of the Take-Up and Implementation of the Well Being Power, 2003–2006 – Baseline report, 2005.

12 The greatest restriction in the United Kingdom is on the ability to raise local taxes.

13 Conservative Party, Control Shift Returning Power to Local Communities: Responsibility Agenda Policy, Green Paper No. 9, 12 (2010).

14 Building the Big Society, *supra* note 4.

15 Vivien Lowndes & Helen Sullivan, *How Low Can You Go? Rationales and Challenges for Neighbourhood Governance*, 86 Public Administration 53 (2008).

16 NALC, *National Association of Local Councils, Annual Report 2009–2010*, (2010).

For arguments in favour of localism are not uncontested.[17] In particular, as critical geographers and political scientists have explored, claims in favour of localism often suggest that localities are separate, both from each other and from wider regional, national or global concerns.[18] Local decisions need take no account of these wider spatial and societal concerns. Further, these devolutionary changes can also represent a rolling back of the obligations of the state and a contemporaneous understanding of localised responsibility. Localism can be both empowering and embody the 'core precepts ... [of] neo-liberal policies of personal responsibility, competition, efficiency and reduced assistance, where rhetoric about self government is used to signal a retreat of the state from the neighbourhood arena as people are called to take charge of their own well-being in line with claims that (over)intervention will distort market signals, fostering and sustaining "dependency" in the local populace'.[19] This 'new emphasis on the personal responsibilities of individuals, their families and their communities for their own future wellbeing and on their own obligation to take active steps to achieve this'[20] may be achieved through governmentality,[21] but as the examples here show, this focus on local responsibility and decision-making can also be achieved through quite straightforward regulatory rules.

One implication of using regulatory means to achieve this self-responsibility is that while social scientists often understand localisation as a dynamic process, understanding the locality, for example, as 'the repository of forces and activities that flourish or disintegrate into patterns of place-centred distinctiveness',[22] lawyers and administrators generally work with a locality in fixed, delineated terms. There is in administrative and land-use law and practice a deep (though not always articulated) connection between understandings of private property and local government; both having a fixed, spatial footprint and delineated boundaries capable of two-dimensional expression on a map.[23] This has the consequence that significantly different legal regimes can apply either side of a boundary line. As residential communities have become spatially 'governmentalised',[24] they have

17 These points are explored in more detail in ANTONIA LAYARD *Law and localism: the case of multiple occupancy housing* LEGAL STUDIES (2012) forthcoming.

18 ASH AMIN, *Local Community on Trial*, 34 ECONOMY AND SOCIETY, 612 (2005).

19 JULIE MACLEAVY, (Re)Analysing Community Empowerment: Rationalities and Technologies of Government in Bristol's New Deal for Communities, 46 URBAN STUDIES, 849 (2009).

20 NIKOLAS ROSE, The Death of the Social, 25 ECONOMY AND SOCIETY 327 (1996).

21 *Id.*

22 TIM O'RIORDAN & CHRIS CHURCH, Synthesis and Context, GLOBALISM, LOCALISM & IDENTITY (Tim O'Riordan ed. 2001).

23 Although in practice the extent of this curtilage or boundary is not always precise, NICHOLAS BLOMLEY, Flowers in the Bathtub: Boundary Crossings at the Public-Private Divide 36 GEOFORUM 281 (2005). *See also Skerritts of Nottingham, Ltd. v. Secretary of State*, [2001] Q.B. 59, 67 (Walker L.J.) (UK).

24 ROSE, *supra* note 20, at 353.

become subjects of regulatory geography in their own right, with spatial and place-based effects.

Certainly this separation and autonomy should not be overstated, since the ability of each locality to make effective decisions on its own is inevitably shaped by its relation to other forms of legal, economic and social governance, as well as its constitutional context.[25] Similarly, conventional assumptions of a trade-off between democracy and capacity require a more nuanced approach, in light of multilevel, multi-actor and e-enabled 'new governance'.[26] Nevertheless, the separation inherent in local government jurisdictions has underscored criticisms that such local autonomy can lead to 'power without responsibility'[27] and an emphasis on local self-interest[28] and, conversely, can lead to poorer and less powerful localities being left to fend for themselves.[29] This apparent isolation has provided one justification for the American Hope VI program that has enabled residents from poorer localities to transfer to wealthier ones, accessing higher quality services (even if social networks between new and existing residents in the wealthier neighbourhoods are not as effective as might be desired).[30] Similarly, there are significant debates to be had about the connection between localities and broader concerns for social justice,[31] environmental sustainability[32] or economic development.[33] So far, however, both the separation and interaction has been less well recognised in England where localism is predicated on separation, with each locality spatially delineated, and a line enclosing and separating one locality from the next.

---

25 David J. Barron, A Localist Critique of New Federalism, 51 Duke L.J. 434 (2002).

26 Lowndes & Sullivan, *supra* note 15.

27 Orlando E. Delogu, *Dilemma of Local Land Use Control: Power without Responsibility*, 33 Me. L. Rev. 15 (1981).

28 Sheryll Cashin, *Localism, Self-Interest, and the Tyranny of the Favored Quarter: Addressing the Barriers to New Regionalism* 88 Geo. L.J. 1985 (2009).

29 Amin, *supra* note 18.

30 Mark L. Joseph, Robert J. Chaskin & Henry S. Weber, *The Theoretical Basis for Addressing Poverty Through Mixed Income Development*, 42 Urban Affairs Review 369 (2007); Henry G. Cisneros, Lora Engdahl & Kurt L. Schmoke, From Despair to Hope: Hope VI and the New Promise of Public Housing in America's Cities (The Brookings Inst, 2009).

31 Richard Briffault, *Our Localism: Part I – The Structure of Local Government Law*, 90 Colum. L. Rev. 1 (1990); Richard Briffault, *Localism and Regionalism*, 48 Buff. L. Rev. 1, 15–18, (2000); Gerry Frug, *The City As a Legal Concept*, 93 Harv. L. Rev. 1057 (1980).

32 US Council on Environmental Quality, *The Quiet Revolution in Land Use Control* 1–3 (1971); John. R. Nolon, *In Praise of Parochialism: The Advent of Local Environmental Law*, 26 Harv. Envtl. L. Rev. 366 (2002); Jamison E. Colburn, *Localism's Ecology: Protecting and Restoring Habitat in the Suburban Nation*, 33 Ecology L. Q. 945 (2006).

33 Amin, *supra* note 18.

Again, in the United States this legal and spatial separation has long been recognised in concerns over exclusionary zoning, where maps delineate localities with different land-use rules inside and outside of the line. The enclosure, both legal and spatial, enables localities to look inwards, putting the interests and desires of their residents before broader, regional or national concerns about housing, welfare or diversity. The separation between one locality and the next is also highlighted by the limited ability of non-residents to challenge zoning laws that exclude them as a result of their inability to reside in the place of their choice.[34] This poses a genuine dilemma since there is something powerful in localism and place-based action that regulators and policymakers would like to capture. In England this autonomy and the pursuit of local identity is frequently translated into a legal system predicated upon conceptual and jurisdictional separation where localities are distinct from each other, even if these boundaries are often overlapping (when school 'catchment areas' for example overlap with healthcare 'primary care trusts' or local neighbourhoods under the Localism Act 2011). This requires thought about how localism can understand localities and places as connected and relational as critical geographers suggest yet can also operate within a legal system that relies on fixed, delineated spatial and legal distinctions. A progressive localist agenda in England and elsewhere needs to be alive to both these concerns.

Secondly, arguments in favour of localism also raise definitional concerns with scholars cautioning that we should not conflate different, though related, understandings of the term. When local government and constitutional lawyers address localism, they are often concerned with 'local autonomy' and the ability to make decisions for a given jurisdiction. This can, and should be, distinguished from local democracy,[35] a long-standing philosophical goal[36] and a policy and legislative aim[37] where citizens are encouraged and facilitated to take part in local decision-making (although there are significant critiques of such projects[38]). While local democracy is concerned with decision-making as part of a broader political project, local autonomy empowers the locality in its own right. These are intertwined in land-use formulations of localism that are concerned with localism as a 'reflection of local identity' capturing 'the capacity to define and express local identity through political activity'.[39] As the three land-use interventions

34 *Warth v. Seldin*, 422 US 490 (1975). *But see Village of Arlington Heights v. Metro.* Housing Development Corp, 429 US. 252 (1977).

35 Lawrence Pratchett, *Local Autonomy, Local Democracy and the 'New' Localism* 52 Political Studies 358 (2004).

36 John Stuart Mill, Considerations on Representative Democracy (New York, Harper & Bros 1862); Carole Pateman, Participation and Democratic Theory (Cambridge Univ. Press 1970).

37 European Charter of Local Self-Government, Council of Europe, 1985, article 4.3.

38 G. Mohan & K. Stokke, *Participatory Development and Empowerment: The Dangers of Localism*, 21 Third World Quarterly 247 (2000).

39 Pratchett, *supra* note, 35.

explored here demonstrate, land-use laws already provide some ability for English communities to express their local identity in residential form. These initiatives pave the way for further localist residential measures aimed at empowering communities, particularly at the neighbourhood or 'nano' scale. The question is whether local identities should be exclusively formulated by existing residents with little thought given to the impact on those 'outside'.[40]

Again this concern has been explored within analyses on exclusionary zoning where land-use identity is also at the heart of the reasoning in favour of the exclusion. In the United States this was confirmed in the case of *Village of Belle Terre et al v Boraas et al*,[41] where an ordinance prohibiting multiple occupation by more than two unrelated residents (unless they were household servants) was upheld by the Supreme Court as a valid instance of municipal land-use planning premised on a valid exercise of the State of New York's 'police power'. Justice Douglas held it to be permissible to zone for 'a quiet place where yards are wide, people few, and motor vehicles restricted are legitimate guidelines in a land-use project addressed to family needs'. Such an ideational project, he held, can rely on the police power 'to lay out zones where family values, youth values, and the blessings of quiet seclusion and clean air make the area a sanctuary for people'[42] using zoning ordinances to give physical effect to an idea of what the locality should be like. Here then, land-use laws are used to realise a spatial and social vision on the ground, pursuing a local identity. In the case of *Belle Terre*, the village was to be a 'family place', implementing a local preferred identity, even if this excludes some uses (and users) that do not conform to this vision.

Lastly, advocating localism requires justification, a contribution that is strikingly lacking in political and policy announcements that often draw simply on the 'romance of local community'.[43] For scholars, this raises questions about the desirability of strong group autonomy. In a land-use context, outside of shared

---

40 These interrelationships between 'insiders' and 'outsiders' have been well considered in debates on gentrification. *See* NEIL SMITH, *Toward a Theory of Gentrification: A Back to the City Movement by Capital, Not People* APA JOURNAL 538–548; LORETTA LEES, *A Reappraisal of Gentrification: Towards a 'Geography of Gentrification'*, 24 PROG. HUM. GEOGR. 389; DANNY DORLING, PHIL REES *A Nation Still Dividing: The British Census and Social Polarisation 1971–2001*, 35 ENVIRONMENT AND PLANNING A 1287-1313 (2003). They are also well represented in the analysis of the experiences of residents moving into mixed income neighbourhoods through the Hope VI program. *See* EDWARD G. GOETZ, *Clearing the Way: Deconcentrating the Poor in Urban America*, 25 (The Urban Inst. Press 2003); SUSAN CLAMPETT-LUNDQUIST, *Moving Over or Moving Up? Short-Term Gains and Losses for Relocated HOPE VI Families*, 7 CITYSCAPE 57 (2004); Mark Joseph, *Early Resident Experiences at a New Mixed-Income Development in Chicago*, 30 JOURNAL OF URBAN AFFAIRS 229 (2008).

41 416 US 1 (1973).

42 *Id.* at 9.

43 AMIN, *supra* note 18, at 618.

residential units or a company town,[44] a contractarian philosophy is unlikely, so that philosophical underpinning is more likely to draw on a communitarian approach which rejects an overly individualistic conception of self, reflecting a belief that human beings flourish when they interact with others. Despite the apparent similarities between property and place, with both delineated by fixed boundary lines, a locality is not the same as a house. While the ability to exclude visitors from private residential property has long been recognised,[45] if we are to permit existing residents to pull up the drawbridge to their residential community in the same way then, ultimately, 'a theory of insiders and outsiders that justifies the exercise of autonomy in its name' is still required.[46] Why should existing residents be able to restrict the ability of other potential residents to live where they choose?

For 'localism does not just happen',[47] it is a normative claim that requires articulation if it is not to become a 'local trap',[48] begging the question, but not explaining why decisions should be made at the local level. While theoretical arguments in favour of localism can be made on grounds of economic efficiency[49] or participatory democracy,[50] the claim in the land-use context is conventionally based on a spatial and temporal understanding of community. Localities are said to be more than the aggregate of individuals who live close to one another; they are 'communities – groups of people with shared concerns and values – distinct from those of the surrounding world and tied up with the history and circumstances of the particular places in which they are located'.[51] It is this common interest predicated on shared experience and difference from 'the surrounding world' that is said to underpin a claim for local rather than regional or national decision-making. The difficulty with this justification, of course, is that localities do not comprise a single community, but are sites of multiplicity and diversity. In practice, even if this is not always legally acknowledged, boundaries are dynamic and overlapping, they do not enclose single homogenous communities, each separated from the next.

---

44 While restrictions could be included in privately concluded covenants, such as those at Poundbury in Dorset or in Bournville in Birmingham, these are exceptional in the United Kingdom although conditions on property maintenance can be included in licensing conditions. Martin Knox & David Alcock, Approaches to community governance: Models for mixed tenure communities (Anthony Collins Solicitors, Birmingham) 3 (2002).

45 *Entick v. Carrington,* 19 State Trials 1029 (1765).

46 Richard C. Schragger, *The Limits of Localism*, 100 Mich. L. Rev. 373, 374 (2002).

47 *Id.*

48 Mark Purcell, *Urban Democracy and the Local Trap,* 43 Urban Studies 1921 (2006).

49 Charles Tiebout, *A Pure Theory of Local Expenditures*, 64 J. Pol. Econ. 416 (1956).

50 Pateman, *supra* note 36; Mill, *supra* note 36.

51 Briffault, *supra* note 30, at 17.

Moreover, these reasons for prioritising local decision-making are rarely articulated in practice. The primary political justification for localist land-use policies in England is that it produces 'better' localities, understood in the examples considered here as communities that are more rural, sustainable or viable than they would be if local decisions could not be made: as the previous Labour Government expressed, 'Localism matters. Local people care most about what happens outside their front doors; they care about whether their community is safe, attractive and one where people want to live. Not only do they care about these things, local people often know more than anyone about how their area can be improved and where the capacity lies to achieve those improvements'.[52] These are effectively judgments about expertise, with an assumption that the community knows best. Such lay knowledge may have much to recommend it in terms of procedural justice, enabling communities to protect an aspect of land use that they deem valuable, but no explanation is given for how these are substantively 'better' decisions.

The difficulty is that these assessments of what 'works' in the land-use context are often qualitative and subjective. They cannot be measured (however imperfectly by GDP, employment rates or health indices). The three instances of land-use regulation discussed in this chapter aim to limit social changes in locations of concern, to ensure that rural locations do not become 'dormitory towns', that urban residential neighbourhoods are not taken over by 'studentification' or that national parks flourish all year round and are not deserted outside of high days and holidays. The initiatives respond to local concerns about residential changes that alter the character of a neighbourhood.[53] New residents, be they commuters, young multiple occupants or holiday makers, alter demand for local community facilities, reducing the need for local schools, libraries or post offices which consequently decline. Their entry into the community requires local retail, commercial services and recreational facilities to restructure to suit the lifestyles of the newly predominant population.[54]

Overall, it appears that what is considered 'better' is actually 'preferred', with local decision-makers giving spatial form to locally determined identity, for example, as a rural, family or year-round place. These are, in practice, complex debates, often assuming a unitary community and a certain spatial authenticity or *genius loci*[55] living 'the right way' in a place while also empowering local communities to protect an aspect of land use that they deem valuable, giving

52 MAKING SENSE OF LOCALISM, (JO COLES, YVETTE COOPER & NICK RAYNSFORD eds, London, Smith Inst. 2004).

53 Press Release, DCLG, Local Powers for Councils to Protect Communities and Improve Standards in the Private Rented Sector (Jan. 27, 2010).

54 DCLG, Evidence Gathering – Housing in Multiple Occupation and Possible Planning Responses Final Report, at 7 (2008).

55 C. NORBERG-SCHULZ, GENIUS LOCI. TOWARDS A PHENOMENOLOGY OF ARCHITECTURE (London, Academy Editions 1980).

them self-determination and maintaining spatial identity and distinctiveness. The difficulty comes if this focus on identity becomes a claim for authenticity; that rural residents *should* be local (from this village not rehoused from the nearest city) or family neighbourhoods *should* be preserved rather than used by sharers. As critical geographers have explored, this static, fixed understanding of place and locality can be regressive,[56] leading to a suggestion that people are 'out of place' and do not belong.

This is inevitably a question of balance. Localism may be desirable to empower communities to shape their own local environment free from national or regional interference. It may enable local communities to protect an aspect of land use they deem valuable, maintaining local distinctiveness and identity. Since place-shaping laws and policies restrict both uses and users, critical land-use lawyers should continue to evaluate local restrictions carefully to ensure that the importance attached to protecting that which is deemed valuable is balanced against the exclusionary or restrictive effects for those who cannot live in the community of their choice.

While the examples of English localist planning rules in this analysis do not necessarily implement binary lines of exclusion, they pattern residential geographies in subtle and incremental ways. Even if they do not determine directly who can live where, these rules can restrict by proportion or percentages or on the basis of qualitative assumptions about what constitutes a rural, balanced or sustainable community. This intervention is justified in recognition of the benefits, both procedural and substantive, localism can bring. These initiatives are concerned both with self-determination and local identity, challenging the otherwise uncontrolled effects of the market. Nevertheless, while residential localism may have much to recommend it, critical land-use lawyers should evaluate its possible exclusionary and restrictive effects.

Case Studies in Residential Localism

Prioritising Rural Affordable Housing for 'Locals'

While there are several routes by which affordable housing can be constructed in the United Kingdom, in rural areas (in communities with fewer than 3,000 residents) one leading mechanism is development on rural exception sites. These developments provide small-scale affordable housing, often of approximately six

56 David Harvey, Justice, Nature & the Geography of Difference (Oxford: Blackwell 1986); Jon May, Globalization and the Politics of Place: Place and Identity in an Inner London Neighbourhood 21 Transactions of the Inst. of British Geographers 194 (1996); Tim Cresswell, In Place/Out of Place: Geography, Ideology, and Transgression, Univ. of Minnesota Press 1993); David Sibley, Geographies of Exclusion: Society and Difference in the West (New York and London, Routlege 1995).

to eight houses, following an application submitted by a quasi-public body such as a Registered Social Landlord (RSL) to build on a site that would not normally be released for housing. Affordable housing projects are often promoted and pursued by the community themselves, identifying local housing needs, agreeing a Village Design Statement, determining the character of the development, identifying acceptable sites and encouraging a local landowner to make suitable land available at a discounted price. In many ways, rural exception site housing provides the model for the community right to build now contained in the Localism Act, 2011.

Under central government guidance, each local rural exception site policy 'should seek to address the needs of the local community by accommodating households who are either current residents or have an existing family or employment connection, whilst also ensuring that rural areas continue to develop as sustainable, mixed, inclusive communities'.[57] It is local decision-makers who draft the precise priorities in each rural location, and there is no standard version of a local connection condition. Local formulations have proliferated throughout the country: the requirement is simply that that local occupancy conditions can be introduced for 'households who are either current residents or have an existing family or employment connection' with the precise formulation of the requirement to be established by the local authority.[58] In general, such conditions take the form of a cascade, where first one group is offered and then another. The approach taken by North Cornwall District Council is fairly typical here: applicants have to (1) be resident in the parish or adjoining parishes to the development for the last three years, or (2) previously have been resident in this area for five years at some point in the past, or (3) have close family connection to this area for a minimum of five years where a caring dependency relationship can be established, or (4) have a permanent job in this area for the last three years and have a demonstrable need to live closer to their employment.[59] Once built, these properties must be used for affordable housing according to these criteria in perpetuity and this obligation will be capable of legal enforcement.[60]

These inclusionary initiatives build on a narrative of shortages in rural housing caused by outsiders, with insufficient provision for rural residents who have been born and raised in a local environment where they cannot, once they reach independence, afford to live. This reflects a recognition that, as the Rural Economy and Affordable Housing Committee Report[61] concluded in 2008: 'migration from

57 DCLG, Planning Policy Statement 3: Housing (2010).

58 DCLG, Delivering Affordable Housing, 16[63] (2006).

59 They also have income restrictions, *see* NORTH CORNWALL DISTRICT COUNCIL, AFFORDABLE HOUSING EXPLAINED: A GUIDE FOR PARISH COUNCILS, available at http://www.cornwall.gov.uk/pdf/AffordableHousingParishPack.pdf, (last visited Jan., 22 2011).

60 A.S.106 (agreement setting out the terms of the obligation).

61 Led by the Cornish Liberal Democrat MP Matthew Taylor, a longtime campaigner for rural affordable housing. *See* MATTHEW TAYLOR, LIVING WORKING COUNTRYSIDE: THE TAYLOR REVIEW OF RURAL ECONOMY AND AFFORDABLE HOUSING (London, DCLG 2008).

urban to rural areas on a permanent basis is the primary driver of demand for housing and consequently unaffordable house prices'.[62] Locals, particularly young families and workers, have been priced out and inclusionary planning measures can be used to construct affordable housing to enable them to stay in the locality.

One widespread justification for this prioritisation for existing local residents is strongly articulated by Shucksmith, who claims that in addition to a belief that rural communities should not become 'gated communities' for the better off:

> there is the overriding consideration of social justice. No one can claim a statutory right to stay in the village where they were born and bred – unless they have been granted the right-to-buy their publicly owned property – but there is surely a limit how far from home the next generation is expected to move: if Birmingham is the nearest place with affordable accommodation for those brought up in a Worcestershire village, it offends a sense of natural justice to expect such a move.[63]

It is this widely accepted linkage between identity and locality that justifies the local connection criterion, prioritising affordable housing for locals in rural locations, with discomfort expressed by parish councils if the locality criterion is to extend beyond a tightly drawn area. Regional and national housing priorities can lead to offers of accommodation being made to residents that parish councils and local residents believe lack 'clear local credentials', particularly if sufficiently local residents cannot be identified within a short period of time.[64] Competing policy demands to allocate much-sought housing to those identified as homeless, even when individuals live in the next village or the nearest town, have sometimes led to disagreements. Housing associations can regard the new housing as 'their' resource, to allocate according to evaluations of housing need, while parish councillors and local residents, who have often worked hard to ensure that these houses would be built in their locality, view these new homes as 'their' or 'their village's' housing.[65]

The concerns here are not simply with a 'birth right' or priority conferred by existing residence. They draw on a linkage between identity, lifestyle and residence. Land use rules have been locally developed to prioritise potential residents from a single parish, disadvantaging potential residents who may live only a short car-ride

---

62 *Id.* at 115; *see also* Richard Best & Mark Shucksmith, *Homes for Rural Communities*, in Report of the Joseph Rowntree Foundation Rural Housing Policy Forum 1, 25–26 (2006).

63 *Id.*

64 Nick Gallent & Phillip Bell, *Planning Exceptions in Rural England: Past, Present and Future*, 15 Planning Practice and Research 375 (2000).

65 Richard Yarwood, Parish Councils, Partnership and Governance: The Development of 'Exceptions' Housing in the Malvern Hills District, England, 18 J. of Rural Studies 275, 286 (2002)

away sometimes on the basis that their behaviour is perceived as likely to clash with tranquil visions of rural life[66] (particularly if they come from nearby cities). This appears to draw on quite set ideas of rural living, even though different people in the same locality reveal multiple, complex discourses of rurality.[67] Ultimately this has meant that, despite its attractions and central government support, the rural exceptions policy has so far not been a great success. Limited numbers of houses have been built at considerable cost and effort, while rural parish councils, disappointed with the allocation of housing, are subsequently often uninterested in participating in new exception sites' developments.[68] A clearer conceptual understanding of the rationale for localism and an awareness of its emphasis on separation and distinctiveness would help to resolve these debates about who should be subsidised to live in the countryside and why.

Indeed, it is striking that prioritising applicants with a 'local connection' over those without contrasts markedly with national housing criteria that are based on 'priority need' for rehousing in existing social housing regardless of local origins.[69] The rural approach also contrasts with the strategy adopted in urban areas. In the London Borough of Kensington and Chelsea, for example, residents will be eligible for affordable housing after having lived in the borough for just six months, with priority given to key workers and existing council and housing association tenants.[70] When Kensington attempted to introduce an urban 'local connection' equivalent, it was ridiculed in the press.[71] While in rural locations, rootedness, cultural coherence and a preservation of local identity are understood as significant, in urban areas, housing is prioritised for 'key workers' and (through minimum income requirements) to those already contributing financially to the economy. These tensions will continue to underpin the newly proposed localist

66 *Id.* 272

67 Ray Pahl, Class and Community in English Commuter Villages, 5 Sociologia Ruralis 5 (1965); Chris Philo, Neglected Rural Geographies: A Review, 8 J. of Rural Studies 193 (1992); Paul Cloke, Paul Milbourne & Chris Thomas, Living Lives in Different Ways? Deprivation, Marginalization and Changing Lifestyles in Rural England 22 Transactions of the Inst. of British Geographers, 210 (1997).

68 The allocation rules are generally made at the county level rather than by the village itself. This will reflect local housing needs over a broader regional area as well as attempting to prioritise residents from the village itself. These tensions, particularly when there are insufficient 'locals' requiring the housing, has resulted in ill feeling if new residents come from nearby towns, to fulfil council housing obligations, instead. Affordable Rural Housing Commission: Final Report (Department of Environment, Food and Rural Affairs, 2006).

69 Andrew Arden et al., Housing Law (Sweet & Maxwell 2007).

70 Affordable Home Ownership, available at http://www.rbkc.gov.uk/housing/findingahome/affordablehomeownership.aspx (last visited Jan., 31 2011).

71 Jill Sherman, *Super-Rich Barred as Kensington Keeps It in Family*, The Times Newspaper, November 14, 2005; *see also Kensington's Drive to Keep Out Outsiders*, Estates Gazette, February 18, 2006.

provisions giving communities a 'right to build' in their locality if sufficient residents approve of the proposal without obtaining planning permission. Both in this new initiative and under existing rural exception site housing provisions, there may be good reasons for restrictive land-use rules and practices that prioritise locals but disadvantage outsiders. To be coherent, however, these debates require a clearer understanding of localist land-use law and policy and its potentially restrictive effects.

Localism and Multiple Occupation

In some urban neighbourhoods, increasing concentrations of multiple occupants have contributed to rapid and highly localised changes in residential geography. Student residents have become a particular concern for some, though by no means all, residents, with lurid media coverage suggesting that 'here come the students – and there goes the neighbourhood'.[72] Worried about an increase in denser, more 'cheek by jowl' living, critics of this intensification have for some time argued that using a property for multiple occupation should automatically require planning permission and that this should be refused in some locations, including in streets close to city centres and universities that are already 'saturated' with students and other multiple occupants. This has led to restrictive measures implemented through the concept of 'change of use'.[73] If the use of a property changes, in particular from one regulatory use class to another, the property owner will need to apply for planning permission for this change of use. In the case of multiple occupation, local authorities have drawn maps delineating specific locations where no more permissions for such a change of use will be granted. Inevitably, this then excludes further multiple occupants, restricting their ability to live where they wish.

Land use regulation of multiple occupation by unrelated residents and occupation by a single individual, couple or family proceeds on the assumption that these types of land use are different. This is in many ways a difficult claim to maintain since using a property either as a 'dwelling house' or for 'multiple occupation' entail very similar activities including sleeping, eating and leisure. In practice, it is the very subtlety of these distinctions that underpinned nuanced and detailed judicial decision-making determining just when a single household becomes a house in multiple occupation:[74] the key test for planning authorities,

72 Louise Tickle, *Here Come the Students – and There Goes the Neighbourhood*, *Education Guardian*, May 15, 2007.

73 The Town and Country Planning (Use Classes) (Amendment) (England) Order 2010 SI No. 653.

74 *Barnes v. Sheffield CC*, (1995) 27 H.L.R. 719, 722–726 (UK); *Simmons v. Pizzey*, (1979) A.C. 37; *R (on the application of Hossack) v. Kettering BC*, [2003] 2 P & CR 34 (UK); *Birmingham Corp. v. MHLG*, (1964) 1 Q.B. 178; (1963) 3 All E.R. 688 (UK); *Secretary of State for Env't., Transp. and Regions v. Waltham Forest LBC*, [2002] EWCA (Civ) 330 (Eng.).

planning inspectors (on appeal) and the courts was whether residents lived together 'as a single household'[75] with judges concluding that these questions were ones of 'fact and degree', distinguishing between residents who came to the property as a 'pre-formed group' for a 'predetermined period' from those who came to the property one by one, for largely indefinite and dissimilar periods[76] or between 'the family kind of picture' and 'the typical pattern of a house in multiple occupation'[77] Complaining that this provided insufficient certainty on the ground, leading to 'paralysis' for communities wanting their decision-makers to limit the numbers of houses in multiple occupation,[78] politicians, neighbourhood groups and planners campaigned for increased certainty in distinguishing between 'dwelling houses' and houses in multiple occupation.

Responding to these campaigns, the outgoing Labour Government introduced a regulation in 2010 replacing these qualitative investigations into whether or not residents lived as a single household with a simple numerical limit.[79] Now whenever three or more unrelated residents live together, the property is no longer a 'dwelling house',[80] it is now a house in multiple occupation: this 'change of use' requires planning permission, which can be refused if the application does not accord with the provisions of the local plan or satisfy other 'material considerations'; the regulation applies throughout England, whether or not localities are concerned with multiple occupation. Responding to complaints of bureaucracy for landlords and local authorities alike, this new regulation was amended by the new coalition Conservative-Liberal Democrat Government within months of coming into force. Automatic planning permission for changes of use from a dwelling house to a house in multiple occupation was granted throughout the country:[81] the scheme was tweaked, however, to allow local planning authorities to choose to opt out of this scheme, rescinding the automatic 'permitted development' and requiring (and refusing) planning permission for changes from a dwelling house to a house in multiple occupation in locally determined areas.

The revised regulatory regime on multiple occupation consequently has a significant localist kick. Introducing the changes, the housing minister explicitly characterised them as devolution, stating that decisions on houses in multiple

75 ODPM Circular 03/2005, para. 77; Town and Country Planning (Use Classes) Order 1987, under the C3 use class. For the new regime, *supra* note 73.

76 *Rogers v. Islington LBC* (2000) 32 H.L.R. 138, 145 (Per Nourse LJ).

77 *Barnes v. Sheffield City Council* (1995) 27 H.L.R. 719.

78 For example, Alan Simpson, MP for Nottingham South: The *Barnes v. Sheffield* decision has paralysed local authorities such as mine and many other university towns and cities, House of Commons Standing Committee on Bills, Home Energy Conservation Bill, 2002, col. 106.

79 *Supra* note 73.

80 Under use class C3, The Town and Country Planning (Use Classes) Order 1987, SI No. 764.

81 The Town and Country Planning (General Permitted Development) (Amendment) (England) Order 2010 (Amendment) (England) Order SI 2010 No. 654.

occupation 'should reflect local priorities expressed through the local plan, rather than nationally imposed rules'.[82] Exercising these local powers, entire cities, including Manchester and Portsmouth, are considering withdrawing automatic permissions to convert a house into a house in multiple occupation, while other local authorities are designating neighbourhoods deemed to already have too many houses in multiple occupation. This enables local decision-makers to draw upon centrally facilitated local government discretion to require an application for planning permission, whilst then consulting with local neighbourhoods to issue maps and guidance, identifying and delineating those streets where planning permission for changes of use from a dwelling house to a house in multiple occupation would no longer be permitted once a set proportion or percentage of houses are already multiply-occupied in a delineated area. After these thresholds have been reached, no further permissions to convert will be granted and no additional multiple occupants will be able to move in.[83] With percentages imposing a ceiling of 5–30 per cent multiple occupants,[84] these locations are to have a majority of individuals, couples or families as residents with a minority of multiple occupants. The rationale for these restrictions is that these limits ensure that neighbourhoods are 'sustainable' or 'balanced'.

There are strong parallels here with the case-law on exclusionary zoning, epitomised in the decision in *Belle Terre*. There are differences: notably that under the English rules multiple occupants are restricted, rather than excluded altogether.[85] Yet in both cases, local decision-makers, motivated by preferences expressed in their communities often at the neighbourhood or 'micro-local' scale, are able to use principles of residential localism to shape the place even though there is a question in the context of multiple occupation about which type of resident is restricting the choices of the other. Existing residents began this campaign for greater regulatory control on multiple occupation by arguing that they were being pushed out by rent-seeking landlords and anti-social students. Since 2010, regulations now limit the ability of multiple occupants to live in areas they might otherwise prefer (particularly in locations close to the city centre and higher education facilities). Both local residents and multiple occupants can claim to have been driven out, the former by the uncontrolled market, the latter by

82 Grant Shapps, House Of Commons Hansard June 17, 2010: Column 55WS.

83 This means that there is no increase in the number of multiple occupants. Given the fluid nature of such occupancy, the actual occupants might change.

84 DCLG, *supra* note 54, at 25–28.

85 In *Belle Terre*, the ordinance requiring single family occupation applied to the village as a whole so that no unrelated multiple occupation was permitted within the village. In England, unrelated multiple occupation is limited locally by quota (by percentages) or by introducing areas of restraint' where additional multiple occupation will only be permitted in exceptional circumstances. Some multiple occupation will already be permitted within these locations but no further shared houses can be established without a grant of planning permission which, within these areas, will almost never be granted.

regulation. Nevertheless, while there may be limited sympathy for students, these restrictions on multiple occupation affect all multiple occupants, the majority of whom are young and single, working migrants or economically inactive, with the poorest of these characterised as 'vulnerable, with little financial power or muscle in the market place'.[86] These are not value neutral debates. The ability to substantially reorder patterns of residential geography through planning law requires careful evaluation and analysis.

Restrictions on Second Homes: Attempted Exclusion

In England, as in many countries throughout the world, coastlines and rural landscapes attract wealthy residents on a part-time basis, buying houses as a 'second home'. The sharp increases in house prices in some parts of Devon, Cornwall and the Lake District has led local politicians to call for restrictions to be imposed on the use of both existing and new build properties in popular and contested areas, in particular, in national parks. Empirical analyses of the causes of sharp increases in house prices have indicated that 'migration from urban to rural areas on a permanent basis is the primary driver of demand for housing and consequently unaffordable house prices', and that 'there is no clear evidence that second homes or holiday lets greatly affects affordability for local people'.[87] Nevertheless, as commentators broadly agree, there are 'micro-crises'.[88] In some villages and communities, levels of second-home ownership exceed 50 per cent, changing the nature of the community, leading to the closure or reduction of local schools and services and becoming 'ghost towns' in winter. The concerns about second homes in many ways echo those about multiple occupation, though they are concerned with under-occupation or de-intensification rather than intensification of use. In both cases, however, patterns of residential geography are altered by the unrestricted operation of the market. Yet in the context of second homes, calls for regulatory intervention have so far been rejected by central government.

Recognising that these 'hotspots' of second-home ownership occur, the call for legal intervention is a localised one. As one politician, Andrew George, MP for the Cornish holiday town of St Ives and the nearby Isles of Scilly, argues: 'Local planning authorities should be given the tools not to outlaw all second homes but to outlaw excessive second-home ownership in many parts of the country'.[89] Such a proposal was made by the 2001 Exmoor National Park Authority draft Local Plan, when it outlined its suggested residential planning policies for the national park that runs along the north coast of Devon in the south west of England. Here

86 DCLG, *supra* note 54, at 11.

87 Taylor, *supra* note 61, at 115.

88 The Taylor report notes there are 64 wards (1%) with more than 20% of the housing stock recorded as second homes including 'micro-crises' in St Minver in North Cornwall (43%) and Beadnell in Berwick-upon-Tweed (42%). *Id.*

89 *House of Commons Hansard*, Jul 14, 2004, Column 463WH.

officials included a policy to control the 'change of use of existing dwellings to second homes' to address the rate of increase in second-home ownership on Exmoor National Park where at least 23 per cent of properties are occupied as second homes.[90] A similar proposal was also included in the Liberal Democrat manifesto, proposing that local authorities should be enabled 'to require specific planning permission for new second homes in areas where the number of such homes is threatening the viability of a community'.[91] Such a localist land-use policy could enable local communities to restrict second-home ownership in 'honeypot' coastal or rural villages. Drawing on a parallel with concentrations of multiple occupation, villages that consider themselves to have 'too many' second homes could draw up planning policies justifying refusing applications for further 'conversions' from using a property as a dwelling house to using it as a second home. Planning restrictions could enable communities to define themselves in terms of full-time residents.

When the Taylor Committee on the Rural Economy and Affordable Housing reported in 2008, it recommended examining 'the options for trialling planning rules limiting change of use of full time homes to part time occupation (as second homes or holiday lets), in one or more of the National Parks'.[92] This would require local or national park authorities to be able to determine that a change from using a house as a dwelling house to using it for less than a set period requires planning permission and to refuse it where 'too many' second homes are already deemed to exist: such a proposal was also made by the Affordable Rural Housing Commission in 2006, who devised an 'opt-in' scheme that is remarkably similar to that now in existence for houses in multiple occupation.[93]

The question is why local restrictions on second-home ownership have been consistently opposed by central government. Both the previous Labour Government and the current coalition government reject such a policy for reasons that are not always clearly defined, though they are often claimed to be 'for legal reasons',[94] arguing both that second homes are difficult to define,[95] although second homes have long been distinguished from 'main' residences for tax and

90 Exmoor National Park Local Plan 2001–2011, 64 *available at* http://www.exmoor-nationalpark.gov.uk/index/living_in/planning/local-plan.htm (last visited Jan., 31 2011).

91 *Liberal Democrat Manifesto* (2010) 81.

92 Taylor, *supra* note 61, recommendation 22.

93 Affordable Rural Housing Commission, *supra* note 68, 65.

94 According to then The Parliamentary Under-Secretary of State for the Environment, Transport and the Regions (Mr. Chris Mullin), House of Commons Hansard, 9 Feb 2000: Column 110WH. The current Conservative [Minister] argues rather opaquely that 'there are serious difficulties in how that can be done, not least because, for the first time, we are bringing the ownership of an asset into consideration of whether it was a material planning use or not', Andrew Stunnel, House of Commons Hansard, 8 Jun 2010: Column 310.

95 House of Commons Hansard, 26 Feb 2002: Column 1176W.

local planning purposes[96] or that planning restrictions on use as a second home 'would be close to impossible' to enforce[97] even though there is good evidence to the contrary. In small, close-knit communities, cases of unauthorized second-home ownership (that contravened restrictive covenants) have already come to light, with residents having no difficulty in illustrating under-use. In *Caradon v Paton*, for example, Mr Castle, a councillor, gave evidence (sworn in an affidavit) that 'his watch on the properties established that the pattern of occupation suggested that they were occupied simply for short-term holiday use, one or two weeks at a time'.[98] Similarly, in Appledore, a village particularly popular with second-home owners, Terry Bailey, born and bred in the village, chose to illustrate how many homes were occupied only occasionally by poking black bin bags through the letter boxes of those properties which lay empty for months at a time.[99] With an asset as valuable as a property and the potential requirement to compel owners to live there full-time, there are good reasons to suggest that concerns about enforcement are overstated. At the very least a pilot project, as suggested by the Taylor Commission,[100] could be introduced over a trial period to investigate the feasibility of such a change.

In practice, while often couched in terms of legal impossibility, the reasons for refusal may have more prosaic grounds. The common sense explanation is a function of economic class and status. Wealthy owners of second homes have more political clout than younger or immigrant renters of multiple occupancy property. Further, while the discourse on second homes is very much a rural one, some urban areas, particularly in London,[101] have some of the highest rates of second-home ownership with professionals using their urban 'pied-à-terre' during the week and returning home at the weekends. Most Members of Parliament are themselves second homeowners for this purpose and can resist the pressures from localities far outside the 'Westminister village' calling for stronger controls on second homes. This restraint also fits in with prevailing assumptions about recreation and property ownership. Owning a second home is also a highly valued aspiration for many that live outside rural or coastal areas, who dream of a 'retreat' away from their daily lives. While local communities clamour for change, the concern does not reverberate at a national scale. Reform seems extremely unlikely.

---

96 *Frost (Inspector of Taxes) v. Feltham*, [1981] 1 WLR 452 (UK); *See* Alan Murdie, *Home Sweet Home?* 148 Solicitors J. (2004).

97 Nick Gallent, Alan Mace & Mark Tewdwr-Jones, *Dispelling a Myth? Second Homes in Rural Wales*, 35 Area 271, 272 (2000); Daniel Scarf, *When Is a Home Not a Home? When It's on Exmoor*, J. of Planning & Envtl. L. 1175 (2002).

98 *Caradon v. Paton*, (2001) 33 H.L.R. 34, [6].

99 *Second Homes Biggest Threat*, Western Morning News (Truro), Feb. 4, 2004.

100 Taylor, *supra* note 61, at 118.

101 Second homes as a percentage of total chargeable dwellings by council tax valuation band and by area classification, 2007/08, CLG, 2008, *available at* http://www.ruralcommunities.gov.uk/files/Second_Homes_2007-08.xls (last visited Jan., 31 2011).

Conclusion

There is a delicate balance to be struck between localism and exclusion or restriction in the land-use context. Residential geographies can be patterned by both the market and by regulatory intervention with both regulation and the lack of regulation capable of having progressive or regressive effects. Moreover, while any disputes can be presented as bilateral, between insiders and outsiders, in practice these tensions draw on uncertainties about the degree of separation, justification or the ability to pursue a local spatial identity. They question, for example, the extent to which coastal or rural areas belong to permanent resident locals or whether owner occupiers should be able to resist landlords by imposing restrictions on sharing houses (and sharers).

These questions rest on an assumption about the extent to which residential localism promotes a restrictive, inward-looking understanding of place, or whether it preserves spatial difference and identity, ensuring the preservation of situated knowledge, practices and traditions. For the 'defensive localisation',[102] which each of these three examples to some extent embody, is not necessarily regressive.[103] There may be good reasons to preserve 'family', 'rural' or 'coastal' neighbourhoods rather than developing 'non-places' where flow and throughput are more important than place.[104] Yet this must be a balanced debate. Policymakers and regulators, at both the local and the national scale, should consider the parties in these ideational projects. It is important to analyse the actors: who is acting defensively and who are they are trying to exclude? The realities of politics and power matter in housing; they should not be ignored.

As long-standing discussions on exclusionary zoning have explored, these are not value-free debates. Legislative mechanisms are applied to questions of expertise (creating communities that are 'sustainable' or 'balanced'), which are not necessarily best resolved at the local level (aspects of homelessness or vacation patterns may be better assessed beyond the local). Critical geographers have suggested that to be progressive, places should be understood relationally, as dynamic and connected, characterised by 'routes not roots'.[105] Yet as long as these questions about localism's scales, meanings and rationales remain unresolved,

102 Arturo Escobar, *Culture Sits in Places: Reflections on Globalism and Subaltern Strategies of Localization* 20 Political Geography 139 (2001); Arturo Escobar, Territories of Difference: Place, Movements, Life, Redes (Duke Univ. Press 2008).

103 Noel Castree, *Differential Geographies: Place, Indigenous Rights and 'Local' Resources*, 23 Political Geography 133 (2004)

104 Manuel Castells, The Information Age: Economy, Society and Culture, The Rise of the Network Society 1 (Oxford, Blackwell 1996); Marc Auge, Non-Place: Introduction to an Anthropology of Supermodernity (London, Verso 1995).

105 Doreen Massey, For Space (London, Sage 2005); John Allen, Doreen Massey & Alan Cochrane, Rethinking the Region (London, Routledge 1988), Ash Amin and Nigel Thrift, Cities: Reimagining the Urban (Cambridge, Polity Press 2002).

these land-use initiatives and their sanctioning or refusal by central government,[106] will continue to be controversial.

Acknowledgement

The paper on which this chapter is based has benefited greatly from the thoughtful and thought-provoking comments by participants at the 2010 Association of Law, Property and Society Conference in Washington DC and at a seminar at Cardiff Law School. It has also been improved substantially by the careful and insightful editing of Michael Diamond.

106 This is required in the United Kingdom.

Chapter 3

De-concentrating Poverty: De-constructing a Theory and the Failure of Hope

Michael Diamond

Introduction

> Our nation is moving toward two societies,
> one black, one white – separate and unequal[1]

Racial segregation has been a problem in the United States for generations. Despite the passage of the Fair Housing Act in 1968,[2] many of the nation's communities remain highly segregated by race. The economic segregation of the poor has also been a major problem although until about 25 years ago it had commanded far less attention. Given the high correlation between poverty and race, the combination of racial discrimination and the limited availability of affordable housing has had the effect of thrusting the poor into (or creating) neighborhoods with concentrated pockets of extreme poverty. Many commentators have claimed that this concentration of poverty has produced enormously negative societal consequences.

In 1987 William Julius Wilson, then a University of Chicago sociologist, published his influential book, *The Truly Disadvantaged*.[3] While Wilson was not the first to point out the negative effects of concentrated poverty, the book fomented a revolution in housing policy. Wilson argued that the concentration of poverty, the very high percentage of people with incomes below the poverty line living within a defined geographic community, resulted in severely negative societal externalities far in excess of what would be expected for isolated circumstances of individual poverty.[4]

Wilson's observations led to a series of federal and local policy prescriptions, each having the ostensible goal of de-concentrating poverty in high-concentration

---

1 US Nat'l Advisory Comm'n on Civil Disorders, Report Of The National Advisory Commission On Civil Disorders (1968) [hereinafter Kerner Commission Report].

2 42 U.S.C. §§ 3601–3619 (2006).

3 William Julius Wilson, *The Truly Disadvantaged: The Inner City, The Underclass, and Public Policy* (1987).

4 This argument, while accepted by many social scientists and policy-makers, has been strongly contested, a point to which I will return later in this chapter.

neighborhoods. Among the resulting legislative initiatives was the HOPE VI program for the redevelopment of public housing.[5] Congress also adopted a demonstration program, Moving to Opportunity (MTO),[6] in which low-income residents were given special §8 vouchers in order to move to other, often suburban, low-poverty neighborhoods. There were also several local programs designed to accomplish the same result.[7]

Even before *The Truly Disadvantaged* was published, there had been efforts to break up the racially concentrating effects of federal public housing policy. For example, *Hills v Gautreaux*[8] challenged the racially segregated siting of public housing by the Chicago Housing Authority (CHA). The litigation resulted in a consent decree that ultimately allowed more than 7,000 households to move to less segregated housing in the Chicago metropolitan area.[9] Due, again, to the high correlation between class and race, particularly in public housing, the extreme racial segregation that was the focal point of the *Gautreaux* suit also resulted in a very high concentration of poverty in those Chicago neighborhoods.[10]

There is, however, a certain irony to the development of and ardor for these governmental programs, since a major contributing cause of racial and (to a great extent) economic segregation in many residential communities had been the housing and housing finance policy of federal and local governments. For example, beginning in the 1930s and continuing, certainly at least, through the 1960s and early 1970s, the Federal Housing Administration (FHA), The United Stated Department of Housing and Urban Development (HUD), and their predecessors

---

5 Quality Housing and Work Responsibility Act of 1998, Pub L. No. 105–276, 112 Stat. 2461, 2473–74 (1998) (codified at 42 U.S.C. § 1437v (2006)).

6 Moving to Opportunity for Fair Housing, Pub. L. No. 103-120, § 3, 107 Stat. 1148 (1993) (codified at 42 U.S.C. § 1437f (2006)).

7 One of the oldest and most widely utilized is Inclusionary Zoning. Inclusionary Zoning (which may be mandatory or voluntary, depending on the jurisdiction) requires developers to include a certain percentage of affordable units in their residential developments of more than a certain number of units. In exchange, the developer receives some form of regulatory relief, often a density bonus above what the zoning regulations would ordinarily allow or fast-track processing of permits. The percentage of affordable units and the targeted income of lower income residents varies by jurisdiction. *See, e.g.*, Montgomery County, Md., Code § 25A–1 (2006).

8 425 US 284 (1976).

9 Molly Thompson, *Relocating from the Distress of Chicago Public Housing to the Difficulties of the Private Market: How the Move Threatens to Push Families Away from Opportunity*, 1 Nw. J.L. & Soc. Pol'y 267, 270 ("The Gautreaux Program ended in 1998 after relocating approximately 7100 families." (citing Leonard S. Rubinowitz & James E. Rosenbaum, Crossing the Class and Color Lines: From Public Housing to White Suburbia 39 (2000))).

10 Of course, the fact that the original neighborhoods contained large public housing projects almost guaranteed the high poverty concentrations that accompanied the racially discriminatory siting policies of the CHA.

and affiliates had an explicit policy of segregating the races and, as time went on, of displacing residents in predominantly black communities in the name of redeveloping "blighted" urban neighborhoods.[11]

For a particularly stark example of the interplay between racial segregation and concentrations of poverty, one, again, need look no further than the policies concerning the siting of public housing developments that were challenged in *Gautreaux*. For decades, public housing developments, which came to house some of the nation's poorest families, were placed in predominantly minority neighborhoods.[12] These developments, large, highly segregated, and housing an extremely poor population, contributed mightily to the considerable concentration of poverty in those communities (in fact, often *causing* the high concentration of poverty) while also reinforcing the preexisting pattern of segregation.[13]

The *Gautreaux* litigation, begun in 1966, was initiated by residents in segregated public housing operated by the CHA.[14] The litigation resulted in a consent judgment that called for the dispersal of CHA residents to less racially segregated communities, which, incidentally, were also often less poor. Under the consent decree program, CHA residents were given vouchers that allowed them to move to other housing accommodations and about 7,000 households took advantage of the program.

After *Gautreaux*, several programs, both federal and local, were initiated to the point that today, the effort to de-concentrate poverty has become an accepted, if not the preeminent, anti-poverty choice in federal and many local policy circles.[15] The de-concentration policy, however, has met with substantial criticism from a range of commentators including academics, community activists and policy-makers as well as from many residents who are (or who are threatened to be) subjected to the de-concentration policy. The criticism has been about both the practical implementation and performance of the programs and about more conceptual issues concerning their very nature.

On the practical level, studies have shown repeatedly that many of the hoped-for fundamental benefits of de-concentration have not been achieved. For example, low-income residents have failed, for the most part, to build social capital when they have moved into higher-income neighborhoods or when they returned to

---

11 *See, e.g.*, Kenneth T. Jackson, *Crabgrass Frontier: The Suburbanization of the United States*, 195–218 (1985).

12 *See Gautreaux*, 425 US at 286–87.

13 The governmental policies were not, of course, the sole cause of the segregated communities. In fact government policy typically reflected public attitudes at the time. These attitudes were also often shared by the government policymakers.

14 While conditions in the various public housing developments were often deplorable and while the social environment was dangerous and unsatisfactory, the case was about the discriminatory siting and resident placement in these developments.

15 Even the Low Income Housing Tax Credit program, the other major governmental affordable housing initiative, permits some mixing of income levels.

redeveloped HOPE VI neighborhoods.[16] Moreover, there has not been appreciable gain for the economically integrated low-income residents in their employment or income status.[17] Instead, there is substantial evidence that such residents have suffered significant economic or other hardship due to higher housing costs,[18] higher costs of daily living,[19] and problems with transportation.[20]

On the conceptual level, critics have focused on the destruction of preexisting communities[21] and the elimination for many people of the social safety net that their old communities provided for them.[22] Some take the critique even further and suggest that, as was claimed to be the case with Urban Renewal and the Interstate Highway program, the current de-concentration programs are deliberately designed to and, in most cases do, displace African-American families and communities.[23]

In this chapter I add my own critique to the literature on the de-concentration of poverty.[24] Part of my concern is about implementation. For example, even if all of the supposed benefits were available to relocating residents (which they

16 Melody L. Boyd et al., The Durability of Gains from the Gautreaux Two Residential Mobility Program: A Qualitative Analysis of Who Stays and Who Moves from Low-Income Poverty Neighborhoods, 20 Hous. Pol'y Debate 119, 125 (2010).

17 Edward G. Goetz, Better Neighborhoods, Better Outcomes? Explaining Relocation Outcomes in HOPE VI. 12 Cityscape 2, 9 (2010).

18 Larry Buron et al, the hope vi Resident Tracking Study 99 (2002), available at http://www.urban.org/uploadedpdf/410591_HOPEVI_ResTrack.pdf: Susan J. Popkin, The HOPE VI Program: What has Happened to the Residents, in Where Are the Poor to Live: Transforming Public Housing Communities 83 (Larry Bennett et al., eds, 2006).

19 Boyd et al., *supra* note 16, at 125; Susan J. Popkin et al., A Decade of HOPE VI: Research Findings and Policy Challenges 45 (2004), http:// www.urban.org/UploadedPDF/411002_HOPEVI.pdf.

20 James Rosenbaum et al., New Capabilities in New Places: Low-Income Black Families in Suburbia, in the geography of opportunity: race and housing choice in metropolitan america 168 (Xavier de Souza Briggs ed., 2005).

21 Stephen Steinberg, The Myth of Concentrated Poverty, in The Integration Debate: Competing Futures for American Cities 213, (Chester Hartman & Gregory Squires eds, 2010)

22 This includes financial support from friends and relatives as well as other support such as child care and transportation assistance.

23 *See, e.g.*, Steinberg, *supra* note 21. ("It is debatable whether integration efforts bestow on poor African-Americans economic or sociological benefits or, rather, destroy non-white political power, sense of community, culture, and neighborhood-based support systems.") (quoting William P. Wilen & Wendy L. Stasell, Gautreaux and Chicago's Public Housing Crisis: The Conflict between Achieving Integration and Providing Decent Housing for Very Low-Income African Americans, in Where Are Poor People to Live? Transforming Public Housing Communities *supra* note 18, at 239, 249); David Imbroscio, "[U]nited and Actuated by Some Common Impulse of Passion": Challenging the Dispersal Consensus in American Housing Policy Research, 30 J. Urb. Aff. 111 (2008).

24 While the critique will focus primarily on the HOPE VI program, which is by far the largest of the federal de-concentration programs, the concerns that I and others have

are not), the aggregate number of households being relocated by these programs represents only a tiny portion of the households living in highly concentrated neighborhoods.[25] Moreover, the destroyed affordable housing in poor communities is not being replaced on a one-for-one basis. The result is an increasing gap between the demand for decent affordable housing and the supply.[26] This is particularly troubling for the lowest income residents who comprise a significant percentage of those who live in public housing. Because the private market cannot economically house them and there are no other governmental programs designed to do so, the units lost due to de-concentration will never be replaced.[27] The result is increased homelessness, more people "doubling up" in units, and more people paying a very high percentage of their household income for rent, thereby leaving other household needs unmet.

My main critical focus, however, will be on the conceptual problems of de-concentration. In particular, I am apprehensive about the social, cultural, and political ramifications of destroying existing communities. Despite popular conceptions, poor communities, just as other communities, contain networks and institutions that are valuable to the residents of those communities and to society. For just this reason, many people faced with involuntary dislocation under one of the de-concentration programs resist the move. Moreover, those who are forced to move often move back to their original or to a similar neighborhood at their first opportunity.[28] The consequence is that the forcible de-concentration of poverty in one neighborhood often creates new or worsening concentrations in other neighborhoods. This presumably unintended consequence, a result of the

---

expressed are applicable, to a great extent, to the other federal and many local programs. Where critiques do not have general applicability, I will discuss the distinctions to be made.

25 As of 2008, 72,265 households had been relocated from HOPE VI developments, which represented 98% of the planned relocation. There were 91,802 units demolished, 95% of the planned demolition: 72,196 units were constructed or rehabilitated, 65% of the planned total of 111,059. Of these planned new or rehabilitated units, about 55% will go to public housing residents although only about 24% of the original households had returned to the completed HOPE VI development of the planned 38% of households to return. G. Thomas Kingsley, Appendix A: Scope and Status of the Hope VI Program, in From Despair to Hope: Hope VI and the New Promise of public housing in American cities 300 (Henry C. Cisneros & Lora Engdahl eds, 2009). Kingsley discounts the net loss of units by pointing out that many of the destroyed units were unoccupied and many of these were "vacant and uninhabitable" (although he concedes that the number of habitable but unoccupied units is not reliably known). *Id.*

26 J. Peter Byrne & Michael Diamond, Affordable Housing, Land Tenure, and Urban Policy: The Matrix Revealed, 34 Fordham Urb. L.J. 527 (2007).

27 It is not an adequate response to say that a large number of the demolished units were uninhabited or even that they were uninhabitable. The fact is that those units were in existence to serve the extremely low-income population but they have permanently been taken out of the inventory.

28 Boyd et al., *supra* note 16, at 122.

lack of affordable housing throughout the economy, suggests the weakness, if not the failure, of the de-concentration policy.

It does not follow that we, as a society, should encourage concentrated poverty. Economic integration has many advantages. In fact, to the extent that de-concentration programs are voluntary, that is, to the extent that residents of concentrated low-income communities want to move to mixed-income, mixed-race communities, they should be encouraged. On the demand side, support, both financial and technical, should be made available by government to residents of high-concentration neighborhoods. On the supply side, greater support should be provided for the development and preservation of affordable units throughout the economy and fair housing laws should be strictly enforced to allow unfettered mobility.

The compulsory destruction of communities and involuntary displacement of residents, however, is another matter. Such actions are, to my mind, immoral, impractical and incoherent. They should be replaced with policies that provide for strengthening existing communities and for increasing the availability of affordable housing in higher income communities. The latter should be accompanied by mobility counseling and rental or purchase subsidies so that low-income households generally would be able to choose whether to move from their original communities to higher income neighborhoods and have the ability to do so if that is their choice

The alternative that I will develop later in this chapter is that we must strengthen existing low-income communities through appropriate interactive institutions (schools, health care, day care, job training, economic development, and so on). We should concentrate on making existing low-income communities into places where residents are proud to reside. These would be places where residents might retain the social ties and the supports available in their communities while at the same time offering them some of the benefits theorized by the advocates of mixed-income communities.

Low-income communities are fundamentally similar to other, higher-income, communities: there are people with talent and ambition; there are social connections that are valuable to existing residents; and institutions that can provide the link between the talent, ambition and connections that already exist in the broader community. Offering residents a realistic choice between moving to mixed-income, mixed-race communities or remaining in a significantly improved, socially and economically viable original community, is a better model of addressing the problems of concentrated poverty.

In this chapter I lay out the nature of the concentration problem and some of its causes and consequences, and then I go on to describe current de-concentration programs and examine the major successes and disappointments of these programs. I elaborate on the criticisms that have already been leveled against them and add my own to the queue. Finally, I propose an alternative to the current focus on the de-concentration of poverty.

The Concentration of Poverty

Long-term poverty has been publicly recognized as a problem in the United States at least since the 1960s when President Lyndon Johnson initiated his War on Poverty.[29] Since that time, there have been countless federal, state, and local programs designed to combat both individual and systemic poverty. Despite these programs, poverty has persisted and the gap between those who have and those who have not has widened.[30] Moreover, poverty in the United States has become increasingly concentrated.[31] In 2000 more than 6.7 million people lived in communities of concentrated poverty.[32]

Several explanations have been offered for the increased concentration of the very poor in particular neighborhoods. A superficially benign explanation is Wilson's claim that the de-segregation of housing led to the voluntary outmigration of relatively wealthier African-Americans from the racially (but not economically) segregated urban neighborhoods in which they lived to other neighborhoods, often in the suburbs.[33]

---

29 President Lyndon B. Johnson, Annual Message to the Congress on the State of the Union (Jan. 8, 1964). I recognize that the War on Poverty, during the mid 1960s, attempted a multifaceted approach to fighting poverty and met with, at best, mixed success. Later in this chapter, I will attempt to distinguish my approach from the earlier effort.

30 Carmen DeNavas-Walt et al., US Census Bureau, Income, Poverty, and Health Insurance Coverage in the United States: 2010, at 4 (2011), *available at* http://www.census.gov/prod/2011pubs/p60-239.pdf ("Approximately 31.6 percent of the population had at least one spell of poverty lasting 2 or more months during the 4-year period from 2004 to 2007."). The Gini index (also known as the Gini coefficient) is a traditional measure of income inequality. *See id.* at 10. "The Gini index was 0.469 in 2010. Except for the 1.5 percent decline in the Gini index between 2006 and 2007, there were no other statistically significant annual changes since 1993, the earliest year available for comparable measures of income inequality. Since 1993, the Gini index is up 3.3 percent." *Id.*

31 Daniel T. Lichter et al., *The Geography of Exclusion: Race, Segregation, and Concentrated Poverty* 2 (Nat'l Poverty Ctr., Working Paper No. 11–16, 2011) ("We document a 25 percent increase in the number of poor places during the post-2000 period (and growing shares of poor people living in them) after deep and widespread declines in concentrated poverty during the economic boom of the 1990s.").

32 Alemayehu Bishaw, US Census Bureau, US Dep't of Commerce, Areas with Concentrated Poverty: 1999, at 3 tbl.1 (2005), *available at* http://www.census.gov/prod/2005pubs/censr-16.pdf (2.8% of approximately 281 million United States citizens – approximately 7,868,000 people – lived in census tracts with 40% or more of residents living in poverty at the time of the 2000 Census); Claudine Gay, *Moving Out, Moving Up: Housing Mobility and Political Participation of the Poor* 2 (Harvard University, Working Paper, 2008) (unpublished paper on file with the author).

33 *See* Wilson, *supra* note 3, at 49 ("… I emphasized that inner-city neighborhoods have undergone a profound social transformation …. as reflected not only in their increasing rates of social dislocation (including crime, joblessness, out-of-wedlock births, female-headed families, and welfare dependency) but also in the changing economic class structure

Those left behind were, to a great extent, households without the financial means to leave. The problems caused by the exodus of working class and, middle- and upper-income African-Americans from their communities were exacerbated by the loss of well-paying industrial jobs in the urban centers. Thus, remaining families not only lost what Wilson thought was the social adhesive that kept the communities together and well functioning, but also the means for those who remained to obtain well-compensated employment.[34]

Other commentators have pointed to several less benign causes. These include persistent racial discrimination and the lingering effects of consciously implemented governmental interventions in markets that were intended to segregate citizens by race and economic class.[35] Examples of these policies include the explicit early guidelines of the Federal Housing Administration concerning mortgage availability for African-Americans;[36] the segregated siting of public housing developments; the Interstate Highway program; and the Urban Renewal program. Each of these programs pushed people into highly segregated neighborhoods and physically isolated those neighborhoods, or forced people to remain in them. Later, when it became expedient for governments to recapture the land or to dislocate existing communities (after government policies had helped to segregate the neighborhoods), government programs often permitted or required bisecting or bulldozing these communities in the name of further societal progress. A few examples should suffice to demonstrate governmental complicity in the concentration of poverty.

Beginning in the 1930s, through the Home Owners Loan Corporation (HOLC) and the FHA, the federal government deliberately steered funds away from African-American neighborhoods and from African-American applicants for

---

of ghetto neighborhoods. I pointed out that [previously] these neighborhoods featured a vertical integration of different income groups [who] all resided more or less in the same ghetto neighborhoods. I also stated that the very presence of working- and middle-class families enhanced the social organization of inner-city neighborhoods. Finally, I noted that the movement of middle-class black professionals from the inner city (*sic*) followed in increasing numbers by working-class blacks, has left behind a much higher concentration of the most disadvantaged segments of the black urban population …").

34 *Id.* at 38–41.

35 Prior to desegregation, the governmental policies affected minorities regardless of class. After desegregation, much of the discrimination resulted in the social and economic isolation of low-income minorities who had insufficient political or economic power to fight these policies and insufficient resources to escape the isolation.

36 The practice of "redlining" was created by the Home Owners Loan Corporation and later adopted by FHA. Redlining draws its name from FHA's practice of rating neighborhood quality by color scheme. The lowest quality neighborhoods, often reserved for those in which African-Americans resided, were coded red. *See* Douglas S. Massey & Nancy A. Denton, American Apartheid: Segregation and the Making of the Underclass 51 (1993).

mortgages even if they were financially qualified for the loan.[37] This practice, which continued for several decades after the creation of these agencies, contributed to highly segregated neighborhoods and a low rate of urban homeownership among African-Americans.[38]

In addition to the restrictions placed on the ability of minorities, particularly African-Americans, to purchase homes or even to live in integrated communities, federal and local policies concerning public housing placements and occupancy added to the segregation and isolation of minorities, and to the concentration of poverty.

The result, if not the intent, of the public housing program of the United States was to segregate the races, to concentrate the disadvantaged in inner cities, and to reinforce the image of suburbia as a place of refuge for the problems of race, crime, and poverty.[39]

The *Gautreaux* litigation led to a change in these policies. The District Court found, in *Gautreaux v Chicago Housing Authority*,[40] that CHA had selected sites for public housing and had assigned tenants to those sites on the basis of race:[41] the parties then entered into a consent decree by which lotteries were established for current African-American residents of (or those on the waiting list for) public housing in Chicago. The winners of the lotteries obtained §8 vouchers and housing counseling to assist them in obtaining housing in predominantly white neighborhoods in the Chicago metropolitan area. At its conclusion, approximately 7,100 families were relocated under the program.[42]

Two other, non-housing federal programs also had significant influence in disrupting or isolating minority communities. Starting in the late 1940s and the

37 For an interesting history of these federal programs, *see* Jackson, *supra* note 11, at 195–218.

38 "A government offering such bounty to builders and lenders could have required compliance with a nondiscrimination policy … Instead, FHA adopted a racial policy that could well have been culled from the Nuremberg laws. From its inception FHA set itself up as the protector of the all-white neighborhood. It sent its agents into the field to keep Negroes and other minorities from buying houses in white neighborhoods." Charles Abrams, Forbidden neighbors 214 (1955).

39 Jackson, *supra* note 11, at 219.

40 296 F. Supp. 907 (N.D. Ill. 1969).

41 "Uncontradicted evidence submitted to the District Court established that the public housing system operated by CHA was racially segregated, with four overwhelmingly white projects located in white neighborhoods and with 99 1/2% of the remaining family units located in Negro neighborhoods and 99% of those units occupied by Negro tenants." *Id.* at 910.

42 James E. Rosenbaum et al., *Can the Kerner Commission's Housing Strategy Improve Employment, Education and Social Integration for Low-Income Blacks, in* Race, Poverty, and American Cities 275 (John Charles Boger & Judith Welch Wegner eds, 1996); Alex F. Schwartz, Housing Policy in the United States: An Introduction 167 (2006).

early 1950s, the Urban Renewal program[43] and the Interstate Highway program[44] each wrought havoc on existing communities, almost always low-income minority communities.

Urban Renewal (which was known as Urban Redevelopment prior to the passage of the Housing Act of 1954) was intended to redevelop areas that had been designated as slums. Local governments, with significant assistance from the federal government, acquired land subject to the slum designation and made it available to private developers for redevelopment. There have been many criticisms of the program, both as to its goals and its effects. For example, Peter Marcuse has claimed that the supporters of Title I of the Housing Act of 1949 (the Title that created the urban redevelopment program) were not concerned with rehousing slum dwellers, but with tearing down slums – at least those casting a blighting influence on major business areas.[45]

The result was the displacement of entire communities without provision for the return of former residents. Moreover, urban renewal eventually was used for more than slum clearance as many neighborhoods that were not slums were also bulldozed.[46] Despite the destruction of whole neighborhoods in which many residents had low or very low incomes, little or no new replacement housing was built to accommodate those displaced. Thus, large numbers of low-income displacees moved to other neighborhoods with existing low-cost housing, creating or exacerbating high-concentration poverty neighborhoods.

The Federal Highway Act was passed in 1956 and had similarly doleful consequences on low-income minority communities. First, because land in and around poor communities was often cheaper and because political opposition there was likely to be less intense, the government often exercised its eminent domain rights to take such land for its right of way, thus disrupting the lower-income communities by displacing many of its residents.[47] Second, the communities that remained were often isolated by the new highways that cut them off from other

43 Michelle Wilde Anderson, *Mapped Out of Local Democracy*, 62 Stan. L. Rev. 931, 942 (2010) ("[I]n the past, such movement of individuals through displacement (such as urban renewal programs) has shown only sporadic success at advancing race and class integration, and it has meant land loss for minority families and the demolition of stable, historically rooted communities."). "As previously noted, urban renewal and redevelopment programs have a dark and extensive history of displacing low-income minority communities in order to make way for land uses that benefit political majorities." *Id.* at 949 n.57.

44 Federal-Aid Highway Act of 1956, Pub. L. No. 84–627, 70 Stat. 374 (1956).

45 Peter Marcuse, *Housing Policy and the Myth of the Benevolent State*, *in* Critical Perspectives on Housing 255 (Rachel B. Bratt et al., eds, 1986).

46 The Supreme Court approved such actions in *Berman v. Parker*, 348 US 26 (1954).

47 *Cf.* Jon Hanson & Kathleen Hanson, *The Blame Frame: Justifying (Racial) Injustice in America*, 41 Harv. C.R.–C.L. L. Rev. 413, 449 (2006) ("The Federal Highway Act funded a highway system to link cities to growing suburbs, permanently destroying much predominantly minority, low-income housing to build roads on which poor, car-less minorities rarely drove. Such targeted infrastructure development also led to depreciation

urban amenities. [48] Such communities became, almost literally, "the other side of the tracks."

Ironically, many of the current government programs designed to de-concentrate poverty are actually seeking to undo the effects of prior government policies that led to, or at least assisted in, the concentration in the first place. Perhaps this policy shift resulted from a good faith reconsideration of earlier judgments, a natural evolution of societal and governmental social vision. As already noted, Wilson's work called attention to significant negative externalities that he claimed were associated with the concentration of poverty: it is also possible, though, that the second thoughts about concentrated poverty reflect no more than the current response to changing preferences of the white middle class whose members want to return to reinvigorated cities. Moreover, there was pressure on government by developers who wished to cater to the desires of the prospective middle class occupants by developing what they considered to be underused urban land.

The Movement to De-concentrate Poverty

As the concentration of poverty accelerated,[49] Wilson's work called attention to what he claimed were the significant negative externalities associated with it.[50] Congress, as well as many state and local legislatures, accepted the idea that concentrations of poverty created these externalities and that they, in turn, led to social and financial costs to local jurisdictions and to many individuals and families. Legislative bodies began to consider ways to reduce the concentration of poverty and thus to reduce the public costs associated with the perceived pathologies.

Two distinct approaches have been utilized by governments in attempting to alleviate the concentrations of poverty. The first involves dispersing the poor from dense, high-concentration neighborhoods to other, less poor, areas. This approach

---

or significantly lower appreciation in black areas than in white areas, further concentrating wealth among the population already controlling the most assets.") (citations omitted).

48 *See* Oliver A. Pollard, III, *Smart Growth: The Promise, Politics, and Potential Pitfalls of Emerging Growth Management Strategies*, 19 Va. Envtl. L.J. 247, 260 (2000) ("Planners of the Federal Highway Act of 1956 declared that the effect of the massive highway building program would be 'to disperse our factories, our stores, our people; in short, to create a revolution in living habits.' This is precisely what has occurred." (quoting William H. Whyte Jr, *Urban Sprawl*, *in* The Exploding Metropolis 133, 144 (1957))).

49 The growth of concentrated poverty has been explosive. Edward G. Goetz, citing studies by Danziger and Gottschalk and Jargowsky, both of which used a 40% threshold for concentration, has pointed out that between 1970 and 1990, the number of high poverty neighborhoods more than doubled and the number of people living in these neighborhoods grew from 4.1 million to 8 million. Edward G. Goetz, Clearing the Way: Deconcentrating the Poor in Urban America 25 (2003).

50 Wilson, *supra* note 3, at 21–22.

is exemplified by federal programs such as *Gautreaux* and Moving to Opportunity. On a local level, many jurisdictions have adopted Inclusionary Zoning programs,[51] and programs modeled on MTO. San Diego, for example, has implemented a local program known as Choice Communities[52] to assist low-income residents to move from high-concentration neighborhoods to higher-income communities.

The other approach adopted by many jurisdictions is to bring wealthier residents into previously high-concentration communities. HOPE VI represents the federal effort in this regard, while local programs such as the District of Columbia's New Communities Program[53] attempt to replicate HOPE VI on a local level. Some critics attack these programs as spurring the market phenomenon of gentrification, the purchasing of property in formerly low-income areas by affluent buyers desirous of urban living environments. Often, but not always, the affluent buyers are of a different race than the lower-income original residents.[54]

In implementing these programs, governments adopted the theory that by de-concentrating the poor, the negative externalities associated with concentration would be reduced. Residents who were able to reside in mixed-income communities, a stated goal of the de-concentration effort,[55] could be expected to obtain the benefits that Wilson thought existed in black communities prior to

51 *See* Nicholas Benson, Note, A Tale of Two Cities: Examining the Success of Inclusionary Zoning Ordinances in Montgomery County, Maryland and Boulder, Colorado, 13 J. Gender Race & Just. 753 (2010) ("First enacted in communities on the East and West Coasts more than forty years ago, inclusionary zoning is now implemented in 250 local communities across the United States. In total, these inclusionary programs have generated an estimated eighty to ninety thousand affordable housing units since their inception.") (citation omitted).

52 San Diego Housing Commission Choice Communities, http://sdhc.org/Rental-Assistance/Rental-Assistance-Participants/Request-to-Move/Choice-Communities/ (last visited Sept. 23, 2011).

53 Office of the Deputy Mayor for Planning and Economic Development, New Communities, The District of Columbia, http://dmped.dc.gov/DC/DMPED/Projects/New+Communities (last visited Sept. 23, 2011).

54 Some have argued that gentrification is beneficial to the lower-income residents who are able to remain in gentrified communities. *See, e.g.*, J. Peter Byrne, *Two Cheers for Gentrification,* 46 How. L.J. 405 (2003). Others, including the author, believe that the poor who remain will face severe economic and social hardship that will lead to their eventually leaving the neighborhood. In either event, the critics claim that the original community has been destroyed and the remaining residents become outsiders in the new social organization of the neighborhood.

55 It should be noted that some critics have suggested that the goal of HOPE VI was not offering the original residents the opportunity to reside in mixed-income communities but rather to redevelop the public housing site into a mixed income community. *See, e.g.*, Susan Clampett-Lundquist, Moving Over or Moving Up? Short-Term Gains and Losses for Relocated HOPE VI Families, 7 Cityscape 57, 58 (2004).

de-segregation; role modeling, social control and social networking leading to economic improvement for the poor.[56]

Professor Mark Joseph, a critic of the programs designed to implement mixed-income communities, has restated Wilson's cataloging of the supposed benefits of such programs. Their goals, he says, are:

- the creation of social interaction and social networks between the higher and lower income residents that could lead to better employment opportunities;
- the establishment of social control;
- role modeling; and
- creating better access to goods and services due to the social and human capital of the higher-income residents.[57]

Many of these supposed benefits, Joseph observes, attempt to rectify defects that the policy-makers supposed existed in the low-income residents themselves, a reworking of the conventional bromide about the "undeserving" poor. They do not respond to defects in the social or economic structures of society that caused (or at least contributed to) the economic problems of many low-income people.[58] This is only one of several critiques of the de-concentration policies that have been adopted. Other critics doubt the sincerity of the stated program goals[59] and still others decry the destruction of community, regardless of the motivations for doing so.[60] Moreover, commentators, both critics and supporters alike, point out that many of the stated goals of the programs have not been met and some of these commentators think they cannot be met.[61] In the sections that follow, I will address these criticisms, beginning with evidence of the failure of the programs to achieve many of their stated goals.

Outcomes of the De-concentration Programs

In this section, I examine studies analyzing only the various federal programs. This is due, in part, to the relatively recent advent of many of the local programs

56 *See* Wilson, *supra* note 3, at 30.

57 Mark Joseph, Early Resident Experiences at a New Mixed-Income Development in Chicago, 30 J. Urb. Aff. 229, 233 (2008).

58 *Id.* Joseph goes on to observe that mixed-income development does not address the underlying causes of persistent poverty.

59 Imbroscio, *supra* note 23 at 112 (in the context of discussing relocation in New Orleans after Hurricane Katrina).

60 *See* Steinberg, *supra* note 23; Imbroscio, *supra* note 23.

61 *See* Goetz, *supra* note 17, at 6 (residents who are displaced by HOPE VI typically move to better neighborhoods but improvement in the quality of their lives ".... is mixed, being quite modest in most cases and frequently non existent.").

(with the exception of Inclusionary Zoning which originated more than 30 years ago) and the relative paucity of data on the newer local initiatives. It is also important to keep in mind here the variety of goals that have been attributed to these programs. They run from the redevelopment of blighted communities to the reduction in the concentration of poverty so as to improve the quality of life and economic opportunities for lower-income residents to the reduction of the social costs of the concentration of poverty. There has been a good deal of success on the redevelopment front, but not as much on the improved opportunities for the poor, or in the reduction of social costs to society.

The most visible measure of success has been purely physical. It has involved the demolition of highly distressed and very dense public housing developments and the replacement of these projects with new, lower-density developments with a substantial number of new units going to market rate buyers and renters. Many critics have pointed to the governmental emphasis on redeveloping toxic sites rather than on rehousing the poor in mixed-income developments.[62] One frequent writer about HOPE VI, Susan Popkin, has noted that even the research on the program done by HUD focuses primarily on neighborhood benefits, not on those displaced by the programs.[63]

For the displacees, the benefits are less clear. Many move to better housing and to neighborhoods with less overall poverty and crime[64] although even these benefits are subject to qualification and come with significant costs. Other benefits, such as more social capital leading to more and better employment and wages, social integration, and better health and educational outcomes are not supported by the evidence.[65] In fact, there is some evidence suggesting the overall condition of displacees may have worsened. The remainder of this section will be devoted to these findings.

Levels of Poverty De-concentration and Racial Integration

I begin this discussion with what should be an alarming reality. A huge percentage of the residents of public housing projects subject to the HOPE VI program are

62 *See, e.g.*, Clampett-Lundquist, *supra* note 56, at 57. Clampett-Lundquist points out that nearly one half of those displaced from public housing due to HOPE VI relocate to other public housing projects. Only approximately 11% are slated to return to the redeveloped HOPE VI community. For those slated to return, the "temporary" relocation time may be four or five years. *Id.* at 57. Many others moved to other high-poverty neighborhoods. *Id.* at 66.

63 Popkin, *supra* note 18, at 68.

64 *Id.* at 70; *see also*; Popkin et al., *supra* note 19 at 30; Goetz, *supra* note 17, at 5.

65 In fact, the studies on benefits for movers to mixed-income communities are mixed, but all find that there is little or no improvement in employment or income for such movers.

African-American or Latino, as are the residents of the communities surrounding those sites.[66] Moreover, 80 per cent of the residents on HOPE VI sites have total income below the poverty line.[67] Reducing this overwhelming race and class segregation was one of the major stated goals of the de-concentration programs, but the results have been far from encouraging.

Even if the de-concentration programs were highly successful in relocating former residents to mixed-income, mixed-race communities, the total number of persons relocated would comprise only a tiny portion of the poor who lived in communities segregated by race and/or class.[68] But, of course, the programs are not highly successful in such relocation. Very few displaced residents of Public Housing end up in truly mixed-income communities. Kingsley et al., for example, found that as of 2000, 49 per cent of the residents displaced from HOPE VI sites went to other public housing developments while 31 per cent obtained §8 vouchers and moved to private housing. Of these, many moved to nearby neighborhoods with income and racial demographics much like the neighborhoods they left. The remaining 20 per cent received other HUD assistance, no assistance at all, or were unaccounted for.[69]

Many researchers have found that while the rate of poverty in the communities to which displacees moved is significantly lower than in their original communities, it is still quite high.[70] Moreover, the communities to which displacees moved remained highly segregated by race.[71] Nevertheless, many commentators have lauded the reduction of poverty rates from more than 60 per cent on average to approximately 27 per cent.[72] Few of these commentators, however, discuss the fact that the poverty rate on HOPE VI sites has been enormous. Thus, the mere destruction of the public housing site and the dispersal of its residents to

---

66 Popkin et al., *supra* note 19, at 8.

67 *Id.* at 9. HUD targets the poorest to live in public housing and only the poorest would live there.

68 In 2000, more than 25% of the urban poor (6,700,000 people) lived in neighborhoods with poverty rates of greater than 30%.

69 G. Thomas Kingsley et al., *Patterns of Section 8 Relocation in the HOPE VI Program*, 25 J. URB. AFF. 427, 429 (2003).

70 For example, Kingsley et al., found that the average poverty rate in census tracts containing public housing developments was 38% while the rate in tracts with HUD assisted housing averaged 22% and those containing §8 voucher holders averaged 19%. The poverty rate in census tracts with HOPE VI designated public housing averaged 61%. The tracts to which displacees of these projects moved averaged 27%. *Id.* at 433.

71 Popkin et al., *supra* note 19, at 29; Popkin, *supra* note 18, at 69. *See also* Kingsley et al., *supra* note 70, at 428, where the authors point out that, while these problems do not characterize the program as a whole, in many cities displacees wind up in seriously distressed, high-poverty neighborhoods not far from their original site.

72 Kingsley, *supra* note 70, at 433.

other communities, even if near the original site, would place those residents in neighborhoods with much lower rates of poverty.[73]

Two additional facts are worth noting in this regard. Many of the communities to which displacees moved were "fragile" and had high rates of poverty even prior to the influx of the former HOPE VI residents.[74] This influx pushes these communities towards higher concentrations of poverty, albeit sometimes remaining below the recognized danger threshold of 30 per cent.[75] In addition, the evidence suggests that many displacees who moved to lower-poverty neighborhoods moved back to their original neighborhood (or to one geographically close to it) within a few years.[76]

Levels of Social Capital and the Benefits Derived from it

Access to neighborhood resources may depend, at least in part, on the degree to which residents have or can form social networks within resource-rich neighborhoods.[77]

One of the major assumptions underlying Wilson's theory about the effects of concentrated poverty was that the very poor needed higher-income people in their neighborhoods to act as role models, to assert a degree of social control, and to provide a level of social capital that would translate into better employment and income opportunities for them. Even if one accepted Wilson's underlying assumption, there are two significant problems with the de-concentration initiatives that emanated from his theory. First, the mixed-income communities Wilson described prior to desegregation were organic. While they were created as a result of a pernicious social policy, they were of longstanding duration and were characterized by limited entrance or exit by residents. People had important commonalities, both demographic and experiential, that bound them together. The communities created by de-concentration programs were artificially constructed, often with unwilling participants on each side.[78] The second problem, which

73 Rachel Dwyer, *The Limits of the Deconcentration of Poverty: The Spatial Context of the Poor* 11 City & Community (2012).

74 Popkin, *supra* note 18, at 83.

75 *Id.* at 13 ("As people leave a poor neighborhood it gets less poor while some other neighborhood gets more poor"); *see also* Goetz, *supra* note 17, at 15; Popkin, *supra* note 18 at 69 (stating that people who move from HOPE VI sites still face extremely poor and segregated communities); Clampett-Lundquist *supra* note 54 at 58 (stating that nearly 50% of displacees moved to other public housing projects); but compare Kingsley *supra* note 70, at 428, who states that while one might expect many former residents to cluster in "a small number of less poor, but still fragile, neighborhoods" which then become destabilized, this did not characterize the HOPE VI program overall.

76 Boyd et al., *supra* note 16, at 122.

77 *Id.* at 124.

78 Imbroscio, *supra* note 23 at 117.

derives from the first, is that in these communities, there is very little meaningful social interaction taking place among the higher-and lower-income residents.[79] Moreover, there is little evidence that living in these communities improves the life chances for the poor.[80]

These findings should not be entirely unexpected. The concept of community generally requires some element of commonality among the theoretical members.[81] What, one might ask, other than geography would qualify as a common bond among the HOPE VI displacees and higher-income residents of an existing community to which they moved? This lack of commonality is exacerbated when one considers that, for the most part, the move by the displaced HOPE VI residents was involuntary[82] and the reception of them by the members of the receiving community was rarely welcoming.[83]

The absence of social capital contributed to disappointing results for other important goals of de-concentration such as increased employment and earnings opportunities. A much more subtle negative effect was the loss of social capital that had existed in the displacees' original communities. While a more detailed discussion of both of these issues will be presented later in this chapter, a comment from one of the displaced public housing residents aptly describes the feelings of many displacees:

> I mean, I understand what they were trying to do. I do understand what they were trying to do and they were trying to give people better opportunities, but to force people away, to force people away from their family, their support system. You know, just common things that people need to have. It's not beneficial.[84]

This absence of social capital was a major factor in limiting new low-income residents in mixed-income communities from achieving some of the other goals of the de-concentration initiatives. For example, the data regarding the success of the low-income movers to mixed-income communities in finding better employment or increasing income is bleak. This is true both for the adult movers and for their children after they became adults.[85] In fact, participants in mobility programs may actually do worse than non-participants in being able to use contacts to find employment.[86] This is the result not only of the lack of social contact between

---

79 Popkin et al., *supra* note 19, at 23; Clampett-Lundquist, *supra* note 56, at 69.

80 Popkin, *supra* note 18, at 70.

81 Mark L. Joseph et al., *The Theoretical Basis for Addressing Poverty Through Mixed Income Development*, 42 Urb. Aff. Rev. 369, 383 (2007).

82 Popkin, *supra* note 18, at 71.

83 Boyd et al., *supra* note 16, at 124 (stating that while blacks tend to want integrated neighborhoods, whites do not).

84 *Id.* at 135 (quoting Nikki, a resident displaced by the Gautreaux Two program).

85 *Id.* at 122 (concerning Gautreaux Two relocation).

86 Boyd et al., *supra* note 16, at 125.

the economic classes: it is also due to the fact that many of the displacees have lower educational attainment, fewer employment skills and less work experience than their higher-income neighbors. Therefore, the jobs for which they would be qualified are limited and are less likely to be the type that the higher-income neighbors would be aware of.[87]

There are other obstacles to employment for displacees. Assuming, as is often the case, the lower-income residents do not own cars, transportation to places of employment may be difficult.[88] The availability of child care may determine whether a resident can take an available job.[89] Moreover, there are a series of health-related barriers, including asthma, diabetes, and obesity that prevent many displacees from obtaining employment.[90] These barriers are independent of the existence of systemic discrimination, which also remains an obstacle for minorities in actually obtaining available jobs for which they are qualified.[91]

Costs to Displacees

There are other, non-employment-based problems associated with the move to mixed-income communities. While there is evidence that displacees who moved to mixed-income communities lived in better housing and safer neighborhoods,[92] there is also evidence that the move imposed significant costs on them. These include both direct and indirect financial costs. The indirect costs include the loss of social networks and the benefits these networks provided, such as material goods, child care, and informal social control.[93]

In addition to the emotional and indirect financial costs of moving away from social networks, there were direct financial costs as well. These included higher costs for needs such as transportation and child care which often made it difficult for many movers to afford food and other necessities. Perhaps more surprisingly, *housing* costs increased for many people who moved to the private market. The increase was due primarily to utility costs, which were previously covered in their

87 *Id.* at 125; Popkin et al., *supra* note 19, at 23; Clampett-Lundquist, *supra* note 56, at 71 ("[N]one [of the low-income residents surveyed] reported having learned of a job opportunity from a new neighbor but several had while in public housing."); *see also* Joseph, *supra* note 58, at 234.

88 Boyd et al., *supra* note 16, at 136; *see also* Goetz, *supra* note 17, at 9.

89 Goetz, *supra* note 17, at 9.

90 Alastair Smith, Joint Ctr. for Hous. Stud. of Harv. Univ., *Mixed-Income Housing Developments: Promises and Reality* 26 (2002), *available at* http://www.jchs.harvard.edu/publications/W02-10_Smith.pdf.

91 *See* Joseph et al., *supra* note 82, at 399.

92 Popkin, *supra* note 18, at 70.

93 Clampett-Lundquist, *supra* note 56, at 69.

public housing rents, but were no longer covered by the §8 voucher provided to displacees.[94]

The psychological costs were also high. Aside from the obvious sense of distance from friends, movers felt a sense of stigma and alienation in their new communities.[95] Displacees often felt as if they were being monitored by a disapproving community. They also reported a sense of relative deprivation in comparison to their higher-income neighbors.[96] One commentator has pointed to the "de-mobilizing" effect of being poor and living in a community of plenty[97] which results in the lower-status individuals experiencing feelings of alienation.[98] One other area of cost should also be mentioned although it is more ephemeral than some of the others. This is the loss of influence concerning neighborhood issues suffered by those who moved to mixed-income communities. The loss is the result of several factors: the newness of the movers to the community and the associated lack of social capital that has already been mentioned; the relatively greater sophistication of the preexisting residents; and the greater financial and political resources of those residents. This loss is partially offset by the relatively greater level of goods and services in the community, many of which one could hypothesize substantially all residents would desire. Nevertheless, these goods and services typically cater to the wishes of the higher-income residents and, in any case, are often obtained without input from or, in many cases, consideration of the needs of the new, lower-income residents.[99]

Critiques of the De-concentration Programs and Strategy

In this section, I discuss the practical and theoretical criticisms that have been (or could be) leveled against the de-concentration concept and programs. Among the most basic complaints is that, even if the programs were highly successful in achieving their stated goals, their scale is so small in comparison to the need that they make minimal impact into the racial and economic segregation of the poor. But, of course, the programs, as I demonstrated in the previous section, have not met many of their stated goals. In addition, the implementation of the programs has imposed substantial costs both on the displacees and on those who remain in concentrated low-income neighborhoods.

---

94 Popkin, *supra* note 18, at 83.

95 Gray, *supra* note 33 at 16; Mark L. Joseph, *Is Mixed-Income Development an Antidote to Urban Poverty*, 17 Housing Pol'y Debate 209, 217 (2006).

96 Robert J. Chaskin & Mark L. Joseph, *Building "Community" in Mixed Income Developments: Assumptions, Approaches, and Early Experiences*, 45 Urb. Aff. Rev. 299, 303 (2010).

97 Gay, *supra* note 33, at 10.

98 *Id.* at 16.

99 Joseph, *supra* note 96 at 216.

Study after study has shown that there has been little neighboring between the higher-and lower-income residents of a mixed-income neighborhood.[100] There has been little social capital developed and little or no improvement in employment status, hours worked or overall income.[101] Mental health outcomes for the low-income residents were mixed. While many movers reported a greater sense of well-being in their new community, others reported a sense of alienation, stigma and relative deprivation.[102] Research has not shown that the provision of "basic" resident services in mixed-income communities has led to improved obesity and mental health outcomes for displacees.[103] Similarly, several studies show no positive educational outcomes for the children of movers.[104] Many, in fact, did not change schools, but continued attending their original school.[105] For those who did change schools, there has been little interaction between the new students and their higher-income classmates.[106] Even where such interaction existed, the low-income students did not consider their classmates as role models and they had little or no interaction with the parents of their new classmates.[107] Conversely, many lower-income students also reported feelings of racism, stigma, and isolation.[108]

The failures of these programs to achieve their goals in reference to those who moved to mixed-income neighborhoods is all the more striking because these who moved into the mixed-income settings were selected only after a rigorous screening process designed to identify the most stable and upwardly mobile public housing residents. Hard-to-house families, on the other hand, were offered very little as they were shunted to other public housing projects or allowed to move with their §8 voucher to other high-poverty neighborhoods geographically and demographically close to their original communities.[109]

In order to be eligible to move into a mixed-income community, public housing residents had to:

---

100 Popkin et al., *supra* note 19, at 23; Clampett-Lundquist, *supra* note 56, at 69; Smith, *supra* note 91, at 2; Joseph, *supra* note 96, at 217.

101 Joseph, *supra* note 96, at 217; Popkin et al., *supra* note 19, at 23; Goetz, *supra* note 17, at 9.

102 Gray, *supra* note 33, at 16.

103 Marjorie Austin Turner, et al., *Estimating the Public Costs and Benefits of HOPE VI Investments: Methodological Report*, at 35 (2007) ("Existing research provides no evidence that a mixed-income redevelopment scenario with 'basic' resident services would lead to improvement in resident obesity or mental health problems. However, 'enhanced' services could reasonably be expected to yield significant improvement in resident health.") Urban Insitiue, *available at* http://www.urban.org/url.cfm?*ID*=411497.

104 Goetz, *supra* note 17 at 8.

105 Clampett-Lundquist, *supra* note 56, at 71. Goetz *supra* note 17, at 8.

106 *Id.* at 71.

107 Goetz, *supra* note 17 at 11.

108 Gray, *supra* note 33, at 16.

109 Goetz, *supra* note 17, at 7.

- be in compliance with their existing lease;
- be working at least 30 hours per week;
- have no unpaid utility bills;
- have no criminal record; and
- pass a drug test.[110]

The fact that those who moved to mixed-income neighborhoods did not achieve the success that was predicted for them raises the question that many have asked: can proximity alone influence social relations?[111] The answer seems to be no. The creation of community, the creation of relationships that encourage interaction with and concern for others requires significant commonalities among the members.[112] These commonalities are not immediately apparent when low-income people of color move into communities of middle-and upper-income white residents. Thus, the expectation of employment opportunities and social support emanating from the higher-income residents for the benefit of the new, lower-income residents appears to be unrealistic.

These implementation failures are not, however, the main problems associated with the de-concentration strategy. The main problems are conceptual. There are three major theoretical difficulties associated with the de-concentration strategy. First, it breaks up existing communities on the supposition that they are valueless or, worse, toxic, and cannot be made to function adequately. The break-up is undertaken without consultation with the residents of those communities and in disregard of the wishes of many of them. Second, it is based on the premise that, somehow, economic integration will compensate for structural flaws in the economic and social systems. It ignores systematically imposed educational and skills deficits brought on by past discrimination and turns a blind eye to current prejudice. Third, it caters heavily to the needs of business interests and middle-income, predominantly white, homebuyers. In this way, it is reminiscent of the racially based displacement of poor people that occurred under the Urban Renewal and Highway programs, programs that regularly served the interests of people other than those displaced.

The Break-up of Existing Communities

A widespread view of low-income communities, particularly those of color, is that they are dysfunctional. This is even more pronounced when the community is in a public housing development. This view is the theoretical basis for the de-concentration strategy. However, low-income communities generally function

110 Joseph, *supra* note 58, at 236; Smith, *supra* note 91, at 23.

111 Joseph et al., *supra* note 82, at 381–82.

112 Smith goes so far as to say homogeneity is necessary for a high level of interaction. Smith, *supra* note 91, at 26.

well, albeit without the various accoutrements of wealth. Most adults work, interact in traditional ways, rely on their friends and neighbors, and obey the law. In fact, William Ryan et al. found "… contrary to conventional wisdom, people at different income levels display pretty much the same distribution of values, social attitudes and lifestyles."[113]

What, then, accounts for the alacrity with which we seek to disrupt existing communities? One answer might be the replacement of a decaying physical infrastructure. If that is all that is being sought, however, it could be done without the destruction of otherwise serviceable housing or, it could be done with allowing all who want to return to the redeveloped community to do so. If what is sought is improvement of the quality of life for residents of the disrupted community, again, the method chosen seems unsuited to the task. For those who move to mixed-income communities, they do gain better housing and better physical infrastructure. They do not gain much social capital and, in fact, may lose much of the benefit provided by social capital in the old communities. A more pressing question is what happens to those who do not move to mixed-income communities?

The evidence is clear that those chosen to move to mixed-income neighborhoods are (in conventional terms) the highest achievers among the local residents. Thus, the problems first suggested by William Julius Wilson, that is, the drain of talent and resource from minority communities due to desegregation, is repeated by the "creaming" of the public housing residents. Those who move to other public housing projects or into private housing in "fragile" nearby communities are left to fend for themselves without counseling or social services associated with the move. Given the de-concentration theory, this would be likely to exacerbate the problems of those displaced to other low-income communities and of the communities to which they move.

But it is also clear that, despite their obvious problems, low-income communities also have strengths. They certainly contain networks of personal connections that make many residents reluctant to leave them.[114] In addition, there are often well-functioning institutions, both public and private, that address many of the needs of local residents. While there may not be a sufficient number of these institutions and those that exist may not have sufficient resources to meet all of the needs of those who live there, nevertheless, they do provide a basis for a different way of thinking about concentrated poverty.

Concerning social services, there is an efficiency associated with providing these services, which essentially everyone agrees is a necessary ingredient in the battle against poverty, in a confined geographic area. It is certainly more difficult and more costly to provide such services across a wide geographic area and with

---

113 Quoted in Joseph et al., *supra* note 82, at 392. Ryan, however, goes onto note the difference between values and actions.

114 In fact, Goetz found that in a Seattle Hope VI project, 60% of those displaced thought that their old neighborhood was a better place to live than their new one. Goetz, *supra* note 17, at 11.

widely dispersed recipients.[115] Again, this is not to say that society should restrict the poor to certain neighborhoods. It is to suggest that such neighborhoods exist and that they offer numerous benefits to the residents. Instead of destroying them, governmental policy could focus on making them stronger and more beneficial to those who live in them and to those who might want to.

De-concentration and Structural Flaws

American society has been plagued by the problem of persistent, systemic poverty. For centuries and across cultures, however, society has viewed this problem as being primarily attributable to the poor, themselves. Distinctions between poverty and pauperism, between the "deserving" and the "undeserving" poor, have dominated policy as well as common discourse. For centuries in England and the United States, distinctions were made between those who suffered poverty due to conditions beyond their control such as advanced age, infancy, disability, or sickness and all others who were said to be lazy, unambitious, drunkards or criminals.[116] The latter group was labeled as paupers or the undeserving poor and was largely cut off from assistance. The former group, labeled the deserving poor, obtained various forms of assistance from their communities, from charities, or from the state.[117] These characterizations were often highly correlated with race, but the symbiosis between race and poverty was rarely examined.

Even recently, there have been labels of the poor that suggest the blame for poverty lies with the poor, themselves. Terms such as the "culture of poverty" and the "underclass" have been used in the past several decades to describe certain groups of poor people. The culture of poverty was first brought to public consciousness by Oscar Lewis. He used the term to describe several "traits" that he ascribed to the poor. The culture, he said:

> … tends to perpetuate itself from generation to generation because of its effects on the children. By the time the slum children are six or seven, they have usually absorbed the basic values … and are not psychologically geared to take full advantage of … increased opportunities that may occur in their lifetimes.[118]

---

115 Smith, *supra* note 91, at 25.

116 For an interesting historical view of distinguishing and labeling the poor, *see* Herbert J. Gans, The War against the Poor: The Underclass and Antipoverty Policy 11–26 (1995).

117 Labels such as these certainly continued into the latter part of the twentieth century and were used by mainstream media, individuals, and institutions. Ronald Reagan used the term "welfare queen" in his 1976 presidential campaign. *See "Welfare Queen" Becomes Issue in Reagan Campaign*, NY Times, Feb. 15, 1976, at 51.

118 Gans, *supra* note 117, at 24 (quoting Oscar Lewis, *The Culture of Poverty*, *in* On Understanding Poverty 188 (Daniel P. Moynihan ed., 1968)).

Michael B. Katz pointed out that the culture of poverty concept was not intended to classify the poor. He claims, however, that it did just that. Most commentators, according to Katz, recognized that the "culture of poverty" did not apply to all poor people. Rather, it placed in a class by themselves those whose behaviors and values converted their poverty into an enclosed and self-perpetuating world of dependence. Although some of its exponents located the sources of poverty in objective factors such as unemployment, the new concept resonated with traditional moral definitions.[119]

Similarly, the term "the underclass," which started as an academic concept, was transformed into a popular and pejorative label for urban African-Americans. Beginning with Gunnar Myrdal's use of the term underclass "to describe the victims of deindustrialization,"[120] the term went through a series of definitions until the 29 August 1977 issue of *Time Magazine* did a cover story entitled, "The American Underclass: Destitute and Desperate in the Land of Plenty."[121] The article went on to describe, in particularly negative terms, the personal attributes of poor, urban African-Americans. The term as a pejorative label had entered the popular consciousness.

The HOPE VI program and many other de-concentration programs have at their core, albeit often tacitly, a similar belief in the moral and intellectual incapacity of many of the poor, particularly poor people of color.[122] Among the central claims for these programs is the social control and role-modeling that will result when the poor are living with higher-income neighbors. Recall William Julius Wilson's lament that desegregation resulted in the removal of the social adhesive that had allowed African-American communities to function and that gave young people role models and hope for the future.[123] The structural flaws in the society are not addressed by the de-concentration strategies. The question might be asked as to how mixed-income communities will end racial discrimination? How will they create millions of jobs that offer a living wage? How will they offer better basic and vocational education to poor young people? As Mark Joseph has said:

> … it is unlikely that mixed-income residence by itself can promote observable change in the short or medium term. In terms of employment, the roles of macrostructural factors-the strength of the economy, the availability of accessible jobs for which residents are qualified and for which they will be fairly considered-cannot be influenced by simply relocating to a mixed-income development.[124]

119 Michael B. Katz, The Undeserving Poor 16 (1989).

120 Gans, *supra* note 117, at 27.

121 *Id.* at 32.

122 Joseph, *supra* note 58.

123 Wilson, *supra* note 3, at 38–41.

124 Joseph et al., *supra* note 82, at 399.

The Cynical View of Community Redevelopment

The final theoretical critique of de-concentration programs that I will discuss is that they often serve the interests of people other than the low-income residents who are subject to their disruptions. There are several interest groups who stand to benefit by the redevelopment of formerly low-income inner-city neighborhoods. These include local governments looking for greater tax income from development and from the higher-income residents who will occupy these redeveloped spaces. A second constituency is higher-income buyers who are looking for safe and convenient urban living experiences. Third are the real estate developers who are seeking valuable "underutilized" land to redevelop and sell. Next, there are merchants who would not have ventured into the former neighborhoods but might now hasten to serve the higher-spending new occupants. Finally, there are those who might wish to minimize the political organization and potential power of low-income residents. This can be accomplished by dispersing them to areas where they will be overshadowed in numbers, financial resources and social and political networking by their higher-income neighbors. It might also be accomplished merely by breaking up existing constituencies and networks.

These concerns are reminiscent of those expressed in connection with the Urban Renewal program in the 1960s when the process of destruction of African-American communities in the name of slum removal and redevelopment came to be known, in James Baldwin's term, as "Negro Removal."[125] Massey and Denton argue that Urban Renewal was enacted at the behest of white elites. Their goal was to stop the spread of African-American neighborhoods that might threaten their elite enclaves. Thus, entire black neighborhoods were razed and redeveloped for other uses. These areas became a buffer against the expanding black ghetto while at the same time forcing the former residents into other highly segregated neighborhoods, or into newly constructed public housing projects that were placed in African-American neighborhoods and were, of course, themselves highly segregated.[126]

The political similarities between Urban Renewal and HOPE VI are stark. In each case, there was a public rhetoric of offering assistance to those in need, of redeveloping highly distressed communities. I am sure there were many, policy-makers and citizens alike, who pursued these programs in the belief that what they were doing was beneficial to the poor. And, to be fair, in many cases there was improvement in the quality of life of low-income residents who moved as a result of the de-concentration programs, particularly in the lives of those who

125 During Urban Renewal's heyday, the 1950s and 1960s, hundreds of thousands of units of low-cost housing was destroyed and millions of people, mostly poor and African-American, were displaced from their homes and communities. There was very little assistance in relocating the displaced families and the typical rent costs for these families went from about $60 per month to about $195 per month. *See* Katz, *supra* note 120, at 136.

126 Douglas S. Massey & Nancy A. Denton, *supra* note 37, at 55–56.

moved voluntarily. Most displaces, however, were involuntarily displaced. This meant that connections, support networks and, to use the encompassing term, communities, were disrupted.[127]

It also meant that, since more housing units were destroyed than were replaced, displacees were largely shunted to neighborhoods with significant vacancy rates or to where they could double up. These tended to be other low-income neighborhoods with high or growing concentrations of poverty. As a consequence of the stringent eligibility requirements for residents to move to mixed-income communities, many of the involuntary displaces were hard-to-house households which often put additional strains on the new communities to which they moved. Already inadequate social services were stretched even thinner when the need was for far greater support.

Finally, whatever political power and organizing opportunities existed in the original neighborhoods was disrupted, if not destroyed, by the displacement that resulted from the de-concentration programs. For the movers to mixed-income communities, the loss is obvious. The movers became a small minority in a new community in which they had few ties and in which new ones proved difficult to create. For the displacees who moved to other low-income communities, they entered new settings in which their old connections had been weakened and they needed access to existing networks that were likely to have preexisting hierarchies and social norms.

Community-building Alternatives to De-concentration

The movement to de-concentrate poverty is based upon the supposition that communities with very high concentrations of poverty involve insurmountable problems for the residents of those communities and for society. Sometimes, this is true. More often, it is not. Communities, and this term connotes something more than merely an aggregate of individuals living in a defined geographic space, suggests important connections among people and between people and place. They serve important personal and societal ends so that when destroyed, something valuable is lost. I, and many others, have argued that even when undertaken with the best of intentions (which is often the case), destruction of communities in the name of de-concentration of poverty has had this destructive effect.

There may be situations when community destruction may serve some greater good, even for the people who are displaced by the destruction. Consider, for example, the removal of residents from an unsafe building or from a neighborhood in jeopardy due to life-threatening pollutants. There may even be situations when the dangers, even overwhelming dangers, come from other residents, or situations

127 Moreover, whatever benefits, limited thought they may have been, that were realized by voluntary movers, such benefits were unlikely to be produced for the involuntary displaces. Popkin, *supra* note 18, at 71.

where any semblance of social order has broken down. In cases like these, most people, even, perhaps, critics of de-concentration, would say that the displacement, the destruction of what remains of community, would be appropriate. But these cases are rare. What is more common is the destruction of viable communities, albeit communities with significant social and economic problems.

To be clear, I am not arguing blindly for the preservation of high-concentration communities. I do argue that in a just society such communities would not be forced to exist. But they do exist, often as a result of governmental policy and therefore, in my view, society has obligations to them and to their residents. Residents of high-concentration neighborhoods who want to move should be assisted, financially, emotionally, and practically, to do so. Those who wish to stay should be able to do so in safety and dignity. For this to happen, however, there needs to be a combined place-based and people-based strategy. Housing and the physical infrastructure must be improved. Existing community institutions must be identified and strengthened. New institutions must be created that address currently unmet needs. Individuals must be given the opportunity to gain skills that will help them achieve both economic improvement and life satisfactions.

The first element of this multifaceted program is the production of an adequate supply of decent affordable housing. This should be accomplished in both low-income communities and in other communities throughout the economy. As a corollary to the construction or rehabilitation of affordable units, subsidies of various sorts should be available to low-income households that would allow them to live, to the greatest extent possible, where they choose. This might be accomplished through such programs as Housing Choice vouchers,[128] the District of Columbia's Local Rent Supplement program,[129] and Inclusionary Zoning.[130]

In order for these programs to work effectively, there must be active enforcement of federal and local fair housing laws. Too often, the "not in my backyard" syndrome or outright discrimination has prevented the racial and/or economic integration of neighborhoods. These obstacles might be overcome with a more rigorous enforcement policy by governments at all levels.

However, the creation of additional affordable housing and housing support, while necessary, is not sufficient to improve the quality of neighborhoods, or to reap the benefits thought to be derived from the economic integration strategy. To obtain these benefits there must be a comprehensive program of:

- social services, including health, educational, youth development, and other services;
- economic development, including small business development by local residents, the attraction of outside employers to the community, and job training and readiness programs;

---

128 42 U.S.C. § 1437f (2006).

129 D.C. Code Ann. § 6–226 (2011).

130 *See supra* notes 7, 52 and accompanying text.

- financial services including financial literacy training, the creation and/or attraction of financial institutions such as commercial banks, credit unions and Community Development Financial Institutions; and
- political organizing and education.

Such ideas are not new. As early as the 1960s, during the Great Society and the War on Poverty, various programs were initiated with the idea of providing more comprehensive and holistic services to poor neighborhoods and families. Programs such as the Community Action Program[131] and Model Cities[132] were designed to provide comprehensive and coordinated community-based physical and human development activities. In addition, The Office of Economic Opportunity funded many Community Development Corporations in poor communities throughout the nation.[133] These programs were place-based efforts to combat poverty and to improve existing communities. Their lack of success can be attributed to a variety of causes, including inadequate funding, lack of long-term commitment, and political misjudgements and missteps, not to mention the intransigency of the structural obstacles to success.[134]

Since the demise of the Great Society programs, there have been a series of local, typically privately initiated, programs that have attempted and, to a great extent, have succeeded in improving local communities. These programs have been called, generically, Comprehensive Community Initiatives, or CCIs.[135] Perhaps the most well known is the Dudley Street Neighborhood Initiative (DSNI) near the Roxbury-Dorchester neighborhoods in Boston. In its more than 25 years of operation, DSNI has engaged in the development of decent affordable housing, the improvement of the local public schools, youth and parenting programs, and in organizing collaborative efforts with other neighborhoods.[136]

The goal of the CCIs is to involve residents in indentifying and prioritizing local problems and planning and implementing sustainable solutions to them. While funding for such initiatives has largely been private with some local

---

131 This program called for the establishment of local Community Action Agencies that included "maximum feasible participation of the residents." These CAAs were to design and coordinate development activities and service provision in low-income communities. Economic Opportunity Act of 1964, Pub. L. No. 88–452, § 202, 78 Stat. 508, 516 (1964).

132 Demonstration Cities and Metropolitan Development Act of 1966, Pub. L. No. 89–754, 80 Stat. 1255 (1966).

133 Economic Opportunity Amendments of 1972, Pub. L. No. 92–424, § 712, 86 Stat. 688 (1972).

134 For an interesting discussion of these programs and their political history, *see* Robert Halpern, Rebuilding the inner city, 106–148 (1995).

135 For a recent listing of research work on CCIs, *see* Chris Walker, Bibliography: Research on Comprehensive Community Initiatives (2010) *available at* http://www.instituteccd.org/library/1402.

136 For a history of DSNI, *see* Peter Medoff & Holly Sklar, streets of hope: the fall and rise of an urban neighborhood (1994).

government support, the diversion of some of the federal funds currently used for HOPE VI and similar dislocating programs could significantly enhance the number and scope of the community initiatives. While these initiatives are not panaceas for the problems of poor communities, they have been shown to have potential for more comprehensive place-based improvements and to do so while leaving existing communities intact.

Conclusion

I have attempted in this chapter to provide a counterpoint to the perceived wisdom of a policy of involuntarily de-concentrating poverty. I have pointed out that the policy has failed to produce many of the benefits expected of it and has caused a good deal of harm to those displaced by it. I have also pointed out that even if the goals had been substantially met and the harms had been averted, the small scale of the policy leaves it far from being a solution for concentrated poverty. As Edward Goetz has pointed out:

> Mobility programs face a paradox-they must remain small to remain politically viable but smallness ensures they will never address concentrated poverty adequately.[137]

Moreover, given the screening process by which residents are selected to move to less poor communities, commentators have raised considerable doubt as to whether the benefits that have been shown to occur do so because of the effects of a new neighborhood and their lower concentrations of poverty or because of the personal and family characteristics of those who have successfully moved.[138] In fact, Alastair Smith points out that very little research has been done on the question of whether mixed-income solutions are even necessary. He asks whether other strategies can achieve the same goals in low-income communities.

What comes with mixed income is a bundle of housing attributes that allow policy-makers to say how well it works. If you provide very-low-income people with good management, good maintenance and housing that blends in, mixed income may not be necessary.[139]

Nevertheless, I do not intend this chapter to be a condemnation of mobility programs. So long as such programs are truly voluntary and are accompanied with appropriate support, they should be a part of the policy arsenal arrayed against poverty. In this chapter, however, I do argue for greater recognition of the importance and, indeed, the capacities of existing communities. By addressing

137 Edward G. Goetz, *The Reality of Deconcentration* (2004) *available at* http://www.nhi.org/online/issues/138/deconcentration.html.

138 Gay, *supra* note 33, 5.

139 Smith, *supra* note 91 at 21, quoting Rachel Bratt.

the structural causes of poverty and segregation and by preserving and improving existing communities, society can provide real choices to lower income citizens as to where to live.

Acknowledgement

I would like to thank my friends and colleagues, Peter Byrne, Mike Seidman and Gerry Spann for their extremely useful comments on various drafts of this chapter. I also want to acknowledge the exemplary research assistance of Jared Lamb.

Chapter 4

Evaluating Legal Models of Affordable Home Ownership in England

Susan Bright and Nicholas Hopkins

Introduction

In England, the majority of households live in homes that they own.[1] Home ownership is not only the majority tenure, but is also the tenure of choice,[2] part of the dream of modern life,[3] and to aspire to home ownership is seen as 'normal'.[4] Rising house prices have, however, meant that traditional home ownership has become unaffordable for a significant proportion of the population.[5] This has not tempered the UK government's desire to extend home ownership rates yet further. Even when the rate of owner-occupation was in the region of 70 per cent, the Labour government declared its commitment to extending this to 75 per cent.[6]

1 67.9% in England in 2008–9. This represents a fall from the previously attained peak of 70.9%. Department for Communities and Local Government, English Housing Survey: Household Report 2008–09, at 10 tbl.1.1 (2010), http://www.communities.gov.uk/documents statistics/pdf/1750765.pdf.

2 Department for Communities and Local Government, Public Attitudes to Housing in England: Report based on the results from the British Social Attitudes Survey 5 (2011) reports that 86% would choose to buy if they had a free choice. The preference for home ownership has remained consistently high despite fluctuations and variations within age groups. A review of attitudes between 1975–2007 is provided by Alison Wallace, *Public Attitudes to Housing* (Joseph Rowntree Foundation 2010).

3 The connection between home ownership and the 'American Dream' is considered by Lorna Fox-O'Mahony, *Homeownership, Debt, and Default: The Affective Value of Home and the Challenge of Affordability*, *in* Affordable Housing and Public-Private Partnerships 169, 170–175 (Nestor M. Davidson & Robin Paul Malloy eds, 2009).

4 Craig M. Gurney, *Pride and Prejudice: Discourses of Normalisation in Public and Private Accounts of Home Ownership*, 14 Housing Stud. 163, 179 (1999).

5 *See Shared Ownership: Facts & Figures*, Promoting Shared Ownership, http://www.shared-owner.co.uk/_media/static/SO-the_facts.pdf (last visited Feb. 8, 2011) (Promoting Shared Ownership is a group of 21 housing associations. Chapter 2 of this work is especially relevant).

6 HM Treasury & Office of the Deputy Prime Minister, The Government's Response to Kate Barker's Review of Housing Supply (2005).

This has meant that new and different ways of enabling homes to be purchased have been developed, and the promotion of low-cost home ownership (LCHO) has become a central plank of English housing policy in order to expand the opportunity to own.

In this chapter we analyse the legal routes used to deliver LCHO in England where there is some element of public subsidy involved. Subsidy is provided in one of two ways. Some schemes use what we call 'subsidy forgiveness', in which a grant or discount is given to the individual purchaser and which is either initially non-recoverable, or is written off over time.[7] Other schemes seek to ensure that the subsidy component remains available for public use in the longer term.[8] In these subsidy 'retention' or 'recapture' schemes, the subsidy is either never released to the individual purchaser or becomes repayable on future sale. The aim of this chapter is to evaluate how effective these legal models are at delivering the stated policy objectives of LCHO rather than to question the policies themselves.

The major route to LCHO in England in the last three decades has been through the Right to Buy (RTB) given to council tenants.[9] RTB has been incredibly popular, in part because it was built on a generous subsidy forgiveness model; but RTB sales have withered, and the high costs of RTB – both in economic terms and in relation to the impact it has had on the affordable housing stock – have been recognised.[10] In recent years, alternative models have been promoted under the umbrella of LCHO, ranging from grants towards house purchase, through part-ownership schemes, to co-operative housing models. Whereas RTB was driven

---

7 Subsidy forgiveness is characteristic of the Right to Buy (RTB) discussed further in this chapter.

8 For example, shared ownership and shared equity schemes discussed further in this chapter.

9 Councils are directly elected local government authorities. In contrast with federal systems of government, they derive their formal legal powers and duties from Parliament. For an account of local government in the UK, *see, e.g.*,, SIR WILLIAM WADE AND CHRISTOPHER FORSYTH, ADMINISTRATIVE LAW (10th ed., 2009) (Chapter 4). Local authorities, together with similar public institutions, dominated public sector housing until the 1980s. It is estimated that around 2.5 million dwellings have been sold to council tenants though the Right to Buy. STEVE WILCOX, UK HOUSING REVIEW 2009/2010, tbl.20d (2010), *available at* http://www.york.ac.uk/res/ukhr/ukhr0910/tables&figures/pdf/09-020a-d.pdf; *see also infra* note 27. Shared ownership, the next largest low-cost home ownership scheme, accounts for around 120,000 properties. HOMES & COMMUNITIES AGENCY, COUNCIL OF MORTGAGE LENDERS AND NATIONAL HOUSING FEDERATION, SHARED OWNERSHIP: JOINT GUIDANCE FOR ENGLAND ¶ 4 (2010) [hereinafter SHARED OWNERSHIP: JOINT GUIDANCE FOR ENGLAND].

10 *See, e.g.*, HOUSING CORPORATION (UK), A HOME OF MY OWN: THE REPORT OF THE GOVERNMENT'S LOW COST HOME OWNERSHIP TASK FORCE 59–82 (2003) [hereinafter A HOME OF MY OWN]. The Coalition Government seeks to stem this decline and has introduced new rules to reinvigorate RTB from 2 April 2012: http://www.communities.gov.uk/news/housing/2123194.

by the single-minded mission of giving people what they want – full ownership – the newer models are more sophisticated and take account of a wider range of objectives. They are sold to purchasers through a range of 'products' designed for particular categories of purchaser and/or types of property.

In order to evaluate these products, this chapter:

a. Explains the legal frameworks used to deliver the main LCHO products available in England;
b. Explores the potential benefits of home ownership to the individual in the form of wealth creation, 'mainstreaming' and security of place;
c. Sets out key additional policy objectives of LCHO, in particular introducing and supporting tenure mix (sustainable communities) and sustaining the opportunity for continued use of the subsidy to provide access to LCHO for intermediate income households; and
d. Evaluates the extent to which the different products available deliver both the individual benefits of home ownership and support the wider policy objectives.

Through this evaluation, our chapter feeds into two key debates that reflect the theme of this collection. The first of these debates is the identity of the individual as a homeowner. In other work, we have used the English model of shared ownership as a lens through which to explore the problematic nature of the label 'home ownership'.[11] In the context of a deeply ingrained dichotomy between an owner and a renter, the label of 'ownership' generates 'a range of expectations and understandings in the mind of the consumer',[12] opposed to those associated with being a 'mere' renter.[13] In this chapter, we consider the ability of a suite of products to deliver the benefits of home ownership to the individual. The second debate concerns the wider objectives now attributed to schemes aimed at expanding home ownership; in particular the desire to create sustainable mixed communities. Hence, in this way, we are concerned both with the identity of the individual as a homeowner and with the role of home ownership in the community. At its heart, our chapter is a study of how the twin policy objectives of delivering the benefits of home ownership to the individual whilst creating sustainable mixed communities are translated by and through different legal models.

11 Susan Bright & Nicholas Hopkins, Home, Meaning and Identity: Learning from the English Model of Shared Ownership, 28 HOUSING, THEORY & SOC'Y 377 (2011).

12 *Id.* at 17.

13 *Id.* at 14–17.

The Legal Frameworks

As already mentioned, a variety of products are potentially available as routes into affordable home ownership. In this chapter, we have chosen to group them together into three main headings: schemes delivering full ownership, part-ownership schemes and co-operative housing models. Although there are some differences between the individual products available within these headings, the groupings that we have chosen enable us to draw out what we think are some of the key issues that emerge when seeking to evaluate routes to LCHO.

Table 4.1 below provides a summary of the key aspects of each scheme, with a fuller explanation being given in the text following.

Table 4.1 Different LCHO Models

Full Ownership	
Scheme	**Legal Framework**
RTB/RTA*	Purchaser acquires freehold of current rented property at discounted price
Cash incentive scheme	Purchaser acquires freehold of property on the open market with help of a grant
Part-ownership	
Shared ownership	Purchaser buys a 'share' of the house value; minimum share usually 25% Purchaser acquires long lease (usually 99 years) Housing provider retains freehold Purchaser pays rent on 'non-purchased' share Purchaser can (usually) 'staircase' up to full ownership
Shared equity	Purchaser buys a 'share' of the house value; minimum share usually 70–80% Purchaser acquires freehold 'Non-purchased' share is subject to subsidised mortgage Purchaser can 'staircase' up to full ownership
Co-operative Housing	
Mutual home ownership	Purchaser given medium term lease (20 years) Occupation payment linked to income Equity purchase through share in fund

* The Right to Acquire (RTA) is a scheme similar to the RTB but applicable to certain tenants of housing associations. See infra text following notes *38, 40.*

Schemes Delivering Full Ownership

Under schemes that deliver full ownership, the purchaser acquires a freehold of the house.[14] There are two main LCHO programs that can lead to this. The first, a Cash Incentive Scheme, involves a subsidy in the form of a cash grant, which is given to the purchaser who is then free to purchase a property in the open market.[15] There may be a condition that if the property is sold within a certain period of time, a proportion of the grant has to be repaid, and the grant may be hedged around with various other conditions, for example relating to the size of the property that can be purchased.[16] The individual has no legal right to such a grant and its availability will be at the discretion of local councils or other social landlords.[17] In practice, the use of grants tends to be restricted to areas in which there is great housing demand as they can be used as a means of encouraging existing social renters to move out of their present housing, thereby releasing the home for another family in housing need.[18]

The second main route is the RTB. In outline, this gives existing council tenants the right to purchase their current home at a discounted price.[19] This was first introduced as a legal right in 1980, following the election of the Conservative

---

14 We assume, throughout, that the property purchased is a house. For complex legal reasons to do with the enforceability of covenants, flats and apartments can only be sold on leases and not as freeholds. So that we can focus on evaluation of the various LCHO models, we have chosen to avoid the additional layer of complication that may arise if the property bought is a flat or apartment and thus must be leasehold. For further discussion of the legal complexities of flat ownership in English law, *see* BEN MCFARLANE, NICHOLAS HOPKINS & SARAH NIELD, LAND LAW: TEXT, CASES AND MATERIALS 965–988 (2009).

15 The statutory basis for the scheme is contained in the Housing Act, 1988, c. 50, § 129 (Eng.).

16 Under the Housing Act, 1988, c. 50, § 129 (Eng.), local housing authorities have wide discretion as to whether to operate a Cash Incentive Scheme and, if they choose to do so, the scheme 'shall contain such provisions as the local housing authority considers appropriate'. Schemes are therefore able to reflect local housing needs and priorities. The exact terms of schemes differ and may change year on year. The comments in this section reflect schemes that have been or are being offered, but given both the local and temporal operation of individual schemes, references to particular schemes are not provided.

17 The ability to offer Cash Incentive Schemes is currently restricted to local housing authorities, but is expected to be extended to other social landlords by the Localism Bill, 2010–11, H.C. Bill [126] cl. 149 (Eng.).

18 This statement reflects the wider strategic outcome the scheme can be used to achieve identified in A HOME OF MY OWN, *supra* note 10, at 95 para 44 and the ability of local housing authorities to devise terms for individual schemes that reflect local housing needs and priorities.

19 The RTB is the topic of extensive discussion in housing literature in the UK. For textbook accounts *see, e.g.,*, SUSAN BRIGHT, LANDLORD AND TENANT LAW IN CONTEXT 743-759 (2007); JILL MORGAN, ASPECTS OF HOUSING LAW 396–412 (2007). For further analysis *see* COLIN JONES & ALAN MURIE, THE RIGHT TO BUY: ANALYSIS AND EVALUATION OF A HOUSING

Party to power in the 1979 general election.[20] Prior to that point in time, it had been possible for individual local authorities to facilitate and allow discretionary sales, but the willingness of local authorities to do so was a political football, as is shown by the variation in the number of sales according to whether the Conservative Party or the Labour Party was in power: during three Conservative years (1971–1973) there were 97,426 sales of dwellings by public authorities in England and Wales, compared to 13,470 sales in the three successive years of a Labour government.[21] When the RTB was introduced (giving a legally enforceable RTB), the number of annual sales to sitting council tenants soared, reaching a peak of 170,600 RTB home sales in England in 1982–1983.[22] The operation of the RTB was relatively simple. There was a statutory scheme setting out the various qualification requirements and the level of discount available (which was based on the length of prior occupation of the council home), as well as setting out the process to be followed in order to exercise the right. As the purchaser of a house would get the freehold, the end result was that the purchaser would look like any other homeowner and the lender financing the purchase would be able to take a legal charge over the property in the traditional manner. Admittedly, the purchaser would have no choice as to which property could be purchased as the right only applied to their current home, and this also meant that they would remain in an area of predominantly social rented housing, but the RTB proved to be extremely popular. According to the then Conservative Secretary of State for the Environment, the *leitmotif* underlying the scheme was that it would deliver 'what people wanted' by fulfilling a 'deeply ingrained desire for home ownership'.[23] Even the Labour Party had, a few years earlier, remarked that home ownership meets a 'basic and natural desire'.[24] RTB delivered what people wanted with great success, at least if the number of people choosing to exercise their rights is anything to go by: more than 2.5 million RTB sales occurred in Great Britain in the period 1980 to 2008.[25] This success is not surprising as it not only tapped into people's dreams

---

POLICY (2006); PETER KING, HOUSING POLICY TRANSFORMED: THE RIGHT TO BUY AND THE DESIRE TO OWN (2010).

20 Housing Act, 1980, c. 51, (Eng.).

21 *Id.* at 23 tbl.2.3 (2006) (table is titled *Sales of dwellings by public authorities (England and Wales) 1960–80*).

22 *See* 272 PARL. DEB., H.C. (6th ser.) (1996) 3–4W (UK).

23 976 PARL. DEB., H.C. (6th ser.) (1980) 1445 (UK) (Michael Heseltine, Conservative Secretary of State for the Environment).

24 DEPARTMENT OF THE ENVIRONMENT, HOUSING POLICY: A CONSULTATIVE DOCUMENT, 1977, Cm. 6851, at 50, ¶ 7.03.

25 WILCOX, *supra* note 9. The number of sales may in fact be higher. Jones and Murie note that between 1979–2003 over 2.7 million dwellings were sold by councils into home ownership. JONES & MURIE, *supra* note 20, at 54 tbl.4.2 (2006) (table is titled *Public sector dwelling sales into home ownership 1979–2003*). The authors explain that while this number is not confined to RTB sales, the larger figure is a more appropriate reference as not all sales taking place under the RTB are officially recorded as such.

and aspirations, but it did so in a way that gave a significant financial incentive, and enabled them to become owners without having to move. Although the level of discount available varied over time, it was generous from the start – the initial maximum discount for houses was 50 per cent, and at one point was as much as 70 per cent on sales of flats.[26] Once the RTB had been exercised, the new owner was free to sell the house on the open market.[27] If the resale occurred within a specified period of time (initially three years), then some of the discount had to be repaid (the amount repayable depending on timing of the resale), but after the expiration of this repayment period the purchaser was free to keep the whole of the sale price received.[28]

As is argued for in the somewhat controversial book by Peter King, *Housing Policy Transformed*, the RTB was a resounding success when measured against the single-minded policy goal of allowing tenants to become owner-occupiers whilst breaking the influence that councils had over housing.[29] RTB has always, however, been subject to much criticism by housing policy commentators.[30] It contributed to the 'residualisation' of council housing as the better-off tenants living in the nicer properties tended to be the ones who exercised the RTB, leaving the less attractive properties under council control rented to those on lower incomes.[31] Over time it was also alleged that the RTB could be used for profiteering.[32] These concerns led to further restrictions being imposed on the RTB. Thus, the period within which resale can trigger repayment of the discount was extended to five years in 2004[33] and the level of discount was restricted to a maximum discount

26 The initial discount for houses was 33% following three years of qualifying residence, with a further 1% for each complete year of tenancy, to a maximum of 50%: Housing Act, 1980, c. 51 § 1(3) and 7(1) (Eng.) (now repealed). The more generous discounts for flats were provided in the Housing and Planning Act, 1986, c. 63 §2(2)(b) (Eng.) which gave an initial discount of 44%, rising at 2% per annum to a maximum of 70%. Over time the initial period of residence required has been varied and the discounts available became less generous: Bright, *supra* note 20, at 748, 753-754. The Coalition Government has increased the maximum discount from 2 April 2012: http://www.communities.gov.uk/news/housing/2123194.

27 But this changed in 2005: Housing Act, 1985, c. 68, § 156A (Eng.) (introduced by the Housing Act, 2004, c. 34 (Eng.)) provides that if there is a disposal within ten years, the property must first be offered back to a social landlord at full market value.

28 Bright, *supra* note 20, at 754–755.

29 King, *supra* note 20, at 66.

30 For an overview of its impact, *see* Bright, *supra* note 20, at 160–164. For more detailed analysis, *see* generally Jones & Murie, *supra* note 20 (especially Chapter 12).

31 *See, e.g.*, *id.* at 210–211.

32 *See* Nicholas Hopkins & Emma Laurie, *Housing or Property? The Dynamics of Housing Policy and Property Principles in the Right to Buy*, 26 Legal Stud. 65 (2006).

33 Bright, *supra* note 20, at 754–755.

of £16,000 in areas of housing pressure.[34] In addition, to address concerns over the impact on the availability of stock, a right of pre-emption is now built into RTB sales so that if the purchaser sells the house within ten years, it must be offered back to the local authority for purchase at market values.[35] RTB sales are no longer occurring on the scale that they did in the first couple of decades.[36] Of course this is also not surprising; the number of nice council homes available for RTB has been significantly reduced, partly by the fact that so many homes have already been sold, but also because much rented stock has been transferred from local authorities to housing associations.[37] There is a similar scheme available to certain tenants of housing associations, which is known as the right to acquire (RTA), but this right has always been more limited in both scope and availability.[38] Additionally, the limits to the RTB that have been introduced in recent years make it less obviously attractive to council tenants, and even more recently the economic downturn and constraints on mortgage lending have also played their part in reducing RTB sales.[39]

---

34 Housing (Right to Buy) (Limits on Discount) (Amendment) Order SI 2003/498. The Coalition Government has increased the maximum cap discount to £75,000 from 2 April 2012: http://www.communities.gov.uk/news/housing/2123194.

35 *Supra* note 28.

36 In 2009–10, there were only 3,100 RTB sales in England. Department of Communities and Local Government, Social Housing Sales to Sitting Tenants, England, 2009–10 (2010), http://www.communities.gov.uk/publications/corporate/statistics/socialhousingsales200910.

37 Housing associations are 'independent, non-profit-distributing organisations governed by voluntary boards to provide mainly rented housing at below market rents'. David Mullins & Alan Murie, Housing Policy in the UK 178 (2006). Since the 1980s, local authority (council) housing has declined while the role of housing associations in providing social housing has increased. The sale of council homes to tenants through the Right to Buy and the transfer of other council housing stock to housing associations through 'large scale voluntary transfers' have both been significant causes of this shift. Bright, *supra* note 20, at 7–8. It has been predicted, in respect of England, that housing associations 'will soon be the second largest form of housing tenure next to owner occupation'. Morag McDermont, Governing Independence and Expertise: The Business of Housing Associations 1 (2010).

38 The Right to Acquire (RTA) was introduced by the Housing Act, 1996, c. 52 (Eng.). It applies only to properties built or acquired on or after 1 April 1997 and the discounts available range from £9,000 to £16,000 depending on the location of the property. Bright, *supra* note 20, at 758. In the period from its introduction to 2009–2010 just 2,670 homes had been sold through the RTA. Department of Communities and Local Government, Social Housing Sales to sitting tenants, England, 2009–10, at 9 (2010), http://www.communities.gov.uk/publications/corporate/statistics/socialhousingsales200910.

39 Official statistics show that in England, while sales had been declining over a four year period, they fell sharply by 76% between 2007–2008 and 2008–2009 (with a further fall of 20% recorded for 2009–2010). Department of Communities and Local Government, Social Housing Sales to sitting tenants, England, 2009–10 tbl.2 (2010), http://www.communities.gov.uk/publications/corporate/statistics/socialhousingsales200910 (the table

Part-ownership

RTB was limited in scope as it applied only to council tenants. Likewise, cash grants are usually only made to enable existing council tenants to move on and free up council housing stock.[40] To reach other groups unable to access traditional home ownership, different schemes have been developed that enable the purchase of part, as against the whole, of the equity in the house. This is sometimes referred to as 'intermediate tenure', but we prefer to use the label 'part-ownership' for three reasons. First, the phrase 'intermediate tenure' is not used consistently and the different uses of the term may mislead. In particular, intermediate tenure is sometimes used to disclose a policy goal under which part-ownership is generally seen as a stepping stone into full ownership, rather than intended to be a permanent form of tenure.[41] This policy goal is of particular importance in delivering the benefits of home ownership to the individual as studies have shown that it is schemes that enable purchasers to progress to full ownership that most satisfactorily fulfil individuals' aspirations for home ownership.[42] In a limited range of circumstances, however, shared ownership cannot be a stepping stone to full ownership and there is a cap on the amount of equity that the purchaser can acquire. This is the case,

---

is titled *Total Right to Buy sales in England)*. The decline between 2007–2008 and 2008–2009 has been linked to the fall in the housing market caused by the recession. KING, *supra* note 20, at 63.

40 The Cash Incentive Scheme is intended to operate alongside the RTB, but not in conjunction with it. Hence, local housing authorities typically specify in the terms of their individual schemes that a cash grant cannot be used to buy an existing rented home under the RTB. To enable a tenant to do so would be to confer a double benefit from the public purse as the tenant would obtain a discount on the purchase price of their existing rented home through the RTB.

41 In addition to highlighting the transitional status of a tenure, 'intermediate tenure' has sometimes been used to capture the fact that the tenure is neither rental nor open-market ownership (which is how it is used in A HOME OF MY OWN, *supra* note 10) and sometimes it is used to indicate that the housing is priced somewhere between subsidised social rents and open-market prices (this latter appears to be the meaning understood by the Department of Communities and Local Government). S*ee* DEPARTMENT OF COMMUNITIES AND LOCAL GOVERNMENT, *Definitions of general housing terms*, http://www.communities.gov.uk/housing/housingresearch/housingstatistics/definitiongeneral/ (last visited Feb. 12, 2011). For further discussion of the definition of intermediate housing, *see* Sarah Monk & Christine Whitehead, *Introduction, in* MAKING HOUSING MORE AFFORDABLE: THE ROLE OF INTERMEDIATE TENURES 1, 8–11 (Sarah Monk & Christine Whitehead eds, 2010).

42 Simon Pinnegar, Vivienne Milligan, Dana Quintal, Bill Randolph, Peter Williams & Judith Yates, *Innovative Financing for Home Ownership: The Potential for Shared Equity Initiatives in Australia* 34 (Australian Housing and Urban Research Institute Position Paper No. 137, 2008), *available at* http://www.ahuri.edu.au/publications/projects/p70394; s*ee also* PATRICK ALLEN, SHARED OWNERSHIP: A STEPPING STONE TO HOME OWNERSHIP 18 (1982). A survey of purchasers of early shared ownership schemes found '[t]he nearer respondents are to full ownership the happier they appear to be with the scheme'. *Id.*

for example, in respect of 'designated protected areas'. These are geographical areas prescribed by statute in which there is considered to be an overriding need to protect the supply of affordable housing (both rented and owned).[43] Shared ownership may also be used in this limited way in warden-assisted homes for elderly residents. Secondly, even where the intention is to provide a stepping stone to full ownership, the practical reality for many purchasers is that this bigger step into full ownership is never taken and part-ownership becomes, for the individual, a permanent tenure.[44] Thirdly, while purchasers of current part-ownership schemes have the *right* to move further towards full ownership when they are able to afford to do so (outside the exceptional schemes referred to above), and indeed there may also be an expectation that they will exercise this right,[45] the traffic is not entirely one way. Provision can also be made for purchasers to reduce their share of the equity, and even to revert wholly to renting.[46] Although providers are not obliged to enable so-called 'downward staircasing' or 'flexible tenure', its availability has been described as a 'strong moral imperative' in the context of the increased risk of repossession during the global economic crisis.[47] Notably, it is being promoted not only for the benefit of the individual,[48] but also as a means of retaining property within the affordable home ownership sector.[49] Part-ownership is also supported as part of the government's 'Mortgage Rescue Scheme' for 'priority' homeowners[50] in England at risk of homelessness through repossession, to enable them to convert from full ownership to a part-ownership arrangement with a social housing provider. The number of home owners who have converted to part-ownership is tiny,[51] but the scheme reflects the need for provision of affordable home ownership

43 Leasehold Reform Act, 1967, c. 88 sched. 4A, ¶ 4A (Eng.) (inserted by the Housing and Regeneration Act, 2008 c. 17) and the Housing (Right to Enfranchise) (Designated Protected Areas) (England) Order 2009/2098; *see also* SHARED OWNERSHIP: JOINT GUIDANCE FOR ENGLAND, *supra* note 9, 7–10, 51–58.

44 *See infra* note 65.

45 *See infra* text accompanying notes 86, 88.

46 DEPARTMENT OF COMMUNITIES & LOCAL GOVERNMENT, ASSISTING SHARED OWNERS AT RISK OF REPOSSESSION: FLEXIBLE TENURE - QUESTIONS AND ANSWERS 4 (2010), *available at* http://www.communities.gov.uk/publications/housing/flexibletenurequestions [hereinafter ASSISTING SHARED OWNERS].

47 *Id.*

48 The individual benefit is twofold: first, retaining the benefit of owner-occupation; and, secondly, avoiding the negative effects connected with repossession.

49 *Id.*

50 Those with dependent children, pregnant women and others considered vulnerable through old age, mental or physical disability or other special reason. The Mortgage Rescue Scheme is open both to those who bought their homes on the open market with mortgage finance in the usual way and those who have become full owners through a transitional tenure. For details, *see* DIRECTGOV, http://www.direct.gov.uk (last visited Feb 14, 2011).

51 Monitoring statistics covering the period from the inception of the Mortgage Rescue Scheme in January 2009 to the first quarter 2011 show only 41 households converted

other than at the point of entry into the housing market, in contrast to the focus of schemes that provide a first 'foot on the property ladder'. It also provides an alternative to a return to renting for those for whom full home ownership has ceased to be affordable.

Although the number of part-owned units is relatively small (around 135,000 homes as at March 2009),[52] the expansion of this form of ownership remains a part of government policy.[53] Part-ownership schemes are currently marketed collectively under the label of HomeBuy, but this marketing tool hides the fact that there are two very different legal models being used here. Indeed, language is used very deceptively in relation to these products, and is little understood.[54]

---

to part-ownership (in the form of shared equity, see later text). In the same period, over 2,500 households converted from homeowners to renters (on an assured shorthold tenancy) through 'Government Purchase to Rent' also available under the Mortgage Rescue Scheme. DEPARTMENT OF COMMUNITIES & LOCAL GOVERNMENT, MORTGAGE RESCUE MONITORING STATISTICS –MARCH QUARTER 2011 (2011), *available at* http://www.communities.gov.uk/publications/corporate/statistics/mortgagerescuestatisticsq12011.

52 HOMES & COMMUNITIES AGENCY, DATA COMPENDIUM: A COLLATION OF PUBLISHED DATA ABOUT THE INTERMEDIATE MARKET 26 ¶ 75 (2010), *available at* http://www.homesandcommunities.co.uk/public/documents/Data-Compendium-autumn2010.pdf. The text accompanying these figures refers to homes owned by housing associations 'on a leasehold basis where the purchaser had not acquired 100% equity (ie on shared ownership terms)', but the footnote referenced at this point suggests that this includes not only shared ownership, but also shared equity properties where the purchaser has not acquired 100% of the equity. Both terms are discussed below in the text. The definitional confusion within official documents illustrates just how little understood these products are.

53 DEPARTMENT OF COMMUNITIES & LOCAL GOVERNMENT, THE COALITION: OUR PROGRAMME FOR GOVERNMENT 12 (2010), http://www.communities.gov.uk/documents/corporate/pdf/1657233.pdf [hereinafter THE COALITION: OUR PROGRAMME FOR GOVERNMENT]. The coalition government's programme for affordable homes for the period 2011–2015 gives priority to 'affordable rent' schemes (rented at 80% of market value), but states that consideration will be given to the inclusion of 'affordable home ownership proposals, where it is a local priority and offers value for money'. DEPARTMENT OF COMMUNITIES AND LOCAL GOVERNMENT & HOMES & COMMUNITIES AGENCY, 2011–15 AFFORDABLE HOMES PROGRAMME – FRAMEWORK 20 ¶ 4.1 (2011), *available at* http://www.homesandcommunities.co.uk/public/documents/Affordable-Homes-Framework.pdf [hereinafter AFFORDABLE HOMES PROGRAMME – FRAMEWORK]. In respect of the two major schemes discussed in the text that accompanies this note, shared ownership will form the main element of affordable ownership offerings, 'to ensure that households on a range of incomes can be assisted', (*Id.* at ¶ 4.9) but equity loans (shared equity) will be considered if they are 'the most appropriate home ownership option for the local area and agreed with the local authority'. *Id.* It has since been announced that of the first 80,000 affordable homes to be provided within the new programme, 79% will be rented and 21% will fall within low-cost home ownership. http://www.homesandcommunities.co.uk/affordable-homes.

54 *See supra* note 42 above for one illustration of confused language. This is not a new phenomenon: Alder similarly accuses the 'co-ownership tenancies' pioneered in the 1960s

The two major schemes are commonly distinguished according to whether they offer 'shared ownership' or 'shared equity'.[55] Broadly, take-up of these schemes depends upon the income level of the purchaser. Those on lower incomes tend to be limited to shared ownership schemes as the part purchased can be as little as 25 per cent of the full value of the property, whereas shared equity schemes usually require a minimum purchase of 70–80% of the full value.[56] As will now be seen, the legal details of how the schemes work are quite different.

Although referred to as shared ownership, there is in fact no ownership that is shared at law under this scheme. The purchaser is granted a long lease of the house (usually 99 years) in return for the capital sum paid, whilst the housing provider retains the freehold to the property.[57] Where the homes are provided with grants from state funds, as will usually be the case, there are certain prescribed clauses that must be included in the leases.[58] In practice, most shared ownership leases will be on the terms of the model leases provided by the Homes and Communities Agency (HCA), and formerly the Housing Corporation.[59] In recognition of the

---

of being a misnomer. John Alder, *Co-operative Housing Associations – An Alternative Tenure – Part 1*, Conv. & Prop. Law., May-June 1988, at 187, 192 (1988).

55 The existence of these two distinct schemes is well established despite the lack of consistency in the nomenclature used. Useful explanations of the operation of each scheme is provided by Shared Ownership: Joint Guidance for England, *supra* note 9, in respect of shared ownership and Communities and Local Government, HomeBuy Direct: A Buyer's Guide (2009) http://cfg.homesandcommunities.co.uk/public/documents/HCA_HomeBuy%20brochure_201109.pdf, [hereinafter HomeBuy Direct Buyer's Guide] in respect of shared equity. *See* further the description of individual schemes at http://www.direct.gov.uk/en/HomeAndCommunity/BuyingAndSellingYourHome/HomeBuyingSchemes/DG_4001347 (last accessed 12 July 2011).

56 The difference in affordability between the schemes and the percentage of the property that the purchaser must be able to buy is acknowledged in A Home of My Own, *supra* note 10, at 61–62, 9–10, 64–65, 13–16. Individual schemes vary as to the level of equity loan available. For example, in HomeBuy Direct, which is based on shared equity, the minimum share that must be purchased is 70%. HomeBuy Direct Buyer's Guide, *supra* note 56, at 8. The scheme is discussed further below note 82 and text. Funding for the HomeBuy Direct scheme ceased to be available from 30 September 2010. A new scheme, FirstBuy, launched in April 2011 requires a minimum purchase of 80%. http://www.homesandcommunities.co.uk/firstbuy. *See* generally, in relation to that scheme, Homes & Communities Agency, *FirstBuy Buyers' Guide* (2011), http://www.homesandcommunities.co.uk/sites/default/files/our-work/firstbuy-buyers-guide-010711.pdf. An 80% minimum purchase will become the norm. The Affordable Homes Programme – Framework, *supra* note 54, ¶ 4.10 caps the equity loan for shared equity schemes approved within the period of the programme (2011–2015) at 20%.

57 Shared Ownership: Joint Guidance for England, *supra* note 9, 5.

58 *Id.* 13.

59 The Homes & Communities Agency is the national housing and regeneration agency for England. It is a public body funded by the Department of Communities and Local Government and created by the Housing and Regeneration Act 2008. Housing and

fact that only part of the value has been purchased, the purchaser is still required to pay a rent on the unpurchased share of the property.[60] The rent is set at a level intended to be affordable,[61] but even so, the combination of having to finance the equity share purchased, carry the repairing costs and paying rent on top does mean that the total cost can be difficult to maintain for those on the lowest incomes. In line with the intermediate nature of the tenure, it is possible for the purchaser to 'staircase' up the proportion that is owned, and provision is made for the freehold to be transferred once the purchaser's share reaches 100 per cent.[62] In practice, the majority of shared owners do not appear to move from this intermediate tenure to full ownership. Figures vary but, at the highest, only a quarter of shared ownership purchasers eventually staircase to 100 per cent ownership.[63]

Shared ownership purchasers are, therefore, leaseholders. In English law, it is never possible for the purchaser to 'own' land in any absolute sense; instead what is owed is an 'estate' in the land, which is essentially land for a time. The most expansive estate that can be owned is the freehold, which is effectively unlimited in duration. The other estate, the leasehold, exists for a fixed period of time. But the difference between freehold and leasehold estates runs deeper than their duration. A leasehold is carved out of a freehold and creates an ongoing relationship between the leaseholder and the freeholder as landlord. In this sense, the leasehold is a subservient estate to the freehold. In legal terms, the relationship is founded on a contract which sets out the various rights and responsibilities of the landlord and leaseholder. Studies have shown that leasehold ownership can lead to certain frustrations as it reduces the autonomy of the individual to treat

---

Regeneration Act, 2008, c.17 (Eng.). Some of its functions were previously exercised by the Housing Corporation, a body abolished by the same statute. *Id.* The Homes & Communities Agency publishes two model shared ownership leases, one for the purchase of a house and one for a flat. http://cfg.homesandcommunities.co.uk/model-leases-for-housing-association-use-from-april-2010.htm [hereinafter the model lease].

60 Shared Ownership: Joint Guidance for England, *supra* note 9, 5.

61 No more than 3% of the unpurchased share. Homes and Communities Agency, *Affordable Housing Capital Funding Guide*, http://cfg.homesandcommunities.co.uk/nbhb-rents (last visited Feb. 14 2011).

62 Provision for the leaseholder to staircase to 100% and own the property outright is a mandatory term of the lease for schemes provided with state funds, other than for properties in designated protected areas (explained above note 45. *See* Homes and Communities Agency, Shared Ownership: Joint Guidance for England, *supra* note 9, 6 and schedule 5 of the model lease for a house).

63 Simon Graham, *The role of shared ownership in the future housing market – a discussion paper* 10 (2010), http://www.shared-owner.co.uk/_media/static/May_2010-The_role_of_shared_ownership_in_the_future_housing_market-a_discussion_paper.pdf, refers to data from the National Housing Federation that suggests on average 25% of shared owners staircase to 100%. Tenant Services Authority, Existing Tenants Survey 2008, at 23 (2008), *available at* http://www.tenantservicesauthority.org/upload/pdf/ETS_technical_report.pdf, says a much lower figure, 8%, had increased their share (at all) since moving in.

the house as their own.[64] The leaseholder may, for example, be unable to make any alterations to the property without the landlord's consent. A shared ownership leaseholder is also vulnerable to losing the home if they fall behind with *either* the mortgage payment on the purchased share *or* the rental payment in respect of the lease. This latter point can have an especially hard and unjust impact, as is illustrated in the County Court case of *Richardson v Midland Heart*.[65] In this case the purchaser, Miss Richardson, entered a 99-year shared ownership lease with the housing association Midland Heart.[66] She paid £29,500 for a 50 per cent stake, and paid rent on the unpurchased share.[67] Significantly, there was no mortgage in this case. In 2003, Miss Richardson had to move into a women's refuge.[68] This led to her owing a great deal of rent under the shared ownership lease as the housing benefit that she had depended on ceased to be payable.[69] In 2005, Miss Richardson attempted to sell the property, which was now valued at £151,000.[70] For reasons that are not entirely clear from the report of the decision, the housing association nonetheless used the rent arrears as grounds for terminating the lease under what is known as Ground 8, which gives a mandatory ground for possession.[71] The judge has no discretion and must order possession.[72] The consequence was that Miss Richardson lost her home. But what made the decision especially shocking is that she also lost all the capital that she had invested in the property. The £45,000 uplift destined to her on a sale represented, according to the judge, a 'windfall' for the housing association.[73] Although the housing association chose to make an *ex gratia* payment of the initial investment (not the uplifted value, and less rent arrears and various costs), at law she was not entitled to anything.[74]

In order to ensure that the housing stock is available to those meeting the landlord's eligibility criteria rather than being placed on the open market, the shared ownership lease also contains restrictions on sale: the way that the lease is structured encourages the shared owner who is planning to market the property to notify the landlord of his or her plans, rather than market the property for sale

64 Ian Cole & David Robinson, Owners Yet Tenants: The Position of Leaseholders in Flats in England and Wales, 15 Housing Stud. 595 (2000).

65 [2008] Landlord & Tenant Reports 31 (Eng.).

66 *Id.* at 2.

67 *Id.*

68 *Id.* at 3.

69 *Id.* at 4.

70 *Id.* at 5–6.

71 Housing Act 1988 sched. 2, Ground 8.

72 Housing Act 1988 sched. 2 distinguishes between 'grounds on which court must order possession' (Part I of the schedule, generally referred to as mandatory grounds) and 'grounds on which court may order possession' (Part II of the schedule, generally referred to as discretionary grounds). In this schema, Ground 8 is a mandatory ground for possession.

73 Landlord & Tenant Reports, *supra* note 66, at 24.

74 *Id.*

through an estate agent in the way that a conventional or traditional[75] owner-occupier would. The landlord then has the opportunity to nominate a purchaser.[76] Once this process is triggered, sale may be protracted: it is only if the landlord does not exercise its rights (or the nominated purchaser fails to exchange contracts), that the shared owner is then able to sell the property on the open market.[77] Further, within the sale process the shared owner does not necessarily have the same freedom to negotiate the sale price enjoyed by a conventional owner-occupier.[78] If the shared owner has staircased to 100 per cent, the restrictions on sale appear even more prescriptive: before any sale can take place on the open market, the property must be offered back to the (former) landlord at a price determined by an independent valuation.[79] This right of pre-emption lasts for 21 years.

Shared equity, which is also referred to as 'equity shares', operates quite differently. In such schemes, the purchaser buys a freehold to the property (the same title that would be bought by a traditional owner-occupier),[80] but only a proportion of the value of the equity (typically between 70–80%).[81] The 'purchased' share will usually be funded (at least in part) by a commercial mortgage and secured by a first legal charge.[82] The balance, the unpurchased share, is funded by an equity loan which is secured as a (usually) second legal mortgage.[83] This unpurchased share represents the subsidised component: the exact payment arrangements under the equity loan may differ between schemes, but typically there is an initial interest-free period in which no payments are made after which a low interest is charged, rising incrementally each year; for example, in HomeBuy Direct, one of the programmes that uses the shared equity model of part-ownership, no interest is

75 By which we mean a person who buys full title on the open market, with any mortgage provided by a commercial lender.

76 *See, e.g.*, clauses 3.19–3.20 of the model lease for a house dealing with alienation.

77 *Id.*

78 The sale process triggers an independent valuation which the vendor is then encouraged to treat as a maximum sale price. *See, e.g.*, clause 3.20.4 of the model lease for a house.

79 *See, e.g.*, the right of pre-emption contained in sched. 5 part 2 of the model lease for a house.

80 HomeBuy Direct Buyer's Guide, *supra* note 56, at 1 puts the point starkly: 'you will still have 100% title to your home'.

81 *Supra* note 57.

82 The expectation a commercial mortgage will be used is acknowledged in the HomeBuy Direct Buyer's Guide, *supra* note 56, at 1.

83 Where the cost of the equity loan is split between the Homes and Communities Agency and the property developer, each will have an equally ranked charge. *See id.* at 14 in respect of HomeBuy Direct and Homes & Communities Agency, *FirstBuy Prospectus* 5 (2011), http://www.homesandcommunities.co.uk/sites/default/files/our-work/firstbuy-prospectus_0.pdf in respect of FirstBuy.

paid on the equity loan for the first five years, after which a fee of 1.75 per cent per annum is paid, rising each year by the Retail Price Index plus 1 per cent.[84]

As with shared ownership, it is possible to staircase up and thereby increase the proportion of the equity purchased.[85] The introduction of, and incremental increase in, interest payments is intended to encourage staircasing as well as to ease financial pressures during the initial period of ownership.[86] When the property is sold on by the purchaser, the amount that the borrower has to repay to the second lender is linked to the value of the home.[87] Thus, on this model, the subsidy component is repaid in a way that keeps the value of the subsidy in line with rising property values. This does, however, have repercussions for the shared equity owner on a sale. Although the property is sold on the open market, the amount repayable may be determined by reference to an independent valuation.[88] If the actual sale price falls below this valuation, the percentage payable is still calculated by reference to the higher figure.[89] If, however, the actual sale price exceeds the valuation, then the amount payable is determined according to the actual price attained.[90] In this way, the shared equity owner acts as guarantor that the amount of the subsidy repaid is commensurate with the property value.

Whereas the lease documentation for shared ownership is now in a very standardised form, there is more variety with the legal structuring of shared equity purchases. There are, however, features common to both models. Under both shared ownership and shared equity, the purchaser is responsible for the full costs of repairs to the property even though they own only a part of the equity. This feature of the schemes has been a source of criticism for purchasers since the introduction of shared ownership.[91] Purchasers' concerns have been cast aside in part on the basis that responsibility for repairs is part and parcel of being an 'owner'.[92] In the context of shared ownership, the imposition of liability for repairs and maintenance thus chimes with the general claim that 'the shared owner has the normal rights and responsibilities of a full owner-occupier'.[93] In shared equity, it is

84 *Id.* at 1, 12. This pattern of interest payments will be adopted in shared equity schemes introduced in the coalition government's programme for affordable homes for the period 2011–2015. Department of Communities and Local Government & Homes & Communities Agency, *supra* note 57, at 21. It is adopted in the FirstBuy scheme: Homes & Communities Agency, *supra* note 57, 45.

85 HomeBuy Direct Buyer's Guide, *supra* note 56, at 11.

86 *Id.* at 13.

87 *Id.* at 9.

88 *Id.* at 10.

89 This appears implicit in relation to HomeBuy Direct and is explicit in the terms of a precedent shared equity agreement logged with the authors. *See id.*

90 This is the position in the terms of a precedent shared equity agreement logged with the authors.

91 Allen, *supra* note 43, at 17.

92 *Id.* at 21.

93 Shared Ownership: Joint Guidance for England, *supra* note 9, at 6.

consonant with the fact that from the outset the purchaser will have '100% title to [their] home'.[94] Under both models there will probably be a prohibition on making physical alterations to the property without the landlord's written consent. Even though this consent cannot be unreasonably withheld, it is a constraint not found in traditional home ownership. Under both models, requirements of consent to subsequent borrowings have been put in place that are designed to limit, or at least to exercise some control over, the purposes for which additional loans are taken.[95]

There is an alternative legal model that can be used to deliver part-ownership. In English law, co-ownership of land is given effect under a trust.[96] Trusts of land arise, for example, whenever a home is co-owned by a married couple, civil partners or cohabitants. The proportion owned by each party is reflected in his or her beneficial share. The same device could have been utilised to provide for LCHO with the provider of the public subsidy becoming a beneficial co-owner together with the purchaser(s). The trust has some advantages particularly over the shared ownership lease. It is an existing and familiar legal device for achieving co-ownership and avoids the need to impose a lease in the case of houses.[97] To date, however, trusts have not been favoured for LCHO. While there is no clear reason why this is the case, it may be no more than an accident of legal history. While co-ownership of the home is now pervasive, it is a relatively recent

---

94 HomeBuy Direct Buyer's Guide, *supra* note 56, at 1.

95 A mortgage protection clause (MPC) is a prescribed term of the shared ownership lease (on which *see supra* note 60). In the clause that has been used in leases since 6 April 2010, the landlord underwrites losses arising on borrower default. Additional borrowings are protected by the MPC only if approved by the landlord. Although the MPC is not explicitly so-confined, it seems that additional borrowings will only be possible for staircasing or to comply with covenants under the lease. Shared Ownership: Joint Guidance for England, *supra* note 9, at 16. At the least, the potential liability of landlords under the MPC will impact on their willingness to give approval for loans for other purposes. Bright & Hopkins, *supra* note 11, at 9–10. Borrowing outside the MPC remains possible, but will be less commercially attractive to the lender. In shared equity, further borrowings require the consent of the provider of the subsidised mortgage (known as the HomeBuy Agent). The HomeBuy Direct Buyers' Guide, *supra* note 56, at 16, advises that '[a]dvances to be used for staircasing or repaying the Agency's contribution will usually be welcomed. Advances for other purposes will be considered by the National HomeBuy Agent on a case by case basis'.

96 The use of a trust as the vehicle for co-ownership is a distinctive feature of English land law. In the absence of an express trust, a statutory trust is imposed in every conveyance to joint owners through the Law of Property Act 1925, ss 34 and 36. For further discussion on the regulation of co-ownership in English law *see* Ben McFarlane, Nicholas Hopkins & Sarah Nield, *supra* note 15, at 593–635.

97 For further discussion, *see* Trowers & Hamlins LLP, Shared Ownership Trusts: Delivering Low Cost Home Ownership (2007), http://www.trowers.com/attachments/published/1615/Shared%20ownership%20trusts%20delivering%20low%20cost%20home%20ownership.pdf.

phenomenon.[98] Prior to the Trusts of Land and Appointment of Trustees Act 1996, the trust imposed on the co-owned home (the 'trust for sale') was far from fit for purpose as the rights and responsibilities of the trustees and beneficiaries reflected an expectation that co-ownership would typically arise in relation to investment property rather than the home.[99] Hence, as the legal models for LCHO evolved in the 1970s and 1980s, the co-ownership trust would have appeared far from an ideal device. Conversely, by the time of the 1996 Act, the legal models for LCHO were perhaps too entrenched to then be superseded by the trust.

Co-operative Housing Models

Only a tiny proportion of UK housing (0.6 per cent) is based on co-operative models,[100] and this is nearly all rental housing for low-income groups. The idea of mutual home ownership (MHO) is, however, being developed as a way of filling a gap in the intermediate housing market.[101] The details of potential models are still

98 In Great Britain (ie, England, Scotland and Wales), home ownership rates increased dramatically after World War II (from 26% in 1945, 60% in 1984). Ray Forrest, Alan Murie & Peter Williams, Home Ownership: Differentiation and Fragmentation 57, tbl.3.1 (1990) (table is titled 'Housing Tenure in Great Britain, 1914–1988 (percentage of dwellings)'). There are no statistics indicating whether a dwelling is in sole or joint ownership, but a survey of married and formerly married people conducted for the Law Commission and published in 1972, showed that there was a marked increase in the rate of joint ownership that began in the 1960's and was continuing. 1972–73 (274) The Law Commission (Law Com. no. 52). Family Law. First report on family property: a new approach, at 8. Co-ownership rates are likely to have continued to increase since then given the increased economic activity of women: between 1971–2008 employment rates for women rose from 56%–70%, Office of National Statistics, Social Trends No. 39, at 48–9 (Matthew Hughes ed., 2009), and the development of informal means of acquiring rights in the home since the 1970s, particularly the constructive trust. *Pettitt v Pettitt* [1970] A.C. 777 (appeal taken from Eng.); *Gissing v Gissing* [1971] AC 886 (appeal taken from_Eng.).

99 The difficulties with the trust for sale were well recognised and are reflected in the Law Commission's work leading to the Trusts of Land and Appointment of Trustees Act, 1996, c. 47 (Eng.)., The Law Commission Report No 181, *Transfer of Land: Trusts of Land* (1989).

100 Commission on Co-operative and Mutual Housing, Bringing Democracy Home 5 (Nic Bliss ed., 2009), *available at* http://www.ccmh.coop/sites/default/files/Commission%20Report.pdf [hereinafter Bringing Democracy Home].

101 The idea is being developed in particular by CDS Co-operatives and the Accord Housing Group. We base our comments on the model supported by CDS Co-operatives, which is discussed in, CDS Co-operatives, A Simple Guide to Mutual Home Ownership (2005), https://docs.google.com/fileview?id=0BwtFGmkmSl96OTkwM2NiYTItOTNhYy00OTRlLWEwMzctMzk1MzVkYmZlZDAw&hl=en_GB [hereinafter A Simple Guide to Mutual Home Ownership]; Community Finance Solutions, Community Land Trusts: A Practitioner's Guide app. 5.3a (2007), http://www.communitylandtrusts.org.uk/resources/publications; CDS Co-operatives, A Consumer's Guide to Mutual Home Ownership 3rd

evolving, but they are built around co-operative ideals that enable individuals to build capital assets. In essence, a locally based entity (usually a community land trust) would own the land on which the homes are built.[102] The element of public subsidy is likely to be in the provision of the land at no, or low, cost;[103] and the value of this land is never passed through to individuals buying into the scheme.[104]

Under the MHO scheme, homes are built on the land of the community land trust by a co-operative society which is controlled by its members, who will also be the occupiers of the homes.[105] The individual occupier is given the right to occupy by a lease – under the MHO model it is a fixed term lease of 20 years (it cannot be longer because of the impact of enfranchisement laws, which enable tenants to require the landlord to sell the freehold to them).[106] But the individual never owns an equity share in the property itself; instead the individual has the opportunity to build a capital asset through investing in an investment fund held by the mutual home ownership society.[107] The MHO Society takes out a single mortgage loan and the occupiers have to pay monthly charges to cover the mortgage and servicing costs.[108] Effectively, the occupiers pay a 'service charge and rent, *plus*'. The actual amount that any individual occupier has to pay will be based upon their income, and the 'plus' component will determine the size of the equity share that that individual acquires.[109] Linking occupation payments to income levels ensures that this is an affordable housing product, but also provides great flexibility as the price may change as income levels rise or drop for the individual.[110] Again, there can be a large variety in the way that the asset-building dimension works. The model which differs the most from the other home ownership products considered in this chapter is one in which the growth that the purchaser is able to take from

---

DRAFT (2008), http://www.cds.coop/about-us/mutual-home-ownership/A%20new%20way%20of%20owning%20a%20stake%20in%20your%20home.pdf [hereinafter A CONSUMER'S GUIDE TO MUTUAL HOME OWNERSHIP].

102 Usually a 'community land trust' (recognised in English statute law in the Housing and Regeneration Act, 2008, c.17, §79(1)), or a 'local housing trust'. *See* Chris Handy, *Community Land Trusts*, 13 J. HOUSING L. 83–6 (2010).

103 The need for low-cost land to be made available has operated as a major constraint on the development of community land holding vehicles.

104 *See infra* note 168 and following text.

105 A CONSUMER'S GUIDE TO MUTUAL HOME OWNERSHIP, *supra* note 102, at 3, 6–7.

106 *Id.* at 10.

107 The cost of building the homes is divided into £1,000 'equity shares' that form the capital asset held by members. Further details on how these shares are accrued, bought and sold is contained *id.* at 3–4, 7–8, 11.

108 *Id.* at 3.

109 *Id.* at 3–4.

110 *Id.* at 8. The underlying principle, explained *id.* at 3 is that housing costs remain at between 35%–40% of the household income.

the trust when he or she moves on is linked to local wage levels rather than to property values.[111]

The MHO idea has been developed particularly from models found in the United States and Australia[112] where co-operative housing is more common, but has been tailored for the UK housing context. It fits well with the localism agenda being developed by the coalition government that took power in 2010 and the coalition government agreement contains a commitment that the government 'will create new trusts that will make it simpler for communities to provide homes for local people'.[113] But even if MHO in some form does move beyond the planning stage, it will always remain a fairly niche market as it is dependent upon local people showing enthusiasm and commitment to the model.

Individual Benefits of Homeownership

In this chapter we explore the impact that these different routes to home ownership have on both the individual and the wider community. Inevitably, we have to be selective in the criteria that we use to measure this against. In relation to the individual, we are looking at the ability of the schemes to provide the individual with both the financial and the non-financial benefits of home ownership. This section of the chapter explains what we mean by this. The following section then looks at the main community objectives that have come to the fore in recent discussions of LCHO programmes. We will then, in the final section of this chapter, evaluate how the different routes to LCHO fare against these measures. There is a myriad of ways in which home ownership is claimed to provide benefit to individuals, but for ease we are grouping them into three main categories: wealth creation, mainstreaming and security of place.[114] Each of these terms needs some further explanation.

Wealth Creation

The core financial benefit lies in ownership of the capital value of the home, that is, in wealth creation. This brings a number of advantages (as well as risks), including

---

111 For fuller discussion and explanation of this point, *see infra* note 144 and following text.

112 The influence of schemes in these jurisdictions is acknowledged in A Simple Guide to Mutual Home Ownership, *supra* note 102. A brief overview of the operation of co-operative tenures internationally is provided in Pat Conaty, Johnston Birchall, Steve Bendle & Rosemary Foggitt, Common Ground – for Mutual Home Ownership 66 (2003), http://www.neweconomics.org/sites/neweconomics.org/files/Common_Ground.pdf.

113 The Coalition: Our Programme for Government, *supra* note 54, at 12.

114 We explore the benefits of home ownership to the individual more fully in Bright & Hopkins, *supra* note 11.

the safety of a foot on the housing ladder, the opportunity for accumulating an asset base, the liquidity and utility of having collateral that can be borrowed against for a variety of purposes and, ultimately, the prospect of financial security with a long-term reduction in housing costs. Access to this investment function is the key to distinguishing an owner from a renter, as the renter's interest in the home is confined to its use value, that is, the home as a consumption good only. The policy objectives for HomeBuy state in stark terms that, 'homes are not just places to live; they are assets. Supporting people on lower incomes to achieve home ownership can help to encourage social mobility and address these economic inequalities'.[115] This statement chimes with evidence that home ownership is desired for the investment potential and opportunity for individual gain that it provides,[116] although there are commentators who challenge the economic prudence of the homeowner putting all of their eggs in one basket.[117]

115 Office of the Deputy Prime Minister, Homebuy: Expanding the Opportunity to Own, Final Regulatory Impact Assessment 3 (2005), *available at* http://www.communities.gov.uk/documents/housing/pdf/142385.pdf.

116 For a recent example, *see* Pinnegar et al., *supra* note 43, at 44. Reporting on discussions in focus groups of two schemes, one based on individual equity and the other on community equity, the authors note '[w]hile the benefits provided by both schemes … were acknowledged and welcomed, the role of the home as an asset became more emphasised when the schemes were discussed'. *Id.*

117 *See, e.g.*, Lee Anne Fennell, *Homeownership 2.0*, 102 Nw. U. L. Rev. 1047 (2008). She seeks to 'start a conversation', *Id.* at 1053, for a model of home ownership that decouples the use and investment functions and gives home owners a choice of how much risk they take of factors (such as trends in the housing market) that are outside their control. *See also* Christine Whitehead & Judith Yates, *Increasing Affordability Problems – A Role for Shared Equity Products? Experience in Australia and the UK*, 21 Housing Fin. Int'l 16, 17 (2007). They note '[t]heory would say that the owner should at least transfer some of the risks involved in owning this specific housing asset to others … This both provides greater financial flexibility and frees up funds from the housing asset to allow the individual household to invest in other investments with different risk profiles'. *Id.* The ability of existing English models of shared ownership and shared equity models to reduce the risks of home ownership is considered by Christine Whitehead, Shared Ownership and Shared Equity: Reducing the Risks of Home-Ownership? (2010), http://www.jrf.org.uk/publications/shared-ownership-shared-equity. She notes that these products can address the risks of housing market volatility and those associated with a particular dwelling (such as the impact on market value associated with the neighbourhood and neighbours) as the impact of price change is shared between the owner and provider. Whitehead suggests that this 'in principle, allows the SO or SE purchaser to diversify into other parts of the housing market and into other types of asset, both reducing their holding of specific risk and enabling a portfolio that better reflects the level of risk they are prepared to take on'. *Id.* at 6.

Mainstreaming

For many, becoming a homeowner gives a sense of having 'arrived', and having achieved the dream. Whether home ownership is in fact necessary for the non-financial benefits associated with it to be attained remains the subject of debate.[118] Hiscock, Keans, MacIntyre and Ellaway report that the psycho-social benefits of ownership (represented in their study by the home as a haven, as a site of autonomy and as providing social status) are not necessarily to do with tenure, but with a wide range of factors such as wealth, location, housing type and being in a settled relationship and work.[119] However, even their study found that many interviewees 'saw owner-occupation as the only worthwhile tenure'.[120] Reporting on a study of low-income American homeowners, Rohe and Stegman concluded that home ownership had a significant effect on overall life satisfaction, even though it did not affect people's self-esteem or sense of control.[121] While the picture that emerges is therefore undoubtedly complex, it is apparent that home ownership is desired and perceived as a source of some possibly ill-defined, non-financial benefits. This is reflected in research conducted for the Australian Housing and Urban Research Institute (AHURI). In their report on the potential for low-cost home ownership schemes in Australia, they note that 'most participants [who took part in their study] were looking for a stepping stone that helped them realise 'the dream', rather than a variant thereof'.[122]

Security of Place

We use this term to refer to a non-financial benefit, linking it to the idea of ontological security that provides a sense of the reliability of things and place.[123] Security of place depends upon the extent to which the owner has choice about whether to stay in the home or perhaps to move from it. There are various ways in which home ownership reinforces security of place. A homeowner will rarely

118 Lorna Fox, Conceptualising Home: Theories, Laws and Policies 232–236 (2007) (responding to the claims famously made in Peter Saunders, A Nation of Home Owners (1990)).

119 Rosemary Hiscock, Ade Kearns, Sally MacIntyre & Anne Ellaway, *Ontological Security and Psycho-Social Benefits from the Home: Qualitative Evidence on Issues of Tenure*, 18 Housing, Theory & Soc'y 50, 62 (2001).

120 *Id.* at 61.

121 William M. Rohe & Michael A. Stegman, *The Effects of Homeownership on the Self-Esteem, Perceived Control and Life Satisfaction of Low-Income People*, 60 J. Am. Plan. Ass'n 173 (1994).

122 Pinnegar et al., *supra* note 43, at 34.

123 The phrase is captured by Giddens, who defines it as: 'The confidence that most people have in the continuity of their self-identity and in the constancy of their social and material environments.' Anthony Giddens, The Consequences of Modernity 92 (1991).

be forced to move unless there are financial difficulties,[124] in contrast to a renter who may have to move simply because the lease term ends or because a legally recognised ground (or reason) for ending the lease can be proved. In the private rented sector in England, it is unusual for a new renter to have any security of tenure beyond the contractual term date. This makes it very difficult for private tenants to build a sense of place and community.[125]

Even if there are financial difficulties, some forms of home ownership enable there to be flexibility in relation to financial payments. This is particularly so in the case of MHO where the principle underlying the amount that an occupier has to pay reflects his or her income at that point in time. This means that if times are hard and the income suddenly drops, the occupier may still be able to remain in his or her home.

Community Benefits: Widening the Policy Focus Beyond the Individual

As LCHO programmes evolved, their initial focus rested firmly on delivering the benefits of home ownership to the individual. This is reflected most clearly in the RTB which, as we have seen, pursued the single-minded policy goal of allowing tenants to become owner-occupiers. But delivering the benefits of home ownership to individuals also characterised early shared ownership schemes. Shared ownership pre-dates the RTB, with early schemes pioneered in Birmingham in 1975.[126] Between 1975–1979, some 24 local authorities sold homes on a shared ownership basis.[127] These schemes pursued the primary objective of expanding home ownership, coupled with the further objective of providing a stepping stone to full home ownership for lower-income households and those with no deposit.[128] The introduction of the RTB reduced reliance on shared ownership. The RTB discount made full home ownership affordable and ensured that the scheme became the principal means through which existing council tenants purchased their home. At that stage it was anticipated that shared ownership would provide a route to home ownership for younger or newly established households or those

124 Compulsory purchase (eminent domain) would be one instance of where there may be a move forced for non-financial reasons.

125 *See, e.g.*, Liam Reynolds, Shelter Safe and Secure? The Private Rented Sector and Security of Tenure 24-26 (2005), http://england.shelter.org.uk/__data/assets/pdf_file/0017/48041/Safe_and_Secure.pdf.

126 Allen, *supra* note 21, at 23. Schemes have been traced to the formation of new model housing associations in the 1960s. David Cowan, *Shared Ownership: Some Problems of Law and Policy*, 13 J. Housing L. 56 (2010) (citing Ray Forrest, Stewart Lansley & Alan Murie, A Foot on the Ladder?: An Evaluation of Low Cost Ownership Initiatives (1984)).

127 Allen, *supra* note 21, at 1.

128 *Id.* at 20.

from outside the public rented sector; that is, households falling outside the RTB scheme.

The turning point in English political attitudes towards LCHO came with the launch in 2003 of the government's Sustainable Communities Action Programme.[129] At that time, the government's commitment to increasing levels of home ownership and the development of LCHO became enmeshed with the idea of creating sustainable communities. Such a community was considered to require '[a] well-integrated mix of decent homes of different types and tenures to support a range of household sizes, ages and incomes'.[130] Within the wider objective of achieving a sustainable community, home ownership was seen as '[giving] people a bigger stake in their community, as well as promoting self-reliance'.[131] The Action Programme led to the creation of the government's LCHO Task Force whose report, 'A Home of My Own', was published in November 2003. The overarching ethos of the Report is the idea that fulfilling individual aspirations for home ownership, or delivering the benefits of home ownership to the individual, does not provide sufficient justification for expanding LCHO. Hence, the Task Force explains that filling the 'aspirations gap' between those who are homeowners and those who would like to be 'is not an end in itself'.[132] Homeownership can achieve a number of objectives which 'can translate into benefits for individual and benefits to society'.[133] The conclusions of the Task Force in turn underpinned the development of HomeBuy – at the time, a label envisaged to be used for a simplified portfolio of LCHO products based on shared equity, but which has come to be used as a generic brand for government-funded shared ownership and shared equity schemes. The Office of the Deputy Prime Minister's consultation on HomeBuy that was carried out subsequent to the work of the Task Force therefore states as the key objective: "[w]e want to help more people to own a home where this helps to achieve their aspirations, and where it helps to meet additional objectives, such as those identified by the Home Ownership Task Force".[134] These 'additional objectives' include creating mixed, sustainable

129 Office of the Deputy Prime Minister, Sustainable Communities: Building for the Future (2003), *available at* http://www.communities.gov.uk/documents/communities/pdf/146289.pdf.

130 *Id.* at 5. This is one of the requirements given in the Report in response to the question 'what makes a sustainable community?'.

131 *Id.* A similar sentiment is expressed in parallel developments in the social rented sector. The introduction of 'choice-based lettings' aimed to promote sustainable communities on the basis that tenants who are involved in decisions about their home are more likely to have a longer term commitment to the locality. *See* Department of the Environment, Transport and the Regions, Quality and Choice: A Decent Home for All 79 9.7 (2000), http://www.communities.gov.uk/documents/housing/pdf/138019.pdf.

132 A Home of My Own, *supra* note 10, at 38.

133 *Id.*

134 Office of the Deputy Prime Minister, Consultation Paper: HomeBuy – Expanding the Opportunity to Own 9 para 2.1 (2005), *available at* http://www.communities.gov.uk/

communities and freeing up existing social housing by encouraging tenants to move into home ownership.[135] In this chapter, our focus on the creation of mixed and sustainable communities reflects the broader policy objective within which LCHO has been located. In the English political landscape, it is unsurprising that this shift in emphasis occurred during the Labour government, in contrast to the focus on the individual benefits promoted though the RTB by the Conservatives.

Sustainable Communities: Creating Mix

A mixed community does not necessarily imply the inclusion of owner-occupation. It could, for example, consist of a bipartite mix of private and affordable/social rented housing. The inclusion of home ownership may be seen as important in building a sustainable community, however, as it is home ownership that gives an individual a 'stake' in the community and promotes self-reliance. As McKee explains, the political assumption underlying the policy rhetoric of mixed communities 'is not only that mono-tenure public housing estates have "failed", but that owner-occupation is the solution to solving the "problem" of poor communities by "reconnecting" them to mainstream society'.[136] Within this, LCHO is important in providing an affordable route to home ownership in the context of a mixed community. Tenure mix is, therefore, part of a mixed community. But income mix may also be important. There could, for example, be a community of mixed rental and ownership properties which are only available on the open market (or available only as affordable housing units). The implicit assumption behind the rhetoric of sustainable mixed communities is that both tenure and income mix are desirable. This requires there to be rental properties, owner-occupied properties, market properties and affordable properties.

Sustaining Mixed Tenure Communities

For a community to be sustainable, the tenure mix must be sustained over time – the idea being that a community that ceases to contain a tenure mix ceases to be sustainable. This means that home ownership must remain accessible to low- and intermediate-income households over time. The best way to achieve this is for *both* the particular stock to remain available as LCHO rather than being released onto the open market on resale *and* for the subsidy to continue to be available in a form that ensures the stock remains affordable. The following paragraphs consider

---

documents/housing/pdf/142115.pdf.

135 For a list of the wider objectives *see* A HOME OF MY OWN, *supra* note 10, at 38.

136 Kim McKee, *Promoting Homeownership at the Margins: the Experience of Low-Cost Homeownership Purchasers in Regeneration Areas*, 4 PEOPLE, PLACE & POL'Y ONLINE 38, 39 (2010), http://extra.shu.ac.uk/ppp-online/issue_2_290710/documents/homeownership_margins_ lowcost_regen_areas.pdf.

how these goals of stock retention and continuing availability of subsidy can be delivered.

Sustainable Communities: Stock Retention

With new developments, LCHO is one of a mix of housing that can be built, and when planning laws have been used to require intermediate housing to be built as part of new sites, this 'on-site' provision has been shown to make an important contribution to mixed communities.[137] RTB has also introduced mix into formerly council rented estates. Whether LCHO can sustain mixed communities in the longer term will depend in part on what happens to the intermediate housing stock on future sales. The clearest route is to ensure through 'stock retention' that each unit sold in the LCHO market is kept within that market, which requires there to be limits on the resale of the property. Typically, this is done in the UK through rights of first refusal and rights of pre-emption which require the property to be offered back to the original housing provider on resale, and for a system of valuation to be applied.[138] This enables the housing provider to re-offer that unit as LCHO to a new household. For the individual, the inability to sell the property through estate agents in the usual way may make the experience feel less like mainstream ownership

Sustainable Communities: Continuing Affordability

As seen above, there are two main forms that the provision of subsidy takes: subsidy forgiveness and subsidy retention/recapture. The fact that with subsidy forgiveness schemes there is no requirement for the subsidy be repaid,[139] means that it is effectively a 'gift' to the individual from the public purse. As such, irrespective of the potential for such a scheme to create a mixed community (for example, by turning a community of council tenants into a mixed community of owner-occupiers and council tenants), it does not provide the opportunity for the subsidy to be used to provide access to LCHO for subsequent low and intermediate income households. The Low Cost Home Ownership Task Force was doubtful as

137 Sarah Monk & Christine Whitehead, *Conclusions*, *in* Making Housing More Affordable: The Role of Intermediate Tenures 261, 268 (Sarah Monk & Christine Whitehead eds., 2010) (and references therein). For more detailed discussion of the relationship between planning and intermediate housing, *see* Tony Crook & Christine Whitehead, *Intermediate Housing and the Planning System*, *in* Making Housing More Affordable: The Role of Intermediate Tenures 101 (Sarah Monk & Christine Whitehead eds, 2010).

138 Compare the US where restrictive covenants have been used. *See*, *e.g.*, James J Kelly Jr., *Homes Affordable for Good: Covenants and Ground Leases as Long-Term Resale-Restriction Devices*, 29 St. Louis U. Pub. L. Rev. 9 (2009).

139 Unless resale occurs within the specified period of time that requires the subsidy to be repaid in whole or part.

to whether subsidy forgiveness schemes are ever appropriate: '[g]iven that people are gaining a capital asset that will normally appreciate, we think it is reasonable to recoup the subsidy wherever this is possible which leads to a re-think of the use of grants and discounts in the future'.[140] It suggested, therefore, that 'in the future, grants and discounts should be limited to achieving wider strategic outcomes not just to help people into home ownership'.[141] This reflects the ethos of the Task Force's Report that providing the benefits of home ownership to the individual does not in itself provide sufficient justification for LCHO. There must be a wider justification for making a gift from the public purse.

In contrast, subsidy recapture requires the owner to repay the subsidy component to the provider upon future sale. Again, there are lots of variations as to how this operates. The shared equity scheme works this way as the second loan (representing the non-owned equity) is repaid on sale at current property values. Assuming that property prices have risen since the initial purchase, this means that the subsidy repayment will similarly be higher than the original amount loaned. The risk of negative equity may also be split proportionately between the parties, or the original purchaser may be liable to repay at least the original subsidy. Subsidy recapture at current property values does not, however, necessarily ensure that access to *affordable* home ownership is sustained over time. If wage increases do not keep pace with property values, then recapturing the subsidy in this way will not enable an equivalent property to be made affordable to an intermediate income household: the affordability gap the subsidy is needed to fill has increased.[142]

140 A Home of My Own, *supra* note 10, at 93. It should be acknowledged, however, that the public purse is also used to subsidise the costs of home ownership through Support for Mortgage Interest (SMI) payments provided as part of the social security system. While directed at providing assistance with interest payments, not the capital sum, the effect of SMI is to help the homeowner retain their capital asset.

141 *Id.* at 95.

142 Community Finance Solutions, Placeshaping: A Toolkit for Urban Community Land Trusts 66 (2008), http://www.communityfinance.salford.ac.uk/pdf/Urban_tools__complete.pdf, provides a worked illustration: 'A £60,000 mortgaged share in a property valued at £100,000, bought at the end of 2001 on a household income of £17,000, became worth £120,000 at the end of 2007. An income of £34,000 would be needed to buy this yet average incomes over the 6 year period have risen around 30% to ~£22,000. So the home has become unaffordable and no longer meets the needs of the community'. The report shows that the value realised can be capped with reference to the property value increase, or by reference to average earnings. The worked example of the CLT Resale Formula in Building and Social Housing Foundation, Equity Sharing with Community Land Trusts: Delivering Sustainable Low Cost Home Ownership by Locking in Value in Perpetuity (2006), *available at* http://www.bshf.org/published-information/publication.cfm?thePubID=21F46BEA-15C5-F4C0-993C6311518A3D40 (an information paper to the government's Shared Equity Taskforce), appears to assume that through the use of restrictive covenants the share of the capital uplift that the purchaser gets on resale is limited; in the worked example it is limited to 25% of the uplift. The paper draws on the use of restrictive

Continuing affordability is therefore best achieved if the amount of the equity that the owner can retain on resale is not a direct reflection of value of the equity that the owner possesses, but is capped in some way. Thus, the owner may be allowed to keep only a specified percentage of the uplift in value of the owner's share, or repayment may be linked to an affordability measure such as a local wage index. This would ensure that the housing provider recovers sufficient funds for the subsidy to be ploughed back into housing at a level that ensures forward looking affordability. This kind of provision has been discussed in England in the context of co-operative housing,[143] but is not replicated in any currently available English schemes that we are aware of. Capping the personal gain in this way does, of course, mean that the wealth created for the individual is more limited; and this limitation means that LCHO delivered in this way is unlikely to have mass appeal. It will also make it very difficult for the individual to 'move up the housing ladder'.

Legally, subsidy recapture is relatively straightforward – it simply requires the subsidy to be secured by a second mortgage. This is in contrast to the more complex provisions restricting onward sale that are necessary to achieve stock retention. The provider of the subsidy is sometimes described as a 'silent partner',[144] but this description is not commonly used in relation to English LCHO schemes and would be misleading where (as may usually be the case) the subsidy provider retains some input over decisions affecting the use of the property. Although subsidy recapture provides the opportunity for the subsidy to be used to provide access to LCHO to another intermediate income household, there may be no obligation that the subsidy is reinvested in another LCHO property or (if it is) within the same community. Hence, subsidy recapture does not necessarily do anything to help promote a *mixed* sustainable community over the long term.

The goals of creating and maintaining mixed communities and preserving affordability over time are therefore best achieved if there is both stock retention and subsidy retention that caps the individual gain by linking it to an affordability measure. Only in this way is the subsidy both trapped within a specific unit and at a level that ensures that if house prices have risen more rapidly than wages (as is common), it can be used to enable future low and intermediate households to access LCHO.

---

covenants in the USA and it is far from clear that covenants would be the appropriate legal device in English law. For a discussion of different ways in which the resale price can be 'controlled' *see* James J. Kelly, Jr, *Land Trusts that Conserve Communities*, 59 DePaul L. Rev. 69, 81–82 (2009).

143 *E.g.*, A Consumer's Guide to Mutual Home Ownership, *supra* note 102, at 11–12.

144 *See, e.g.*, Pinnegar et al., *supra* note 43, at 27.

Table 4.2 Evaluating LCHO Models

Full Ownership						
Scheme	**Community impact**			**Individual impact**		
	Introduces income/ tenure mix	Sustains tenure mix over time	Sustains opportunity for access to equity growth	Wealth	Main-streaming	Security of place
RTB/RTA	Achieved for tenure	Achieved, but not guaranteed	Not achieved	Achieved	Achieved	Achieved
Cash incentive scheme	Not achieved	Not achieved	Not achieved	Achieved	Achieved	Achieved
Part-ownership						
Shared ownership	Achieved	Achieved	Achieved	Achieved, but with risk	Limited	Achieved, but with risk
Shared equity	Achieved	Limited	Achieved	Achieved	Limited	Achieved
Co-operative Housing						
Mutual home ownership	Limited to non-market mix	Achieved for non-market mix	Achieved	Limited	Not achieved	Limited

Evaluation

Table 4.2 provides a snapshot evaluation of the three routes to affordable home ownership discussed in this chapter, measured against the potential community and individual benefits that we have identified. The schemes within each route are assessed as having 'achieved', 'not achieved' or achieving to a limited extent ('limited') the particular forms of community and individual impact. This evaluation must be understood in conjunction with the accompanying text.

As can be seen, none of the models of affordable home ownership fully achieves all of the community and individual benefits. Inevitably there has to be a trade-off. Of course, for the earlier schemes, particularly RTB, the community benefits we discuss were never part of the objective – it is only since the launch in 2003 of the Sustainable Communities Action Plan that the use of LCHO to deliver community benefits has been a policy goal.[145] The need for 'trade-offs' between objectives was acknowledged in the work of the Low Cost Home Ownership Task Force.[146] Housing literature recognises that tensions exist in seeking to deliver both the individual and community benefits of home ownership.[147] Writing about affordable housing (not specifically affordable home ownership), Diamond discusses what he terms the 'conflict of competing goods'.[148] This expression is used to capture the conflict between different housing goals that most people would agree are socially and morally desirable. Diamond explains that it is impossible to maximise each competing goal and therefore society is 'put to the choice among incommensurables'.[149] The tension between individual and community benefits can aptly be described, as such, a conflict[150] and is reflected in attempts to balance the creation of mixed sustainable communities against delivering the benefits of home ownership to the individual.

Schemes providing full ownership are most successful in delivering the benefits of home ownership to the individual. Indeed, the position of purchasers under such schemes may be almost analogous to that of a traditional owner-occupier. The RTB/RTA operates on the basis of subsidy forgiveness, subject to the subsidy being clawed back in the event of a re-sale within an initial period. Greater variety

145 The RTB was incorporated into the sustainable communities programme: ODPM, *Sustainable Communities: Homes for All* 9 ¶ 1.22 (2005) states 'Right to Buy will continue ... to give people more choice and promote mixed communities'. A critical evaluation of its contribution to sustainable communities is provided by Jones & Murie, *supra* note 20 (Chapter 8). It may further be suggested, in light of King's analysis, King, *supra* note 20, that an attempt to incorporate the RTB into this wider objective is misplaced. On King's account, the simplicity of the scheme in pursuing a single-minded policy goal is integral to its success. *Id.* at 66–67. The limitations on the ability of the RTB to deliver mixed sustainable communities is further discussed in the text that follows.

146 A Home of My Own, *supra* note 10, at 9 para 5.

147 *See, e.g.*, Pinnegar et al., *supra* note 43, at 11.

148 Michael Diamond, *Affordable Housing and the Conflict of Competing Goods: A Policy Dilemma*, *in* Affordable Housing and Public-Private Partnerships 1 (Nestor M. Davidson & Robin Paul Malloy eds, 2009).

149 *Id.* at 1.

150 Diamond refers to 'the competition between the provision of decent, affordable shelter and the creation of wealth for homeowners'. *Id.* at 3. While this could cover the policy choice between an affordable rented home or individual home ownership, some of the issues that arise reflect the choice between individual and community benefits in the context purely of affordable home ownership. Hence, Diamond explains, 'to the extent that society seeks to preserve an affordable housing unit for the long term, it must restrict the wealth that an owner can derive from the sale or rental of that property. To the extent the owner is able to demand full market value for the unit, it would likely be too expensive, either as a purchase or as a rental, for a low income resident'. *Id.*

may be found in the Cash Incentive Scheme where the terms of the grant are determined by the individual local authority. In relation to mainstreaming, the RTB/RTA is subject to the limitation, which may be significant, that the purchase is limited to the current rented home rather than offering a choice of property.[151] On the Cash Incentive Scheme choice may be restricted in terms of the size of property (based on number of bedrooms) that can be purchased.

As has been noted, it is now considered that the provision of grants and discounts that provides the basis of the RTB/RTA and Cash Incentive Scheme should be 'limited to achieving wider strategic outcomes'. The Cash Incentive Scheme does not help to provide mixed communities as the recipient of the grant leaves their social rented home to buy as an owner-occupier on the open market. However, the scheme does free up the social rented home currently occupied by the recipient of the grant for a person in greater need of social rented housing and, as we have noted, this is one of the other wider objectives that has been associated with the provision of LCHO. The RTB introduces a bipartite tenure mix by bringing owner-occupation into a previously mono-tenure public rented community, though as it is existing tenants who buy their home, there is no change in the income mix in the neighbourhood. Although the tenure mix may be sustained over time (the purchased unit remaining in the owner-occupation sector, subject to the right of pre-emption that is now built into RTB sales), it is not guaranteed: there are no controls on the number or percentage of properties within a particular estate that can be sold. Hence, an entire estate could move from a mono-tenure public rented community to a community of owner-occupiers. As the scheme is based on subsidy forgiveness, the RTB does not sustain the opportunity for future low- and intermediate-income households to access equity growth. Further, unlike the Cash Incentive Scheme, the RTB does not free up or make available social housing for a person in greater need. Indeed, under the Conservative governments of the 1980s and 1990s, Local Authorities were prevented from using the capital sums received through the RTB to re-invest in new housing, although under the reinvigoration of the RTB announced by the Coalition government in 2012 properties sold under the RTB are to be replaced by new homes for affordable rent'.[152]

The provision of wider community objectives alongside the individual benefits of home ownership has been an overt policy goal of part-ownership schemes since the launch of the Sustainable Communities Action Programme. The schemes highlight the difficulty in balancing these objectives and illustrate the trade-offs that inevitably result. The introduction of part-ownership into a community creates a tenure/income mix, although the nature of that mix is dependent on the particular scheme or product concerned. As we have noted, both shared ownership and shared equity are marketed under HomeBuy. Different HomeBuy schemes or products may be targeted at particular groups of purchaser and/or particular

151 *See, e.g.*, Pinnegar et al., *supra* note 43, at 37–38.

properties.[152] Where property is purchased in a new build development,[153] the scheme may create a mix of affordable and open market home ownership in a community that may otherwise have become exclusively open-market ownership. Social HomeBuy, that enables social tenants to become part owners of their home, may introduce part-ownership into a community of social renters.

Both part-ownership models (shared ownership and shared equity) sustain the opportunity for future intermediate income households to access equity growth, but each achieves this differently and this difference impacts on the ability of schemes to sustain a tenure mix over time. The restrictions on sale and rights of pre-emption in the shared ownership lease provide the opportunity for the subsidy to be retained in the individual unit and, by doing so, enables the tenure mix to be sustained over time: in contrast, in current shared equity schemes, the property will invariably be sold on the open market with the subsidy recaptured on sale as a proportion of the market value. Therefore, there is the opportunity for the subsidy to be used to provide access to equity growth for future households even though, as we have noted, there is no obligation that the subsidy will be reinvested and even if the subsidy is reinvested this may not take place within the same community. This point has particular resonance in the English context where housing demand is not evenly spread and market 'hot-spots' (for example, in London and the South East) typically arise in areas where there is a lack of land available for future development. The loss of the housing unit by a sale on the open market means that shared equity, in contrast to shared ownership, is limited in its ability to sustain a tenure mix over time. Neither scheme is able to ensure full affordability for future generations; as mentioned earlier, if property prices have risen at a faster pace than earnings, there may need to be a bigger subsidy to enable low earners to buy any share.

Although part-ownership schemes provide many of the benefits of home ownership to the individual, it is not the same thing as full – traditional – home ownership. As is the case with all LCHO schemes, the individual does not have complete freedom as to which property to buy; only certain stock can be bought through LCHO.[154] Shared ownership is likely to feel less 'mainstream' than shared equity, because of the fact that shared ownership is given effect through a lease. Long leases of houses do exist in the owner-occupier market, but they are very

---

152 HM Government, Laying the Foundations: A Housing Strategy for England 56 (2011).

A list of current products can be found at HomeBuy, http://www.homebuy.co.uk (last visited Feb. 21, 2011).

153 Through either New Build HomeBuy (shared ownership) or HomeBuy Direct or FirstBuy (shared equity).

154 Although free choice is not impossible, at one point there was 'Open Market HomeBuy' which did enable an individual to find a property on the open market and then purchase through the shared equity scheme.

much the exception[155] and there is generally no legal reason why a lease needs to be used. Research has demonstrated that long leaseholders experience confusion as to their status, which is summed up in Cole and Robinson's description of them as 'owners yet tenants'.[156] The use of a lease for shared ownership of a house therefore brings part-ownership into an already problematic category. The terms of the lease impose rights of pre-emption on sale and exercise a degree of control over further borrowing that are not experienced by traditional owner-occupiers. The ambiguity of status has been commented on by shared owners: '... at the end of the day the property will never be yours. You can partly buy it but you have to pay rent on the rest of it'.[157] It has further been noted that shared ownership "... could be the worst of both worlds offering neither the security of social renting nor the freedom and independence of owner-occupation".[158] In this respect, the limitations imposed on shared equity purchasers are less apparent, but are still present. Purchasers under shared equity hold 100 per cent of the legal title from the outset and are not subject to limitations on sale (other than the fact that sale triggers repayment of the subsidy). However, the property is still not fully 'theirs' and the provider of the subsidy is not merely a 'silent partner',[159] but retains input into decisions affecting the use of the property, particularly for subsequent borrowing which requires the consent of the provider of the subsidised loan.

Both shared ownership and shared equity are capable of delivering the benefits of wealth creation and security of place to the individual. Shared equity appears better equipped to do so, however, because of the particular risks in the shared ownership lease powerfully illustrated by the *Richardson v Midland Heart* case.[160] Part owners, like full home owners, have the opportunity for wealth creation through increases in property values (and the corresponding risk of falling values). Equally, part owners are vulnerable to loss of their home if they are unable to maintain payments on a mortgage used to purchase their 'share' of the home (while shared equity purchasers must also pay interest on the subsidised loan). However, where possession proceedings arise following mortgage default, courts at least have discretion to postpone possession[161] and, if the home is lost through mortgage

155 Long leaseholds of house account for just 4% of owner-occupied housing stock. Department for Communities and Local Government, English Housing Survey Live Tables, tbl.S305 (2006), http://www.communities.gov.uk/housing/housingresearch/housingsurveys/surveyofenglishhousing/sehlivetables/owneroccupiersincluding/?view=Standard ('Percentage of households who own their home freehold and leasehold', data from 2005-06).

156 Cole & Robinson, *supra* note 65, at 595.

157 Housing Corporation & Chartered Institute of Housing, Housing Aspirations and Shared Ownership 10 (2008), http://www.cih.org/publications/pftf/pdfs/Aspirations.pdf.

158 *Id.*

159 *Cf.* Pinnegar et al., *supra* note 43, at 27.

160 [2008] Landlord & Tenant Reports 31 (Eng.). The decision in the case is discussed in *supra* note 66 and accompanying text.

161 Administration of Justice Act, 1970, c.31, §36 (Eng.).

possession, the part owner, like the full owner, is entitled to any financial equity that remains following the discharge of the outstanding debt and costs. The shared owner, however, is vulnerable to the additional risk of possession proceedings for non-payment of *rent*. Possession then may be mandatory, not discretionary, and the financial consequences are Draconian – leaving the shared owner with no legal entitlement to the return of their investment or any uplift in the value of the property. It should be acknowledged, however, that this particular risk could be removed by ensuring that tenants of registered providers of social housing are not subject to Ground 8.[162]

In light of the current policy objectives, limitations on the ability of part-ownership to deliver the benefits of home ownership to the individual can, to an extent, be explained as representing a trade-off with benefits provided to the community. Hence, for example, the right of pre-emption in a shared ownership lease that detracts from the individual's benefits of home ownership nevertheless helps sustain a tenure/income mix over time; but it would be wrong to attribute all compromises to such a trade-off. It does not explain, for example, the imposition of additional risks through reliance on shared ownership as the method of delivery when other legal models (shared equity and co-ownership trusts) are available. More generally, in a social and political context in which expectations are built around the 'dream' of home ownership, part-ownership inherently represents a compromise for those for whom the mainstream of full ownership remains an unaffordable aspiration. It is unsurprising to find that not all limitations are attributable to balancing individual and community benefits when it is recalled that the legal models of shared ownership and shared equity themselves pre-date the recognition of wider benefits to the community as an explicit policy goal.

MHO has been developed as a means of 'couching aspirations for individual assets in a community safety net'.[163] Its ethos lies firmly in the collective.[164] The tenure mix achieved is limited to the extent that schemes are based exclusively on the provision of affordable housing (both rented and owner-occupied) to the exclusion of private or market-based housing. The mix is sustained over time as assignments of leases through which individuals occupy their home take place

---

162 The Law Commission recommended the abolition of Ground 8 in the social rented sector. Law Commission, Report No. 297, 1 Renting Homes: The Final Report 20–21 para 1.43–1.50 (2006), *available at* http://www.lawcom.gov.uk/docs/lc297_vol1.pdf. Even in the absence of implementation of the Report, the same result could be achieved through the terms of the shared ownership lease.

163 Bringing Democracy Home, *supra* note 101, at 6.

164 *See, e.g., id.* at 25. 'Co-operative and mutual housing is particularly relevant within a wider changing cultural shift from individualism to collective, communitarian, ethical and environmental approaches ... It may be that co-operative and mutual housing sits alongside trends such as car sharing, recycling, use of low energy appliances and local produce and positive responses to the Co-operative Bank's and Co-operative Group's ethical policies.' *Id.*

through the co-operative.[165] This is to ensure that units are not sold at a premium.[166] Ensuring the retention of the subsidy to help future low and intermediate households lies at the heart of the scheme. The subsidy (in the form of the free or low-cost provision of the land) is held in the community land trust and does not fall into the ownership of the individual occupier. Indeed, the community land trust is 'designed to extract the land from the market and retain it as a public asset'.[167] There are significant limitations on the ability of MHO to deliver the benefits of ownership to the individual. Wealth creation (through the purchase of equity shares) may be capped, for example by being linked to the regional average wage index rather than house prices. Where average wages do not keep pace with property values, this may mean it becomes unaffordable for the individual to leave the co-operative. The extent to which security of place is achieved will depend on terms and length – of the tenancy used – but one of the models being proposed at the moment provides a 20-year term. MHO does not represent the mainstream, or purport to do so. Instead, it is promoted as a means of enabling people to achieve some of the aspirations they have for home ownership while representing 'an option of choice for some people because of its shared sense of belonging, identity in communities and mutual support structures'.[168] For the individual, the difference between traditional home ownership, or even part-ownership, and MHO, is reflected most potently in two respects. First, in the de-coupling of the wealth creation function of home ownership from property values, and secondly, in the fact that what is owned is not the home, but shares. With its emphasis on the community, the attraction of co-operative housing lies in a lifestyle choice. It may represent, in essence, a positive decision not to enter the mainstream housing market.

Conclusion

In this chapter we have evaluated the legal models of affordable home ownership in England against their ability to provide both the benefits of ownership to the individual and a wider community benefit represented by the creation of sustainable mixed communities. As seen, there is an inevitable trade-off between the maximisation of benefits to the individual and benefit to the community. The result is a suite of products that are much less attractive to the individual than the earlier RTB. We have also seen that not all of the compromises that are made can be attributed to that trade-off. The choice of legal model used to deliver LCHO also impacts on the experience of the purchaser. The common difficulty for all forms of LCHO is that individuals' aspirations for ownership are constructed

165 Conaty et al., *supra* 113, at 66.

166 *Id.*

167 *Id.* at 4.

168 Bringing Democracy Home, *supra* note 101, at 27.

around traditional owner-occupation. In their different ways, and to different degrees, by departing from those aspirations, each of the legal models we have examined ultimately challenges established understandings of what 'ownership' really means.

Acknowledgement

We are grateful to Dr Emma Laurie, University of Southampton, for her comments on a previous draft.

Chapter 5
Foundations of Federal Housing Policy

David J. Reiss

The federal government has a bewildering array of housing programs funded with tens of billions of dollars every year.[1] In the broadest strokes, these include:

- The Federal Housing Administration ("FHA"), which provides mortgage insurance on loans made by FHA-approved lenders;[2]
- The Government National Mortgage Association, which insures mortgage-backed securities ("MBS") backed by federally insured or guaranteed loans;
- The Federal National Mortgage Association ("Fannie Mae"), Federal Home Loan Mortgage Corporation ("Freddie Mac"), and the Federal Home Loan Bank System, which issue MBS and invest in mortgages and mortgage-related products;[3]
- Project-Based Rental Assistance, which provides supply-side funding to increase the stock of affordable housing;
- Section 8 Housing Vouchers, which delivers demand-side subsidies to individuals and families seeking housing in the private market;
- Housing Counseling Assistance;
- Supportive Housing for the Elderly;
- Disabled Housing; and
- HOPE (Housing Opportunities for People Everywhere) VI Grants, which replaces dysfunctional public housing projects with mixed-income housing and vouchers.[4]

---

1 *See* Office of Management and Budget, A New Era of Responsibility: Renewing America's Promise at 74 (2009), *available at* http://www.gpoaccess.gov/usbudget/fy10/pdf/fy10-newera.pdf (providing Fiscal Year 2010 budget overview).

2 The Federal Housing Administration was created during the Depression to incentivize lenders to originate mortgages with longer terms.

3 In addition to the FHA, the federal government created a variety of other specialized housing finance entities. Ginnie Mae is an instrumentality of the federal government. Fannie, Freddie and FHLBS are government-sponsored enterprises ("GSEs"). Fannie Mae and Freddie Mac, the two largest GSEs, are owned by private shareholders but have a public mission to create a liquid secondary market for residential mortgages. They are currently in conservatorship and under the control of the US government.

4 *See* US Dep't of Hous. & Urban Dev., Fiscal Year 2009 Justification for Estimates, *available at* http://www.hud.gov/offices/cfo/reports/2009/cjs/introduction.pdf; *see* Richard

And recently, the Department of Housing and Urban Development created "a new Energy Innovation Fund to catalyze private sector investment in the energy efficiency of the Nation's housing stock," as well as a "a new Choice Neighborhoods Initiative to make a range of transformative investments in high-poverty neighborhoods where public and assisted housing is concentrated."[5] Indeed, each new administration, whether Democratic or Republican, makes its own additions to the federal housing edifice. HUD's most recent Strategic Plan, for instance, incorporates an extraordinarily broad range of goals, including improving health, child development, and economic security outcomes for various populations.[6]

On top of these direct expenditures on housing, the federal government makes hundreds of billions of dollars more in tax expenditures.[7] "Tax expenditures" refer to "those revenue losses attributable to provisions of the Federal tax laws which allow a special exclusion, exemption, or deduction from gross income or which provide a special credit, a preferential rate of tax, or a deferral of tax liability."[8] For instance, a mortgage interest deduction reduces income subject to taxation by an amount equal to a taxpayer's mortgage interest payments in order to encourage investment in housing. The other significant housing-related tax expenditures are the:

- deductibility of state and local property tax on owner-occupied homes;
- capital gains exclusion on home sales;
- exclusion of net imputed rental income;
- exception from passive loss rules for certain rental loss;
- credit for low-income housing investments; and
- accelerated depreciation on rental housing.[9]

The Tax Policy Center estimates that tax benefits to homeowners in 2005 amounted to $147 billion, while direct aid to renters amounted to $41 billion in the same

---

K. Green & Stephen Malpezzi, A Primer on US Housing Markets and Housing Policy 89–95 (2003).

5 Office of Management and Budget, A New Era of Responsibility: Renewing America's Promise at 74 (2009), *available at* http://www.gpoaccess.gov/usbudget/fy10/pdf/fy10-newera.pdf (providing Fiscal Year 2010 budget overview).

6 US Dep't of Hous. & Urban Dev., HUD Strategic Plan FY 2010–2015 (2010).

7 *See* Stanley S. Surrey, Pathways To Tax Reform: The Concept of Tax Expenditures 6–7 (1973). Tax expenditures are typically made "to achieve various social and economic objectives." Stanley S. Surrey, *Tax Incentives as a Device for Implementing Government Policy: A Comparison with Direct Government Expenditures*, 83 Harv. L. Rev. 705, 706 (1970).

8 Congressional Budget and Impoundment Control Act of 1974, Pub. L. No. 93–344, § 3(3), 88 Stat. 297, 299 (1974) (codified as amended at 2 U.S.C. § 622(3)).

9 US Census Bureau, The 2009 Statistical Abstract: The National Data Book 307 tbl.459 (2009), *available at* http://www.census.gov/prod/2008pubs/09statab/fedgov.pdf.

year.[10] The greatest benefits for homeowners accrue to the wealthy, with 72 per cent of all the income tax benefits accruing to those making more than $75,000 per year, while only a negligible amount goes to those making less than $40,000 per year.[11]

Given the size of federal housing expenditures (not to mention state, county, and municipal programs), it is unsurprising that housing's regulatory web is also immense and intricate, including as it does:

- the newly created Federal Housing Finance Agency;[12]
- the newly created Consumer Financial Protection Bureau;
- the Department of Housing and Urban Development;
- the Federal Reserve Board;
- the Federal Trade Commission;
- the Office of the Comptroller of the Currency; and
- the National Credit Union Administration.

Trying to derive a principled understanding of federal housing policy in the face of such enormous expenditures and extraordinary complexity is no easy task. Indeed, my quest to identify one or a few "first principles" of American housing policy might even be described as quixotic. Nonetheless, I have undertaken this task because our muddled housing agenda has left debates surrounding housing policy confused and unproductive. The vast housing policy literature—spread as it is through the economics, policy, legal, sociology, and other bodies of scholarship—reflects that confusion.[13]

It is difficult to provide a generally accepted definition of "housing policy." At its broadest, it can refer to government efforts to shape "the dynamic relationships between housing markets and economic, demographic, and social trends."[14] More typically, however, housing policy refers to government efforts to increase housing affordability.[15]

10 Adam Carasso et al., *The Trend in Federal Housing Tax Expenditures*, Tax Notes, Feb. 28, 2005, at 1081.

11 Adam Carasso, *Who Receives Homeownership Tax Deductions and How Much?* Tax Notes, Aug. 1, 2005 (using FY2004 data).

12 The FHFA replaced the Office of Federal Housing Enterprise Oversight (Fannie and Freddie's regulator) and the Federal Home Loan Board (the FHLB System's regulator).

13 *See generally* Tim Iglesias, *Our Pluralist Housing Ethics and the Struggle for Affordability*, 42 Wake Forest L. Rev. 511 (2007) (reviewing housing literature in various disciplines).

14 Joint Ctr. for Hous. Studies, Harvard University, *About Us*, http://www.jchs.harvard.edu/aboutus/index.html (last visited Nov. 6, 2011).

15 *See, e.g.,* Ctr. for Hous. Policy, *Center Mission and Goals*, http://www.nhc.org/about/Center-Mission-Goals.html ("[T]he Center helps to develop effective policy solutions at the national, state and local levels that increase the availability of affordable homes."); Alex F. Schwartz, Housing Policy In The United States 1 (2006) (looking at

This chapter aims to clarify debates in the housing policy field by providing a taxonomy of principles that are relied upon explicitly and implicitly in debates regarding the proper goals of housing policy. I proceed as follows. First, I survey current opinion about housing policy in order to begin my inquiry into principles of federal housing policy. And second, I identify the particular principles that inform federal housing policy. To be clear, this chapter does not take a position on which principles of housing policy are preferable; it merely seeks to set forth the options. I leave the development of a particular position on housing policy to a later day.

Cataloguing Current Opinion on Housing Policy

Identifying possible first principles for a field as complex and conflicted as housing policy is difficult. This chapter, however, will take a catholic approach to the categorizing of possible principles, setting forth all that are put forth in good faith by those who write about housing. By "principle," I mean a rationale that is widely accepted to justify a particular policy. By "first principle," I mean a rationale that is fundamental to the policy that it is meant to justify. In other words, a "principle" may treat housing policy as a means to another policy end, whereas a "first principle" treats housing policy as an end in itself. So to begin, we must roughly indicate what the goals of housing policy are.

I begin my inquiry by surveying current opinions regarding housing policy. From one useful perspective, the field may be surveyed via five broad "housing ethics."[16] The use of the term "ethics" is substantively similar to my use of the term "principles." But such "ethics" are intended to be more descriptive, while my "principles" are intended to be used as tools of evaluation. As such, this ethics-view accepts that even contradictory ethics can coexist as political priorities shift, while I argue that those seeking to shape housing policy should attempt to identify and resolve such conflicts so that housing policy does not work at cross purposes with itself.

With this caveat in mind, the iteration of the five ethics is useful because they do reflect many of the broadly held intuitions that we have about housing policy. The five ethics identified are:

- Housing as an Economic Good;
- Housing as Home;
- Housing as a Human Right;

"primary policies and programs designed to make decent and affordable housing available to Americans of modest means."). The role of tax expenditures like the mortgage interest deduction is often underemphasized in discussions of housing policy, notwithstanding their budgetary impact.

16 Tim Iglesias, *supra* note 13, at 511.

- Housing as Providing Social Order; and
- Housing as One Land Use in a Functional System.[17]

The "Housing as an Economic Good" ethic treats housing as any other commodity and asks how government policies will distort the functioning of the market for housing. The "Housing as Home" ethic explores the impact of policy on personal liberty, privacy, and security. The "Housing as a Human Right" speaks to how a policy furthers the goal of making decent housing available to all. The "Housing as Providing Social Order" ethic speaks to how a housing policy will impact the community as it currently exists. And the "Housing as One Land Use in a Functional System" ethic speaks to how a policy will impact the broader society, in particular the infrastructure, education, and workforce sectors.

These five housing ethics are a useful survey of housing policy generally, but the "Housing as an Economic Good," and the "Housing as a Human Right" ethics play a greater role in *federal* housing policy in particular. Given the historic role that the states play in land use, law enforcement, and landlord/tenant law, it is not surprising that the federal government is not nearly as involved in implementing the other three ethics.

The "Housing as an Economic Good" ethic is embedded throughout all federal housing policy discussions. Many past programs have come to be criticized for their unintended distortions of the housing market, which can reduce the supply and affordability of housing in the long-term even if they reduce the cost of housing in the short-term.[18] Rent control is the most commonly discussed example of a policy with a negative unintended distortion of the housing market, with economists nearly universal in their judgment that rent control ultimately reduces the supply of rental housing, particularly for low-income families, thereby increasing the aggregate cost of such housing.[19] While very popular with those in rent regu-

---

17 *Id.* Michael Diamond and J. Peter Byrne also attempt to provide some order to the vast literature about affordable housing. Michael Diamond & J. Peter Byrne, *Affordable Housing, Land Tenure, and Urban Policy: The Matrix Revealed,* 34 Fordham Urb. L.J. 527 (2007).

18 Edward L. Glaeser & Joseph Gyourko, Rethinking Federal Housing Policy 29–32 (2008) (discussing various ways that localities regulate housing).

19 In a 1990 survey, roughly 93 per cent of economists agreed absolutely or conditionally with the statement, "A ceiling on rents reduces the quantity and quality of housing available." Richard M. Alston, J.R. Kearl & Michael B. Vaughn, *Is There a Consensus Among Economists in the 1990's?*, 82 Am. Econ. Rev. 203, 204 (1992). Furthermore, it is now commonly understood that rent regulation generally reduces rents for only controlled units while depressing the creation of new housing, thereby increasing average rents for the rental sector as a whole. *See* Glaeser & Gyourko, *supra* note 18, at 58–62 (2008). While recognizing this traditional disapproval of rent control in the form of a price ceiling, a small number of revisionists have urged that this harsh opposition be relaxed in the face of "second-generation" rent control, or "rent stabilization." Richard Arnott, *Time for Revisionism on Rent Control?*, 9 J. Econ. Perspectives 99 (1995). Defenders of this

lated units, the policy has fallen out of favor as it appeared that rent regulation did not keep down rents generally but, rather, just for those in rent regulated units.[20]

The affordability aspect of the "Housing as a Human Right" ethic is also thoroughly imbued in housing policy debates. This ethic is typically more of the guiding force behind federal *rental* housing policy than federal *homeownership* policy.

Somewhat surprisingly, largely missing from the current discourse on housing policy is what appears to me to be a completely separate sixth housing ethic or principle: "Housing as a Bulwark of Democracy." Reaching back at least as far as the time of Jefferson, the idea of the yeoman farmer who owns his homestead, is financially self-sufficient, and acts the part of a democratic citizen is central to America's vision of itself.[21] I will argue below, however, that it is fundamental to an understanding of federal housing policy. Perhaps it is so deeply ingrained in the broader American ethic that it does not particularly surface in debates regarding housing policy.

An insight into the contemporary dialogue on housing policy may be gleaned from the national housing platforms of the Democratic and Republican parties. It is worth quoting the platforms in full because those two documents reflect two of the dominant housing ethics at play today in federal housing policy. I **bold** possible references to the "Housing as a Human Right" ethic and I *italicize* possible references to the "Housing as an Economic Good" ethic.

The 2008 Democratic National Platform states that:

We will ensure that the foreclosure prevention program enacted by Congress is implemented quickly and effectively so that at-risk **homeowners can get help and hopefully stay in their homes**. We will work to reform bankruptcy laws to *restore balance between lender and homeowner rights*. Because we have an obligation to prevent this crisis from recurring in the future, we will *crack down on fraudulent brokers and lenders* and *invest in financial literacy*. We will pass a Homebuyers Bill of Rights, which will include establishing new lending standards to **ensure that loans are affordable** and fair, provide adequate remedies to make sure the standards are met, and ensure that homeowners have *accurate*

---

more flexible form of oversight believe that, theoretically, "it is possible to design a set of rent regulations that results in an improvement in efficiency over the unrestricted market equilibrium." *Id.* at 110. However, even economists that have applauded this flexible approach have acknowledged the practical limitations that the political process imposes on effectively targeting the appropriate households. *See, e.g.*, *id.*; Aaron S. Edlin, *The New Palgrave: Surveying Two Waves of Economic Analysis of Law*, 2 Am. L. & Econ. Rev. 407, 419–420 (2000).

20 Glaeser & Gyourko, *supra* note 18, at 58–62. *But see* Arlo Chase, *Rethinking the Homeownership Society: Rental Stability Alternative*, 18 Brook. J.L. & Pol. 61 (2009) (arguing that modest rent regulation should be resurrected as a housing policy tool to provide for housing stability in market economy).

21 Thomas Jefferson, The Essential Jefferson xvi (Jean M. Yarbrough ed., 2006) (discussing Jefferson's idealization of the "yeoman farmer" in Query XIX of Jefferson's Notes on The State of Virginia).

and complete information about their mortgage options. We will support **affordable rental housing**, which is now more critical than ever. We will implement the newly created **Affordable Housing Trust Fund** to ensure that it can start to support the **development and preservation of affordable housing** in mixed-income neighborhoods throughout the country, restore cuts to public housing operating subsidies, and fully fund the Community Development Block Grant program. We will work with local jurisdictions on the problem of vacant and abandoned housing in our communities. We will work to end housing discrimination and to ensure equal housing opportunity. We will **combat homelessness** and target homelessness among veterans in particular by expanding proven programs and launching innovative preventive services.[22]

This platform is imbued with the two main federal housing ethics, but especially "Housing as a Human Right." This ethic is seen in the efforts to promote the development and support of affordable rental housing and to combat homelessness. The "Housing as an Economic Good" ethic is seen, to a lesser extent, in efforts to correct for various market failures caused by information asymmetries between homeowners and lenders and unlawful practices by mortgage market players.

The Republican platform echoes many of the concerns of the Democratic platform, but emphasizes the "Housing as Economic Good" ethic:

Homeownership remains key to creating an *opportunity society*. We support timely and **carefully targeted aid** to those hurt by the housing crisis so that affected individuals can have a chance to trade a burdensome mortgage for *a manageable loan that reflects their home's market value*. At the same time, government action must not implicitly encourage anyone to borrow more than they can afford to repay. We support energetic federal investigation and, where appropriate, *prosecution of criminal wrongdoing in the mortgage industry and investment sector. We do not support government bailouts of private institutions. Government interference in the markets exacerbates problems in the marketplace and causes the free market to take longer to correct itself. We believe in the free market as the best tool to sustained prosperity and opportunity for all.* We encourage potential buyers to work in concert with the lending community to educate themselves about the responsibilities of purchasing a home, condo, or land.

Republican policy aims to make owning a home more accessible through *enforcement of open housing laws*, **voucher programs, urban homesteading** and—what is most important—*a strong economy* with low interest rates. Because **affordable housing is in the national interest**, any simplified tax system should continue to **encourage homeownership**, recognizing the tremendous social value that the home mortgage interest deduction has had for decades. In addition, sound housing policy should recognize the needs of renters so that apartments and multifamily homes remain important components of the housing stock.[23]

22 Democratic Nat'l Convention Comm., The 2008 Democratic National Platform: Renewing America's Promise 25 (2008).

23 Republican Nat'l Comm., 2008 Republican National Platform 28 (2008).

As noted, the Republican platform emphasizes the "Housing as an Economic Good" (that is, as a commodity) ethic most of all, with its reliance on the free market; its wariness of government interference in the market; and its promise to punish those who illegally interfere with the market. But the Republican platform does not completely ignore the "Housing as a Human Right" ethic, with its reference to vouchers and affordable housing for owners and renters alike. While the two platforms reflect other housing ethics as well, to some small extent, it is clear that each party has chosen to identify itself with one of the two main federal housing ethics.[24]

Continuing our survey of "current opinion," it is also helpful to assess the views of the major special interest groups representing the housing industry. Because these groups are major players within the industry, they have the potential to greatly influence the opinions of policymakers. Their views mostly echo the two main ethics, with a particular emphasis on "Housing as a Human Right." This emphasis may be seen as a moral position in line with this ethic, but it is also certainly consistent with the financial interests that these groups represent as well.

The National Association of Home Builders strives to create an environment in which:

- All Americans have access to the housing of their choice and the opportunity to realize the American dream of homeownership.
- Builders have the freedom to operate as entrepreneurs in an open and competitive environment.
- Housing and those who provide it are recognized as the strength of the nation.[25]

The first bullet point, of course, reflects the "Housing as a Human Right" ethic and the last two reflect the "Housing as an Economic Good" ethic.

And the Mortgage Bankers Association "invests in communities across the nation by ensuring the continued strength of the nation's residential and commercial real estate markets; expanding homeownership and extending access to affordable housing to all Americans and supporting financial literacy efforts."[26] The National Housing Conference, which draws its membership from every segment of the

24 The "Vision Statement" of the National Council of State Housing Agencies (which includes as members the housing finance agencies of every state) focuses on the affordability ethic: its concise vision is of an "affordably housed nation." National Council of State Housing Agencies, About NCSHA, http://www.ncsha.org/about-us.

25 Nat'l Ass'n of Home Builders, Mission and Vision, http://www.nahb.org/page.aspx/generic/sectionID=88 (last visited Sept. 12, 2010); Nat'l Ass'n of Realtors, NAR Overview, http://www.realtor.org/realtororg.nsf/pages/NAROverview (last visited Sept. 12, 2010).

26 Mortgage Bankers Ass'n, About MBA, http://www.mbaa.org/AboutMBA (last visited Sept. 12, 2010).

housing industry, promotes "policies, programs and legislation that help to provide affordable and suitable housing in a safe, decent environment."[27] Unsurprisingly, housing advocates share this vision, but they come to that conclusion directly from their mission. The National Low Income Housing Coalition, for instance, "is dedicated solely to achieving socially just public policy that assures people with the lowest incomes in the United States have affordable and decent homes."[28]

Federal Housing Policy Principles

Now that we have surveyed some of the leading current opinions regarding housing policy, let us return to the question posed at the start: what are the goals of housing policy? But before reaching that question, we must first answer a threshold question: what broader social policy is housing policy a part of?

In broad brush, housing policy typically involves the redistribution of income either to lower-income households or to a politically favored class of households such as homeowners. But housing policies do not merely attempt to redistribute income. Rather they typically tie the income redistribution to the households' housing consumption.[29] Contrast, for instance, the Earned Income Tax Credit to the Section 8 voucher program: the former offers a no-strings-attached tax refund to lower-income households for the sole purpose of redistributing income; the latter indirectly redistributes income to a similar population in the form of a housing subsidy, with the more concentrated goal of improving housing opportunities. Thus, while a housing policy may flow from broader social policies, it necessarily has elements that are intrinsically related to housing.

This brings us back to the main question that I seek to answer: what are the goals of housing policy? We must first ask whether there are goals of housing policy that are goods in themselves, and we must distinguish them from those that are means to other ends. For example, if a goal is to ensure that Americans live in safe, well-maintained and affordable housing, such a goal would be a good in itself. On the other hand, if a goal of housing policy is just a particular application of the general principle of promoting economic efficiency, as suggested by the

---

27 Nat'l Hous. Conference, http://www.nhc.org/ (last visited Sept. 12, 2010).

28 Nat'l Low Income Hous. Coalition, http://www.nlihc.org/template/index.cfm (last visited Sept. 12, 2010). Other advocacy organizations emphasize similar goals. *See, e.g.*, Neighborworks America, http://www.nw.org/network/aboutUs/mission/default.asp (last visited September 12, 2010) (stating that mission of this Congressionally-created not-for-profit is to create "opportunities for people to live in affordable homes, improve their lives and strengthen their communities.").

29 There are, of course, exceptions. The deduction of interest for a home equity loan of up to $100,000 is an example of a housing policy that is not tied to a household's housing consumption, because the proceeds from such a loan may be used without limitation without impacting the deductibility of the interest.

"Housing as an Economic Good" ethic, then such a housing policy goal would be a means to a more general end.

As we seek to identify what is unique to housing policy, we can set aside goals that treat housing as a means to a more general end. This does not mean that we ignore them in our policy discussions, just that we ignore them as we attempt to systemize our thinking about housing policy as a distinct field. As such, I reject "Housing as an Economic Good" as a candidate for a first principle of federal housing policy, at least in its purest form.[30] I also reject straightforward income redistribution as a candidate because a housing policy intended to achieve that end would see housing as a mere means to that general redistributional end.

What then is the aim of a housing policy? The answer to this is not immediately clear. As noted, many assert that a fundamental goal of housing policy is to assist Americans to live in a safe, well-maintained and affordable housing unit. Such a view would be consistent with a rights-based view of "Housing as a Human Right." Another similar, but more modest, expectation is that housing policy should promote a specialized form of income redistribution that ensures that the income transferred is consumed in increased housing. This view may be derived from the "Housing as an Economic Good" ethic in its recognition that the political decision to redistribute funds should be made within a market framework. Finally, one might argue that homeownership and stable housing is fundamental to the American notion of citizenship. And, indeed, that is how many politicians have approached the question, applying the "Housing as a Bulwark of Democracy" ethic. There are, of course, many other principles that impact housing policy debates, but I begin the discussion with these three broad and broadly held ones.[31]

Safe, Well-maintained and Affordable Housing

Let us start with the principle that Americans should live in well-maintained, safe and affordable housing. What does that mean? What is the actual function of housing? Many consider it to be as fundamental as food and clothing as it addresses basic survival needs. The right to adequate housing is enumerated in the United Nation's "Universal Declaration of Human Rights," and closer to home, the US Congress has enshrined the "goal of a decent home and a suitable living environment for every American family" as part of its national housing policy.[32]

30 To be clear, Iglesias is certainly right that considerations of his "Housing as an Economic Good" ethic are reflected in nearly every policy discussion regarding housing. That just happens to be a different discussion than the one intended in this article.

31 *Arthur P. Solomon* attempted a similar project in *A National Policy and Budgetary Framework for Housing and Community Development*, 5 AREUEA J. 147 (1977) (providing "an analytic foundation for a national policy and budgetary framework for housing, housing finance, and community development").

32 Universal Declaration of Human Rights, art. 25, § 1, G.A. Res 217A, U.N. GAOR, 3d Sess., 1st plen. mtg., UN Doc. A/810 (Dec. 12, 1948); 42 U.S.C. §1441 (2009) (setting

Our discussion of what "safe, well-maintained and affordable housing" is cannot end there, however, as the concept of "well-maintained" and "safe" housing has changed over time. Reaching back at least as far as Jacob Riis's HOW THE OTHER HALF LIVES, society has taken an interest in implementing government programs that attempt to raise the minimum standard of decent housing for all.[33] The advocacy of Riis and others led to the Tenement Housing Law of 1901, which was "the first major advance in the fight against the tenement slum."[34] Over time, the quality of the housing stock has improved because of increases in the standard of living as well as the implementation of construction and housing codes that aimed to preserve housing and protect consumers.[35] And as the housing stock has improved, the meaning of "safe" and "well maintained" housing has also evolved.

Whereas indoor plumbing could not be taken for granted 100 or even 50 years ago, it can now.[36] And while inadequacies remain for too many Americans in terms of dangerous wiring, poor heating, vermin infestation, and exposure to lead paint and mold, as a whole, physical housing conditions have seen a transformation for the better. But whereas an inquiry into the quality of the housing stock was once limited to the condition of individual units, a comparable inquiry today would look to the housing stock as part of the fabric of its broader environment: being safe in one's home is no longer considered sufficient if one's community is unsafe; educa-

---

forth 1949 Congressional declaration of national housing policy). The Cranston-Gonzalez National Affordable Housing Act reinforced this notion by stating, "[t]he objective of national housing policy shall be to reaffirm the long-established national commitment to decent, safe, and sanitary housing for every American …." Pub. L. No. 101–625, § 102, 104 Stat. 4079 (1990).

33 Francesco Cordasco, *Introduction* to JACOB RIIS, HOW THE OTHER HALF LIVES, AT VI (Garrett Press 1970) (1890).

34 *Id. at viii.*

35 John Emmeus Davis, *Between Devolution and the Deep Blue Sea: What's a City or State to Do?*, *in* A RIGHT TO HOUSING: FOUNDATION FOR A NEW SOCIAL AGENDA 364, 376 (Rachel G. Bratt, Michael E. Stone & Chester Hartman. eds, 2006). Although building codes have generally improved conditions, their lack of flexibility have, in many instances, inhibited the adoption of efficiency optimizing constructive practices, thus limiting their net benefits. *See, e.g.*, JERRY J. SALAMA, MICHAEL H. SCHILL & JONATHAN D. SPRINGER, FURMAN CENTER FOR REAL ESTATE AND URBAN POLICY, REDUCING THE COST OF NEW HOUSING CONSTRUCTION IN NEW YORK CITY: 2005 UPDATE 69–74 (2005).

36 GLAESER & GYOURKO, *SUPRA* NOTE 18, AT 29–32 (citing US CENSUS BUREAU, DECENNIAL CENSUS, LONG FORM HOUSING CHARACTERISTICS (1940–2000)). *But see* RACHEL G. BRATT, MICHAEL E. STONE & CHESTER HARTMAN, *Why a Right to Housing Is Needed and Makes Sense: Editors' Introduction, in* A RIGHT TO HOUSING: FOUNDATION FOR A NEW SOCIAL AGENDA, *supra* note 35, at 1, 3, 5 (noting that poor housing "quality is still a problem facing millions of Americans" in terms of dangerous wiring, poor heating, vermin infestation and exposure to lead paint and mold and that HUD found in 2003 that about 5% of households have incomes less than 50% of Median Area Income; pay more than 50% of income in rent; and live in severely inadequate quarters).

tion, work, and healthcare opportunities are scarce; and the residents cannot access a reliable transportation network.[37]

The concept of "affordable" has also changed over time. As Edward L. Glaeser and Joseph Gyourko have noted, "a consensus seems to have arisen that housing becomes 'unaffordable' when costs rise above 30% of household income," a consensus that serves as the basis for federal housing policy.[38] But until the early 1980s, these very same federal programs set a 25 per cent ceiling for housing costs for various federal programs.[39] In contrast, much of the debate surrounding anti-foreclosure efforts focuses on determining what maximum percentage of adjusted family income spent on housing can be sustained by a household, with guidelines ranging from 31 per cent to 38 per cent for loan modifications.[40]

In evaluating whether housing is safe, well-maintained, and affordable in the context of contemporary American society, we then might view a primary function of housing to be to provide an environment where a person can enjoy "Life, Liberty and the pursuit of Happiness."[41] And indeed, leading right-to-housing activists use language that has echoes of Jefferson's, with one "characterizing housing as the foundation for life and a launching pad which is fundamental to human development."[42]

In sum, providing safe, well-maintained, and affordable housing has consistently remained a broadly held principle of housing policy, even if the standards for such housing has changed over time.

Specialized Income Redistribution

Another widely held "first principle" of housing policy is that many low- and moderate-income households should receive a specialized form of income redistribution that ensures that the income transferred is consumed in increased housing. One of the main arguments in favor of such a specialized form of income redistribution is that low-income children benefit from policies that require

37 *See* Bratt, Stone & Hartman, *supra* note 35, at 1–2 ("Housing is, or can be, the basic building block for a range of related benefits—personal health and safety, employment opportunities, a decent education, security of tenure, economic security …"). This broader environment of safe and livable neighborhoods was also acknowledged as an essential part of housing policy in the Cranston-Gonzalez National Affordable Housing Act. Pub. L. 101–625, § 102(4), 104 Stat. 4079 (1990).

38 Glaeser & Gyourko, *supra* note 18, at 29–32. *See* Federal Housing Administration, Third Annual Report 10 (1937) (noting that more than 90% of FHA mortgages entailed monthly payments amounting to less than 20% of borrowers income).

39 Alex F. Schwartz, Housing Policy In The United States 23 (2006).

40 Federal Deposit Insurance Corporation, FDIC Loan Modification Program 8–9, *available at* http://www.fdic.gov/consumers/loans/loanmod/FDICLoanMod.pdf.

41 The Declaration of Independence para. 1 (US 1776).

42 Iglesias, *supra* note 13, at 542 (summarizing views of Chester Hartman).

their legal guardians to consume more housing (as opposed to other goods and services).[43]

There are additional rationales for privileging housing expenditures over other household expenditures. First of all, housing is the largest budget item for all households, those of both renters and homeowners.[44] Indeed, in 2005, housing expenses accounted for nearly 32 per cent of all consumer spending by homeowners and nearly 36 per cent for renters.[45] Congress may believe that left to their own devices, people will under-consume housing as a proportion of their income in a manner which is bad for them or, perhaps, bad for their children and their communities.[46] Thus, Congress may use subsidies and tax expenditures to encourage the greater consumption of housing.

Second, given the strong commitment in the United States to a market economy, as compared to other developed nations,[47] some argue that government policies which smooth out the impact of market forces on such a key component of well-being like housing are a necessary palliative for households as they face the unexpected challenges posed by the economy.[48]

Third, and particularly after the homelessness crisis that began in the 1980s, the federal government has also taken a particular interest in preventing homelessness. While this increased interest developed against a backdrop of a long-term decrease in federal funding for low- and moderate-income housing, recent initiatives have more directly addressed the housing situation of the neediest in society:

---

43 Glaeser & Gyourko, *supra* note 18, at 55–56. One might argue that this first principle is just a watered down version of the first candidate discussed above. While that argument is not without some merit, this redistributionist first principle treats housing less as a right and more like a commodity. As such, it is worth separating the two of them out for the purposes of this analysis.

44 Anthony Downs, *Introduction: Why Rental Housing Is the Neglected Child of American Shelter*, *in* Revisiting Rental Housing: Policies, Programs, And Priorities 2 (Nicolas P. Retsinas & Eric S. Belsky eds, 2008).

45 *Id.*

46 Many economists would likely disagree with such a belief. *See, e.g.*, Glaeser & Gyourko, *supra* note 18, at 54 ("Economists generally prefer pure income redistribution to redistribution in-kind.").

47 The United States was recently ranked higher (6) on a 2008 summary of economic freedom than other developed nations such as the United Kingdom (10), Germany (24), Japan (24), France (35) and Italy (66). James Gwartney, Joshua Hall & Robert Lawson, Fraser Institute, Economic Freedom of the World: 2010 Annual Report 17 (2010).

48 *See* Stephanie M. Stern, *Residential Protectionism and the Legal Mythology of the Home*, 107 Mich. L. Rev. 1093, 1132–33 (2009) (arguing that "major stumbling block to adopting a minimal approach to home protection has been the fear that homeowners will founder on the shoals of the free market."). *See also* Rachel G. Bratt *et al.*, *supra* note 42, at 8 ("Housing problems are deeply ingrained in the operation of our economic system and in the ways in which society functions.").

the developmentally disabled; the mentally ill; very low-income families and individuals; and the elderly.[49]

Glaeser and Gyourko rightly point out that policies that require low-income people to consume redistributed income on housing (which is just the flip side of privileging housing over other expenditures) are paternalistic and unsupported by any studies that convincingly demonstrate that low-income households make particularly bad housing choices.[50] They also challenge the belief that many Americans under-consume housing.[51] That being noted, there is no question that much of housing policy is premised on the notion that people (indeed, people of all classes) should receive assistance in offsetting the large expense that housing entails.[52]

This holds particularly true for renters as they tend to be quite a bit poorer than homeowners: in 2005, the median income of renter households was less than half that of owner-occupant households.[53] John Quigley writes that:

> Affordability is clearly the most compelling rationale for polices [sic] subsidizing rental housing. The high cost of rental housing, relative to the ability of low-income households to pay for housing, means that these households have

49 *See, e.g.*, Joel Blau, The Visible Poor: Homelessness In The United States 175–76 (1993) (reviewing government responses to homelessness in the 1980s). The irony of this government interest in homelessness is that the 1980s homelessness crisis was caused in part by government policies that disfavored single room occupancy hotels that were often residences of last resort for very low-income individuals. Brendan O'Flaherty, Making Room: The Economics of Homelessness 176 (1996) (noting that New York City's 1961 zoning amendments were designed explicitly to "discourage subdividing apartments and buildings into small units"). Decreased federal funding for housing disproportionately affects low-income households. *See* Rob Rosenthal & Maria Foscarinis, *Responses to Homelessness: Past Policies, Future Directions, and a Right to Housing*, *in* A Right To Housing: Foundation For A New Social Agenda, *supra* note 18, at 319–320.

50 Glaeser & Gyourko, *supra note 18,* at 55.

51 *Id. passim.*

52 If housing policy was based on a principle of straightforward income redistribution, then it would really be a means to an end, the end being decreased income inequality or the provision of a basic standard of living. Moreover, if it were merely intended to be a way of implementing income redistribution, housing policy would be an incredibly inefficient way to achieve that end. This is because it would limit to housing the ways that the recipients of the income redistribution could spend that money. This would lead to some recipients over-consuming housing when their preference would be to consume other goods (e.g., food) and services (e.g., education) instead. All of this is not to say that income redistribution concerns do not play a role in housing policy. Rather, it is to say that we should be careful not to lose sight of what makes housing policy *housing policy*.

53 Downs, *supra* note 44, at 2.

few resources left over for expenditures on other goods—food, clothing, medicine—that are also necessities.[54]

As such, affordability rationales frequently predominate in the rental housing policy arena.

A variety of programs implement this principle. In addition to programs like housing vouchers that reduce household rent payments for low-income families, the federal government has also implemented a variety of initiatives to make housing more affordable and sustainable for particular renters, such as the special needs populations noted above.[55] If members of these populations are not able to secure and maintain housing because of their inability to earn an income, some argue that society is responsible for providing needy members of these populations with affordable housing. This argument obviously reflects the "Housing as a Human Right" ethic.

A related principle (although rarely stated because of its plainly instrumentalist nature) of some aspects of housing policy is to ensure that low-income people do not cause harm to other members of society. This principle served as a motivating force behind the earliest tenement laws, "to protect the nonpoor who were living in" neighborhoods near to tenement slums, and despite changing standards of political correctness, very much remains in effect today.[56] It is based on the belief that society benefits from low-income households consuming more and better housing, just as it may benefit from them consuming more food (via the Food Stamp program) and medical care (via Medicaid).[57] By providing these households with improved housing as opposed to tax credits, the federal government can ensure that its funds are used specifically for the benefit it wishes to confer.[58] Society's benefit from increased housing consumption by low-income households may take the form of reduced homelessness and increased social cohesion. It may also take the form of the increased public safety that results from building and housing standards that protect the housing stock from casualties such as fire and earthquake

54 John M. Quigley, *Just Suppose: Housing Subsidies for Low-Income Renters*, *in* Revisiting Rental Housing: Policies, Programs, And Priorities, *supra note 44* at 300, 308.

55 *See generally* Libby Perl, Section 811 and Other HUD Housing Programs for Persons with Disabilities (2008), *available at* http://assets.opencrs.com/rpts/RL34728_20081103.pdf (also noting support services funding for such programs are intended to sustain long-term residency).

56 Rachel G. Bratt *et al.*, *supra* note 35, at 1, 2–3.

57 Although housing policy may be modeled after the principles of these programs, it tends to be dissimilar from Food Stamps and Medicaid in practice because it is not an entitlement and lacks comparable funds, and thus fails to reach many individuals who are eligible for assistance. Peter Dreier, *Federal Housing Subsidies: Who Benefits and Why?*, *in* A Right To Housing: Foundation For A New Social Agenda, *supra* note 35, at 111.

58 Glaeser & Gyourko, *supra* note 18, at 54–56.

damage and protect communities from diseases that more easily spread where certain public health measures are not implemented.[59]

Housing as a Bulwark of Democracy

While predominantly relating to homeownership (as opposed to rental) policy, the importance of this principle in American housing policy cannot be overstated. The centrality of homeownership to America's vision of itself as a society of equal citizens reaches at least as far back as Jefferson's idealized "yeoman farmer" and continued through to Lincoln's Homestead Act of 1862, which granted 160 acres to settlers.[60] Jefferson's yeoman farmer was his ideal citizen because he was self-sufficient, earned his own keep, considered himself the equal of anyone else, and jealously protected his liberty and unalienable rights.

America's vision of itself as "yeoman farmers" transformed into that of "homeowners" in the 20th century, when interdependent communities in cities and suburbs began to replace self-sufficient farms. Accordingly, presidents as varied as Herbert Hoover, Lyndon Johnson, Bill Clinton and George W. Bush made homeownership a key element of their agendas.[61] Indeed, the extraordinary lengths that the Bush and Obama administrations have taken to stabilize the housing market during the Great Recession, taking over the privately held mortgage finance giants Fannie Mae and Freddie Mac and committing tens of billions of dollars to head off foreclosures, respectively, evidence the importance that both parties place on homeownership.[62]

While a first principle of housing policy is to make people into better citizens by making them homeowners, the possible non-economic benefits of homeownership are not necessarily limited to the political sphere. As a result, homeownership policy has also been designed at times to encourage these other potential benefits. The connection between homeownership and these non-economic benefits has not, however, been clearly demonstrated.

---

59 Cordasco, *supra* note 33, at viii.

60 JAMES M. MCPHERSON, ABRAHAM LINCOLN AND THE SECOND AMERICAN REVOLUTION 12 (1992).

61 Lawrence J. Vale, *The Ideological Origins of Affordable Homeownership Efforts*, *in* CHASING THE AMERICAN DREAM: NEW PERSPECTIVES ON AFFORDABLE HOMEOWNERSHIP 31–32 (William M. Rohe & Harry L. Watson eds, 2007) (discussing Hoover's efforts to increase the homeownership rate while Commerce Secretary and President); Rachel G. Bratt, *Homeownership for Low-Income Households: A Comparison of the Section 235, Nehemiah, and Habitat for Humanity Programs*, *in id.* at 46–47 (discussing Johnson initiatives); *id.* at 67 (discussing Clinton and Bush efforts).

62 *See, e.g.*, Edmund L. Andrews, *U.S. Sets Big Incentives to Head Off Foreclosures*, N.Y. TIMES, Mar. 5, 2009, at A1 (reporting $75 billion Obama Administration to head off foreclosures); Stephen Labaton & Edmund L. Andrews, *In Rescue to Stabilize Lending, U.S. Takes Over Mortgage Finance Titans*, N.Y. TIMES, Sept. 8, 2008, at A1 (reporting Bush Administration takeover of Fannie Mae and Freddie Mac).

There is a significant amount of scholarship that argues that there are a range of other non-economic benefits from homeownership. These include better outcomes for residents in education, health, and employment.[63] These also include increased civic engagement, as demonstrated through higher levels of volunteerism and participation in community activities.[64] Thus, homeownership policy is often justified by the claim that it helps to achieve better outcomes regarding these non-economic benefits as well.

Some also argue that homeownership encourages wealth accumulation and forced savings (through principal repayment of the mortgage).[65] These goals are consistent with the principle of making contemporary Americans self-sufficient like Jefferson's idealized yeoman farmers. There is plenty of evidence that homeowners have more wealth than renters, although researchers have only recently attempted to demonstrate the extent to which homeownership actually causes that greater wealth accumulation.[66] And while it might come as no surprise that homeowners historically accumulated greater wealth, recent events have at least temporarily put an end to that trend. The boom in housing prices that began in the 1990s, along with easy access to credit, set homeowners up for a fall when housing prices tumbled in the late 2000s. Indeed, more than a third of homeowners were underwater on their mortgages (that is, they owed more than their houses were worth) in 2009.[67]

---

63 Downs, *supra* note 44, at 9. A related argument is that children benefit from living in homes owned by their legal guardians. Empirical research has not, however, convincingly demonstrated that this benefit results from such policies, notwithstanding the fact that numerous studies have been conducted in this area. *See, e.g.*, GLAESER & GYOURKO, *supra* note 18, at 56; David Barker & Eric A. Miller, *Homeownership and Child Welfare*, 37 REAL ESTATE ECON. 279 (2009) (finding that homeownership has little or no effect on children's welfare based on several indicators of well-being).

64 Grace W. Bucchianeri, *The American Dream or The American Delusion? The Private and External Benefits of Homeownership* 3–4, *available at* http://real.wharton.upenn.edu/~wongg/research/The%20American%20Dream.pdf (reviewing literature).

65 *See, e.g.*, Bratt *et al.*, *supra* note 35, at 1, 4.

66 *See, e.g.*, Dia *et al.*, *Do Homeowners Achieve More Household Wealth in The Long Run?*, 6 J. HOUS. ECON. 274 (2007) (providing "first empirical evidence that homeownership, after controlling for other drivers of wealth accumulation, is positively and significantly associated with wealth accumulation over time."); Thomas P. Boehm & Alan M. Schlottmann, *Wealth Accumulation and Homeownership: Evidence for Low-Income Households*, 10(2) CITYSCAPE 225 (2008) (finding "household wealth generally appears to be positively affected by homeownership").

67 Bob Tedeschi, *The Depths of Mortgage Debt*, NY TIMES, Aug. 30, 2009, at RE9 (providing second quarter 2009 data).

Other Principles

There are additional rationales for certain housing policies that are clearly not first principles of a housing policy, but rather are parallel goals, ones that reflect other branches of broader social policy. It is not surprising that quite a few other social policies are enmeshed with housing policy, given the size of the housing sector and its role in the economy. The most important are:

1. ending segregation and other racial inequities which are present in the housing market;
2. increasing socioeconomic diversity;
3. promoting green construction practices and energy efficiency;
4. promoting community and economic development; and
5. preventing sprawl and promoting Brownfield (environmentally contaminated property) development.

Ending Segregation and Other Racial Inequalities

Racial segregation and racial discrimination have always permeated, and continue to permeate, the housing market. This discrimination is also seen as having a pernicious influence on many other aspects of social welfare: education, health, and workforce issues being three of the most important.[68] The federal government has implemented and reinforced policies meant to remove racial bias from the public sphere for decades—a trend that has extended into housing policy. That being said, ending racial discrimination is not so much a principle of housing policy *per se* as it is a fundamental and parallel principle that must be implemented in housing and throughout the rest of society.

It must also be noted that housing policies have often been used to *implement* racist and classist agendas. In the past, these policies were often explicitly racist, as with redlining policies implemented by the Federal Housing Administration. Redlining, the practice of refusing to lend in certain communities, particularly African-American communities, was pioneered by the federal government through the Home Owners' Loan Corporation and the FHA in the 1930s and continued on for decades.[69]

Other housing policies only thinly veiled their discriminatory aims. Urban renewal, sometimes characterized as a policy to improve the life of low-income households, was often implemented in such a way as to force low-income households from their admittedly substandard homes and replace them with buildings

68 Nancy A. Denton, *Segregation and Discrimination in Housing*, *in* A Right To Housing: Foundation For A New Social Agenda, *supra* note 35, at 61, 71.

69 *Id.* at 66.

designed for businesses or higher-income residents.[70] More recently, facially acceptable programs like Housing Opportunities for People Everywhere ("HOPE") VI (discussed below) have been criticized for dispersing poor communities of color and replacing them with higher income residents.[71] The existence of racist and classist policies, whether implicit in the design of the policy or its implementation, must be acknowledged in order to prevent them from being executed.

Another classist policy that bears ongoing examination is the manner in which tax expenditures on homeownership greatly favor wealthy homeowners over less wealthy homeowners and renters.[72] As noted above, 72 per cent of all the income tax benefits accruing to homeowners go to those making more than $75,000 per year, and only a tiny amount go to those making less than $40,000 per year.[73] Such a policy is not innately repugnant like a racist policy, but it should give pause to those who believe that the tax system should be progressive and not regressive.

Increased Socioeconomic Diversity

A related principle is that increased socioeconomic diversity should be incentivized in housing policy. It may be seen as a principle that respects the low-income residents of a gentrifying community and the fabric of the community itself.[74] Socioeconomic diversity may also be seen as necessary for a community to function in a healthy manner.[75] Finally, it may be seen as something that particularly benefits residents of high poverty areas. One major federal initiative, the Moving to Opportunity for Fair Housing demonstration, gave rent vouchers to residents of poor urban areas to move to "low-poverty areas."[76] One of the major rationales for the demonstration is that very low-income families would benefit

---

70 Peter Marcuse & W. Dennis Keating, *The Permanent Housing Crisis: The Failures of Conservatism and the Limitations of Liberalism*, *in* A RIGHT TO HOUSING: FOUNDATION FOR A NEW SOCIAL AGENDA, *supra* note 35, at 139, 144–45.

71 SUSAN J. POPKIN ET AL., A DECADE OF HOPE VI RESEARCH FINDINGS AND POLICY CHALLENGES 3 (2004) ("[T]here is substantial evidence that the original residents of HOPE VI projects have not always benefited from redevelopment, even in some sites that were otherwise successful.").

72 *See supra* notes 7–11 and accompanying text.

73 Carasso, *supra* note 10.

74 LORETTA LEES ET AL., GENTRIFICATION 215 (2007).

75 *See, e.g.*, ALYSSA KATZ, OUR LOT: HOW REAL ESTATE CAME TO OWN US 192–93, 200 (2009) (arguing that the creative classes "who made [New York City] what it is" are being forced out by Wall Street real estate investors); John Ingram Gilderbloom et al., *Why Cities Need Affordable Housing: A Case Study of Houston*, *in* JOHN INGRAM GILDERBLOOM, INVISIBLE CITY: POVERTY, HOUSING AND NEW URBANISM 203 (2008) (arguing that lack of affordable housing policy jeopardizes Houston's future).

76 *See generally* LARRY ORR ET AL., HUD: OFFICE OF POLICY DEV. & RESEARCH, MOVING TO OPPORTUNITY FOR FAIR HOUSING DEMONSTRATION: INTERIM IMPACTS EVALUATION (2003), *available at* http://www.huduser.org/Publications/pdf/MTOFullReport.pdf.

from living among higher-income families.[77] Another major federal initiative, HOPE VI, demolishes dysfunctional public housing and replaces it with mixed-income housing (as well as providing housing vouchers to some of the original tenants who were displaced).[78] Congress' stated objectives for HOPE VI included: (1) improving "the living environment for residents of severely distressed public housing"; (2) revitalizing "sites on which such public housing projects are located and contribut[ing] to the improvement of the surrounding neighborhood"; and (3) providing "housing that will avoid or decrease the concentration of very low-income families."[79] In one program then, HOPE VI encompasses many of the rationales for increasing socio-economic diversity. This parallel principle, like the first one, goes way beyond the scope of a housing policy to touch upon key political goals relating to educational and work opportunities as well as economic development, to name a few.

Promoting Green Construction Practices and Energy Efficiency

Promoting green construction practices and energy efficiency has taken on a greater importance in housing policy in the last ten years. Indeed, it is considered the cutting edge issue throughout the entire construction industry, including the affordable housing sector.[80] Bringing environmental concerns to this sector of the economy makes particular sense given that heating and powering residential buildings are responsible for about 20 per cent of total US CO_2 emissions.[81] To some extent, the principle of housing affordability aligns well with that of green construction as operating costs (energy costs in particular) may be lower with

77 In the interim, there is little evidence that these benefits have been realized. Adults who moved from high- to low- poverty areas did not experience improvements in earnings or economic self-sufficiency; these individuals rarely found employment through their new neighbors, and even reported that decreases in access to public transportation lead to impediments absent from their old neighborhoods. Furthermore, aside from decreased obesity rates, adults also saw very little improvement in physical health. There were, however, significant improvements to the participants' mental health. These short-term effects in adults may not be indicative of potential long-term benefits embodied within the youth of the MTO program, who displayed mixed results based on gender: female teenagers showed positive education and mental health benefits with negligible physical health benefits, while male teenagers showed strong negative effects in the same areas. Jeffrey R. Kling, Jeffrey B. Liebman & Lawrence F. Katz, *Experimental Analysis of Neighborhood Effects*, 75 Econometrica 83, 99–104 (2007).

78 *See generally* Popkin et al., *supra* note 71.

79 42 U.S.C. § 1437v (2009).

80 *See* Jerry Yudelson, The Green Building Revolution 3–6, 129–130 (2008) (reviewing history of green building movement beginning with promulgation of Leadership in Energy and Environmental Design (LEED) standards in 2000).

81 D&R International, Ltd., U.S. Dep't of Energy, 2009 Buildings Energy Data Book 2–24 (2009) (2006 data).

green buildings.[82] But construction costs for green projects are typically higher, at least at present, which raises the cost of construction for each unit.[83] The affordable housing sector is, with its low margins, particularly sensitive to increased cost. And as with the two previous parallel principles, green building is not so much a principle of housing policy, but a parallel principle that seeks to implement environmentally sound practices throughout broad swaths of the economy.

Promoting Community and Economic Development

Promoting community and economic development is often intertwined with housing policy, although not integral to housing policy itself. Community and economic development policy usually sees housing as one element of a broader strategy to ensure the long-term health of a community. Typically, other important elements of a community and economic development policy include transportation, education, and infrastructure objectives, as well as "soft" elements, such as developing social capital in low-income communities.[84]

Preventing sprawl and redeveloping Brownfields While preventing sprawl has become an issue of great concern for state governments with their historical responsibility for land use regulation,[85] federal housing policy may also encompass this principle. Federal activity in this area has not been exceptional—after all, there is no question that, historically, federal transportation, housing finance, and infrastructure policies have had the effect of actually increasing sprawl.[86]

Federal and state governments have also looked to Brownfield redevelopment as an element of housing policy, although they have trodden with care because of the environmental hazards that these properties present.[87] Addressing sprawl

82 Piet Eichholtz *et al.*, *Doing Well by Doing Good? Green Office Buildings*, Am. Econ. Rev. (forthcoming), *available at* http://ssrn.com/abstract=1480215 (noting that while "hard evidence on the financial performance of green buildings is limited and consists mainly of industry-initiated case studies," green buildings appear to have slightly higher construction costs and lower operating costs); Norm Miller *et al.*, *Does Green Pay Off?*, 14 J. Real Est. Portfolio Mgmt. 385, 385 (2008) (arguing that "payoff from wise green investment is easy to justify even if it is based on purely profit motivations").

83 Eichholtz *et al.*, *supra* note 82, at 8.

84 *See generally* William H. Simon, The Community Economic Development Movement: Law, Business, and The New Social Policy (2001).

85 *See* Regina C. Gray, *Ten Years of Smart Growth: A Nod to Policies Past and a Prospective Glimpse into the Future*, 7 Cityscape 109 (2007) (reviewing state and local smart growth strategies).

86 *See generally* Kenneth T. Jackson, Crabgrass Frontier: The Suburbanization of the United States (1985).

87 *See Responsible Housing*, Nat'l. Conf. of State Legislatures, http://www.ncsl.org/?TabId=16767 (last visited April 16, 2010) (advocating that to make Brownfields "available for housing, Congress needs to give states flexibility to immunize project

and Brownfields as part of a housing policy reflects a commitment to sustainable growth.[88] But as with community and economic development initiatives, sustainable growth initiatives are generally much broader than just housing as they reflect environmental, energy, and quality of life concerns as much as housing policy concerns.[89]

Subordinate Principles

While the five parallel principles outlined directly above are best characterized as "goods in themselves," there are also some subordinate principles of housing policy that relate to the size of the housing sector, particularly the mortgage and construction industries, and its importance to the overall economy. These subordinate principles are clearly means to other ends. For instance, finance industry representatives argue for policies that stabilize the mortgage markets, also noting the impact that the mortgage industry has on the health and stability of the overall economy.[90] This has never been clearer than in the Great Recession where stabilizing mortgage lenders was identified as one of the key elements of the government's response to the crisis.[91]

Others argue that affordable housing expenditures by the government can also be counter-cyclical and help to smooth out the boom and bust cycle that characterizes the construction sector.[92] Housing and housing finance industry representatives, therefore, argued for policies that are intended to stabilize the construction and housing sectors during the recent financial crisis.[93]

providers from future federal cleanup liability and provide the necessary funding to assist states in the clean-up of these sites").

88 *See generally* John C. Dernbach & Scott Bernstein, *Pursuing Sustainable Communities: Looking Back, Looking Forward*, 35 URB. LAW. 495 (2003).

89 *Id.*

90 David Reiss, *Fannie Mae and Freddie Mac and the Future of Federal Housing Finance Policy: A Study of Regulatory Privilege*, 61 ALA. L. REV. 907, 922 (2010).

91 *See, e.g.*, *id.* (discussing government attempts to stabilize mortgage finance giants Fannie and Freddie).

92 *See* Iglesias, *supra* note 13, at 548 n.186 (arguing that "[a] primary purpose of the public housing program was to act as an employment program to stimulate the construction industry" during and after the Great Depression).

93 *See, e.g.*, MORTGAGE BANKERS ASS'N, 2009 MBA POLICY AGENDA TO STABILIZE THE HOUSING AND MORTGAGE MARKETS; National Multi Housing Council, http://www.nmhc.org/Content/ContentList.cfm?NavID=424 (last visited Sept. 12, 2010) (proposing policy responses to stabilize industry during credit crisis).

Conclusion

HUD's recently released Strategic Plan is notable for its incorporation of just about all of these first, parallel and secondary principles.[94] The fact that it does not focus solely on first principles does not undercut its legitimacy—it is important to remember that first principles are not necessarily more important goals of government than parallel or secondary principles at any given time. Rather, isolating first principles helps us identify what is intrinsic to housing policy so that we may clearly analyze potential policy choices for housing specifically, as opposed to how they may contribute to some larger goal; in other words, it helps to ensure that housing policies have measurable housing outcomes. And imposing some analytic structure here is of key importance because federal housing policy is a morass. This exercise should help to ensure that monies spent to increase the supply and quality of housing are used efficiently.

In order to work through the morass, it is necessary to identify legitimate first principles of housing policy, then to evaluate housing programs to see whether they are designed to achieve goals consistent with some or all of those principles. Finally, it is necessary to evaluate the effectiveness of housing programs individually and taken together in order to ensure that they do not work at cross purposes. Such an exercise should help to clarify debates surrounding American housing policy as each new presidential administration seeks to put its own stamp on this field.

I have argued that the three first principles that inform federal housing policy are: (i) allowing all Americans to live in a safe, well-maintained, and affordable housing unit; (ii) providing a specialized form of income redistribution that ensures that the income transferred is consumed in increased housing; and (iii) incentivizing Americans to take on the key attributes of Jefferson's yeoman farmer: economic and social self-sufficiency as well as a jealous regard for one's liberty

A housing policy primarily guided by each of these three first principles would look very different from one guided by the other two. One guided by the first would emphasize housing for very low-income households which would not be able to pay market rates for safe, well-maintained, and affordable housing. One guided by the second would likely contemplate some kind of progressive housing subsidy for a range of low- and moderate-income households. And one guided by the third would seek to maximize the homeownership rate for the nation as a whole at whatever income levels are the most efficient for achieving that goal.

Obviously, these principles can all be present—and in tension with one another—within a particular housing policy initiative and across initiatives. In the United States, the typical approach is an often inefficient muddle of programs focused on competing principles. However, the goal of this chapter was not to argue that all housing programs can be rationalized into one coherent whole. This chapter has the much more limited goal of developing a more systematic approach

94 US Dep't of Hous. & Urban Dev., *supra* note 6.

to the evaluation of housing policy. We now have an answer to the question posed at the beginning of this chapter: what are the main goals of housing policy? With this rough outline, we can now move to fill in the details.

Acknowledgement

This chapter is based in large part on David Reiss, *First Principles for An Effective Federal Housing Policy*, 35 BROOKLYN J. INT'L L. 795 (2010). Thanks to Michele Cotton for helpful comments and to Philip Tucker, Hanna Robinson, Frank Marallo, and Kevin Kim for superb research assistance.

Chapter 6

Evolving Ethical Standards in Property Law: A Study of Regulatory Perspectives Toward Home Mortgage Lending Transactions

Vincent Di Lorenzo

Introduction

This chapter is a study of ethical perspectives toward consumer protection in residential mortgage-lending transactions. It contrasts the view of the Congress with that of the federal bank regulatory agencies through an analysis of regulatory actions and Congressional enactments over the course of the last three decades.

The ethical viewpoint embraced by a society is frequently reflected in its laws.[1] The best evidence is a series of statutory or case law developments over a prolonged period of time, rather than an individual enactment that may be motivated by a unique, perceived need for action or a compromise reached to avoid inaction. The question explored in this chapter is whether US society sanctions business practices involving residential property which extract profits from individuals who are unable to protect themselves? More narrowly drawn, the issue is whether US society considers such business practices to be ethical when they involve an essential public good—namely a home.

The evidence presented in this chapter points to a conclusion reached by the US Congress that the answer to that question is "No." What is interesting about this conclusion concerning residential mortgage-lending transactions is that the same evidence exists with respect to other transactions involving consumers' homes. Thus, over the last 30 years the warranty of habitability has been embraced by state legislators and judges. The embrace of a warranty of habitability is a decision to intervene in the free market to protect individuals against substandard housing conditions (significant injury, both financial and, at times, physical) because the

1 The relationship between law on the one hand and ethics or morality on the other hand has been the subject of a great deal of debate. There has nonetheless been recognition of a frequent intersection, what even Austin characterized as a "frequent coincidence" of positive law and morality. *See* H.L.A. Hart, *Positivism and the Separation of Law and Morals*, 71 Harv. L. Rev. 593, 598–599 (1958). This chapter relies on the common motivation or viewpoint that led to statutory enactments over a period of more than three decades to discover the ethical perspective accepted by US society.

legislators or courts have concluded that most tenants cannot effectively protect themselves[2] against exploitation by unscrupulous landlords. This is a reflection of current prevailing standards of ethical conduct in residential landlord-tenant transactions.[3] Similarly, over the last 20 years the warranty of quality has been imposed on builders of new homes by state legislators and courts. Again, intervention in the free market has been justified due to the significant financial injury that would be suffered by homebuyers against which they are unable to protect themselves.[4] Similarly, this reflected current, prevailing standards of ethical conduct.[5] My thesis is that there is an ethical viewpoint reflected in all of these developments, including Congressional decisions to prohibit particular abusive mortgage practices. At times the courts and legislatures have refrained from intervening in the consumer-oriented real estate markets. However, in recent decades, intervention has been more frequent and reflects an ethical viewpoint that business entities should not be permitted to profit by imposing significant financial costs and burdens on consumers of homes (whether homeowners or tenants) when it is found that such consumers are unable to effectively protect themselves.

---

2 *See* Restatement (Second) of Prop.: Landlord & Tenant § 5.1 cmt. b (1977). The courts have imposed an implied obligation on the landlord's part that the premises are suitable for residential occupancy. They have rejected the doctrine of caveat emptor due to the complexity of residential housing systems, the expense of making repairs, and the lack of bargaining power on the part of most residential tenants.

3 *See, e.g.*, Javins v. First National Realty Corp., 428 F.2d 1071, 1081 n.56 (D.C. Cir. 1970) ("[F]or reasons of public policy warranties are often implied into contracts by operation of law in order to meet generally prevailing standards of honesty and fair dealing. When public policy has been enacted into law like the housing code, that policy will usually have deep roots in the expectations and intentions of most people.").

4 *E.g.*, Albrecht v. Clifford, 767 N.E.2d 42 (Mass. 2002) (a warranty protects purchasers from "defects that are nearly impossible to ascertain by inspection" and imposes burdens "on the person who has the opportunity to notice, avoid, or correct" latent defects); Caceci v. Di Canio Const. Corp., 526 N.E.2d 266, 269 (N.Y. 1988) (the parties do not bargain as equals, and the purchaser "has no meaningful choice but to rely on the builder-vendor to deliver … a house reasonably fit for the purpose for which it was intended"); McDonald v. Mianecki, 398 A.2d 1283, 1289–1290 (N.J. 1979) (in the area of home construction the two parties do not bargain as equals). "The purchaser therefore ordinarily relies heavily upon the greater expertise of the vendor to ensure a suitable product …" *McDonald*, 398 A.2d at 1289. "The caveat emptor rule … does a disservice not only to the ordinary prudent purchaser but to the industry itself by lending encouragement to the unscrupulous, fly-by-night operator and purveyor of shoddy work." *Id.* at 1290.

5 *Id.* at 1291 ("[T]he law should be based on current concepts of what is right and just, and the judiciary should be alert to the never-ending need for keeping its common law principles abreast of the times."); *Caceci*, 526 N.E.2d at 270 ("If judges have woefully misinterpreted the *mores* of their day, or if the *mores* of their day are no longer those of ours, they ought not to tie, in helpless submission, the hands of their successors." (citing Benjamin N. Cardozo, Nature of Judicial Process 152 (1921))).

This chapter reveals, however, a schism between Congress and the federal bank regulatory agencies. In the first part of this chapter, the view of the federal regulatory agencies is documented, in the period 1982–2008, the period preceding the current mortgage crisis. The Federal Reserve Board's viewpoint is explored along with that of the other federal regulatory agencies. The finding is that the regulatory agencies relied on market discipline to address possible abusive lending practices, as did the property law doctrine of caveat emptor. In addition, the Federal Reserve Board embraced a net societal benefits test as the determinant for government intervention in the mortgage market. Thus, the Federal Reserve would be willing to intervene in the market only if: (a) consumers suffer substantial injury; (b) against which they are unable to protect themselves; *and* (c) net societal benefits will result from government intervention. A net societal benefits test *requires* a finding that the benefits of government intervention will exceed its costs. No intervention is authorized, and none will occur, unless such a finding is made. This contrasts with cost-benefit evaluations. In cost-benefit evaluations, the benefits and costs of government intervention are *considered*, but there is no requirement that benefits must exceed costs before any action can and will be taken.

As a result of the Federal Reserve's embrace of a net societal benefits test, abusive practices went unchecked through the last decade because the Fed found current practices provided substantial benefits to the industry or, at times, to other consumers, or because a change would impose costs on the industry, and as a result no net societal benefit was thought to result from government intervention. This regulatory view allowed the industry to take advantage of large segments of the public as long as the industry or other members of the public benefited.

In the second part of this chapter, the view of the Congress is explored prior to its recent statutory intervention in response to the mortgage crisis. Congress rejected a reliance on market discipline as well as a net societal benefits test as the standard for statutory intervention during this period. Instead, it recognized the need for government intervention whenever consumers suffered a substantial injury against which they were unable to effectively protect themselves. This is an ethical perspective more in line with the viewpoint that led to the recognition of the warranty of habitability and the warranty of quality by state legislatures and the judiciary. The third part of this chapter then explores whether these contrasting viewpoints have changed in light of the recent mortgage crisis. First, recent amendments to the Federal Reserve's regulations aimed at curbing unfair mortgage-lending practices are examined. The conclusion drawn is that the Fed still adheres to a net societal benefits test as the determinant of the need for government intervention in the mortgage market. Its viewpoint continues to ignore the threshold for government intervention to address abuses in consumer lending transactions that had been embraced by Congress in legislative enactments during the last three decades, and which is consistent with other developments in residential property law during the same period. Second, the recent response of Congress in the 2010 Dodd-Frank Act is explored. In that action, Congress provided a more mixed message. However, overall Congress reaffirmed the ethical viewpoint found in earlier enactments.

Agency Reliance on Market Discipline: 1982—2008

The power of federal banking agencies to regulate unfair mortgage-lending practices comes from three sources: (a) the Federal Trade Commission (FTC) Act;[6] (b) the Home Ownership and Equity Protection Act (HOEPA);[7] and (c) banking law prohibitions against unsafe and unsound banking practices.[8] The last of these statutory powers can be exercised over only banks, thrifts and their affiliates. The first two can be exercised over all lending institutions, either by the Federal Reserve or by the FTC. Power to address unfair mortgage lending under HOEPA is vested in the Federal Reserve and applies to the activities of banks, thrifts, their subsidiaries and affiliates, as well as independent mortgage companies.[9]

The actions of the Federal Reserve evidence a reliance on a free-market approach to address unfair mortgage products and practices whenever HOEPA vested discretion in the Fed. Bank management was relied upon to avoid unfair mortgage loans and, more importantly, consumers were relied upon to protect themselves against unfair mortgage loans.

This is the same viewpoint manifest in the regulatory policies of the other federal bank regulatory agencies over the last three decades. For example, when statutory mandates governing home mortgage-lending transactions were lifted by the Garn-St Germain Act in 1982,[10] the federal regulators were free to impose regulatory restrictions. They chose instead to impose no restrictions at all.

The Office of the Comptroller, for example, relied on bank management to determine which practices were "unsafe." The Comptroller justified this decision in the following terms:

> The Office believes that aside from the regulations, factors such as market forces and management philosophies are the real determinants of banks' real estate lending practices.

6 15 U.S.C.A. §§ 45, 57a(f) (West 2010).

7 15 U.S.C.A. § 1639(l) (West 2010).

8 *E.g.*, 12 U.S.C.A. §§ 1828(o) (safety and soundness in real estate lending by all depository institutions), 1843(c)(8), 1843 (j)(2)(A) (safety and soundness in activities of affiliates) (West 2010).

9 15 U.S.C.A. § 1602(f) (West 2010) (creditor is a person who regularly extends credit and is the person to whom the debt is initially payable). The statute applies to "consumer credit transactions," which would include residential real estate loans. 15 U.S.C.A. § 1602(h) (West 2010) (primarily for personal, family, or household purposes).

10 Pub. L. No. 97–320, § 322, 96 Stat. 1469 (1982) (real estate lending authority of thrifts); Pub. L. No. 97–320, § 403(a), 96 Stat. 1510 (1982) (real estate lending authority of national banks).

> [T]he Office believes that, in the interest of facilitating national banks' ability to respond to market conditions, removal of the restrictions is warranted.
>
> Decisions concerning the forms and terms of national bank lending are properly the responsibility of each bank's directorate and management.
>
> [A]t this time, regulatory restrictions are unnecessary to ensure the safety and soundness of national banks' real estate lending activities. These activities can be monitored and evaluated through various means including the examination process, surveillance procedures, contact with the industry, and economic reviews.[11]

Similarly, after initially proposing to retain some regulatory requirements such as loan-to-value ratios, the Federal Home Loan Board removed all regulatory requirements for real estate loans except for two—a loan could not exceed 100 per cent of the appraised value of the real estate and a home loan could not have a maximum term longer than 40 years.[12] By 1996, even these limited requirements were lifted.[13]

The agencies' most recent revisions of their uniform real estate lending standards came in 2006 and 2007. An interagency guidance on nontraditional mortgage products was issued in October 2006.[14] The guidance was motivated by the increased offering of loans that allowed borrowers to defer payment of principal and, at times, interest, that is, interest only and payment-option adjustable-rate mortgages, and that imposed reduced documentation requirements.[15] The guidance continued to rely on bank management to decide the policies and products that will serve to minimize risks to the banks and thrifts.[16]

While the agencies recognized the consumer protection issues raised by many product offerings, they continued to rely on disclosure to address such concerns.[17] The guidance merely cautioned, but did not require, banks to include

11 Real Estate Lending by National Banks, 48 Fed. Reg. 40,698, 40,699–700 (Sept. 9, 1983).

12 Implementation of New Powers; Limitation on Loans to One Borrower, 48 Fed. Reg. 23,032, 23,035–37 (May 23, 1983) ("For home loans originated in excess of ninety percent of the initial appraised value, an association must obtain private mortgage insurance for that part of the loan balance that exceeds eighty percent of the property's value.").

13 Office of Thrift Supervision, 61 Fed. Reg. 50,951 (Sept. 30, 1996).

14 Interagency Guidance on Nontraditional Mortgage Product Risks, 71 Fed. Reg. 58,609 (Oct. 4, 2006) (final guidance).

15 Interagency Guidance on Nontraditional Mortgage Products, 70 Fed. Reg. 77,249, 77,252 (Dec. 29, 2005) (proposed guidance).

16 Interagency Guidance on Nontraditional Mortgage Product Risks, 71 Fed. Reg. 58,609, 58,613–15 (Oct. 4 2006) (final guidance).

17 More than traditional ARMS, mortgage products such as payment option ARMs and interest-only mortgages can carry a significant risk of payment shock and negative

an evaluation of the borrower's ability to repay the debt at final maturity at the fully indexed rate and assuming a fully amortizing repayment schedule,[18] and to demonstrate mitigating factors supporting the underwriting decision in the event of risk layering, such as reduced documentation loans.[19] Thus, a largely free-market approach continued to be favored with bank management, determining the appropriate policies to employ and products to offer, and consumers determining the risks such products pose for them.

The last interagency guidance on real estate lending was issued in July 2007. It was motivated by concern over the increasing use of adjustable-rate mortgage products with low initial payments based on an introductory rate that expires after a short period.[20] With respect to consumer protection concerns, apart from cautioning that loan underwriting should consider the borrower's ability to repay, disclosure was once again relied upon to protect consumers.[21]

Turning to the Federal Reserve Board, in 2001 the Fed recognized increased reports of abusive loans which:

> [G]enerally included one or more of the following: (1) making unaffordable loans based on the borrower's home equity without regard to the borrower's ability to repay the obligation; (2) inducing a borrower to refinance a loan repeatedly, even though the refinancing may not be in the borrower's interest, and charging high points and fees each time the loan is refinanced, which decreases the consumer's equity in the home; and (3) engaging in fraud or deception to conceal the true nature of the loan obligation from an unsuspecting or

---

amortization that may not be fully understood by consumers. ... [C]ommunication should help minimize potential consumer confusion and complaints, foster good customer relations, and reduce legal and other risks to the institution. *Id.* at 58,616-17. *See also id.* at 58,612; Interagency Guidance on Nontraditional Mortgage Products, 70 Fed. Reg. 77,249, 77,255 (Dec. 29, 2005) ("Institutions should also ensure that consumers have information that is timely and sufficient for making a sound product selection decision.").

18 *Id.* at 58,614.

19 *Id.*

20 Statement on Subprime Lending, 72 Fed. Reg. 37,569, 37,569–72 (July 10, 2007) (final guidance) ("The Agencies are concerned that these products, typically offered to subprime borrowers, present heightened risks to lenders and borrowers. Often, these products have additional characteristics that increase risk. These include qualifying borrowers based on limited or no documentation of income or imposing substantial prepayment penalties or prepayment penalty periods that extend beyond the initial fixed interest rate period.").

21 Fundamental consumer protection principles relevant to the underwriting and marketing of mortgage loans include: approving loans based on the borrower's ability to repay the loan according to its terms; and providing information that enables consumers to understand material terms, costs, and risks of loan products at a time that will help the consumer select a product. *Id.* at 37,574. These were the only two principles announced.

> unsophisticated borrower—for example, "packing" loans with credit insurance without a consumer's consent.[22]

It also recognized evidence of targeting of vulnerable groups. The Board noted:

> Most of the information the Board received about predatory lending is anecdotal, as it was when Congress passed HOEPA in 1994. The reports of actual cases (including additional Congressional testimony by consumers) are, however, widespread enough to indicate that the problem warrants addressing. Homeowners in certain communities—frequently the elderly, minorities, and women—continue to be targeted with offers of high-cost, home-secured credit with onerous loan terms. The loans, which are typically offered by non-depository institutions, carry high up-front fees and may be based solely on the equity in the consumers' homes without regard to their ability to make the scheduled payments. When homeowners have trouble repaying the debt, they are often pressured into refinancing their loans into new unaffordable, high-fee loans that rarely provide economic benefit to the consumers. These refinancings may occur frequently. The loan balances increase primarily due to fees that are financed resulting in reductions in the consumers' equity in their homes and, in some cases, foreclosure may occur. The loan transactions also may involve fraud and other deceptive practices.[23]

The Federal Reserve's response to the four or more abusive practices it had identified was to address only one of these practices—loan flipping—and the one constraint it imposed was a very narrow one. It imposed a prohibition on refinancing a HOEPA loan into another HOEPA loan unless the new loan was in the borrower's interest, and even that prohibition only applied during the first year of the loan.[24] The Federal Reserve did not address lending without regard to ability to repay, concealed costs such as credit insurance, or targeting of vulnerable groups with high fees. It did not even address refinancing of low-rate loans originated through mortgage assistance programs with high-cost loans.[25] The Board used cost-benefit analysis to set aside that proposed prohibition reasoning that, "(w)hile borrowers with low-rate mortgage loans could benefit from the rule, the benefits appear to be far outweighed by the potential compliance burden for all home-equity lenders."[26]

This leads us to explore further the viewpoint of the Federal Reserve with regard to regulatory intervention in the mortgage markets. I examined the

---

22 Truth in Lending, 66 Fed. Reg. 65,604 (Dec. 20, 2001).

23 *Id.* at 65,607.

24 *Id.* at 65,612–13. The Board also prohibited an additional troubling practice, the use of "due-on-demand" clauses in HOEPA loans. *Id.* at 65,611.

25 *Id.* at 65,613.

26 *Id.* The proposed rule would allow such refinancing only when it was in the borrower's interest. The Board did not explain or document the "compliance burden."

speeches of the Federal Reserve Governors addressing mortgage market issues in three periods in which abusive lending practices were being investigated by Congress—1999–2000, 2003–2004 and 2007–2008. All three periods reveal the same regulatory viewpoint. First, there is a preference for free-market solutions to predatory practices, primarily disclosure and consumer education programs. Second, regulatory intervention is determined by cost-benefit analysis and not by Congress' stated goal of protecting consumers against abusive practices. Third, no action is taken until it is expected that net societal benefits will result from intervention.

Reliance on consumers to protect themselves in a largely free market is apparent, for example, from these remarks on the part of Federal Reserve Governor Gramlich in 2000:

> We should all recognize that the best defense against predatory lending is a thorough knowledge on the part of consumers of their credit options and resources. Educated borrowers who understand their rights under lending contracts and know how to exercise those rights can thwart predatory lenders. As the knowledge base of consumers grows, the market for credit-at-any-cost diminishes. Unfortunately, as is usually the case, the best solutions are often the most difficult to implement. A massive educational campaign is needed to bring about this expanded consumer knowledge.[27]

In fairness, Governor Gramlich privately sought greater oversight over risky mortgage loans consumers could not afford, including investigation and oversight of the practices of bank affiliates. This was especially true after risky loan products proliferated in the period after 2004. However, he was rebuffed by other Federal Reserve officials, especially chairman Alan Greenspan.[28] In part this was due

27 Governor Edward M. Gramlich, *Subprime Lending, Predatory Lending*, Remarks at the Federal Reserve Bank of Philadelphia (Dec. 6, 2000), *available at* http://www.federalreserve.gov/boarddocs/speeches/2000/20001206.htm. See also the following remarks by Governor Gramlich eight months earlier:

> Predatory lending would not exist, or would be relatively rare, if prospective borrowers understood the true nature of their loan contracts. The Neighborhood Reinvestment Corporation (NRC) has an active borrower education program to promote just that type of understanding, and many other public and quasi-public agencies are thinking of following suit. To this point, efforts to extend consumer financial education into high schools have proven very disappointing, but there have been some successes with stock market simulation exercises. Perhaps some of these efforts could be extended to predatory lending issues.

Governor Edward M. Gramlich, *Predatory Lending*, Remarks at the Fair Housing Council of New York (Apr. 14, 2000), *available at* http://www.federalreserve.gov/boarddocs/speeches/2000/200004142.htm.

28 Edmund L. Andrews, *Fed and Regulators Shrugged As the Subprime Crisis Worsened*, NY Times, Dec. 18, 2007, at A1.

to the view that the overall benefits of risky loan practices outweighed possible risks[29]—a net societal benefits test being used as the determinant for government intervention.

The net societal benefits viewpoint was the subject of a lengthy analysis of subprime mortgage lending by Federal Reserve Governor Gramlich in 2004.[30] He explained:

> On a social level, one question is whether the gains afforded by these new market developments outweigh the losses. Another question is whether anything can be done to limit foreclosures.
>
> Despite the caveats, the net social evaluation of these trends is probably a strong positive. The 9 million new homeowners, more than half of whom are minorities and many of whom have lower incomes, suggest that credit and ownership markets are democratizing. Millions of lower-income and minority households now have a chance to own homes and to build wealth; and the vast majority of these new homeowners do not appear to be having credit problems. The rates of serious delinquencies and near-serious delinquencies do raise important warning flags and should inspire renewed efforts to prevent foreclosures, but they do not seem high enough to challenge the overall positive assessment.[31]

Governor Gramlich's individual assessment did focus on equal opportunity for low-income borrowers, and the costs and benefits of increased regulation to such borrowers. By contrast, the Federal Reserve Board's assessment of net social benefits with regard to the decision not to prohibit refinancings of low-cost mortgages, discussed above, balanced the benefits of regulation to the borrower against the costs to the industry.

As discussed above, Governor Gramlich did later attempt to persuade other Federal Reserve Board members to increase oversight over risky loan practices, but was rebuffed, in part based on the view that the overall societal benefits of risky loan practices outweighed possible risks.[32]

A related viewpoint voiced at times by Federal Reserve members is one that examines the need for intervention at the macroeconomic level. Federal Reserve Chairman Greenspan's remarks on the dangers of high loan-to-value mortgage

---

29 *Id.* (officials, including Alan Greenspan, praised subprime lenders for helping families buy homes even while they recognized that the loosening of mortgage credit terms increased financial risk).

30 Governor Edward M. Gramlich, *Subprime Mortgage Lending: Benefits, Costs and Challenges*, Remarks at the Financial Services Roundtable Annual Housing Policy Meeting (May 21, 2004), *available at* http://www.federalreserve.gov/boarddocs/speeches/2004/20040521/default.htm.

31 *Id.*

32 *Supra* notes 28–29 and accompany text.

lending illustrate this view. Justifying his conclusion that no government intervention was necessary, Greenspan noted:

> [M]easures of household financial stress do not, at least to date, appear overly worrisome.
>
> About three-fourths of all outstanding first-lien mortgages were originated with a loan-to-value ratio of 80 per cent or less, and in aggregate, the current loan-to-value ratio is estimated to be around 45 percent. Even though some down payments are borrowed, it would take a large, and historically most unusual, fall in home prices to wipe out a significant part of home equity. Many of those who purchased their residence more than a year ago have equity buffers in their homes adequate to withstand any price decline other than a very deep one.[33]

As to the size of the debt burden households are subject to, the analysis was on the same terms:

> To be sure, some households are stretched to their limits. The persistently elevated bankruptcy rate remains a concern, as it indicates pockets of distress in the household sector. But the vast majority appear able to calibrate their borrowing and spending to minimize financial difficulties. Thus, short of a significant fall in overall household income or in home prices, debt servicing is unlikely to become destabilizing.[34]

Under the Federal Reserve's approach, millions of homeowners could be unwittingly subjected to loans that they cannot repay, and therefore subjected to loss of their homes and equity as long as most homeowners were not overburdened and benefits resulted for the economy from such lending. Similarly, vulnerable groups of borrowers could be stripped of equity through excessive interest rates, excessive fees, and excessive prepayment penalties as long as the economy as a whole benefited from unregulated lending practices. In other words, under sanction of law, wealth was transferred from vulnerable groups to business interests in the name of net societal benefit.

In summary, the view of the federal regulatory agencies was that statutory or regulatory restrictions on mortgage practices and products might reduce risks, but did not maximize wealth. The preferred approach was to lift statutory and regulatory restrictions in order to maximize wealth, and to rely on market discipline to avoid excess risk taking. The resort to deregulation did not completely ignore the aim

33 Alan Greenspan, Chairman, Fed. Reserve Bd., *The Mortgage Markets and Consumer Debt*, Remarks at America's Community Bankers' Annual Convention (Oct. 19, 2004), *available at* http://www.federalreserve.gov/boarddocs/speeches/2004/20041019/default.htm.

34 *Id.*

of weeding out unfair or deceptive mortgage practices, since Congress insisted upon it over the years. However, the threshold for regulatory intervention—net societal benefits—relegated that aim to secondary importance behind wealth maximization. Moreover, market discipline was presumed to effectively substitute for government intervention to avoid the emergence or prevalence of unsafe and unfair mortgage products. In the case of unfair mortgage products, the discipline was to be exercised by the consumers, who would presumably avoid unfair, as well as unsafe, mortgage practices and products.

The Congressional Viewpoint Prior to Dodd-Frank

To address the viewpoint of the Congress regarding the proper means to ensure consumer protection in home mortgage-lending transactions, I examined Congressional activity over the course of the last three decades. The question was whether Congress embraced the view that market discipline, including caveat emptor, was the proper means to avoid abusive lending practices. The evidence does not support such a conclusion.

Congress did embrace a free-market approach in one limited sense. In 1980, it preempted state usury limits on first-lien residential mortgage loans.[35] This was done to address the "… adverse effects of usury ceilings on credit availability ..." and ensure the stability and continued viability of the financial system.[36] However, Congress did not embrace a free-market approach in other legislative enactments as the sole or primary means to achieve consumer protections, that is, fairness and equal opportunity in the mortgage loan market. Even the legislative history of the 1980 DIDMCA cautioned that "[i]t is not the intent of section 302 to repeal existing consumer safeguards that the Federal Home Loan Bank Board has adopted with respect to real estate loans, or prevent the Board from enacting consumer safeguards in the future."[37]

A second legislative enactment frequently used as an example of Congressional embrace of a free-market approach is the 1982 Garn-St Germain Act. This is a misunderstanding of the Act. The Act lifted statutory requirements for real estate loans on the part of insured institutions, such as required loan-to-value ratios. However, there is a distinction between lifting statutory requirements for mortgage loans and embracing a free-market approach; that is, relying only, or primarily,

35 Depository Institutions Deregulation and Monetary Control Act (DIDMCA), 12 U.S.C.A. § 1735f-7 (West 2010).

36 S. Rep. No. 96–368, at 19 (1979).

37 *Id.* at 18. The Senate report specifically noted that only state limits that are included in the annual percentage rate are preempted and not other limits such as "... limitations on prepayment charges, attorney fees, late charges or similar limitations designed to protect borrowers." *Id.* at 19.

on market forces to protect consumers against unfair practices and protect the financial system against unsound practices.

Titles 3 and 4 of the Garn-St Germain Act lifted the rigid statutory requirements for mortgage loans originated by federally chartered banks and thrifts, such as stipulated maximum loan-to-value ratios.[38] It substituted a general authorization to make real estate loans, and this authorization was subject to the "restrictions and requirements" the federal regulators may prescribe by regulation or order.[39] The change was made to permit banks greater flexibility in order to meet the needs of first-time homebuyers and effectively compete with less regulated competitors.[40] Congress did not require a free-market approach as a substitute. Rather, statutory mandates were replaced with an authorization of regulatory restrictions.[41] This was recognized by the federal regulators in 1983 when they issued new regulations pursuant to the Garn-St Germain Act.[42] It was the federal regulators that chose to utilize a free-market approach.

Title 8 of the Garn-St Germain Act, otherwise known as the Alternative Mortgage Transactions Parity Act of 1982, allowed non-federally chartered housing creditors to offer alternative mortgage transactions to the extent that

38 For example, prior to its amendment in 1982, 12 U.S.C. § 371, governing the real estate lending powers of national banks, required a maximum loan to value ratio of 90 per cent when the collateral was improved real estate, and required any loan secured by a one to four family residence with a loan to value ratio in excess of 75 per cent to contain installment payments sufficient to amortize the entire principle of the loan within a period of not more than 30 years.

39 12 U.S.C.A. § 371(a) (West 2010) (Comptroller of the Currency); 12 U.S.C.A. § 1464(c) (West 2010) (previously Federal Home Loan Bank Board, and later Office of Thrift Supervision).

40 S. Rep. No. 97–536, at 25–26 (1982). *See also id.* at 13–15 (additional asset flexibility and earnings opportunities are provided to thrift institutions in order to "compete effectively in a marketplace characterized by payment of market interest rates"); S. Rep. No. 97–641, at 88 (1982) (Conf. Rep.) (liberalized provisions in the bill are intended to strengthen the thrift industry so that it may maintain its place as the nation's primary home lender).

41 Pub. L. No. 97–320, § 403(a), 96 Stat. 1510 (1982) (a national bank may make loans secured by interests in "real estate, subject to such terms, conditions, and limitations as may be prescribed by the Comptroller of the Currency").

42 The Office of the Comptroller of the Currency summarized its options in 1983 as follows:

1. Adopt a regulation that reaffirms the limitations that existed under 12 U.S.C. 371 before the 1982 amendment.

2. Adopt a regulation that modifies the limitations that existed under 12 U.S.C. 371 before the 1982 amendment and currently exist in the interpretive rulings.

3. Adopt a regulation that imposes no limitations on national banks' real estate lending and rescinds current regulations which do impose limitations.

Real Estate Lending by National Banks, 48 Fed. Reg. 40,698, 40,699 (Sept. 9, 1983). The Comptroller chose the third option.

such transactions were authorized by federal regulators and subject to the federal regulations governing such instruments.[43] Congress concluded that alternative mortgage transactions were "essential to the provision of an adequate supply of credit secured by residential property necessary to meet the demand expected during the 1980's …"[44] However, it never required that a free-market approach would be used to determine the *terms* of such transactions. Rather, once again Congress authorized regulatory restrictions.[45]

This conclusion was confirmed when Congress revisited its decision to lift statutory mortgage-lending rules. This was done in 1991. The Federal Deposit Insurance Corporation Improvement Act of 1991[46] responded to losses suffered by insured institutions due to risky practices, including risky real estate lending practices. Congress was concerned that banks responded to their eroding market position by putting more funds into higher-risk real estate deals, highly leveraged transactions, and loans to less-developed countries. These investments carried higher yields, but caused many institutions to suffer financial losses.[47] Congress responded by cautioning banks that deposits must be invested wisely and to accomplish this result stated that banks must be "closely supervised."[48] In addition, in the 1991 statute, Congress provided that: "[t]he appropriate Federal banking agencies are required to jointly adopt uniform regulations prescribing standards for real estate lending by insured depository institutions."[49] Thus, in 1991, Congress replaced the option of regulatory restrictions with a requirement of regulatory intervention.

When formulating new standards for real estate lending, the regulators were also directed by Congress to consider three factors: "the risks presented to the insurance funds, the safety and soundness of the institution, and the availability of credit."[50] As in earlier statutory directives concerning safety and soundness requirements, the decision to intervene and type of intervention chosen was not based on a net societal benefits standard. Indeed, such a standard has never been mentioned by the Congress in its consideration of safety and soundness issues.

Access to mortgage credit is an important goal embraced by Congress and it motivated the actions of Congress in 1980 and 1982. It is often overlooked

43 Pub. L. No. 97–320, § 804, 96 Stat. 1469 (1982) (current version at 12 U.S.C.A. § 3803 (West 2010)).

44 *Id.* § 801 (current version at 12 U.S.C.A. § 3803 (West 2010)).

45 *Id.* § 804(a) (current version at 12 U.S.C.A. § 3803 (West 2010)) (transactions by non-federally chartered housing creditors must be "in accordance with regulations governing alternative mortgage transactions as issued" by the federal banking regulators).

46 Pub. L. No. 102-242, 105 Stat. 2236 (1991).

47 H.R. Rep. No. 102–330, at 91 (1991).

48 *Id.* at 95.

49 *Id.* at 136 (emphasis added). This requirement was manifest in section 304 of the Act, Pub. L. No. 102–242, § 304, 105 Stat. 2354 (1991) (current version at 12 U.S.C.A. § 1828(o) (West 2010)).

50 H.R. Rep. No. 102–330, at 136 (1991).

that Congress also embraced a subsidiary goal. In numerous enactments over the last three decades, Congress has embraced the view that lending institutions must avoid abusive practices, including unfair practices, when providing access to credit. This is a restraint imposed on all institutions providing mortgage credit and not just for federally chartered or insured institutions. To achieve this goal, Congress has endorsed government intervention when necessary to avoid unfair lending practices, including outright prohibitions against particular abusive practices. It has not relied solely on market forces to address abusive practices. In addition, it has not embraced a net societal benefits standard as the determinant of a decision to intervene in the mortgage market. Such a standard was not required by the explicit terms or in the legislative history of Congressional enactments prior to 2010. Indeed, it was not even explicitly mentioned except in the legislative history of HOEPA, discussed below.

It is often assumed that the Real Estate Settlement Procedures Act of 1974 (RESPA) is the primary federal response to possible deceptive and abusive practices in the field of mortgage lending and that its response was only disclosure. This leads to the mistaken conclusion that Congress was embracing a free-market approach, namely full disclosure, as a means to ensure that consumers protect themselves. This is only half the story. RESPA is not the only federal enactment addressing abusive mortgage practices, and disclosure was not its only response. When enacting RESPA in 1974 Congress identified two major problems:

1. Abusive and unreasonable practices within the real estate settlement process that increase settlement costs to homebuyers without providing any real benefits to them; and
2. The lack of understanding on the part of most homebuyers about the settlement process and its costs, which lack of understanding makes it difficult for a free market for settlement services to function at maximum efficiency.[51]

As to the justification for government action, it was: (a) significant consumer losses; plus (b) the inability of consumers to protect themselves, that justified government intervention. Net societal benefit was not an additional prerequisite to government intervention. Indeed, Congress noted, "while the making of such payments [referral fees, kickbacks, rebates and unearned commissions for settlement services] may heretofore have been necessary from a competitive standpoint in order to obtain or retain business, and in some areas may even be permitted by state law, it is the intention of section 7 to prohibit such payments, kickbacks, rebates or unearned

51 S. Rep. No. 93–866, at 1, 4 US Code Cong. and Admin. News at 6547 (1974). A third problem was the complexities and inefficiencies in the present system for recording land titles. *See also* the Congressional findings and statement of purposes in the Act, Pub. L. No. 93–533, § 2, 88 Stat. 1724 (1974), which identifies the need to protect consumers from unnecessarily high settlement charges caused by abusive practices.

commissions."[52] Thus, there was recognition of benefits to the industry of existing practices, but a decision to prohibit such practices nonetheless.

As to the response employed by the Congress in RESPA, one response was disclosure.[53] However, a second response was *prohibition* of kickback or referral fee arrangements.[54] This second response addressed the problem of abusive practices that increased settlement costs. Direct government intervention was employed to stop abusive practices in addition to disclosure.[55] Subsequent Congressional responses occurred in 1988 and 1994. Both subsequent responses were similarly two-fold—both disclosure and prohibition of particular abusive practices.

In 1988 Congress addressed consumer concerns regarding home equity loans that had increased fivefold between 1981 and 1986.[56] First, disclosure and advertising requirements were imposed for home equity loans, and second home equity protections were legislated.[57]

Congress wanted to "assure that consumers get necessary and important disclosures before they open home equity loan accounts ... [so as to] enable consumers to understand fully the conditions of this new form of consumer borrowing."[58] This was not, however, Congress' only response. The bill's main sponsor explained that: "H.R. 3011 basically embodies a disclosure approach. However, there are a few areas where restrictions on certain contractual practices used by lenders are warranted." [59] Therefore, the statute required lenders to base variable rate loans on an index that is publicly available and not under the control of the creditor, prohibited unilateral termination of a home equity credit plan

52 S. Rep. No. 93–866, at 5 (1974).

53 This was contained in sections 4, 5, 6 and 7 of the Act providing for uniform settlement statements and advance disclosure of settlement costs. Pub. L. No. 93–533, § 4–7, 88 Stat. 1724 (1974) (current version at 12 U.S.C.A. § § 2605–2606 (West 2010)).

54 This was contained in section 8, Pub. L. No. 93–533, § 8, 88 Stat. 1724 (1974) (current version at 12 U.S.C.A. § 2607 (West 2010)).

55 Indeed section 10 of the Act required the Secretary of HUD to monitor the implementation of the various anti-abusive and disclosure provisions of the bill and report back to Congress on whether there is any necessity for further legislation and the corrective measures that need to be taken. *See* Pub. L. No. 93–533, § 10, 88 Stat. 1724 (1974), and discussion contained in S. Rep. No. 93–866, at 7–8 (1974). Subsequently, the Real Estate Settlement Procedures Act Amendments of 1975 modified section 8 of RESPA to make clear that cooperative brokerage and referral arrangements of real estate agents are exempt from the prohibition against kickbacks and unearned fees. Pub. L. No. 94–205, § 7, 89 Stat. 1157 (1975).

56 134 Cong. Rec. H4,468–02 (June 20, 1988) (statement of Representative Annunzio, co-sponsor).

57 Home Equity Loan Consumer Protection Act of 1988, Pub. L. No. 100–709, §§ 2 (disclosure and advertising requirements), 3 (home equity protections) (1988).

58 134 Cong. Rec. H4,468–02 (June 20, 1988) (statement of Representative Annunzio, co-sponsor).

59 *Id.* (statement of Representative Price).

and acceleration of the outstanding balance (except on the basis of three criteria specified in the statute), and prohibited lenders from unilaterally changing the terms of the home equity credit plan. In 1988, as in 1974, disclosure was not the exclusive response and market discipline on the part of consumers was not the only form of protection embraced. Instead, government intervention was embraced in the form of prohibition of specific abusive practices that had been uncovered.

Congress again addressed abusive lending practices in 1994 with enactment of the Home Ownership and Equity Protection Act. Here, the goal embraced by Congress—not only access to credit, but access to credit without abusive terms—was again witnessed. In addition, its rejection of a free-market approach was made clear. The Senate Report on the Act explains that "[t]he legislation generally prevents lenders from including certain potentially abusive terms ... in high cost mortgages."[60]

Congress had uncovered evidence that some home improvement contractors, second mortgage brokers, and other lenders acted in a "predatory fashion, targeting unsophisticated, low-income homeowners and 'skimming' equity from the neighborhoods through high-rate, high fee loans."[61] Congress' response to these problems it had uncovered was, once again, two-fold. One response was disclosure—a new streamlined disclosure form that provided additional information regarding the risks of high cost loans.[62] However, the second response was a prohibition of identified abusive practices. As the Senate Report on the Act explained:

> The Committee finds that certain loan terms are particularly problematic and often mislead borrowers about the true cost of a loan. Consequently, the legislation prohibits High Cost Mortgages from containing the following terms: prepayment penalties, points on loan amounts refinanced, default interest rates above the rate prior to the default, balloon payments, negative amortization, or prepayment of more than two of the periodic payments.[63]

The final version of the bill enacted by Congress also prohibited loans made without regard to the borrower's ability to repay.[64]

The motivation for Congressional intervention was: (a) losses suffered by low-income residents targeted by reverse redlining, resulting in "skimming" of equity

60 S. Rep. No. 103–169, at 2 (1993).

61 *Id.* at 22.

62 Pub. L. No. 103–325, § 152, 108 Stat. 2160 (current version at 15 U.S.C.A. § 1639 (West 2010)).

63 S. Rep. No. 103–169, at 25 (1993).

64 15 U.S.C.A. § 1639(c)–(h) (West 2010). HOEPA's prohibitions were applied to the abusive lending transactions indentified in Congressional hearings, namely home equity loans and refinancings, and were applied to "high cost loans." 15 U.S.C.A. §§ 1602(w), 1602(aa) (West 2010).

from low-income neighborhoods; and (b) which losses residents could not avoid because they were misled, were unaware of the terms, or were unsophisticated concerning the mortgage market, and were, therefore, taken advantage of by lenders.[65] Once again, net societal benefit was not the determinant of the decision to intervene or not intervene. Rather the determinant was significant consumer losses that consumers could not avoid.

To say that net societal benefit has not determined the decision to intervene is not to say that Congress has not considered the costs and benefits of a proposed action. Thus, the Senate Report cited testimony from the Comptroller of the Currency that the legislation would not impose unreasonable compliance costs or interfere with legitimate financial transactions.[66] In addition, the Senate Committee considered whether the bill would restrict the flow of credit.[67] To avoid this adverse effect, it focused the Act's prohibitions "… on the segment of the home equity loan market most vulnerable to abuse."[68] Most revealing, the Committee recognized that prepayment penalties may compensate a lender if the borrower repays the loan before the date specified by the loan terms—a benefit to the lender. Nonetheless, "[i]n the case of High Cost Mortgages … the broader public interest is served by eliminating barriers that might prevent a borrower from repaying the loan."[69]

Thus, while costs and benefits of proposed government intervention were considered, they were not used to establish a net societal benefits standard as the determinant of a decision to intervene or not to intervene in the mortgage market. Rather, the possible adverse effects of intervention to the industry or to consumers, at times, were addressed by minimizing such adverse effects. At other times, they were ignored because of the public interest in halting abusive loan practices.

In 1994, Congress not only prohibited certain abusive practices it had identified. It also granted the Federal Reserve Board the power to prohibit other unfair, deceptive, or abusive practices that it may uncover in the future.[70] The legislative history explains the approach embraced to address additional abusive practices:

> the Committee also realizes that new products and practices may emerge that facilitate reverse redlining. For this reason, the legislation requires the

65 S. Rep. No. 103–169, at 21–22; *see also id.* at 24 ("the Committee is seeking to prevent unscrupulous lenders from … tak[ing] advantage of unwitting consumers"); *id.* at 25 ("certain loan terms are particularly problematic and often mislead borrowers").

66 *Id.* at 23.

67 *Id.* at 24.

68 *Id.* This was the justification for the annual percentage rate trigger in the definition of high cost mortgages subject to the Act's prohibitions.

69 *Id.* at 26.

70 "(2) Prohibitions, — The Board, by regulation or order, shall prohibit acts or practices in connection with … (A) mortgage loans that the Board finds to be unfair, deceptive, or designed to evade the provisions of this section; and (B) refinancing of mortgage loans that the Board finds to be associated with abusive lending practices, or that are otherwise not in the interest of the borrower." 15 U.S.C.A. § 1639(l)(2) (West 2010).

> Federal Reserve Board to prohibit acts or practices in connection with High Cost Mortgages that it finds to be unfair, deceptive, or designed to evade the provisions of this section, It is the Committee's intention that the Federal Reserve will examine complaints and utilize this legislation to provide adequate protections for consumers under Truth in Lending.[71]

There is one exception to the conclusion that Congress never even explicitly mentioned a net societal benefits standard in its legislative enactments regarding consumer-oriented mortgage market transactions in the period 1974 through 2009.

Regulatory power over unfair lending practices, as opposed to unsafe and unsound lending practices, results from HOEPA and Section 5 of the FTC Act. HOEPA permits the Federal Reserve Board to prohibit acts or practices in connection with "mortgage loans that the Board finds to be unfair, deceptive, or designed to evade the provisions of this section."[72] The Conference Report on the Act explains that, "[i]n making any determination, the Board should look to the standards employed for interpreting state unfair and deceptive trade practices acts and the Federal Unfair and Deceptive Practices Act (15 U.S.C. § 45(a)(1))."[73]

The Congress that adopted HOEPA and included this explanation in the Conference Report is the same Congress that amended the Federal Unfair and Deceptive Practices Act, otherwise known as the FTC Act. The 1994 Amendment provided that:

> The Commission shall have no authority under this section or section 18 to declare unlawful an act or practice on the grounds that such act or practice is unfair unless the act or practice causes or is likely to cause substantial injury to consumers which is not reasonably avoidable by consumers themselves and not outweighed by countervailing benefits to consumers or to competition. In determining whether an act or practice is unfair, the Commission may consider established public policies as evidence to be considered with all other evidence. Such public policy considerations may not serve as a primary basis for such determination.[74]

---

71 S. Rep. No. 103–169, at 27 (1993) (emphasis added).

72 15 U.S.C.A. § 1639(l)(2) (West 2010). This is broader than the scope of other provisions in HOEPA, such as the explicit prohibitions on certain abusive practices, that apply to "a mortgage referred to in section 103(aa)." Section 103(aa) employs the interest rate trigger of greater than 10 percentage points above the Treasury yield on comparable Treasury securities or the fee trigger of points and fees in excess of 8 percent of the total loan or $400, whichever is greater, and excludes home purchase loans. Such section 103(aa) mortgage loans are typically referred to as HOEPA loans.

73 H.R. Rep. No. 103–652, at 162 (1994) (Conf. Rep.).

74 Federal Trade Commission Act Amendments of 1994, Pub. L. No 103–312, § 9, 108 Stat. 1691 (1994) (codified as amended at 15 U.S.C.A. § 45(n) (West 2010)).

This permitted the regulators to claim that in the mortgage markets as well there should be a preference for consumer self-protection. In addition, the regulators could claim that even in the mortgage markets, the threshold for governmental intervention should be based on a net societal benefits standard, as well as an evaluation that examines the costs and benefits not only to consumers, but to the economy as a whole.

This was the agencies' interpretation of Congress' 1994 enactment. The Federal Reserve Board in its July 2008 rule on unfair mortgage practices noted that state deceptive practices law could be the standard used to determine whether to intervene in the mortgage market. However, it chose to adopt the net societal benefits test imposed for non-mortgage transactions as the standard for intervention.[75] Similarly, the other bank regulatory agencies in regulatory guidance on unfair mortgage practices chose to employ the FTC's net societal benefits test.[76]

There is an alternative view. The direction in the Conference Report on HOEPA, that the Federal Reserve should "look to" the standards contained in the FTC Act, does not compel the conclusion that mortgage market regulation through HOEPA must be subject to exactly the same standards and basis for regulatory intervention as is used in the FTC Act.

Indeed, the FTC Act provides expressly that the FTC's power to prevent unfair or deceptive practices does not apply to savings associations, banks, or federal credit unions, among others.[77] Rather, such authority is explicitly granted to the federal banking agencies,[78] including the power to issue regulations governing unfair mortgage acts and practices that are applicable to independent mortgage companies, which is granted to the Federal Reserve Board.[79] One could view the mortgage market as different from the wide range of consumer practices covered by the FTC Act, and therefore favor regulatory intervention more readily. The 1991 legislation, for example, had required regulatory restrictions. In addition, the agencies' interpretation ignores the direction in the Conference report to also "look to" state law.

Most states have not adopted the FTC's current standard for defining unfairness and imposing regulatory restrictions. Rather, they have embraced a more liberal standard that does not include a net societal benefits test.[80] The standard embraced

75 Truth in Lending, 73 Fed. Reg. 44,522, 44,529 (July 30, 2008). The Board stated it "considered" both the FTC standard and state standards, but in fact its analysis is based on the FTC standard, including a net societal benefits test.

76 *See* Unfair or Deceptive Acts or Practices, 72 Fed. Reg. 43,570, 43,573–74 (Aug. 6, 2007).

77 15 U.S.C.A. § 45(a)(2) (West 2010).

78 15 U.S.C.A. § 57a(f)(1) (West 2010).

79 15 U.S.C.A. § 1639(l)(2) (West 2010).

80 Matthew A. Edwards, *The Law, Marketing and Behavioral Economics of Consumer Rebates,* 12 Stan. J. L. Bus. & Fin. 362, 404 n.223 (2006–2007) (most states do not apply the current FTC unfairness standard); *see also* Truth in Lending, 73 Fed. Reg. 44,522, 44,529 (July 30, 2008) ("A number of states follow an unfairness standard formerly used by the FTC.

by most states provides additional evidence of the ethical viewpoint accepted by US society. The Federal Reserve Board admitted this was an alternative basis for intervention available to it, but chose to adopt the net societal benefits test.[81] Other federal banking agencies had made the same admission and the same decision.[82]

Congress responds to particular situations presented to it and typically tailors its response to the narrow situation at hand. In limiting the power of the FTC, Congress was responding to earlier overly broad FTC rules, especially rules aimed at commercial advertising.[83] However, the same Congress responded differently to abusive mortgage practices when it adopted HOEPA. It is a reasonable view that Congress viewed the appropriate threshold for regulatory intervention in the mortgage markets to be different.

In summary, Congress over the years has signaled willingness, perhaps preference, to employ government intervention to ensure fairness in residential mortgage-lending transactions, as well as safety and soundness. Current regulatory policy undermines the goals embraced by Congress. The net societal benefits test leaves consumers with no protection, even when faced with practices against which they are unable to effectively protect themselves. The disparate impact of such a scenario is one disproportionately stripping equity from low-income, as well as minority, residents and communities.

Re-examination of Agency and Congressional Viewpoints in Light of the Mortgage Crisis

The Federal Reserve Board's 2008 Intervention

In 2008 the Federal Reserve Board significantly expanded consumer protections through increased regulation of the mortgage market. All this was done without

---

Under this standard, an act or practice is unfair where it offends public policy; or is immoral, unethical, oppressive, or unscrupulous; and causes substantial injury to consumers.").

81 *Id.* The Federal Reserve stated it "considered" both the FTC standard and the state standards, but in its analysis of the justification for the rules adopted it in fact followed the FTC standard.

82 *E.g.*, Department of the Treasury, Office of Thrift Supervision, Unfair or Deceptive Acts or Practices, Advance Notice of Proposed Rulemaking, 72 Fed. Reg. 43,570, 43,573–74 (Aug. 6, 2007) (OTS notes it has the option of adopting the FTC standard as its principle for regulatory intervention or it could follow the direction of state law models, among others).

83 140 Cong. Rec. S11316–17 (April 11, 1994) (discussion of conference report compromise measure); *see also* S. Rep. No. 103–130, at 13 (1993) (greater guidance is needed on the meaning of unfairness to prevent the FTC from abandoning the principles of the 1980 and 1982 guidance it had formulated); Matthew A. Edwards, *The FTC and New Paternalism,* 60 Admin. L. Rev. 323, 341–42 (2008) (discussing board range of FTC rules during the 1970's including the controversial rulemaking effort aimed at restricting children's television advertising).

any Congressional amendments to HOEPA, confirming that the Federal Reserve had more regulatory power and discretion than it had exercised in the past.

The 2008 amendments to the HOEPA regulations, effective 1 October 2009, significantly broadened the reach of new regulatory prohibitions. It established a category of loans called "higher-priced mortgage loans," in order to subject such loans to additional prohibitions and other consumer protections.[84] Its definition of that new term caused its new regulations to apply to all subprime mortgages.

The Federal Reserve also rejected its earlier reliance on "guidance" rather than regulations to address abusive lending practices. In doing so, it admitted the shortcomings of a reliance on guidance:

> Guidance … is not necessarily implemented uniformly by all originators. Originators who are not subject to routine examination and supervision may not adhere to guidance as closely as originators who are. Guidance also does not provide individual consumers who have suffered harm because of abusive lending practices an opportunity for redress. The new and expanded consumer protections that the Board is adopting apply uniformly to all creditors and are enforceable by federal and state supervisory and enforcement agencies and in many cases by borrowers.[85]

The Federal Reserve issued regulations that add four additional protections, in the form of regulatory prohibitions or requirements, for borrowers with such "higher-priced mortgage loans." Under the new regulations: (a) lenders are prohibited from making a loan without regard to borrowers' ability to repay the loan from income and assets other than the home's value, and a lender must assess repayment ability based on the highest scheduled payment in the first seven years of the loan; (b) creditors must verify the income and assets they rely upon to determine repayment ability; (c) any prepayment penalty is banned if the payment can change in the initial four years, and for other higher-priced loans, a prepayment penalty period cannot last for more than two years; and (d) creditors must establish escrow accounts for property taxes and homeowner's insurance for all first-lien mortgage loans.[86] In addition, the regulations add some protections for all loans secured by a consumer's principal dwelling, even if the loan is not a "higher-priced mortgage loan."[87]

---

84 Truth in Lending, 73 Fed. Reg. 44,522 (July 30, 2008). The Federal Reserve Board will publish the "average prime offer rate," based on a survey currently published by Freddie Mac. A loan is higher-priced if it is a first-lien mortgage and has an annual percentage rate that exceeds this index by 1.5 percentage points or 3.5 percentage points if it is a subordinate-lien mortgage.

85 Truth in Lending, 73 Fed. Reg. 44,522, 44,528 (July 30, 2008).

86 *Id.* at 44,539-60. No "pattern or practice" of making loans without regard to ability to repay needs to be demonstrated, as it was in earlier regulations. *Id.* at 44,543.

87 *Id.* at 44,563. The protections are as follows: (a) "[c]reditors and mortgage brokers are prohibited from coercing a real estate appraiser to misstate a home's value," (b) "[c]

The new Federal Reserve regulations apply to home purchase loans, refinancings, and home equity loans. All of the 2008 regulations were issued on the basis of the Federal Reserve's authority to prohibit acts or practices that are unfair, deceptive, or designed to evade the provisions of HOEPA.[88]

The actions of the Federal Reserve reflect a partial change in viewpoint. On the issue of consumer self-protection, the Board admitted that consumers are often *unable* to protect themselves due to: (a) limitations on price and product transparency; (b) the complexity of products offered and the limits of any form of disclosure to provide an effective means of protection for consumers; (c) misaligned incentives among originators and the lack of transparency regarding the roles and incentives of originators; and (d) the behavioral tendency of limited shopping and limited focus on the part of consumers.[89]

However, what did not change in 2008 is the significant barrier to regulatory intervention in the mortgage markets arising due to the Fed's embrace of a net societal benefits test. The Federal Reserve's proposed rule makes it clear that it decided to intervene in the mortgage market based on a conclusion that the net societal costs of the current regulatory approach far outweighed its benefits.[90] Federal Reserve Chairman, Bernanke, noted:

> Rates of mortgage delinquencies and foreclosures have been increasing rapidly lately, imposing large costs on borrowers, their communities, and the national economy. Although the high rate of delinquency has a number of causes, it seems clear that unfair or deceptive acts and practices by lenders resulted in the

ompanies that service mortgage loans are prohibited from engaging in certain practices, such as pyramiding late fees. In addition, servicers are required to credit consumers' loan payments as of the date of receipt and provide a payoff statement within a reasonable time of request," and (c) "[c]reditors must provide a good faith estimate of the loan costs, including a schedule of payments, within three days after a consumer applies for any mortgage loan," including home improvement loans and refinancings. Press Release, Federal Reserve Board, Board Issues Final Rule Amending Home Mortgage Provisions of Regulation Z (Truth in Lending) (July 14, 2008). For all mortgages, the rule also imposes additional advertising standards. Advertising rules require additional information about rates, monthly payments, and other loan features. The final rule bans seven deceptive or misleading advertising practices, including representing that a rate or payment is "fixed" when it can change. Truth in Lending, 73 Fed. Reg. 44,522, 44,574 (July 30, 2008).

88 15 U.S.C.A. § 1639(l)(2) (West 2010).

89 Truth in Lending, 73 Fed. Reg. 44,522, 44,524–26 (July 30, 2008).

90 The proposed rule discusses the serious levels of delinquency in subprime loans generally and even in near prime loans, the severe consequences of default for borrowers and the entire communities where they are located, the expectation that delinquencies and foreclosure will rise further, and the risks posed not only to borrowers but to creditors. Truth in Lending, 73 Fed. Reg. 1,672, 1,674 (Jan. 9, 2008) (proposed rule).

> extension of many loans, particularly high-cost loans, that were inappropriate for or misled the borrower.[91]

This viewpoint was not only reflected in the motivation for the Federal Reserve's decision to act. It was also reflected in its reaffirmation of its embrace of the FTC's standard for defining unfair practices under the FTC Act as the governing standard under HOEPA as well.[92] The Board stated that it had "considered" both the standards currently applied by the FTC as well as standards applied under similar state statutes.[93] However, when deciding whether to adopt certain regulatory prohibitions, the Board employed the FTC standard, including an analysis of whether injury is outweighed by countervailing benefits to consumers or to competition.[94] It did not analyze whether a practice offends public policy, is immoral, unethical, oppressive, or unscrupulous—the standard employed by most states.

Thus, recent action of the Federal Reserve demonstrates that it continues to adhere to the position that if an act or practice causes or is likely to cause substantial injury to consumers, and the injury is not reasonably avoidable by consumers, the Federal Reserve still will not intervene unless such injury

---

91 Ben S. Bernanke, Chairman, Fed. Reserve Bd., Statement (July 14, 2008), *available at* http://www.federalreserve.gov/newsevents/press/bcreg/bernankeregz20080714.htm.

92 Truth in Lending, *supra* note 87, at 44,529.

93 *Id.* The Board notes that the Conference Report on HOEPA asks the Board to look to the standards under state law and the FTC Act. It also notes that:

> Many states also have adopted statutes prohibiting unfair or deceptive acts or practices, and these statutes employ a variety of standards, many of them different from the standards currently applied to the FTC Act. A number of states follow an unfairness standard formerly used by the FTC. Under this standard, an act or practice is unfair where it offends public policy; or is immoral, unethical, oppressive, or unscrupulous; and causes substantial injury to consumers.

Id. at 44,530 (footnote omitted).

94 *Id.* at 44,543 (prohibition of lending without regard to borrower's ability to repay — Board considers substantial costs to borrowers and communities), 44,554 (prepayment penalties' injuries outweigh their benefits in case of higher-priced mortgaged and HOEPA loans with payment increases after a few years, but for other types of loans the injuries and benefits are much closer to being in equipoise), 44,559 (benefits from escrows for taxes and insurance outweigh costs.). The Board's discussion emphasizes costs and benefits to consumers. However, this is not the Board's only concern. For example, in making its decision regarding the scope of the prohibition on prepayment penalties, the Board considered if prepayment penalties increase market liquidity by permitting creditors and investors to price directly and efficiently for prepayment risk. *Id.* at 44,554. Similarly, when discussing its decision to require tax and insurance escrows, the Board noted the potentially substantial costs to creditors in setting up or acquiring escrow capabilities, and noted that escrows can improve loan performance to the advantage of creditors, investors and consumers alike. *Id.* at 44,559.

outweighs countervailing benefits to society. This creates a legal environment in which the law permits financial exploitation of vulnerable individuals.

Congressional Action in the Dodd-Frank Act

In the Dodd-Frank Act, Congress responded in the same manner as it had when it enacted RESPA in 1974, when it enacted the Home Equity Loan Consumer Protection Act in 1988, and when it enacted HOEPA in 1994. It rejected a reliance on market discipline to address the abusive practices identified and instead prohibited the practices in question. In the 2007–2010 period, the primary cause of concern was mortgage loans made to consumers without regard to the borrowers' ability to repay. Congress was motivated to act due to a concern that consumers had been subjected to "unfair, deceptive and abusive acts that so often trap them in unaffordable financial products."[95] The concern was that this had occurred because many borrowers were not able to protect themselves. This was true because they did not and could not understand or calculate the risks posed by many features of recent mortgage products, such as adjustable-rate mortgages and payment option mortgages.[96] The response of the Congress was not increased disclosure, that is, a reliance on market discipline on the part of consumers. The response was to prohibit residential mortgage loans made without regard to the borrower's ability to repay.[97]

The Dodd-Frank Act reaffirms the view that government intervention is justified when significant consumer losses occur and consumers are unable to effectively protect themselves. This viewpoint is explicitly recognized in the statute's new authorization granted to the regulators to prohibit or regulate additional acts and practices that are found to be "abusive." The standard for government intervention is a finding that an act or practice "(1) materially interferes with the ability of a consumer to understand a term or condition of a consumer financial product or service; or (2) takes unreasonable advantage of (A) a lack of understanding on the part of the consumer of the material risks, costs, or conditions of the product or service; (B) the inability of the consumer to protect the interests of the consumer in selecting or using a consumer financial product or service; or (C) the reasonable reliance by the consumer on a covered person to act in the interest of the consumer."[98]

95 S. Rep. No. 111–176, at 11 (2010). The Senate Report discussed the Senate version of bill, namely S. 3217.

96 *See id.* at 12–13. The Report also discusses the targeting of minority borrowers. *Id.* at 14–15.

97 Dodd-Frank Wall Street Reform and Consumer Protection Act, Pub. L. No. 111–203, § 1411 (2010). The statute also requires the creditor to verify and document the borrower's ability to repay.

98 *Id.* § 1031.

One point of concern regarding the consistency of the ethical viewpoint voiced by Congress with regard to consumer-oriented mortgage transactions is the standard it adopted for prohibition or regulation of additional "unfair" acts or practices, as opposed to "abusive" acts or practices. In the Dodd-Frank Act, Congress adopted the net societal benefits standard found in the FTC Act as the threshold for this regulatory determination and decision to intervene.[99] Does this reflect a change in viewpoint, namely that substantial injury to consumers, against which they are unable to protect themselves, should be tolerated as long as other consumers or industry members receive greater benefit? I think it does not. As noted earlier, the same Congress in the same statutory provision adopted a new federal prohibition directed at "abusive" acts and practices that requires only a finding that consumers are unable to effectively protect themselves.[100] In addition, none of the other consumer protection statutes directed at mortgage lending have reflected such an ethical viewpoint, and ethical perspectives should be based on a series of developments over a prolonged period of time and not upon an individual action.

Conclusion

This chapter has examined the ethical viewpoint of Congress and the federal bank regulatory agencies toward consumer protection in the mortgage market. I examined the viewpoint of bank regulatory agencies and that of the Congress over the last three decades. On one level, this is an analysis of whether regulators have properly effectuated the intentions of Congress. On another level, it is an exploration of the ethical perspective manifest in Congressional decisions. This chapter embraces the view that the actions and viewpoints of Congress taken and recognized repeatedly over an extended period of time are a reflection of the ethical standards accepted by US society. The conclusion drawn is that Congress repeatedly prohibited mortgage practices and products that subjected consumers to significant financial injury (loss) when it found that consumers were unable to effectively protect themselves against such injury. This reflected an ethical viewpoint in US society, namely that business entities should not profit by inflicting significant financial injury on vulnerable individuals. Such a viewpoint, and justification for legal intervention, mirrors the viewpoint and the justification for embrace of consumer protections in residential landlord-tenant transactions (warranty of habitability) and in some residential real estate transactions (warranty

99 *Id.*

100 In addition, the general standard governing regulatory action contained in Title X of the Dodd-Frank Act, as opposed to the unique standard adopted only with respect to "unfair" acts or practices, does not contain a net societal benefits standard. Rather it merely states the regulator shall consider benefits and costs of proposed rules. *Id.* § 1022. This is what Congress has done in past, e.g., in its deliberations leading to enactment of HOEPA.

of quality). As a result of this ethical viewpoint, US law has, to a significant degree, rejected caveat emptor as a governing principle in consumer-oriented real estate transactions. Much has been written of this change in landlord-tenant law, and in the law governing sales of new homes. This chapter documents the same change has occurred in real estate financing, the third major type of real estate transaction that consumers encounter.

Chapter 7
Identity Property and the Inheritance of Family Cottages

Sarah E. Waldeck

During the summer of 2007, a bookstore in a small Michigan resort town had more than 20 copies of a text entitled *Saving the Family Cottage* on its reserve shelf. When I commented on the book's apparent popularity, the shopkeeper informed me that it was outselling the new *Harry Potter*. I was intrigued, but not surprised. In this place where visitors boast about the length of their families' connection to the town, discussions about the fate of the family cottage are common. Everybody seems to want to keep the cottage, but no one is certain they will be able to. This is because family cottages are often identity property, which by its very nature presents particularly difficult inheritance questions.

Margaret Radin famously wrote that there is a relationship between property and personhood. That is, "[m]ost people posses certain objects that they feel are almost part of themselves."[1] In Radin's formulation, such objects are "bound up with the holder"[2] and essential to the self. As such, the loss of these objects harms the individual and interferes with the ability to flourish and develop.

"Identity property" is personhood property ratcheted down. Identity property is closely linked to one's sense of self and family and is valued primarily for what it signifies and embodies, not for its economic worth. As with Margaret Radin's "personhood property," identity property is non-fungible and thus cannot be replaced even by a mostly identical item with the same market value.[3] Unlike personhood property, however, identity property is not essential to human flourishing or self-development. Rather, identity property is cherished because of what it represents about one's family and own history. Identity property can emerge from a wide variety of experiences such as, for example, activities during a formative period in one's life or long-lasting relationships.[4]

Often identity property is connected to familial history. For example, identity property might be the appropriate label for hunting rifles, or for recipes that are written in the hand of the original baker, or for a crystal lowball cocktail glass. All of these items are "heirlooms" in the sense that they can be passed on from one

1 Margaret Jane Radin, *Property and Personhood*, 34 STAN. L. REV. 957, 959 (1982).
2 *Id.*
3 *Id.*
4 I thank Professor Marc Poirier, who suggested the term "identity property" to me.

generation to the next. They are not, however, the only property that an individual might pass along, nor are they necessarily the most valuable or the objects that have been in the family the longest. But all of these objects can have a particular significance because of how they were used by the person who is bequeathing them and how an heir participated in that use. If, for example, Grandma always used a particular recipe on the first day of Christmas, and her granddaughter always spent Christmas with Grandma, then the recipe is both an essential element of the granddaughter's own Christmas and a means by which the granddaughter can maintain a sense of connectedness to her past. A certain cookie during the holidays, or a particular rifle on the opening day of deer season, or a crystal glass for a Friday evening gin and tonic—each can create a sense of continuity though one's own experiences and a sense of seamlessness with the past. Such objects can, however, also raise thorny inheritance questions.

Because of identity property's unique value, its owner is likely to keep the property throughout her life and pass it along at death. The property may be the subject of a specific devise or bequest to a single heir; in that case, others who also cherish the property may be chagrined, but the situation is straightforward and the named beneficiary will simply take the property. What is just as likely, however, is that identity property will fall into a class gift ("All of my property to my children," for example) or pass through intestate succession to multiple takers. In either case, the heirs will own the identity property as tenants in common.

When personal property has been jointly inherited—particularly personal property with little market value—we expect heirs to swap their way out of joint ownership. One child will take the crystal cocktail class, another will take the hunting rifle, and yet another will take the recipe holder. The heirs involved in the informal settlement may have lingering doubts about whether they struck the best possible deal, but joint ownership is fleeting and everyone eventually moves on. (Well, maybe not everyone. A student once told that me that while his aunts were arguing over who was going to take their mother's recipe book, one of them absconded with the book and hid it in the walls of her house, where it remains to this day.)

If, however, the composition of property within the estate forecloses the possibility of an informal swap, matters become more difficult. This scenario is most common when an estate has a single piece of identity property with a high market value. Few heirs will be willing to swap a cocktail glass for a Monet, regardless of how much each reminds them of their father. Unless the heirs are willing to sell the Monet—and if the painting is identity property they likely are not—they will have to find a way to successfully share it.

While some estates, like the one with the Monet, will have *personal* property that both warrants the identity label and has a high market value, another (and more likely possibility) is that an estate will have *real* property that both merits the identity label and has a high market value. This chapter focuses on the inheritance of one such real property example: the family cottage. The available evidence about the inheritance of family cottages suggests that the law of tenancy in common—and thus some of the default rules of inheritance—are ill-suited for identity property.

Family Cottages

First, an explanation of what this chapter means by "family cottage." The term refers to recreational property, not to a primary residence. In ordinary parlance, family cottages are also known as summer houses, or cabins, or are simply referred to by their location: the lake, the Cape, up north, the Shore. They are places of retreat and where grandparents play with grandchildren and cousins play with cousins. In the words of one sociologist who has studied them, family cottages are "used and enjoyed by successive generations to enhance family cohesion through a shared cultural experience, regardless of age or interest ... they are *the* location for extended family gatherings over several generations."[5]

Lest this description summon up only images of the Bush compound in Kennebunkport or the Kennedy estate in Hyannisport, the 2000 Census states that seasonal properties range from "big summer estates on Long Island, time-sharing condos in Fort Lauderdale, or simple fishing cabins in Michigan."[6] In 2009, the median price of "vacation homes" was $150,000 and the typical buyer had an annual household income of slightly more than $97,000.[7] At death, the family cottage is often a decedent's single most economically valuable asset.[8] The available sociological field work further suggests that among those who have inherited family cottages, most owners would not be able to afford the property, but for the fact that the property was jointly inherited and costs are split among multiple owners.[9] Those who own family cottages tend to be economically fortunate in relative terms, but they are not necessarily wealthy.

Statistics about cottage ownership in the United States are hard to come by, and information about how many of these cottages qualify as identity property is harder still. But discrete pieces of information are suggestive. A 2007 survey of American housing reported 4,318,000 seasonal properties; of these, more than half of the owners identified "recreational purposes" as the reason they owned the property and about five per cent of owners described their property as "inherited."[10] Of those surveyed, 89 per cent of individuals who purchased "vacation homes" in 2009

---

5 Judith Huggins Balfe, Passing It On: The Inheritance and Use of Summer Houses ix (1999).

6 US Census Bureau, Housing Characteristics: 2000 5 (2001).

7 Research: Second-Home Market Snapshot, Realtor, May 2009, *available at* www.realtor.org/rmonews_and_commentary_secured/articles/2009/0905.

8 Stuart J. Hollander, Saving the Family Cottage 4 (2007).

9 Balfe, *supra* note 5, at xiii.

10 US Department of Housing and Urban Development & US Department of Commerce, American Housing Survey for the United States: 2007, at tbl.1A–1 (2008).

reported that they would use the property as a "family retreat."[11] As a percentage of housing stock, Maine, Vermont and New Hampshire have the largest number of seasonal properties. Other states with large amounts, either in absolute number or as a percentage of housing units, include Florida, Michigan, Wisconsin, New York, and California.[12]

At their most basic level, family cottages are a kind of home plus. Many scholars have documented the centrality of homes. Homes are the primary site for family interactions and the setting for a variety of interpersonal relationships; a place to establish and maintain everyday routines; and a place to present and project an image of oneself through design and décor. Family cottages (or cabins, or summer homes, or whatever you want to call them) are "the place of … strongest memories, childhood and adult."[13] One researcher has described the family cottage as particularly important because "[i]n a globalized world that many experience as placeless, the cottage may serve as a centre of meaning across the life course even as people relocate their permanent residence."[14] In a survey of cottage owners in the Hayward Lakes area of Wisconsin, respondents verbalized this sense of continuity by contrasting the number of cottages their families had owned (one) with the number of year-round or primary homes they had owned (sometimes as many as eight or ten).[15] In a different survey of second-home owners in Colorado, respondents similarly emphasized this sense of continuity: "It's always just been a special kind of place to go and that didn't change … [A]s you move, from place to place … that was always a constant place that you … knew that would be there."[16] Sociologist Judith Huggins Balfe, who surveyed 125 respondents across 17 states to study the ownership and inheritance of summer houses, writes that such properties "provide a unique sense of stability."[17] Surveys suggest that even individuals who have had just one year-round residence during their adult lives tend to characterize their primary home as a "mere residence" and the cottage as "their emotional home."[18]

Balfe's sociological work has further documented that family cottages are rife with rituals that are repeated year after year. Some of the rituals that families describe can be appreciated by wider audiences, such as particular menus that are

---

11 Research: Second-Home Market Snapshot, *supra* note 7.

12 US Census Bureau, Housing Characteristics, *supra* note 6, at 4–5.

13 Balfe, *supra* note 5, at viii.

14 Daniel R. Williams & Susan R. Van Patten, *Home and Away? Creating Identities and Sustaining Places in a Multi-centred World, in* Multiple Dwelling and Tourism: Negotiating Place, Home, and Identity 32, 38 (Norman McIntyre et al., eds, 2006) [hereinafter Multiple Dwelling and Tourism].

15 *Id.* at 39.

16 Norman McIntyre et al., *Home and Away: Revisiting 'Escape' in the Context of Second Homes*, in Multiple Dwelling and Tourism, *supra* note 14, 114, 124.

17 Balfe, *supra* note 5, at xi.

18 Richard C. Stedman, *Places of Escape: Second-home Meanings in Northern Wisconsin, USA, in* Multiple Dwelling and Tourism , *supra* note 14, 129, 132.

cooked year after year. Others will strike outsiders as at least faintly ridiculous: referring to plants by the names of the deceased family members who planted them, or throwing a birthday party for the house every five years, or keeping a house log in which each entry begins "Dear Grandma," when Grandma has been dead for decades.[19] But all such rituals are significant to the people who engage in them. Moreover, the rituals are intertwined with the cottage, such that the loss of the property would also mean the loss of the ritual.

Many cottages are also property that has passed or will pass from one generation to the next. In one survey of cottage owners, more than 80 percent stated that they intended to give the property to their children at death.[20] In the representative words of one cabin owner from Colorado, "Our dream wasn't just that we would like a place to relax, but it'd be a place where our children and our children's children could ... build family relationships as well."[21] Preserving the cottage is a means of influencing the next generation's personal history, status and values. Current owners also may hope that because the cottage will remain integral to the family, they will as well. Balfe's work shows that individuals who see multiple generations on the same land, "experience a sense of timelessness ... as they connect the present and anticipated future to the past."[22] As Balfe explains, "the inheritance of summer houses ... is among the mechanisms for transmitting the specifics of a family culture to the next generation, providing some of the 'glue' that gives meaning and cohesion to its collective identity."[23]

Tenancy in Common, Familial Bonds, and Partition Actions

Now assume that the owner of a family cottage devises it to "my two children" or dies intestate. Unless the testator has left instructions to the contrary, the children will take the property as tenants in common. Without some alternative arrangement between the siblings, a series of default legal rules familiar to anyone who has taken a basic property course will govern the ownership, use, and management of their common property. Briefly summarized, each co-tenant is entitled to possess the whole property, regardless of the size of her ownership share. Co-tenants receive a proportional share of all rents and profits earned by the property and must pay a proportional share of taxes, mortgages, and other necessary carrying costs. In most jurisdictions, a co-tenant making or paying for repairs has no right to contribution, even when the repairs are necessary. A co-tenant who makes improvements also has no right to contribution.

19 Balfe, *supra* note 5, at 189, 191.

20 Hollander, *supra* note 8, at xiii.

21 McIntyre et al., *supra* note 16, at 124.

22 Balfe, *supra* note 5, at 121.

23 *Id.* at 127.

With respect to every consequential decision about the property, the co-tenant siblings are locked into a bilateral monopoly: that is, neither co-tenant has good alternatives to dealing with the other. If both want exclusive possession of the cottage on July 4, they will have to hash out a compromise among themselves. Neither sibling can resolve the dispute through negotiation with a third party, because no third party has the power to allow one sibling exclusive possession. (Compare the negotiations over the Fourth of July with those that would occur with contractors if the siblings decided to replace the cottage roof. If the siblings did not like the price quoted by one company, they would go elsewhere for a better bid. If, on the other hand, one sibling does not want to vacate on July 3, there is no one to negotiate with besides the other sibling.) Economists typically describe bilateral monopolies as creating high transaction costs; laypeople describe them as creating frustration and inherently complex negotiations.

Standard doctrine describes two different forces as mitigating the bilateral monopoly in which the siblings find themselves: (1) familial bonds; and (2) the right of partition. First, we expect the familial relationship between the siblings to promote cooperation. Robert Pollack, who studies families and marriage, has identified four reasons why familial bonds tend to encourage cooperation:[24] (1) family members are well-positioned to punish and deter non-cooperative behavior, presumably because expulsion from the family network is particularly costly; (2) families are likely to have a great deal of information about a member's character and history, which reduces the transaction costs associated with the informal interactions that yield cooperation; (3) background social norms favor loyalty toward one's family; and (4) humans may have evolved to behave altruistically towards family, particularly those who share the same gene pool.

Balfe's 17-state survey of cottage owners provides some support for the proposition that family members who jointly own property are more likely to cooperate than co-owners who are at arm's-length. For example, one of Balfe's respondents explained:

> At Christmas, when the whole family was assembled, my grandfather distributed Monopoly money to everyone for a mock auction to get an idea of how to divide the estate in his will, according to what people valued most … [P]resumably, spouses and their children could combine their money to bid on the same thing if they wanted to, which is the only way that just one family could get the summer house. Well, no family got together for such a bid … maybe because no-one wanted to exclude their siblings and cousins from sharing it. So in one way the mock auction was inclusive, even if it was great fun. It was also very instructive: Grandfather's view was that you can only keep this going with creativity, not

24 Robert Pollack, *A Transaction Cost Approach to Families and Households*, 23 J. Econ. Literature 581, 585–88 (1965).

> with the law, and that legacy is going to help us settle the issues now that the younger generations are in charge.[25]

This respondent is clearly anticipating that familial bonds and a grandfather's legacy will foster cooperation.

Familial bonds are not always a panacea, however. Some of Balfe's respondents reveal substantial inability to cooperate with their co-owners: "[m]uch as I love my brother, this [place] is driving us apart;"[26] "[w]e got along fine until my parents died and my sister and brother and I inherited the place… [n]ow we have disagreements all the time;"[27] and "[r]elations with my [sister-in-law] got so bad we weren't talking."[28] One interviewee explained:

> My mother is 85 and she can't deal with the rivalry my sister and I feel about the place … She just says, "Can't you just love each other?" We do, of course, but that doesn't settle anything about different standards of maintenance or improvements and all that.[29]

Estate planning guides recount similar cautionary tales, with siblings and cousins fighting over who will use the cottage when; how particular financial obligations should be shared; how the property should be maintained; and so forth.

This is where partition—the standard doctrine's other solution to the bilateral monopoly problem—kicks in. If familial bonds fail to yield cooperation, each co-owner has the unilateral right to exit the tenancy through a partition action. If, say, one sibling files such an action, a court will either order the property to be sold at fair market value (a partition-by-sale), or decree that it be physically divided and apportioned between the tenants (a partition-in-kind). In theory at least, the unilateral right to partition eliminates the bilateral monopoly problem because the siblings are not truly locked-in. If negotiations over July 4 become unbearable, then one sibling can file for partition and altogether exit the tenancy. Moreover, in many cases, exit will not even require the actual filing of a partition action. Even a sibling who prefers that a tenancy continue may capitulate to its end when formal court action seems inevitable. Once the tenancy ends, of course, the siblings are "unlocked" and have no need to consult each other about July 4.

In the context of identity property, however, this tidy explanation of how partition solves the bilateral monopoly problem works only if: (1) "partition" means partition-in-kind; or (2) the mere threat of having to exit is powerful enough to compel cooperation. In a partition-in-kind, the land is divided into discrete parcels that are individually owned by each of the former co-tenants; in a partition-by-

25 Balfe, *supra* note 5, at 131–32.

26 *Id.* at 159.

27 *Id.* at 163–64.

28 *Id.* at 163.

29 *Id.* at 132.

sale, the entire parcel is sold to the highest bidder—either one of the co-tenants or a third party. While courts often profess a preference for partition-in-kind, a robust literature has demonstrated that courts faced with practical concerns, ranging from the existence of a dwelling to topographical features, usually conclude that in-kind division is infeasible and instead order a sale.[30] This *de facto* preference for partition-by-sale is critical. If land were partitioned in kind, our siblings could exit the *tenancy* without having to exit all four corners of the *land*. But in a partition-by-sale, exit means that at least one sibling will actually have to leave the land and therefore lose the identity property.

In some instances—particularly when no co-tenant is confident that she could outbid the others at a partition sale—the mere threat of having to exit may be powerful enough to compel cooperation. As an example, consider this story from one of Balfe's respondents:

> In my years as an estate lawyer in Boston, I saw so much acrimony over shared inheritance that in my own will only one of my children will get this place… So in six months after I die, when my estate is probated, the four children will "duke it out" in lottery fashion as to which one gets all of it. That may seem unfair, but it was the way we always used when dividing scarce desirables when there wasn't enough to go around among the children, whether it was a single piece of candy or use of the family car on Friday night. They'll accept it as fair.

Then, with a twinkle in still-sharp blue eyes, he said:

> Now of course, nothing need prevent them from getting together before the "duking" to make some other arrangement among themselves, so that all can use it in some manner if they want.[31]

This family patriarch is counting on the threat of "winner take all" and the resulting forced exit by the others to provoke cooperation.

An equally plausible scenario, however, is that the threat of a forced exit will foster a *lack* of cooperation. If the filing of a partition action means the loss of the cottage, then partition becomes a nuclear option that needs to be avoided at all cost. This makes it easier for one of the siblings to shirk obligation and engage in other uncooperative behavior, because the sibling knows that she is likely to be let off the hook so that a fight does not culminate in a partition action. Further complicating matters is that the cottage may be identity property for one sibling but not another. These differing subjective values will influence the extent to which each co-tenant is willing to compromise.

---

30 Phyliss Craig-Taylor, *Through a Colored Looking Glass: A View of Judicial Partition, Family Land Loss, and Rule Setting*, 78 Wash. U.L.Q. 737, 753 (2000).

31 Balfe, *supra* note 5, at 129–30.

If physical division—not a forced sale—were the likely outcome of a partition action, partition might be a reliable means of solving the bilateral monopoly problem: co-tenants would suffer the loss of some portion of the identity property, but would not lose *all* of it. When "partition" means partition-by-sale, however, the co-tenants may perceive themselves as locked into the tenancy—and into an ongoing relationship with their co-tenants because a sale is simply unthinkable. In this case, negotiations with co-tenants are likely to be complex and frustrating. In economic terms, the bilateral monopoly will be robust and transaction costs will be correspondingly high.

This is not to say that courts have erred by adopting a *de facto* preference for partition-by-sale. As a practical matter, cottages or other land or objects that might be identified as "identity property" might not neatly lend themselves to physical division. Courts may also find it difficult to balance the interests of co-tenants who value property mostly because of its identity nature and co-tenants who value property mostly because of what it could fetch in the economic marketplace. It is therefore entirely unsurprising that a court would gravitate toward the concreteness of a relatively simple economic inquiry and ask whether the total property will be worth less when it is divided into smaller parcels. Empirical work further suggests that when partition-in-kind is viewed with the benefit of hindsight, one or more co-tenants are often awarded parcels of land that, from a purely dollar-based perspective, are worth substantially less than what was awarded to other co-tenants.[32]

While the judicial preference for partition-by-sale is both predictable and understandable, however, the foregoing suggests that property law lacks a satisfactory default doctrine for situations in which identity property is inherited by more than one individual. Moreover, the dissatisfaction with the law of partition and default rules of tenancy in common is more than just academic. Among those who currently own or anticipate inheriting a family cottage, interest in opting out of the default rules of tenancy in common is strong enough to have spawned law firms that specialize in "cottage planning." The property management systems to which these individuals voluntarily agree provides insight into what fosters cooperation between co-owners of identity property.

Beyond the Law of a Tenancy in Common

Those who seek legal advice about how to preserve the family cottage for themselves or future generations typically are advised to establish a trust or a

32 Manel Baucells & Steven A. Lippman, *Justice Delayed is Justice Denied: A Cooperative Game Theoretic Analysis of Hold-Up in Co-Ownership*, 22 Cardozo L. Rev. 1191 (2001).

limited liability company (LLC).[33] Others simply enter into formal contracts that govern their actions with respect to the property. Each of these forms substantially differs from the others, both in terms of what is necessary to establish the entity and how the entity functions once established. This chapter draws on what co-tenants tend to agree to when they use an LLC, which is currently "hot" among estate planners. For our purposes, however, the precise nature of the legal form is unimportant. Instead, what matters is how these co-owners choose to define their obligations to each other and, particularly, how they address the right of exit.

As one might expect, most formal agreements between co-tenants are aimed at establishing a management system that lowers transaction costs and prevents free-riding. The law of tenancy in common mostly positions co-tenants to act as independent operators. Except for that which is essential to the preservation of the property—mortgages, taxes, and other carrying costs, to which all tenants must contribute—each tenant is free to make their own decisions and then see how the other tenants will respond. Will they contribute to a repair or improvement? Show up on July 4?

The formal management structures that co-owners establish for themselves, in contrast, tend to emphasize owner interdependency. For example, a popular cottage planning text advises that cottages be organized as direct democracies unless there are so many co-tenants that a majority rule becomes "unwieldy."[34] At that point, co-owners are advised to opt for a representative democracy in which decisions are made by representatives of each family branch. If the number of branches exceeds three, the representatives of each branch are advised to appoint a small "management committee" which has the authority to handle all the day-to-day operations of the property. Co-owners might further calibrate the total vote requirement to the significance of the decision, so that some decisions require unanimity or a super-majority, while others require only a simple majority.

The branch concept also influences the assignment of household tasks, scheduling, and the disciplining of members who fail to pay their share of costs. Representatives assign chores such as writing checks or arranging for repairs to the best-suited individual. With respect to use, the typical LLC operating agreement allots a specific amount of use time to each branch and leaves it to members of the branch to allocate the time among themselves. To prevent free-riding, many operating agreements further provide that a branch's right to use depends on the entire branch having fulfilled its financial obligations, so that branch members have incentive to police and make good on the obligations of

33 *See* Hollander, *supra* note 8, at 68–79. Some owners may also choose an S corporation, mainly because they are already familiar with the concept of a "corporation." *Id.* at 73. (The "S election" allows each shareholder to claim a proportionate share of the property tax deduction.) Attorneys and accountants, however, tend to recommend LLCs as a better alternative to S corporations, primarily because LLCs are less fragile entities. *Id.* at 74.

34 Hollander, *supra* note 8, at 119.

their own. In addition, some operating agreements reserve the right to force a defaulting household member to sell his or her share, usually at a price that is far below fair market value.

In addition to creating a management system that explicitly acknowledges the interdependency of co-tenants, formal arrangements between co-tenants in family cottages are aimed at preserving the identity nature of the property. That is, the current owners of the property seek to make sure that it will remain in the family, both for themselves and for future generations. Most LLC operating agreements, for instance, define who can be a member of the LLC. A typical membership clause might state: "No person who is not a descendant of [current owners] may become a member of this company." Or, in a slightly less restricted version: "No person who is not a descendant of [current owners] may become a member of this company without the unanimous consent of the members."[35] A more nuanced version of this sort of clause describes three categories of transfers: those that are automatically permitted (such as a transfer to descendants); those that are permitted only after obtaining the consent of other members (such as a transfer to stepchildren); and those that are prohibited (such as a transfer to an ex-spouse). These clauses, in either their strong or weaker versions, seek to ensure that the family cottage remains exactly that: a cottage that is owned by either *de jure* or *de facto* family and no-one else.

As for the right of exit, it is also customary for operating agreements to greatly reduce the opportunity of individuals to profit from their share of the cottage. To begin, the possibility of unilateral partition is completely off the table; the cottage may only be sold if either all or a majority of members consent. As suggested above, a member who wishes to sell her share may do so, but often only to other family members. A typical operating agreement might further fix the sale price at 20 to 50 per cent less than fair market value and allow the purchasers to make a small down payment and amortize the remaining balance. Some agreements might also constrain the timing of sales to ensure that the LLC never has more than one outstanding debt at a single time. These constraints on the ability to recognize financial gain "(1) [emphasize that] the family's interest in preserving the cottage is more important than the economic benefit the cottage confers upon a single heir; (2) [discourage] an heir from selling … and (3) [compensate] the rest of the family for the burden of finding the money to pay off the former owner through the advantageous price at which the company buys the interest."[36]

These restrictions on exit are stark. The possibility of a straightforward exit through partition is gone. The number of individuals to whom shares can be sold or transferred is severely limited. The amount for which shares can be sold is substantially discounted. An individual may not be able to sell or exit on their preferred timetable; rather, the timing of their sale is dictated by how much debt the commons property has at any one time. All of these constraints elevate the familial

---

35 *Id.* at 82.

36 *Id.* at 111–12.

interest in retaining the identity property over the individual economic interest of any single member. They also comport with the lessons that can be gleaned from the work of the economist Elinor Ostrom and others who have studied successful commons property (albeit property that is much larger in geography and group membership than a family cottage).[37] In many of Ostrom's and others' success stories, the ability of the individual to exit from the commons property is sharply limited. Such restrictions on exit may "enhance [members'] interest in making the best possible use of their rights"[38] and "strengthen the bonds among co-owners and reinforce the rights in the commons, thus facilitating cooperation."[39]

One way to understand how these agreements between cottage co-owners modify the default rules of a tenancy in common is through the lens of property rules and liability rules.[40] Under a liability rule, the holder of an entitlement is told how much they have to be paid to compel the loss of the entitlement. Under a property rule, the holder of an entitlement continues to have the entitlement until they allow someone to purchase it. Property rules allow the holder of a right to determine the value of that right; liability rules allow someone else (typically a court) to place a value on the right. Every tenancy in common potentially has two competing entitlements: the right to own the tenancy property and the right to exit the tenancy. The law of partition entitles a co-tenant to exit through partition and protects the other co-tenant's interest in the tenancy property with a liability rule: so long as the co-tenant is paid their proportional share of fair market value, they have to forfeit their right to the tenancy property. The typical formal operating agreement, however, both makes the terms of a sale unfavorable to the tenant who wishes to exit and narrows the number of individuals to whom the property can be sold. These agreements thus seek to tilt the scales in favor of those who wish to continue the joint ownership and to protect them with a property rule. Those who wish to continue joint ownership may decide to relent and allow a member to exit under terms that are more favorable than those specified in the agreement, but then they—not a court determining fair market value—will determine what price must be paid to bring the joint ownership to an end.

Of course, co-owners do not need an LLC or other formal agreement in order to reject the default rules of a tenancy in common. The default rules allow for substantial private ordering. For example, just because tenants in common have an equal right to possess the cottage does not necessarily mean that they will exercise

---

37 *See* Elinor Ostrom, Governing the Commons: The Evolution of Institutions for Collective Action (1990).

38 Margaret A. McKean, *Success on the Commons: A Comparative Examination of Institutions for Common Property Resource Management*, 4 J. Theoretical Pol. 247, 261 (1992).

39 Hanoch Dagan & Michael A. Heller, *The Liberal Commons*, 110 Yale L.J. 549, 566 (2001).

40 Guido Calabresi & Douglas Melamed, *Property Rules, Liability Rules, and Inalienability: One View of the Cathedral*, 85 Harv. L. Rev. 1089 (1975).

that right. Instead, they are likely to negotiate about when each co-tenant will use the property. A tenant who wants to cash out may be willing to accept less than the fair market value of their share, either because they want the property to stay in their family or because they are selling to their siblings or cousins, or for some other reason. A tenant also may feel compelled to contribute to an improvement that they would not have chosen to make, either because they recognize that they will benefit from the improvement or because they feel some obligation to the family member. Co-tenants might deviate from the rules of a tenancy in common in a hundred different ways; they do not need a legally-enforceable agreement to do so.

In a similar vein, we can question the practical effect of these legal forms. Assume that one of the LLC members has fallen on hard times and is unable to pay their fair share of the cottage expenses. Will the other members penalize their branch of the family by cutting off access to the property? Will they really force their brother or cousin to sell his share? As for the member who is determined to make an improvement, will the other members actually prevent them from doing so at their own expense? The legal agreement is relevant only to the extent that the would-be co-tenants choose to follow and enforce it. But, as already described, the mere existence of the agreement changes the background rules and tilts the legal entitlements in favor of those prefer to enforce its terms.

A New Approach to Fostering Cooperation

The sorts of agreements described above suggest that when identity property is jointly inherited, much could be gained by judicial recognition of alternatives to the default rules of a tenancy in common and the unilateral right of partition. The co-tenants in family cottages or other identity property who argue over use and maintenance and even whether the tenancy will continue are almost always related by either blood or adoption. The conundrum is that identity property—which is partially about family and a sense of one's history—can drive a wedge between family members. Margaret Brinig has written persuasively about the need for family law to encourage a "franchise model," in which family members continue to care about each other, the family name, and even family property long after legal bonds are broken by emancipation.[41] This sort of model, however, can exist only if our legal regime is willing to sacrifice some of its commitment to individualism and market-like behavior. In this context, when there is evidence that default ownership rules may contribute to strife between siblings and cousins and other relatives, the law should do what it can to ameliorate the discontent. Moreover, while empirical evidence about the frequency with which co-tenants opt out of the default rules is incomplete, the market for planning guides advising them how to

41 Margaret F. Brinig, *The Family Franchise: Elderly Parents and Adult Siblings*, 1996 Utah L. Rev. 393, 396.

do so indicates genuine dissatisfaction with the rules. Ever since Norman Dacey published *How to Avoid Probate!* in 1965, estates and trusts reforms have been made with an eye towards reflecting how people prefer to manage their affairs and conduct business.

The insight that the law of tenancy in common treats co-tenants as independent operators, whereas co-tenants seeking to perpetuate their joint ownership emphasize their interdependency, may provide a blueprint for change. When a family cottage or other identity property is the subject of a probate or a partition action, the law can similarly attempt to foster cooperation by acknowledging co-tenant interdependency.

As an example, consider what might unfold between co-tenants if partition actions involving identity property had three potential remedies instead of just two: a partition-in-kind, a partition-by-sale *and* temporal partition. Whereas a partition-in-kind divides property according to its physical dimensions, a temporal partition grants someone the right to use the property for a particular period of time. The remedy is an old one that has long been out of favor, primarily because of fears about inconvenience and potential inequities. But when the subject of the action is identity property, a court could favor temporal partition over partition-by-sale. Temporal partition may increase the length of time that tenants with an identity connection to the property are able to own it. Even more significantly, the possibility of a temporal partition may substantially alter the dynamics of the co-tenancy.

In the typical temporal partition, the co-tenant who wanted out would instead receive the lifetime rental value of her interest in the property, with the interest passing to the co-tenant's heirs or devisees at death. In the most optimistic telling, the temporal partition would allow the other co-tenants to retain the lifetime interest of the departing co-tenant. Depending on the age of the exiting co-tenant, the value of the lifetime interest may be substantially less than the value of the entire interest. Upon the former co-tenant's death, the property interest would pass to that co-tenant's heirs, who would have an interest in the identity that the property represents.

Of course it does not require much creativity to imagine how this rosy tale may go awry. If co-tenants cannot purchase the property interest outright, they may not be able to afford a temporal slice. Depending on the nature of the property, the lifetime interest could be sold to a third party and the remaining co-tenants may find the prospective of dealing with an outsider extremely unattractive. The co-tenant also may devise the interest to someone who does not want it (or whom the remaining co-tenants do not wish to have it), which simply sets the stage for additional negotiations between co-tenants or a future partition action. If, however, the co-tenants who wish to keep the property are able to purchase the lifetime interest, a temporal partition quite literally offers the advantage of "buying time." At a minimum, those who care about the identity property will own it for longer than they otherwise would. Moreover, if the departing co-tenant's interest in the identity property is passed on to someone who wishes to sell it, the other co-tenants may have come into a position to be able to purchase the entire interest outright.

How a temporal partition might actually play out, however, is less important than how the *possibility* of a temporal partition may affect co-tenant behavior. Most disputes between co-tenants do not culminate in a partition action; instead, they are resolved though private bargaining, with each party knowing that the other has the right to exit through a partition action. If temporal division is one possible result of such an action, the threat of partition—currently the nuclear option for those who wish to retain the identity property—becomes much muddier. At present co-tenants bargain against a backdrop in which complete exit from the property is assured; a co-tenant merely has to elect to do so. If judges would consider and sometimes actually order a temporal partition of identity property, the calculations of negotiating co-tenants become more complex. A co-tenant inclined to end a tenancy would have to account for the possibility that a judge would allow only partial exit (and partial financial gain) and that the remainder interest would be in the co-tenant's estate. In other words, the co-tenant would remain partially dependant on their fellow tenants. This diminishment—although not abolition—of the right of exit may serve to foster cooperation within the tenancy.

Of course, favoring temporal partition over partition-by-sale is not the only measure a court might take that acknowledges the interdependency of co-owners. One can also imagine scenarios where probate judges recommend that heirs to identity property engage in a mediation-like process designed to facilitate agreement about how the property will be managed, or that judges order a cooling-off period before an aggrieved co-tenant can file for partition.

All of these judicial actions would reflect a normative judgment about the interests involved, namely, that identity property is important enough to warrant special treatment. But if the readers of this book categorized the property in their own lives, the list of that which is non-fungible and closely linked to one's sense of self and family would likely be very short. The property on that list, however, might matter more than the sum total of all the other categories. A close examination of the formal agreements of co-tenants who opt out of default rules reveals much about the extent to which they value identity property and how an emphasis on interdependence can foster cooperation among co-owners of property. The law cannot guarantee that co-tenants will be able to continue to own their identity property, but it can take steps to promote their net good instead of elevating the interest of those who fail to cooperate.

Acknowledgement

I owe particular thanks to Marc Poirier, Charles Sullivan, and John Nagle for their insights about identity property and to Dwight King and Ellen Bernstein for their research assistance. This chapter draws from: Rethinking the Intersection Between Inheritance and the Law of Tenancy in Common, 87 NOTRE DAME LAW REVIEW 735 (2011).

Chapter 8
The 'Context' of Home: Cohabitation and Ownership Disputes in England and Wales

Andrew Hayward

Introduction

Forty years after the House of Lords' decisions of *Pettitt v. Pettitt*[1] and *Gissing v. Gissing*,[2] the legal principles governing ownership disputes over the family home remain confused and incoherent.[3] The predominant reason is that, in contrast to other jurisdictions which have provided statutory remedies for eligible cohabitants, England and Wales continue to utilise a trusts-based framework.[4] As will be explained, a particular type of trust, namely the common intention constructive trust, has become the key device favoured by the courts to settle these types of dispute: this trust responds to agreements as to beneficial ownership, whether expressly concluded between the parties or inferred from their conduct, and materialises when unconscionability occurs after one party seeks to resile from that agreement. The development of this trust has generated a wealth of inconsistent case law, particularly as the judicial search for common intention is often challenging within the informal context of the home.[5] Linked to this problem of finding common intention is the uneasy tension within the trusts framework between, on the one hand, the courts recognising the family home as a distinct domestic entity, thereby necessitating family-centric considerations when demarcating beneficial ownership, and on the other, merely viewing the home like any other type of real property. These issues, coupled with the lack of clear

1 *Pettitt v. Pettitt*, [1970] A.C. 777 (H.L.) (appeal taken from Eng.).

2 *Gissing v. Gissing*, [1971] A.C. 886 (H.L.) (appeal taken from Eng.).

3 The two House of Lords' decisions are cumulatively referred to as the 'twin peaks' in *Grant v. Edwards*, [1986] Ch. 638 (C.A.) 646 (Nourse LJ) emphasising that judicial navigation of this area is an arduous task.

4 Various states within Australia and Canada provide remedies for eligible cohabitants whereas, closer to home, Scotland has provided limited remedies through the Family Law (Scotland) Act 2006 along with more recently, Ireland, through the Civil Partnership and Certain Rights and Obligations of Cohabitants Act 2010.

5 *See* N. Glover & P. Todd, *The Myth of Common Intention,* 16 Legal Stud. 325 (1996).

direction from the earlier House of Lords' authorities, have necessitated repeated calls for statutory reform.[6]

The recent House of Lords' decision in *Stack v. Dowden*[7] attempts to clarify the current legal regime and provides guidance on the operation of the common intention constructive trust. The methodology employed by the House of Lords to elucidate the trust framework and the cornerstone of the majority's reasoning is the invocation of 'context'. Baroness Hale, representing the majority voice in the House of Lords, states that 'in law "context is everything"'[8] and approaches the family home with recognition that it is a different type of property to commercial property. The unique nature of the home therefore necessitates a bespoke set of trusts principles. Baroness Hale subsequently formulates a context-specific analytical approach to be applied within this 'consumer context'.[9] Here the constructive trust is deemed the correct analytical device and the House of Lords clearly state that it is the common intention of the parties alone that determines its operation. A key motivation for this entrenchment of common intention in *Stack* is to prevent the practice of judges abandoning their search for elusive intention and instead utilising a judicial concept of fairness.

This chapter explores the deployment of context in its various forms within the trust framework in England and Wales and assesses its utility in relation to judicial reasoning. It focuses primarily on joint legal title disputes arising between cohabitants or platonic home-sharers.[10] It will firstly provide an outline of the trust framework utilised in England and Wales to help illustrate the extent to which *Stack* has modified the law. After then analysing the principles of *Stack*, it explores the judicial resort to context and the various meanings of context present in the decision. Context will be analysed from two perspectives; namely the 'context of home' and 'contextual analysis'. As will be shown, the issues discussed in this chapter resonate with the theme of Community, Home and Identity in this collection, particularly in relation to the justifiability and practical implications of creating a home context in England and Wales.

This chapter seeks to question whether the drive towards contextualising the home provides clarification to the trusts framework and whether heightened

6 The Law Commission for England & Wales stated that trusts were 'relatively rigid and extremely difficult to apply, and their application can lead to what many would regard as unfairness between the parties', Law Commission, Cohabitation: The Financial Consequences of Relationship Breakdown (Law Com No 307 Cm 7182, 2007), ¶ 1.27, *available at* http://www.justice.gov.uk/lawcommission/docs/cp179_Cohabitation_Consultation_overview.pdf.

7 *Stack v. Dowden,* [2007] UKHL 17 (H.L.).

8 *Id.* 69.

9 *Id.* 52, 54, 57–58.

10 In England and Wales, married couples and civil partners are excluded from this analysis owing to the courts structured judicial discretion to deal with questions of beneficial ownership of property contained within Part II Matrimonial Causes Act 1973 and sched. 5 Civil Partnership Act 2004, respectively.

contextual analysis actually facilitates the pinpointing of common intention for the purpose of the constructive trust. Separating the domestic context from the commercial context may instinctively appear possible, yet this chapter will illustrate that it is far from straightforward. Similarly, when within this domestic context, the judicial resort to contextual analysis may lend itself to sensitively engaging with facts surrounding the acquisition of property, particularly through appreciating the intricacies of domestic relations. Furthermore, contextual analysis may be a prevailing trend in England and Wales, particularly in light of developments in other areas of law,[11] and it may represent for the litigants involved a palatable method for unravelling the complexities of their individual dispute. Nevertheless, contextual analysis may simultaneously obscure legal reasoning and enable factors to be taken into account that bear tenuous, or even no direct, correlation to the question of intended beneficial ownership. Ultimately, this chapter seeks to question whether a heightened recognition of context within home is a welcome development in this jurisdiction.

The Trusts Framework in England and Wales

As England and Wales do not provide a set of financial remedies for cohabitants to utilise upon relationship breakdown, beneficial ownership of the family home is determined by the parties' 'strict entitlements in equity'.[12] General principles of property law, equity and contract law are therefore applicable. Owing to the rise in owner-occupation and the lucrative nature of property ownership, there is a significant amount of case law which makes it difficult to extrapolate clear legal principles. Indeed, as one judge noted in 1996, it is often 'not easy to reconcile every judicial utterance in this well-travelled area of the law'.[13] The following part of the chapter provides a brief overview of the foundational legal principles governing trusts of the family home disputes in England and Wales.

The case law can be divided into sole and joint legal title disputes. In sole legal title disputes, the sole legal title holder is regarded as absolute owner of the property concerned. However, a non-legal title holder seeking to assert a beneficial interest in that property may do so in numerous ways. This is a two-stage process whereby they must firstly acquire an interest (acquisition stage) and then, secondly, have that interest quantified (quantification stage). One route to be used by a non-legal title holder is pinpointing the presence of an express declaration of trust

11 *See* the recent developments in proprietary estoppel following *Yeoman Row v. Cobbe*, [2008] UKHL 55 (H.L.) and *Thorner v. Major*, [2009] UKHL 18 (H.L.) along with the context sensitive developments in the interpretation of contracts following *Attorney General of Belize v. Belize Telecom Ltd.*, [2009] UKPC 11 (PC) and *Chartbrook Ltd v. Persimmon Homes Ltd.*, [2009] UKHL 38 (H.L.).

12 *Hammond v. Mitchell*, [1992] 2 All ER 109, 112 (Waite J).

13 *Drake v. Whipp*, [1996] 1 FLR 826, 827 (Peter Gibson LJ).

made by the legal title holder that stipulates that the latter would hold the property, as a trustee, on trust for them both in specified shares. This declaration would need to be manifested in writing and signed by the party capable of declaring the trust.[14] The benefits of this type of trust stem from the certainty that it provides, as the declaration of trust represents 'virtually irrebuttable evidence' of the nature and extent of the parties' interests in the property.[15] However, in cases where a non-legal title holder moves into property, after the legal title holder has acquired the property, the likelihood that this trust will be engaged is diminished as it requires positive action by the legal title holder. Consequently, it is the implied trusts, governed by section 53(2) Law of Property Act 1925, that are more frequently applicable and, as a result, litigated in England and Wales.

The implied trusts can be subdivided into the presumed intention resulting trust and the common intention constructive trust. Both trusts are intention based and the courts are unable to impose either trust on a basis of achieving a fair result between the parties. In sole legal title disputes, the presumed intention resulting trust arises where property is purchased or transferred into the name of another and the non-legal title holder has made a financial contribution to the acquisition. Unless it can be shown that the latter intended to make a gift, equity will regard the legal title holder as trustee, holding the property on trust for the non-legal title holder in shares proportionate to their respective contributions. In essence, the beneficial ownership of the property concerned 'results' back to the contributor. After acquisition of an interest under a resulting trust materialises, quantification of the specific share of the beneficial ownership is strictly mathematical and dependent solely on the financial contribution. This device has a historic pedigree[16] and, prior to the early 1970s, was the key device used in disputes concerning the family home.[17] The presumed intention resulting trust, however, responds only to direct financial contributions made at the point of acquisition. Indirect financial contributions, for example where one party pays household bills to enable the other to discharge the mortgage repayments[18] or non-financial contributions for example child care or domestic responsibilities will not trigger a resulting trust.[19]

From the late 1960s onwards, the courts in England and Wales developed another trust to be used to determine beneficial ownership of the family home, namely the common intention constructive trust. The three House of Lords'

---

14 As required by § 53(1)(b) Law of Property Act 1925.

15 K. Gray & S. Gray, Elements of Land Law 7.1.29 (5th ed. 2009). Such express declarations of trust can only be set aside in exceptional circumstances, such as in instances of fraud, mistake or undue influence.

16 *Dyer v. Dyer*, [1788] 2 Cox Eq Cas 92.

17 *See Hodgson v. Marks*, [1971] 2 WLR 1263 (C.A.) for a classic example of its operation.

18 *See Gissing v. Gissing*, *supra* note 2.

19 *See Burns v. Burns*, [1984] Ch. 317 (C.A.).

decisions of *Pettitt v. Pettitt*,[20] *Gissing v. Gissing*[21]and *Lloyd's Bank v. Rosset*[22] provided the operating requirements of this type of trust and cumulatively provided two routes for its acquisition. In sole legal title cases, the first route is where parties have formed an express agreement, or rather, a common intention as to the beneficial ownership. In *Rosset* this represented 'any agreement, arrangement or understanding ... however imperfectly remembered'.[23] This agreement evidences the common intention to share beneficial ownership between the parties and, owing to the informality of dealings in the home, is often pieced together through conversations that may have occurred many years prior to the legal dispute. A second route for acquiring a constructive trust is for an inference of common intention to arise through 'a direct financial contribution to the purchase price or a mortgage repayment' with anything less being unlikely to substantiate a claim.[24] These contributions enable the court to infer a common intention between the parties. After evincing a common intention, the party seeking to rely on such agreement must demonstrate detrimental reliance, namely an altering of their position in reliance on the agreement itself. The requirement of detrimental reliance is significant to justify equity's intervention as without such conduct, equity would be assisting a volunteer. If one party seeks to deny the existence of an antecedent bargain or resile from its terms after the other party has relied on the agreement to their detriment, a court will seek to combat that unconscionable behaviour through the finding of a common intention constructive trust. In England and Wales, this trust is not imposed upon the parties in a remedial manner, but is instead recognised by the court when the requisite elements of common intention and detrimental reliance crystallise.

In stark contrast to the mathematical approach to quantification under the presumed intention resulting trust, the common intention constructive trust adopts a more flexible approach. After *Midland Bank v. Cooke*, which allowed the court to quantify beneficial interests using a broad-brush approach that took into account not merely financial contributions, the common intention constructive trust differentiated itself from the purely financial focus present in quantification under the resulting trust.[25] This approach was further expanded upon in *Oxley v. Hiscock* where Chadwick LJ stated that, in the absence of an agreement between the parties as to beneficial ownership, the court can quantify beneficial interests with regard to what would be fair having regard to the whole course of dealings

20 *Supra* note 1.

21 *Supra* note 2.

22 *Lloyd's Bank v. Rosset*, [1991] 1 A.C. 107 (H.L.)

23 *Id.* at 132 (Lord Bridge).

24 *Le Foe v. Le Foe*, [2001] 2 FLR 970, suggested that indirect financial contributions would suffice for a common intention constructive trust yet has failed to gain subsequent judicial support.

25 *Midland Bank v. Cooke*, [1995] 4 All ER 562 (C.A.).

between the parties.[26] Thus, indirect financial contributions, along with non-financial contributions, could be taken into account at the quantification stage.

Joint legal title disputes, which are the main focus for this chapter, utilise the same trusts, although focus on the secondary quantification stage as opposed to the primary acquisition stage. The reason for this is that joint legal title presupposes that both parties would share at least some of the beneficial interest so the party disputing any allocation does not need to 'acquire' their interest. The joint legal title holders may use express declarations of trust to specify whether they hold the property as tenants in common or joint tenants and in what shares. There has been a consistent judicial effort to emphasise the importance of declaring beneficial interests at the time of acquisition to avoid lengthy and costly legal disputes.[27] Where the beneficial interests are silent, the implied trusts apply. Historically, joint legal title would generate equal division of the beneficial interest as 'equity follows the law'. However, *McKenzie v. McKenzie* illustrated that this equal division could be easily dislodged in favour of unequal shares whether through a resulting trust or constructive trust.[28]

The aforementioned illustrates the varying responses dependent on the type of trust utilised. Whilst express trusts represent a relatively settled area of jurisprudence in England and Wales, the interface between the resulting and constructive trust has generated extensive confusion and contradiction. The following section will outline the recent House of Lords' decision of *Stack* with a view to evaluating whether any clarification has been provided to the modern trusts framework.

Stack v. Dowden

Stack concerned a dispute over a jointly owned family home that was acquired through financial contributions made by both parties.[29] The parties had an enduring

---

26 *Oxley v. Hiscock*, [2004] EWCA Civ. 546 (C.A.).

27 *See Carlton v. Goodman*, [2002] 2 FLR 259, 44 (Ward LJ) and *Crossley v. Crossley*, [2005] EWCA Civ. 1581, 5 (Sir Peter Gibson).

28 *McKenzie v. McKenzie*, [2003] All ER (D) 155. *See also Goodman v. Gallant*, [1986] Fam 106.

29 *Stack* has been widely analysed in the academic community. *See* N. Piska, *Intention, Fairness and the Presumption of Resulting Trust after* Stack v. Dowden, 71 Modern L. Rev. 114 (2008); G. Battersby, *Ownership of the Family Home:* Stack v. Dowden, in *the House of Lords*, 20 Child & Fam. L. Q. 255 (2008); A.J. Cloherty & D. Fox, *Proving a Trust of a Shared Home*, Cambridge L.J. 517 (2007); W. Swadling, *The Common Intention Constructive Trust in the House of Lords: An Opportunity Missed*, 123 L. Q. Rev. 511 (2007); R. George, Stack v. Dowden – *Do As We Say and Not As We Do?*, 30 J. Social Welfare & Fam. L. 49 (2008); R. Probert, *Cohabitants and Joint Ownership: The Implications of* Stack v. Dowden, Fam. L. 924 (2007); R. Probert, *Equality in the Family Home? Stack v. Dowden*, 15 Feminist Legal Stud. 341 (2007).

cohabiting relationship lasting 27 years and there were four children. Had the parties been married, the issue of beneficial entitlement to the property upon relationship breakdown could have been resolved by the wide judicial discretion conferred via the Matrimonial Causes Act 1973. This not being the case in *Stack* meant that, whilst there was joint legal title, beneficial ownership of the property fell to be determined by general trusts principles.

As is common in this area, there was no express declaration of trust to demarcate the parties' respective beneficial interests, although the transfer did contain a declaration that the survivor could give valid receipt for capital money arising from disposition.[30] Ms Dowden provided a greater share of the acquisition costs, particularly through the repayment of the mortgage. Improvements were made to the property by both parties. Household bills were generally in Ms Dowden's name. Both parties kept separate bank accounts and made separate investments. The relationship broke down and Mr Stack sought an order for sale of the property coupled with equal division of the proceeds of sale.

Owing to the longevity of the relationship and the partnership between the parties, the first instance judge awarded an equal division of the beneficial ownership. Ms Dowden appealed and the Court of Appeal held that the property should be divided unequally in a 65/35 division in her favour despite the presence of joint legal title.[31] The Court of Appeal utilised the principles laid down in the earlier decision of *Oxley v. Hiscock*[32] to reach this conclusion, namely an assessment of what would be a fair share having regard to the whole course of dealings between Ms Dowden and Mr Stack. The fact that Ms Dowden had financially contributed more to the acquisition was highly persuasive for the Court of Appeal. Mr Stack appealed, arguing in favour of a 50/50 distribution of the beneficial ownership. The House of Lords upheld the result of the Court of Appeal, but was divided on how it should have been reached.

In the House of Lords, Baroness Hale recognised that the rise in cohabitation in England and Wales meant that these disputes were becoming 'increasingly visible'.[33] More importantly, disputes over the family home were unlike those located in the commercial setting and 'the domestic context is very different from the commercial world'.[34] Linked to this fact, Baroness Hale then explored the current devices used to determine ownership of the family home. Express declarations of trust pinpointing beneficial ownership at the time of acquisition may decrease the

30 Following *Huntingford v. Hobbs*, [1993] 1 FLR 736 (C.A.) and *Harwood v. Harwood*, [1991] 2 FLR 274 (C.A.) this cannot operate as a declaration of trust.

31 *See* E. Cooke, *Cohabitants, Common Intention and Contributions (again,)*, CONV. & PROP. LAW. 555 (2005).

32 *Supra* note 26.

33 *Stack v. Dowden, supra* note 7, 44.

34 *Id.* 69.

high level of litigation, yet are dependent on proactive conveyancing practice.[35] Locking in the beneficial shares at an early stage provided legal certainty, but the esoteric language of land law was more likely to confuse rather than clarify matters for the lay purchaser.[36] The mechanical presumed intention resulting trust facilitates the informal creation of an interest in the home at the time of acquisition, yet responds to financial considerations, which consequently ignore the significance of homemaker contributions. Whilst some have praised the 'clear simple and cheap to apply' presumption of resulting trust, even prior to *Stack* its utilisation was dwindling in frequency owing to the differences in quantifying that trust in comparison to the constructive trust.[37] Ultimately for Baroness Hale, the common intention constructive trust was the key device as it gives primacy to shared party intention and has developed incrementally since *Pettitt* and *Gissing* in response to changing social and economic conditions.[38]

Baroness Hale introduced a new highly structured framework for adjudicating disputes over jointly owned property.[39] This was dependent on a set of analytical starting points and was neatly encapsulated as follows:

> Just as the starting point where there is sole legal ownership is sole beneficial ownership, the starting point where there is joint legal ownership is joint beneficial ownership. The onus is upon the person seeking to show that the beneficial ownership is different from the legal ownership. So in sole ownership cases it is upon the non-owner to show that he has any interest at all. In joint ownership cases, it is upon the joint owner who claims to have other than a joint beneficial interest.[40]

---

35 There is a widespread optimism that the TR1 form, used in England and Wales for transfers of registered title and in use from 1st April 1998 will direct, albeit not compel, parties to declare beneficial interests and thus the problem will eventually disappear. *See Stack v. Dowden, supra* note 7, 52 (Baroness Hale).

36 *See* G. Douglas, J. Pearce & H. Woodward, *Cohabitation and Conveyancing Practice: Problems and Solutions,* CONV. & PROP. LAW. 365, 370 (2008); G. Douglas, J. Pearce & H. Woodward, *Money, Property, Cohabitation and Separation: Patterns and Indications*, in SHARING LIVES, DIVIDING ASSETS: AN INTERDISCIPLINARY STUDY 158 (J. Miles & R. Probert, eds 2009).

37 LORD NEUBERGER, CHANCERY BAR ASSOCIATION ANNUAL LECTURE, THE CONSPIRATORS, THE TAX MAN, THE BILL OF RIGHTS AND A BIT ABOUT THE LOVERS, 10th March 2008, 9.

38 The common intention constructive trust was again emphasised as the primary device in *Abbott v. Abbott*, [2007] UKPC 53 (P.C.) at 4 (Baroness Hale).

39 A key feature of *Stack* is the highly regimented structure it propounded, as recognised by Lord Hope in *Stack v. Dowden, supra* note 7, 3 stating 'The key to simplifying the law in this area lies in the identification of the correct starting point. Each case will, of course, turn on its own facts. But law can, and should, provide the right framework.'

40 *Id.* 56.

This framework was translated into the following legal principles. Joint registration of legal title instigated a heavy burden of equal sharing through a beneficial joint tenancy.[41] This situation reflected a default position, premised on the equitable maxim that 'equity follows the law', and the question, in practice, then became whether the property concerned fell within the domestic context or was commercial property. If the former, it was envisaged that in the vast majority of cases, equal beneficial sharing would remain. This would operate through the common intention constructive trust as opposed to a presumed intention resulting trust.[42] Conversely, if commercial property was involved, the traditional resulting trust would be a more appropriate tool, particularly owing to the fact it recognised the financial contributions of the parties at the time of acquisition. The home was different, and thus mere unequal financial contribution, which satisfied unequal sharing through a resulting trust in a commercial context, would not of itself dislodge equal sharing through a constructive trust in a domestic context.[43]

When discussing domestic cases where an unequal division was appropriate, Baroness Hale advocated contextual analysis and that '[e]ach case will turn on its own facts'.[44] Only 'unusual'[45] or 'exceptional'[46] cases would be capable of dislodging equal sharing in equity. Baroness Hale strongly reiterated that extensive investigation to find a common intention to share the beneficial interest unequally should not be embarked upon lightly owing to the disproportionate costs and the inherent evidential difficulties endemic within the family home context.[47]

Exceptional or unusual cases involved an investigation of whether the parties intended that their beneficial interests should depart from their legal interest and if so to what extent. At this point an extensive and non-exhaustive list of factors could be employed by the court to 'ascertain the parties' shared intentions, actual, inferred or imputed, with respect to the property in the light of their whole course of conduct in relation to it'.[48] The enumerated factors consisted of a blend of property-related and relationship-related elements which would enable the court to evaluate

41 It can be queried whether the majority intended the creation of a presumptive beneficial joint tenancy as opposed to a tenancy in common in equal shares thereby without survivorship.

42 This was to reverse a string of authorities advocating a strict resulting trust approach where there was a joint name conveyance, namely *Walker v. Hall*, [1984] FLR 126 (C.A.), *Springette v. Defoe*, [1992] 2 FLR 388 (C.A.) and *Huntingford v. Hobbs*, *supra* note 30.

43 Baroness Hale at 68 in *Stack* states that challenges to 'the hundreds of thousands, if not millions, of transfers into joint names' should not, in practice, occur merely because of unequal contribution to their purchase. *See Fowler v. Barron*, [2008] EWCA Civ 377 (C.A.), 18 (Arden LJ).

44 *Stack v. Dowden*, *supra* note 7, 69.

45 *Id.* 68–69, 92 (Baroness Hale).

46 *Id.* 33 (Lord Walker).

47 *Id.* 68 (Baroness Hale), 33 (Lord Walker).

48 *Id.* 60 (Baroness Hale).

the parties' common intentions, with examples being any advice or discussions at the time of the transfer, the purpose for which the home was acquired and the nature of the parties' relationship.[49] By not limiting the investigation to financial contributions, the whole course of dealings between the parties would be assessed. Most importantly for the House of Lords, where evidence pinpointing intention was lacking, the court could not abandon the search for common intention and supplement its finding with what would on the facts be termed a fair outcome.

In contrast to Baroness Hale's emphasis on the differentiation of the domestic context and her contextual analysis of the parties' shared lives, the minority judgment of Lord Neuberger downplayed context and the use of an overly formulaic framework. In the absence of statutory reform in this area, the court's role was merely to provide 'clarification and simplification'[50] and the existing, well-established principles of trusts were flexible enough to be deployed without the need for extensive judicial tampering. Lord Neuberger rejected the idea of carving out the family home for separate treatment, as distinct from commercial property, stating that, without legislative provisions dictating otherwise:

> … the same principles should apply to assess the apportionment of the beneficial interest as between legal co-owners, whether in a sexual, platonic, familial, amicable or commercial relationship.[51]

This did not mean that the courts would ignore the domestic or home dimension, as Lord Neuberger noted that the existing framework was not 'static'[52] and could allow differing factual considerations to be taken into account when interpreting intentions as to ownership. The context of the parties' relationship provided the backdrop to the courts' analysis of party interaction when determining beneficial ownership. For Lord Neuberger, a failure to express beneficial interests in a joint legal title case would direct the court to consider contributions at the date of acquisition, thereby triggering a presumed intention resulting trust. In the absence of a contrary common intention, the resulting trust solution was the most appropriate mechanism for resolving the issue. Thus, the presumption of resulting trust could be 'rebutted and replaced' by a common intention constructive trust.[53]

The House of Lords held that the property was to be divided 65/35 in favour of Ms Dowden. The majority believed that despite the starting point of a joint beneficial tenancy between Ms Dowden and Mr Stack, this was 'a very unusual case'.[54] For Baroness Hale there was no pooling of assets for the common good as both parties kept rigidly separate financial affairs. Thus, the parties 'did not

49 *Id.* 69 (Baroness Hale).
50 *Id.* 105 (Lord Neuberger).
51 *Id.* 107.
52 *Id.* 101.
53 *Id.* 124.
54 *Id.* 92 (Baroness Hale).

intend their shares, even in the property which was put into both their names, to be equal'.[55]

Various Meanings of 'Context'

Stack represented the first House of Lords' authority on a joint legal title dispute between cohabitants.[56] Similarly, it was the first decision on the family home since the sole legal title case of *Lloyds Bank v. Rosset*.[57] The latter, decided 16 years prior to *Stack*, provided a rigid and formulaic framework for the acquisition of a beneficial interest in the family home based on express agreements and direct financial contributions.[58] Whilst acquisition of a beneficial interest was not at issue in *Stack*, it was expected by the legal profession and academic community that the decision would provide clarification to the general principles of trusts of the family home.[59] This need for clarification was well-known, particularly as the case law demonstrated a destabilised area of law typified by widespread 'doctrinal fudging'.[60] These hopes have arguably not been satisfied and, as will be demonstrated through the post-*Stack* case law, the current legal framework may still be regarded as a confused 'witch's brew'.[61] In particular, this chapter argues that a key factor that contributed to this ambiguity was the majority's resort to context.

The idea of context utilised in *Stack* can be deconstructed and may arguably have differing meanings.[62] To begin with, the lay person's interpretation and definition of context may, in its most basic and literal form, refer to the circumstances that surround a particular event which consequently contribute to and facilitate the understanding of that event. Traditionally conceived context has a supplemental role enabling the event to be viewed in full recognition of its factual background. Yet, in addition to this non-legal viewpoint, context can be translated into legal regulation in different ways.

55 *Id.* (Baroness Hale).

56 As noted by Baroness Hale in *Stack, supra* note 7, 40.

57 *Supra* note 22.

58 See above for the requisite elements of a claim.

59 The effect of *Stack* on sole legal title disputes is currently perplexing the lower courts as evidenced from *Abbott v. Abbott, supra* note 38; *James v. Thomas*, [2007] EWCA (Civ) 1212 (C.A.); *Morris v. Morris*, [2008] EWCA 257 (C.A.); *Webster v. Webster*, [2008] EWHC 31 (H.C.).

60 J. Miles, *Property Law v. Family Law: Resolving the Problems of Family Property*, 23 Legal Stud. 624 (2003).

61 *Stack v. Dowden*, [2005] EWCA (Civ) 857 (C.A.), 75 (Carnwath LJ).

62 To borrow Lord Walker's technique in *Stack* of counting the amount of times Lord Diplock utilised the word 'infer' in *Gissing v. Gissing, supra* note 2, the House of Lords in *Stack* refer to the word 'context' 28 times.

When one approaches the dichotomy between domestic and commercial settings evinced by the majority in *Stack*, one understanding of context is as a labelling device, whereby in a respective sphere, or rather, *in a particular context*, different principles apply and different normative values operate. A central feature of the majority decision in *Stack* was the differential treatment offered to property depending on whether it fell within the domestic or the commercial context. Thus, one approach that the law could take would be to treat domestic and commercial property as operating in two separate realms. Hopkins has noted this dichotomy and stated, 'we can regulate the home differently, by applying different principles in relation to the home'.[63] Hopkins termed this characterisation a context-specific approach. For Hopkins, this 'would require entirely contextual regulation'.[64] The importance of this context-specific approach is prior classification of the property. Once property has entered this specific realm, principles can be applied that directly address the fact that we are concerned with a domestic property. This is arguably present in the approach that *Stack* advocates through the development of a presumptive beneficial joint tenancy applicable to domestic joint legal title cases.

In contrast to what will be termed the 'context of home,' is the idea of 'contextual analysis' in *Stack*: thus, running alongside a taxonomic approach to different types of property contexts is the idea of contextual analysis or *viewing a specific event in context*. This is utilised when the courts are isolating the parties' common intention for the purpose of the constructive trust. When transposed onto the legal framework from *Stack*, once the property has been classified as domestic, a secondary meaning of context opens up: context shifts from merely possessing an identification function, but instead becomes practical, that is, deployed when scrutinising specific factors or evidence. In disputes over the family home, contextual analysis enables close scrutiny of the prevailing conditions, motivations and most importantly, intentions regarding that specific act of acquisition. Reference to contextual analysis enables the court to look at a variety of facts surrounding acquisition. Similarly, context may also enable scrutiny of events that take place post-acquisition, which are often crucial when looking back in retrospect to demarcate agreements as to beneficial ownership. *Stack* also utilises contextual analysis and when exploring the relationship between Ms Dowden and Mr Stack closely focused on their relationship dynamics both towards the property and also between each other. As Baroness Hale noted, '[t]he context is supplied by the nature of the parties' conduct and attitudes towards their property and finances'.[65]

63 N. Hopkins, Regulating Trusts of the Home: Private Law and Social Policy, 125 L. Q. Rev. 310, 311 (2009).

64 *Id.*

65 *Stack v. Dowden*, *supra* note 7, 90. Lord Hope also discusses the 'wider context of their overall relationship' at ¶ 3.

There are other ways of conceptualising context within the home. Hopkins further explores this and opines that the home can be approached in a context-neutral manner, thus no differentiation between domestic or commercial spheres. However, the courts may utilise contextual analysis of facts as drivers for decisions.[66] In short, the same initial legal framework applies irrespective of the labelling of the property, but contextual analysis has a transformative effective on their application, namely 'context-neutral, outcome specific'.[67] The minority approach in *Stack* demonstrated a preference for a context-neutral, outcome-specific adjudication, and as Lord Neuberger noted, 'while the domestic context can give rise to very different factual considerations from the commercial context, I am unconvinced that this justifies a different approach in principle to the issue of the ownership of the beneficial interest in property held in joint names'.[68]

The majority's approach in *Stack* falls within a context-specific metric and also utilises heightened contextual analysis of the facts. As will be argued, the approach goes beyond the aforementioned minority approach as various factors are investigated which go further than those accepted by Lord Neuberger. The following section of this chapter explores the context of home and contextual analysis with a view to questioning whether the prioritisation of context clarifies the trusts of the family home framework.

The 'Context' of Home

Recognising the differences between the home context and the commercial context is not a new analytical technique for England and Wales. Despite the well-documented failings of the trust regime, there is evidence showing that the courts have manipulated the trust framework by being receptive to context. As a result, *Stack* may merely build upon past judicial practice in numerous ways.

It is trite law that there is no separate and coherent regime for determining ownership of the family home.[69] Strictly speaking, the general principles of property and trusts apply irrespective of the designation of the property. However, the courts have tried to accommodate the interpersonal dimension surrounding trusts operating within the family home context. The common intention constructive trust, as developed through the cases of *Pettitt* and *Gissing*, was developed with the shared home in mind and has been used within the domestic context for decades.[70] The creativity of equity and the vitality of trusts enabled

---

66 N. Hopkins, *supra* note 63, at 311.

67 *Id.* at 313.

68 *Stack v. Dowden, supra* note 7, 107.

69 This is contrasted against the position of married couples and civil partners in *Stack v. Dowden, supra* note 7, 43 (Baroness Hale), 100 (Lord Neuberger).

70 *See* A.J.H. Morris, *Equity's Reaction to Modern Domestic Relationships*, in Trends in Contemporary Trust Law (AJ Oakley eds, 1997) (Chapter 12).

the House of Lords in both cases, albeit more explicitly in *Gissing*, to fashion a response to the particular problems of ascertaining ownership of the family home. Dewar has indicated that in spite of cohabitants being regarded as strangers[71] when dealing with real property, 'allowances'[72] have been made to the fact that, when determining ownership, land has been used for a family purpose. Drawing upon what he regards as a 'highly complex and specialised branch of law',[73] the modern regime of trusts and property law applicable to ownership disputes has undergone 'familialization'.[74] A specialised body of principles has emerged, recognising the context of the home which has in turn developed specifically for application in that area.

However, the fact the common intention constructive trust operates exclusively within the family home does not mean the presence of a coherent legal framework. The trust devices deployed represent an amalgam of conceptually variable entities[75] that find their homes in multiple branches of the law.[76] Thus, drawing on various branches of law, such as property law and family law, means the regulation of ownership of the family home sits precariously between regimes with competing rationales and motivations.[77] Land lawyers, for example, are invariably keen to assert the primacy of certainty in dealings affecting land, especially for third parties, with an emphasis on what was agreed or what contributions were made in the past. Family lawyers favour a more forward-looking, discretionary system to determine ownership, often focusing on future needs.[78] This familialisation trend is problematic for a variety of reasons and it should be noted that Dewar's thesis

71 It should be noted that prior to the conferral of a redistributive discretion in 1970, married couples were also treated as strangers when dealing with ownership of the matrimonial home. A key reason for this was the principle of separate property.

72 J. Dewar, *Land, Law, and the Family Home*, in LAND LAW: THEMES AND PERSPECTIVES 327 (S. Bright & J. Dewar eds, 1998).

73 *Id.* at 328.

74 *Id.* at 328.

75 As noted by Hopkins, *supra* note 63, at 310 comparing common intention constructive trust principles under *Stack* with their subsequent regulation under the Trusts of Land and Appointment of Trustees Act 1996.

76 As Dewar has argued, 'the relevant legal rules must be picked out from the law of conveyancing, real property, trusts, and contract, and from statutes dealing with divorce, children, domestic violence, insolvency, trusts of the land, tenancies and creditor protection' in J. Dewar, *supra* note 72, at 327.

77 A.J. Cloherty & D.M. Fox, *supra* note 29.

78 For an excellent analysis of the competing motivations of property law and family law *see* J Miles, *supra* note 60; R Probert, *Family Law and Property Law: Competing Spheres in the Regulation of the Family Home, in* NEW PERSPECTIVES ON PROPERTY LAW, HUMAN RIGHTS AND THE HOME (A. Hudson ed., 2003). Compare J. Mee, *Property Rights and Personal Relationships: Reflections on Reform*, 24 LEGAL STUD. 414, 418 (2004), noting the 'temptation ... to dismiss property law as narrow and rigid and to praise family law as being flexible and just.'

is premised on the fact that piecemeal endeavours to isolate the home for separate treatment, whether through trusts or legislation, has ultimately provided further 'complexity and internal inconsistency'.[79]

Stack continues this trend and coupled with its use of contextual analysis, explored below, is a classic case of familialisation of trusts. Singling out the domestic context and then closely scrutinising the property and relationship dynamics of the parties when quantifying shares clearly evince this tendency. The following section explores the practical and theoretical difficulties in further developing a separate trust regime for exclusive applicability in the home.

Firstly, there are practical difficulties as carving out a separate regime for the determination of beneficial interests in the home requires the ability to categorise and distinguish home and commercial contexts. Instinctively, distinguishing the family home and the commercial context may appear possible. The text of *Stack* refers to 'domestic consumer context',[80] 'consumer context',[81] 'domestic context',[82] 'cohabitation context'[83] and to the context of a 'home'.[84] All of these labels resonate with the central idea that the property concerned fell within the private sphere as distinct from referring to property purchased at parties operating at arm's-length, possibly as an investment. Yet, problematically, the labelling used in the decision is not consistent. Whilst the members of the House of Lords may have been referring to a specific type of property when using these terms and may not have been as pedantic as to taxonomy, differences arise between these labels. For example, it is arguable that the cohabitation context is different from the home context and these distinctions are visible in the post-*Stack* case law.

Following the ratio of *Stack* alone, the strong presumption of beneficial joint tenancy applied in the 'cohabitation context'. The litigants in *Stack* were in an intimate cohabiting relationship and the discussion of the majority focused on this type of relationship. Lord Hope stated that with cohabiting relationships, 'the place where they live together is their home'[85] and there was a widespread utilisation of the term 'home' in *Stack* as distinct from the mere reference to 'property'. Arguably, this case was concerned with the cohabitation paradigm and many of the reform projects in England and Wales focus on providing remedies for intimate cohabiting relationships. However, shortly after the House of Lords' decision, courts were required to examine whether platonic or familial relationships would fall within the principles of *Stack* and therefore be able to utilise the presumptive beneficial joint tenancy. The courts had to evaluate what types of properties and, incidentally, relationships fell within the domestic context.

---

79 *Id.* at 329.

80 *Stack v. Dowden*, *supra* note 7, 58 (Baroness Hale).

81 *Id.* 52, 54, 57 (Baroness Hale).

82 *Id.* 60, 69 (Baroness Hale), 107 (Lord Neuberger).

83 *Id.* 69 (Baroness Hale).

84 *Id.* 64–65 (Baroness Hale).

85 *Stack v. Dowden*, *supra* note 7, 3.

In *Adekunle v. Ritchie*,[86] decided shortly after the House of Lords' decision in *Stack*, a council tenant utilised a 'right to buy' discount to finance a joint named purchase with her son. After her death, her estate was administered by two of her children who sought sale and subsequent division of the proceeds of sale of the property. Her son contended that as legal joint title holder, his mother's share passed to him by way of survivorship, thereby making him absolute owner. Counsel for the administrators argued that *Stack* did not apply as Baroness Hale envisaged sexual, cohabiting relationships. Judge Behrens rejected this argument and stated that the 'new' principles of *Stack* directly applied by virtue of the fact that the property was a home.[87] The majority's utilisation of the term 'domestic context' in *Stack* meant that the principles were not restricted to intimate cohabiting relationships. At first glance, it appeared that *Stack* instinctively applied irrespective of the nature of the parties' relationship.

However, the presumptive beneficial joint tenancy was dislodged in *Adekunle* as, after initial categorisation of the property as a home, Judge Behren's use of contextual analysis generated an unequal division of the beneficial interest. Whilst the 'primary purpose'[88] of this acquisition was the provision of a home for the mother, Judge Behrens conceded that the fact the parties were not in an intimate sexual relationship had an impact on the application of *Stack*. Judge Behrens stated:

> It may well be, however, that where one is not dealing with the situation of a couple living together it will be easier to find that the facts are unusual in the sense that they are not to be taken to have intended a beneficial joint tenancy.[89]

The home element opened up the application of *Stack*, but when shifting away from the paradigm intimate cohabiting relationship in *Stack*, the parties' relationship in *Adekunle* instigated a predisposition towards the case being exceptional. Despite one of the foundational principles of *Stack* being that financial contributions should not be determinative in this domestic context, Judge Behrens largely followed a presumed intention resulting trust analysis when determining the beneficial interests of the parties. Whilst it is easy to envisage a plethora of home-sharing patterns within the domestic context,[90] *Adekunle* demonstrated that singling out the home and then applying context-sensitive principles may allow further subdivisions based on intimacy or familial ties. This result also seems antagonistic to the purported bright-line principle of the House of Lords in *Stack* that there was a heavy presumption of beneficial joint tenancy. *Adekunle* thus highlighted the

86 *Adekunle v. Richie*, [2007] EW Misc 5.

87 *Id.* 9.

88 *Id.* 66.

89 *Id.* 65.

90 As noted by LAW COMMISSION, SHARING HOMES: A DISCUSSION PAPER (Law Com No. 278, 2002).

risk of further splintering and subdivision of the multi-faceted characterisation of a property as home.

The issue of 'home' arose again in the Court of Appeal decision in *Laskar v. Laskar*.[91] In *Laskar*, the property was purchased by a mother and daughter as joint legal owners. The intention was for the property to be an investment, thereby generating income through renting it out to tenants. The mother and daughter both kept their financial affairs separate.[92] Lord Neuberger, sitting in the Court of Appeal, jettisoned the application of the principles of *Stack*, noting that *Stack* concerned 'a long-term sexual relationship' and the premises were purchased with a view to providing 'a family home'.[93] The lack of communality in the management of their affairs negated a 'home' context and opened up the presumed intention resulting trust traditionally thought to operate in the commercial context. Interestingly, Lord Neuberger recognised that *Laskar* was a 'midway'[94] case between a cohabitation case and a commercial context case. Lord Neuberger also noted that even if *Stack* had applied, this case would be regarded as an exceptional case and the beneficial interest would be divided with reference to the respective financial contributions.

Subsequent case law may suggest a return to the default approach laid down in *Stack*, namely that within the domestic context a strong presumption of beneficial joint tenancy arises. *Fowler v. Barron* concerned a long-term intimate relationship.[95] The property was purchased by Mr Barron and served as a family home for the parties. The Court of Appeal held that this case fell directly within the domestic context and the fact that there were unequal financial contributions to the acquisition of the property did not justify dislodging the beneficial joint tenancy. Arden LJ was keen to endorse the 'essential'[96] reasoning behind *Stack* and emphasised its creation of a 'default rule'[97] behind the separate treatment of the home. Interestingly, and owing to the fact that *Fowler* was the first case dealing with an intimate cohabiting relationship after *Stack*, the fact that the property was used as a home attracted considerable weight. Toulson LJ stated that there was 'nothing at all unusual'[98] about the facts in *Fowler* and stated that an overtly financial outlook would fail to recognise the fact that '... the property served as a family home for the parties and their children from the time of its acquisition until the time of breakdown of the relationship'.[99]

---

91 *Laskar v. Laskar*, [2008] EWCA (Civ) 347.

92 Lord Neuberger, in *Laskar v. Lasker*, invokes the dichotomy between domestic and arm's length arrangements. *Id.* 15.

93 *Id.*

94 *Id.* 17.

95 *Supra* note 43. *See* A. Hayward, *Family Values in the Home: Fowler v. Barron*, 21 Child & Fam. L. Q. 242 (2009).

96 *Fowler v. Barron*, *supra* note 43, 45.

97 *Id.* 34.

98 *Id.* 53.

99 *Id.* 56.

These cases indicate the delicacy involved in distinguishing particular factual contexts and illustrate how the majority in *Stack* appears to have created an elaborate arrangement of legal principles. They also show that the creation of a context of home and the virtues of the presumptive beneficial joint tenancy may arguably be symbolic as contextual analysis generates exceptional cases negating their utilisation. As the above cases have illustrated to varying degrees, singling out the home and distinguishing this context represents a difficult move. There is a lack of precision as to the types of cases that *Stack*'s approach would operate within, which could be attributable to the majority's insouciance with regard to the prefix before context, that is, 'domestic context' or 'cohabitation context'.[100] These fine distinctions add uncertainty into the legal framework especially with regards to practitioners advising clients. It is also arguable that this imprecision empowers the judiciary to generate fine distinctions underneath the umbrella 'context' of the home.[101] A spectrum appears to be emerging in the domestic context with the paradigm intimate cohabiting relationship at one end with a quasi-commercial, albeit familial relationship, at the other end.[102] In turn, the further away from the paradigm relationship, the more likely the case would be regarded as unusual, which suggests *Stack* clearly had a cohabiting relationship in mind when carving out the context of home.

Linked to this spectrum is the fact that problems certainly arise where the property concerned functioned as both a home and also a business for the parties. Where there is a dual function, naturally the question arises of whether the courts should apply the home-centric rules, instigating in particular the presumptive joint tenancy, or should the resulting trust be employed.[103] Even when the case falls within the context of home, the fact that the property may also operate as an investment may mean a subsequent rebuttal of the presumption of beneficial joint tenancy. Although Bridge has argued that the determination of property has been 'resolved relatively satisfactorily by the courts', it is probable that future case law will pose further issues with categorisation.[104]

There are also theoretical problems in developing a separate regime for the home. One motivation that can be discerned for the creation of a separate regime in *Stack* is that it develops a concept of home. Homes are different and require

---

100 Neuberger, *supra* note 37, 14.

101 *See* N. Piska, *Two Recent Reflections on the Resulting Trust*, Convey. & Prop. Law. 441, 446 (2008) for the machinations involved in categorising and subdividing the domestic/commercial contexts.

102 Once it is deemed fully commercial then the *Stack* principles do not apply and the presumed intention resulting trust would appear more appropriate.

103 With regard to sole legal title disputes *see* N. Piska, A Common Intention or a Rare Bird? Proprietary Interests, Personal Claims and Services Rendered by Lovers Post Acquisition, 21 Child & Fam. L.Q. 104 (2009).

104 S. Bridge, *Jones v. Kernott: Fairness in the Shared Home – the Forbidden Territory or the Promised Land*?, Convey. & Prop. Law. 324, 329 (2010).

a legal framework cognisant of the interpersonal dealings between parties when acquiring property. Invoking the idea of home may instinctively seem appealing, particularly for litigants, but various issues arise.

Firstly, there is an underdeveloped concept of 'home' in England and Wales and had the majority engaged more fully with this, the creation of a separate regime may have had more persuasive impact. Understanding and clearly articulating the motivations behind specific treatment would help give clarity to the legal principles. As noted above, the legal regulation of the family home is a patchwork of rules and principles emanating from a variety of sources. As Fox has argued:

> … the extent to which the law seeks to recognise and protect the status of home … varies, in a more or less ad hoc fashion, depending on the context in which the legal issues arise and, particularly, on the right of the competing interest(s) at stake in any given case. Thus, while 'home' interests may be (implicitly) recognised in some legal contexts (usually where the primary aim of legal policy is to promote the home interest) they are also relatively easily dismissed in others. There is not, as yet, a coherent concept of home in law.[105]

Fox has outlined this 'home interest' as a multifaceted concept comprising various elements. Whilst Fox's work is centred in the creditor context, where the creditor clearly has a readily identifiable interest in recouping their financial outlay on the other parties' default, the interests of individuals *inter se* within the home are harder to differentiate. Without reference to a concept of home, the majority in *Stack* did not provide the necessary theoretical underpinning to justify treating domestic property differently. The House of Lords do, however, explore certain aspects identifiable within a 'home interest' that make the home different.

The main component of this home interest, which is evident in *Stack*, is the financial aspect of home, linked to recognition of home as a capital asset. Lord Hope stressed the importance of home ownership owing to its lucrative benefits[106] and Baroness Hale likewise provided a socially sensitive judgment, recognising the importance of homeownership and rising house prices.[107] In particular, Baroness Hale focused on the ideological shift towards owner-occupation and how this has been facilitated further by incentives, such as the 'right to buy' legislation introduced in the 1980s. Because it is 'more advantageous'[108] for an individual who has made a financial contribution to a home to claim ownership rather than merely a return of their capital input, creating a clear and structured system for determining ownership is likely to be integral to the majority's

105 L. Fox, Conceptualising Home, Theories, Laws and Policies 4 (2007); L. Fox, *The Meaning of Home: A Chimerical Concept or a Legal Challenge*, 29 J. L. & Soc'y 580 (2002).

106 *Stack v. Dowden*, *supra* note 7, 2.

107 *Id.* 41.

108 *Id.* 41 (Baroness Hale).

reasoning. This financial element may be linked to the fact that there is a 'pressing social problem'[109] regarding determining ownership of the home and a principled approach is deemed necessary.[110] The focus on starting points and procedure suggested that the practicalities of the separate regime centre on trying to achieve legal certainty or allowing 'everyone to know where they stand'.[111]

The financial ethos within *Stack* is particularly interesting owing to the majority's rejection of the presumed intention resulting trust in domestic cases. Despite the majority treating the home separately, the ultimate outcome of the case rested upon financial considerations and the specific money management pattern within that case. When the courts divined the shared intentions in *Stack*, the unequal division correlated to an outcome capable of being generated under the resulting trust.[112] The cases of *Adekunle* and *Laskar*, discussed above, both demonstrated recognition of the capital value of home and their results were consistent with a resulting trust outcome. Whilst viewing the home as a capital asset reflects a significant dimension of its meanings for these parties, *Stack* and most of the subsequent case law provided a semblance of valuing the home interest, yet ultimately take the law back to financial considerations; a movement that many commentators wanted the law to manoeuvre away from. Subsequent Court of Appeal decisions, such as *Fowler v. Barron*[113] and *Jones v. Kernott*,[114] may indicate a movement away from focusing on financial contributions and this may develop more legal discourse surrounding the home element in *Stack*. However, this indicates that time is needed for clearer principles to develop when unpacking the rationale for separating out the home.

Interestingly, *Stack* does not provide much further indication of the reasons for singling out the home, nor does it unpack *alternative* interests that can be located within the umbrella home interest.[115] Nevertheless, the status of the property as a home has become a central focus through the post-*Stack* case law. Overall, the majority approach of the House of Lords did not convincingly justify the singling out of the home or provide clear principles. Whilst the overarching ethos of *Stack* rests on context, the fluidity surrounding what the majority was referring to renders its invocation inherently problematic. Creating a separate regime for the home opens up a new and unchartered territory for the courts which may in

---

109 *Id.* 2 (Lord Hope).

110 *See* Law Commission, *supra* note 90, on the importance of establishing ownership as between the parties and vis-à-vis third parties.

111 *Stack v. Dowden*, *supra* note 7, 5 (Lord Hope).

112 *See* Lord Neuberger advocating the 'resulting trust solution' in *Stack v. Dowden*, *supra* note 7, 106.

113 *Supra* note 43.

114 *Jones v. Kernott*, [2010] EWCA (Civ) 578.

115 Fox explores these interests such as home as territory, home as self-identity and home as a social and cultural unit in L. Fox, Conceptualising Home, Theories, Laws and Policies, *supra* note 105 (Chapter 4).

turn destabilise the law further because within that regime, context is everything, making outcomes unpredictable. Equally, as has been noted, it is open for the courts to subdivide and splinter the categorisations within the domestic context.

Contextual Analysis

Once property held with joint legal title has been deemed to fall within the 'domestic context', a presumptive beneficial joint tenancy arises. The party challenging this equal division must evince evidence of a shared intention to share unequally. Here the court utilises contextual analysis to determine the common intention of the parties based on a variety of factors. Without utilising fairness, the court has to ascertain a common intention which reflects 'what the parties must, in the light of their conduct, be taken to have intended'.[116] This echoed the Law Commission's holistic approach utilised in their Discussion Paper Sharing Homes[117] as opposed to utilising that of Chadwick LJ advocating 'fairness' as a benchmark in *Oxley v. Hiscock*.[118] Rather than focusing solely on financial contributions to the acquisition of the property, the majority in the House of Lords in *Stack* provided, in paragraph 69, a non-exhaustive list of considerations. These included:

> … any advice or discussions at the time of the transfer which cast light upon their intentions then; the reasons why the home was acquired in their joint names; the reasons why (if it be the case) the survivor was authorised to give a receipt for the capital moneys; the purpose for which the home was acquired; the nature of the parties' relationship; whether they had children for whom they both had responsibility to provide a home; how the purchase was financed, both initially and subsequently; how the parties arranged their finances, whether separately or together or a bit of both; how they discharged the outgoings on the property and their other household expenses.[119]

It was envisaged that contextual analysis would help a trial judge ascertain the true intentions of the parties. The motivation behind this broad investigative technique was that more factors are relevant when ascertaining party intention. *Stack* has therefore expanded the ambit of the investigation. It is also far from contentious to assert that conduct within a domestic setting may have different motivations or may be interpreted differently than equivalent conduct in a commercial setting. As Baroness Hale noted:

116 *Stack v. Dowden*, *supra* note 7, 61 (Baroness Hale).

117 Law Commission, *supra* note 90, at 4.7.

118 *Supra* note 26.

119 *Stack v. Dowden*, *supra* note 7, 69.

> … to put it at its lowest, the interpretation to be put on the behaviour of people living together in an intimate relationship may be different from the interpretation to be put upon similar behaviour between commercial men. To put it at its highest, an outcome which might seem just in a purely commercial transaction may appear highly unjust in a transaction between husband and wife or cohabitant and cohabitant.[120]

The focus of this investigation for the majority was an analysis of party conduct with a view to ascertain intended ownership of property. However, when looking for party intention, how far are the courts focusing the issue of property ownership as opposed to scrutinising the parties' general interaction within the home? Context allows *all* factors relevant to intention to be taken into account, which causes a problem with the accepted judicial exercise when divining intentions. As Dixon has noted, it is difficult for a trial judge to:

> … separate a course of dealings between the parties which goes to the acquisition of the land (allowable) from a course of conduct which goes to the success of the relationship or simply reflects the normal obligations of everyday life (disallowable).[121]

The list of factors within paragraph 69 enables the judiciary to dissect, in minute detail, not only the intricacies of the parties' relationship with the property, but often the relationship between each other. The predicament is the lack of precision in the judicial investigation now that contextual analysis is paramount. It is apparent that subsequent judicial and academic commentary has suggested that the factors set out in paragraph 69 are 'not necessarily reliable indicators of the parties' intention',[122] which from a doctrinal perspective is problematic when party intention is the bedrock of the common intention constructive trust.

Stack and the decisions that followed it have illustrated this difficulty of dividing up permissible and impermissible analysis. In *Jones v. Kernott*,[123] Nicholas Strauss QC noted that certain of the paragraph 69 factors 'have little direct connection

---

120 *Stack v. Dowden*, *supra* note 7, 42, as reiterated in *Abbott v. Abbott*, *supra* note 38, 2 where Baroness Hale stated 'the inferences to be drawn from the conduct of husband and wife may be different from those to be drawn from the conduct of parties to more commercial transactions'. *See* R. Lee, *Stack v. Dowden: A Sequel*, 124 L. Q. Rev. 209 (2008).

121 M. Dixon, *The Never-Ending Story – Co-ownership after Stack v. Dowden*, Convey. & Prop. Law. 456, 458 (2007).

122 *See* G. Douglas, J. Pearce & H. Woodward, *Money, Property, Cohabitation and Separation: Patterns and Indications*, *supra* note 36, at 141 (providing case studies exploring the paragraph 69 factors).

123 *Jones v. Kernott*, [2009] EWHC 1713.

with the property'.[124] Similarly Lord Neuberger noted in *Stack* that the way parties conduct their 'day-to-day living and finances, is in my view, at least of itself, not a reliable guide to their intentions in relation to that ownership'.[125] The majority were indeed cognisant of the difficulty of dividing up property-related and relationship-related enquiries. Baroness Hale criticised the focus of the trial judge in *Stack* on the relationship between Mr Stack and Ms Dowden. She stated:

> ... the judge addressed himself to 'looking at the parties' entire course of conduct together'. He looked at their relationship rather than the matters which were particularly relevant to their intentions about this property. He founded his conclusion on the length and nature of their relationship, which he repeatedly referred to as a partnership, despite the fact that they had maintained separate finances throughout their time together.[126]

Whilst extricating property-related and relationship-related factors is necessary, if determining common intention as to property ownership is paramount, it is conceded that it is problematic in practice. For example, Baroness Hale noted the fact that Mr Stack gave his father's address when directing his post and bank statements. She commented that '[t]he judge made little of this fact, but it might be thought to indicate something about the quality of the parties' relationship',[127] which appears contradictory to the purported search for party intention with respect to property ownership. This is another example of how open-textured heightened contextual analysis can be.

A clearer approach may have been greater emphasis in *Stack* on the fact that the context of the parties' relationship could only be examined insofar as it casts light on the parties' shared intentions vis-à-vis ownership of the property. Lord Neuberger advocated this approach, stating that evidence of the parties' use and enjoyment of the property represented 'vital background',[128] but was not determinative of the matter. Lord Neuberger accepted that 'the domestic context can give rise to very different factual considerations from the commercial context',[129] yet his Lordship favoured harnessing this through the judicial interpretation of facts rather than demarcating out a separate regime for the home and applying heightened contextual analysis. This viewpoint is more logical and may control the scope of contextual analysis advocated in *Stack*. A clearer statement of the parameters of the judicial enquiry could have simultaneously recognised the value

124 *Id.* 19. In the Court of Appeal decision in *Jones v. Kernott*, *supra* note 114, Rimer LJ suspected that trial judges would consider *Stack* as presenting 'something of a challenge'.

125 *Stack v. Dowden*, *supra* note 7, 143 (Lord Neuberger).

126 *Id.* 86 (Baroness Hale).

127 *Id.* 76.

128 *Stack v. Dowden*, *supra* note 7, 143.

129 *Id.* 107.

of holistic analysis of party conduct, whilst ensuring some degree of predictability of outcome.

The paragraph 69 factors in *Stack* also generate complexity when they are applied to given factual scenarios. In particular, their interaction may indicate that certain factors have more weight and the interpretation given to each factor gives insight into the judicial methodology in trusts of the family home cases. In an area where expressly articulated intentions are rare and parties are not expected to operate with documented formality, the long and non-exhaustive list of factors set out by Baroness Hale may appear instinctively appropriate. Yet, does the provision of a non-exhaustive list of factors disguise legal reasoning and permit fairness being employed under the guise of common intention?

Firstly, the breadth of the factors may suggest that the court has an unlimited ability to divine the intentions of the parties. In *Holman v. Howes*,[130] a sole legal title case decided very shortly after *Stack*, Ms Holman argued that the courts reference to the whole course of dealings allowed the court to take into account a myriad of behavioural factors. In particular, it was argued that the upkeep of a private road and subsequent dealing with trees on the property without Mr Howe's supervision,[131] along with his alleged undue influence and unconscionable behaviour towards herself and their daughter,[132] represented post-acquisition factors that could enable the court to divine their intentions. Whilst concerned with quantification in a sole ownership case, the Court of Appeal explored the conduct that could be focused upon to ascertain intention. It is unsurprising that Lloyd LJ regarded these occurrences as 'unilateral',[133] owing to the lack of post-acquisition dealings with Mr Howes and also 'plainly irrelevant'.[134] It was argued that to take these factors into account would be to herald a retreat back to fairness which the House of Lords rejected in *Stack*.

The arguments advanced by counsel in *Holman* illustrated an extreme example of a plea for contextual analysis. Subsequent cases have nevertheless still recognised the 'very wide range'[135] of factors laid down in *Stack*. In the joint legal title case of *Fowler*, discussed above, Arden LJ stated that the tenor of *Stack* required that 'all the circumstances which may throw light on the parties' intentions' could be reviewed.[136] For many it signalled (and this related to the compartmentalisation of the presumed intention resulting trust in this area) that an 'arithmetical calculation of how much is paid by each'[137] was no longer determinative. This analytical trend is certainly not new and bears hallmarks of the liberalised approach endorsed by

130 *Holman v. Howes*, [2007] EWCA (Civ) 877.

131 *Id.* 21.

132 *Id.* 24.

133 *Id.* 31.

134 *Id.*

135 Battersby refers to them as a 'real cause for concern', *supra* note 29.

136 *Fowler v. Barron*, *supra* note 43, 41.

137 *Stack v. Dowden*, *supra* note 7, 69 (Baroness Hale).

Midland Bank v. Cooke[138] and *Oxley v. Hiscock*.[139] Those cases stated that when quantifying beneficial interests, a broad-brush holistic approach could be adopted, looking at the whole course of dealings between the parties. There appears to be an inconsistency, as despite *Stack* creating a set of principles for the home and providing a non-exhaustive list of considerations, certain factors have, in reality, had more impact than others, which may create within the paragraph 69 factors a hierarchical structure.

Taking *Stack* as the template, the majority of the House of Lords decided on unequal division based on the fact Ms Dowden had made greater financial contributions to the purchase of the property,[140] coupled with a lack of pooling of resources through keeping 'rigidly separate'[141] financial affairs. Unequal financial contribution is inherently problematic as it merely takes us back to the resulting trust. Baroness Hale was also keen to stress that Ms Dowden earned more than Mr Stack, yet with regard to the 'give and take' nature of cohabiting relationships mentioned in *Stack*,[142] does this ability to contribute more really render the case exceptional? The approach utilised in *Adekunle*, discussed above, is informative on this point as Judge Behrens appears to have endorsed the reasoning of *Stack*, but directs his mind to the resulting trust and then contrasts that outcome with the 'holistic approach' necessary under *Stack*.[143] Financial interactions of the parties utilised when determining intentions indicate a judicial retreat to factors focused on in the pre-*Stack* case law. This could be indicative of what Lord Neuberger has referred to as a '*de facto* resulting trust apportionment'.[144]

So, embedded within the common intention constructive trust framework of *Stack*, a resulting trust analysis finds a place as an initial comparator. Arithmetical calculations clearly still loom large, which again suggests the artificiality of the claim that the court is applying a presumptive beneficial joint tenancy with departure from this only in 'exceptional' cases. The arrangement of the parties' finances was also determinative in *Stack*, suggesting that the courts focus on whether the parties pool their assets for the common good.[145] Despite Lord Hope intimating that there was a pooling of assets,[146] this element of reasoning in *Stack* has been subject to extensive, and justifiable, criticism. Through viewing,

138 *Midland Bank v. Cooke*, [1995] 2 FLR 915.

139 *Supra* note 26.

140 *Id.* 88 (Baroness Hale).

141 *Id.* 92 (Baroness Hale).

142 *Id.* 3 (Lord Hope).

143 *Adekunle v. Ritchie*, *supra* note 86, 68.

144 NEUBERGER, *supra* note 37, 17.

145 This feature was recognised in *Adekunle v. Ritchie*, *supra* note 86, 64 as a justification for *Stack's* departure and the presence of a joint bank account in *Abbott* intimated towards equal division (albeit the latter was a case concerned with a married couple). Similarly, in *Fowler* this pooling of assets was important and suggested that the presumption of beneficial joint tenancy should not be rebutted.

146 *Stack v. Dowden*, *supra* note 7, 11.

in context, the parties' course of dealings and how they managed their financial affairs, the majority extrapolated a clear intention to share the beneficial interest of the property unequally. However, as Burgoyne and Sonnenberg have indicated, trying to understand intentions and how parties deal with money is a 'potential minefield'[147] and there is a clear paucity in the evidential basis for this outcome. As noted by Miles and Probert, had the majority in *Stack* engaged with empirical research governing financial management patterns, they may have discovered that separate financial affairs are not so unusual.[148] It could be argued that, whilst *Stack* has endorsed close contextual analysis of the whole course of dealings between the parties, this adds to the legal uncertainty surrounding the principles, particularly for practitioners advising clients.

Both the majority and minority in *Stack* accepted that the inquiry should be context-driven and sensitive to the facts. Lord Hope stated that a 'more practical, down-to-earth, fact-based approach'[149] is necessary in the domestic context and Baroness Hale explicitly noted that 'each case will turn on its own facts'.[150] However, within this area, there is an almost ritual incantation that facts in the family home context are often scant,[151] and as Arden LJ notes in *Fowler*, the court must 'simply do the best it can'.[152] Problematically, this evidential issue was further emphasised through *Stack*, placing a large onus onto the trial judge to unravel often contested facts only for the open texture of *Stack* to allow the decision to be subsequently overturned on appeal. *Stack* is noteworthy for the now accepted variance that different court compositions can have when confronted with the same set of facts.

For many, the presumption of a beneficial joint tenancy could be regarded as acceptable, particularly with regard to certainty for third parties, if the lower courts would follow Baroness Hale's statement that cases of departure from equality would be 'very unusual'[153] and that rebuttal was 'not a task lightly to be embarked on'.[154] Although some have questioned the legitimacy of a presumption of a joint tenancy as opposed to a tenancy in common,[155] a key issue lies in the fact that in reality the presumption can be rebutted relatively easily. It appears likely that the reason for this is the heightened contextual analysis that *Stack* permits. Without any clear guidance on what factors make a case exceptional, it is unsurprising that

147 C. Burgoyne & S. Sonnenberg, *Financial Practices in Cohabiting Heterosexual Couples: A Perspective from Economic Psychology*, in Sharing Lives, Dividing Assets: An Interdisciplinary Study 103 (J Miles & R Probert eds, 2009).

148 J. Miles & R. Probert, *Sharing Lives, Dividing Assets: Legal Principles and Real Life*, in Sharing Lives, Dividing Assets: An Interdisciplinary Study 15 (2009).

149 *Stack v. Dowden*, *supra* note 7, 3.

150 *Id.* 69.

151 As noted in *Adekunle v. Ritchie*, *supra* note 86, 51, 55–58.

152 *Fowler v. Barron*, *supra* note 43, 2 (Arden LJ).

153 *Stack v. Dowden*, *supra* note 7, 69.

154 *Id.* 68.

155 Neuberger, *supra* note 37, 13.

of the post-*Stack* case law, a significant proportion of cases have been regarded as 'exceptional'.

Conclusion

Stack has been subject to extensive critical evaluation over the past four years. Whilst academics can criticise its methodology, its aim for ameliorating the hardship surrounding orthodox trust principles appears understandable. *Stack*, in this respect, represents a beneficial decision for highlighting the need for reform in England and Wales of this notoriously complex area of law. Another important feature of *Stack* was the way it placed modern ownership disputes within a system of attempted law reform and Baroness Hale's judgment provided a significant narrative of the various attempts within this area.[156]

However, the majority decision and the emphasis on context have the potential to confuse rather than clarify the trust framework. The reason for this is that the creation of a new framework, specifically created for the home, lacks precision and clearer principles are needed. Whilst the home is given specialised treatment, the use of a separate regime permits highly fact sensitive subdivision depending on the relationship dynamics within the property concerned. This vividly illustrates a tension between concepts of home and identity; two themes of this collection. Cases have demonstrated the difficulty of categorising property, and even where the principles of *Stack* do apply within the context of home, the sanctioning of contextual analysis creates uncertainty for practitioners and litigants. This exposes a possible contradiction in Baroness Hale's approach, as it embodies both an overly formulaic approach based on categorisation of properties and starting points, which is at the same time overly fluid owing to the extent of contextual analysis making a case exceptional. Thus, the symbolic principle that the home is different invariably yields to the practice of heightened contextual analysis rendering cases exceptional. In short, it is unfortunate that *Stack* can, as Dixon has noted, be regarded as 'all things to all judges'.[157]

As evidenced by extensive litigation, the open-texture of *Stack* sanctions expansive interpretation and unpredictable judicial embellishment. This quality of *Stack* may also encourage the post-*Stack* case law to trespass into the 'forbidden territories' of fairness.[158] Although fairness is not the determinant for ascertaining beneficial ownership, a context-sensitive, non-exhaustive list of factors may militate towards either a disguised, or occasionally an overt, fairness computation. In absence of legislative intervention and for the sake of clarity, surely the time

156 *Stack v. Dowden*, *supra* note 7, 46.

157 Dixon, *supra* note 121, at 460. *See* Probert, *Cohabitants and Joint Ownership: The Implications of Stack v. Dowden*, *supra* note 29, at 929, who states the main result of *Stack* may simply be to generate a discussion of 'what exactly its implications are'.

158 *Stack v. Dowden*, *supra* note 7, 145 (Lord Neuberger).

has come for an authoritative judicial statement indicating what the courts are in fact doing when deciding ownership disputes over the family home. A preferred solution, however, would be statutory reform. As the issues surrounding trusts of the family home have generated acute issues for decades, the allure of legislation seems irresistible. A key virtue would be the fact that legislation would provide a clear rationale behind its operation which would help justify and defend any award granted. Legislation in England and Wales providing financial remedies for specified categories of cohabitant would permit entry for a class of litigants into the protective realm of family law and would avoid the vagaries surrounding the trust framework.[159] Yet, for the time being, the context-driven principles of *Stack* are more likely to bedevil than help clarify this well-travelled area of law.

Acknowledgement

The author would like to thank Lorna Fox O'Mahony, Clare McGlynn, Nick Piska and Christopher Bevan for their helpful discussions and comments on an earlier draft. A section of this chapter was presented at the Association for Law, Property and Society Annual Meeting in Washington DC on 4th–5th March 2010. All errors and opinions remain my own.

159 Law Commission, *supra* note 6.

Bibliography

Books, Law Review Articles, and Other Sources

"Welfare Queen" Becomes Issue in Reagan Campaign, NY TIMES, Feb. 15, 1976, at 51.

1867 Voter Registration Records, Texas State Library and Archives Commission, MF Reel VR-4.

A.J. Cloherty & D. Fox, *Proving a Trust of a Shared Home*, 66 CAMBRIDGE L.J. 517 (2007).

A.M. GIBSON, THE LIFE AND DEATH OF COLONEL ALBERT JENNINGS FOUNTAIN (1956).

A.S. Edlin, *The New Palgrave: Surveying Two Waves of Economic Analysis of Law*, 2 AM. LAW & ECON. REV. 407 (2000).

Adam Carasso, *Who Receives Homeownership Tax Deductions and How Much?*, 108 TAX NOTES 591 (2005), *available at* http://www.taxpolicycenter.org/UploadedPDF/1000804_Tax_Fact_8-01-05.pdf.

Adam Carasso, C. Eugene Steuerle & Elizabeth Bell, *The Trend in Federal Housing Tax Expenditures*, 106 TAX NOTES 1081 (2005), *available at* http://www.urban.org//UploadedPDF/1000750_Tax_Fact_2-28-05.pdf.

A.J.H. Morris, *Equity's Reaction to Modern Domestic Relationships*, *in* TRENDS IN CONTEMPORARY TRUST LAW (AJ Oakley ed., 1997).

Alan Greenspan, Chairman, Fed. Reserve Bd., *The Mortgage Markets and Consumer Debt*, Remarks at America's Community Bankers' Annual Convention (Oct. 19, 2004), *available at* http://www.federalreserve.gov/boarddocs/speeches/2004/20041019/default.htm.

Alan Murdie, *Home Sweet Home?*, 148 SOLICITORS J. (2004).

Alastair Smith, Joint Ctr. for Hous. Stud. of Harv. Univ., *Mixed-Income Housing Developments: Promises and Reality* (2002), *available at* http://www.jchs.harvard.edu/publications/W02-10_Smith.pdf.

ALEMAYEHU BISHAW, US CENSUS BUREAU, US DEP'T OF COMMERCE, AREAS WITH CONCENTRATED POVERTY: 1999 (2005), *available at* http://www.census.gov/prod/2005pubs/censr-16.pdf.

ALEX F. SCHWARTZ, HOUSING POLICY IN THE UNITED STATES: AN INTRODUCTION (2006).

ALISON WALLACE, PUBLIC ATTITUDES TO HOUSING (2010).

Allison Brownell Tirres, American Law Comes to the Border: Law and Colonization on the US/Mexico Divide, 1848–1890 (2008) (unpublished Ph.D. dissertation, Harvard University).

Allison Brownell Tirres, *The View from the Border: Law and Community in the Nineteenth Century*, *in* 2 TRANSFORMATIONS IN AMERICAN LEGAL HISTORY: ESSAYS in Honor of Morton J. Horwitz (Daniel W. Hamilton & Alfred L. Brophy, Harvard Law Sch., eds, 2011).

Andrew Arden et al., Housing Law (2007).

Anna Louise Fahy, Chinese Borderland Community Development: A Case Study of El Paso, 1881–1909 (2001) (unpublished master's thesis, University of Texas at El Paso).

Anthony Downs, *Introduction: Why Rental Housing Is the Neglected Child of American Shelter*, *in* Revisiting Rental Housing: Policies, Programs and Priorities 1 (Nicolas P. Retsinas & Eric S. Belsky eds, 2008).

Anthony Giddens, The Consequences of Modernity (1991).

Ariela J. Gross, Double Character: Slavery and Mastery in the Antebellum Southern Courtroom (2000).

Ariela J. Gross, *The "Caucasian Cloak": Mexican Americans and the Politics of Whiteness in the 20th-Century Southwest*, 95 Geo. L.J. 95 (2006).

Arturo Escobar, *Culture Sits in Places: Reflections on Globalism and Subaltern Strategies of Localization*, 20 Pol.Geography 139 (2001).

Arturo Escobar, Territories of Difference: Place, Movements, Life, Redes (2008).

Ash Amin & Nigel Thrift, Cities: Reimagining the Urban (2002).

Ash Amin, *Local Community on Trial*, 34 Econ. & Soc'y 612 (2005).

Ben McFarlane, Nicholas Hopkins & Sarah Nield, Land Law: Text, Cases, and Materials (2009).

Ben S. Bernanke, Chairman, Fed. Reserve Bd., Statement (July 14, 2008), *available at* http://www.federalreserve.gov/newsevents/press/bcreg/bernankeregz20080714.htm.

Benjamin N. Cardozo, The Nature of Judicial Process (1921).

Bob Tedeschi, *The Depths of Mortgage Debt*, NY Times, Aug. 30, 2009, at RE9.

Brendan O'Flaherty, Making Room: The Economics of Homelessness (1996).

Building and Social Housing Foundation, Equity Sharing with Community Land Trusts: Delivering Sustainable Low Cost Home Ownership by Locking In Value in Perpetuity (2006), *available at* http://www.bshf.org/published-information/publication.cfm?thePubID=21F46BEA-15C5-F4C0-993C6311518A3D40.

Building the Big Society (2010), *available at* www.cabinetoffice.gov.uk/media/407789/building-big-society.pdf.

Burgoyne, C. & S. Sonnenberg, *Financial Practices in Cohabiting Heterosexual Couples: A Perspective from Economic Psychology*, *in* Sharing Lives, Dividing Assets: An Interdisciplinary Study 103 (J. Miles & R. Probert eds, 2009).

C. Norberg-Schulz, Genius Loci: Towards a Phenomenology of Architecture (1980).

Carmen DeNavas-Walt et al., US Census Bureau, Income, Poverty, and Health Insurance Coverage in the United States: 2010 (2011), *available at* http://www.census.gov/prod/2011pubs/p60-239.pdf.

Carol A. O'Conner, *A Region of Cities, in the Oxford Encyclopedia of the American West* (Clyde A. Milner, II, Carol A. O'Connor & Martha A. Sandweiss eds, 1994).

Carol Rose, *Comedy of the Commons: Custom, Commerce, and Inherently Public Property*, 53 U. CHI. L. REV. 711 (1986).

CAROLE PATEMAN, PARTICIPATION AND DEMOCRATIC THEORY (1970).

CDS CO-OPERATIVES, A SIMPLE GUIDE TO MUTUAL HOME OWNERSHIP (2005), https://docs.google.com/fileview?id=0BwtFGmkmSl96OTkwM2NiYTItOTNhYy00OTRlLWEwMzctMzk1MzVkYmZlZDAw&hl=en_GB.

CDS CO-OPERATIVES, A CONSUMER'S GUIDE TO MUTUAL HOME OWNERSHIP (THIRD DRAFT), http://www.cds.coop/about-us/mutual-home-ownership/A%20new%20way%20of%20owning%20a%20stake%20in%20your%20home.pdf.

CHARLES ABRAMS, FORBIDDEN NEIGHBORS (1955).

CHARLES CUTTER, THE LEGAL CULTURE OF NORTHERN NEW SPAIN, 1700–1810 (1995).

Charles Tiebout, *A Pure Theory of Local Expenditures*, 64 J. POL. ECON. 416 (1956).

Chris Handy, *Community Land Trusts*, 13 J. HOUSING L. 83 (2010).

Chris Philo, *Neglected Rural Geographies: A Review*, 8 J. RURAL STUDIES 193 (1992).

Chris Walker, Bibliography: Research on Comprehensive Community Initiatives (2010), *available at* http://www.instituteccd.org/library/1402.

Christine Whitehead & Judith Yates, *Increasing Affordability Problems—A Role for Shared Equity Products? Experience in Australia and the UK*, 21 HOUSING FIN. INT'L 16 (2007).

CHRISTINE WHITEHEAD, SHARED OWNERSHIP AND SHARED EQUITY: REDUCING THE RISKS OF HOME-OWNERSHIP? (2010), http://www.jrf.org.uk/publications/shared-ownership-shared-equity.

Claudine Gay, Moving Out, Moving Up: Housing Mobility and Political Participation of the Poor (Harvard University, Working Paper, 2008).

Clifford A. Perkins, *Reminiscences of a Chinese Inspector*, 17 J. ARIZ. HIST. 181 (1976).

COLIN JONES & ALAN MURIE, THE RIGHT TO BUY: ANALYSIS AND EVALUATION OF A HOUSING POLICY (2010).

COMMISSION ON CO-OPERATIVE AND MUTUAL HOUSING, BRINGING DEMOCRACY HOME (Nic Bliss ed., 2009), *available at* http://www.ccmh.coop/sites/default/files/Commission%20Report.pdf.

COMMUNITY FINANCE SOLUTIONS, COMMUNITY LAND TRUSTS: A PRACTITIONER'S GUIDE (2007), http://www.communitylandtrusts.org.uk/resources/publications.

COMMUNITY FINANCE SOLUTIONS, PLACESHAPING: A TOOLKIT FOR URBAN COMMUNITY LAND TRUSTS (2008), http://www.communityfinance.salford.ac.uk/pdf/Urban_tools__complete.pdf.

Conrey Bryson, *A Man Named Aoy*, 35 Password 95 (1990).

Craig M. Gurney, Pride and Prejudice: Discourses of Normalisation in Public and Private Accounts of Home Ownership, 14 HOUSING STUD. 163 (1999).

D&R International, Ltd., U.S. Dep't of Energy, 2009 Buildings Energy Data Book 2–24 (2009).

Dallas Morning News, Feb. 10, 1886.

Dallas Morning News, Jan. 21, 1886.

Daniel R. Williams & Susan R. Van Patten, Home and Away? *Creating Identities and Sustaining Places in a Multi-centred World, in* MULTIPLE DWELLING AND TOURISM: NEGOTIATING PLACE, HOME, AND IDENTITY (Norman McIntyre et al., eds, 2006).

Daniel Scarf, *When Is a Home Not a Home? When It's on Exmoor*, J. PLAN. & ENVTL. L. 1175 (2002).

Daniel T. Lichter et al., The Geography of Exclusion: Race, Segregation, and Concentrated Poverty (Nat'l Poverty Ctr., Working Paper No. 11–16, 2011).

Danny Dorling & Phil Rees, *A Nation Still Dividing: The British Census and Social Polarisation 1971–2001*, 35 ENVTL. & PLAN. A 1287 (2003).

David Cowan, *Shared Ownership: Some Problems of Law and Policy*, 13 J. HOUSING L. 56 (2010).

DAVID DORADO ROMO, RINGSIDE SEAT TO A REVOLUTION: AN UNDERGROUND CULTURAL HISTORY OF EL PASO AND JUÁREZ, 1893–1923 (2005).

DAVID HAMER, NEW TOWNS IN THE NEW WORLD: IMAGES AND PERCEPTIONS OF THE NINETEENTH-CENTURY URBAN FRONTIER (1990).

DAVID HARVEY, JUSTICE, NATURE AND THE GEOGRAPHY OF DIFFERENCE (1986).

David Imbroscio, *"[U]nited and Actuated by Some Common Impulse of Passion" 1: Challenging the Dispersal Consensus in American Housing Policy Research*, 30 J. URB. AFF. 111 (2008).

David J. Baron & Gerald E. Frug, *Defensive Localism: A View of the Field from the Field*, 21 J. L. & POL. 261 (2005).

David J. Barron, *A Localist Critique of New Federalism*, 51 DUKE L.J. 434 (2002).

DAVID J. WEBER, THE SPANISH FRONTIER IN NORTH AMERICA (1992).

DAVÍD MONTEJANO, ANGLOS AND MEXICANS IN THE MAKING OF TEXAS, 1836–1986 (1987).

DAVID MULLINS AND ALAN MURIE, HOUSING POLICY IN THE UK (2006).

DAVID SIBLEY, GEOGRAPHIES OF EXCLUSION: SOCIETY AND DIFFERENCE IN THE WEST (1995).

Deed Records, Books B & E, El Paso County Records, MS 132, C.L. Sonnichsen Special Collections Department, University of Texas at El Paso.

Democratic Nat'l Convention Comm., The 2008 Democratic National Platform: Renewing America's Promise (2008).

Department of Communities and Local Government, Assisting Shared Owners at Risk of Repossession: Flexible Tenure—Questions and Answers (2010), *available at* http://www.communities.gov.uk/publications/housing/flexibletenurequestions.

DEPARTMENT OF COMMUNITIES AND LOCAL GOVERNMENT, ENGLISH HOUSING SURVEY: HOUSEHOLD REPORT 2008–09 (2010), http://www.communities.gov.uk/documents/statistics/pdf/1750765.pdf.

Department of Communities and Local Government, Mortgage Rescue Monitoring Statistics—March Quarter 2011, *available at* http://www.communities.gov.uk/publications/corporate/statistics/mortgagerescuestatisticsq12011.

Department of Communities and Local Government, Public Attitudes to Housing in England (2011).

Department of Communities and Local Government, The Coalition: Our Programme for Government (2010), http://www.communities.gov.uk/documents/corporate/pdf/1657233.pdf.

Department of Communities and Local Government, Homes and Communities Agency, 2011–15 Affordable Homes Programme—Framework (2011), *available at* http://www.homesandcommunities.co.uk/public/documents/Affordable-Homes-Framework.pdf.

Department of Communities and Local Government, Definitions of General Housing Terms, http://www.communities.gov.uk/housing/housingresearch/housingstatistics/definitiongeneral/.

Department of Communities and Local Government, Social Housing Sales to Sitting Tenants, England 2009–2010 (2010), http://www.communities.gov.uk/publications/corporate/statistics/socialhousingsales200910.

Department of the Environment, Housing Policy: A Consultative Document, 1977, Cm. 6851, at 50.

Department of the Environment, Transport and the Regions, Quality and Choice: A Decent Home for All (2000), *available at* http://www.communities.gov.uk/documents/housing/pdf/138019.pdf.

Directgov, http://www.direct.gov.uk (last visited Feb 14, 2011).

Doreen Massey, For Space (2005).

Doris Wallingford Busalacchi, History of the Federal Judiciary District of Western Texas (1950) (unpublished seminar paper, University of Texas at El Paso) (on file with author).

Douglas S. Massey & Nancy A. Denton, American Apartheid: Segregation and the Making of the Underclass (1993).

Duncan Kennedy, *Three Globalizations of Law and Legal Thought: 1850–2000*, *in* The New Law and Economic Development: A Critical Appraisal (David M. Trubek & Alvaro Santos eds, 2006).

E. Cooke, *Cohabitants, Common Intention and Contributions (Again)*, 2005 Conveyancer & Prop. Law. 555 (2005).

Edmund L. Andrews, *Fed and Regulators Shrugged As the Subprime Crisis Worsened*, NY Times, Dec. 18, 2007, at A1.

Edward A. Leonard, *Rails to the Pass of the North*, 48 Password 11 (2003).

Edward G. Goetz, *Better Neighborhoods, Better Outcomes? Explaining Relocation Outcomes in HOPE VI*, 12 Cityscape 2 (2010).

Edward G. Goetz, Clearing the Way: Deconcentrating the Poor in Urban America (2003).

Edward L. Glaeser & Joseph Gyourko, Rethinking Federal Housing Policy (2008).

EDWARD T. PRICE, DIVIDING THE LAND, EARLY AMERICAN BEGINNINGS OF OUR PRIVATE PROPERTY MOSAIC (1995).

El Paso Bureau of Information, The City and County of El Paso, Texas, Containing Useful and Reliable Information Concerning the Future Great Metropolis of the Southwest, Its Resources and Advantages for the Agriculturalist, Artisan, and Capitalist 62 (1886).

El Paso Herald, June 1, 1881.

ELINOR OSTROM, GOVERNING THE COMMONS: THE EVOLUTION OF INSTITUTIONS FOR COLLECTIVE ACTION (1990).

Erika Lee, *Enforcing the Borders: Chinese Exclusion Along the U.S. Borders with Canada and Mexico, 1882–1924*, 89 JOURNAL OF AMERICAN HISTORY 54 (2002).

Francesco Cordasco, *Introduction* to JACOB RIIS, HOW THE OTHER HALF LIVES (1970).

G. Battersby, *Ownership of the Family Home:* Stack v. Dowden *in the House of Lords*, 20 CHILD & FAM. L. Q. 255 (2008).

G. Douglas, J. Pearce & H. Woodward, *Cohabitation and Conveyancing Practice: Problems and Solutions*, 2008 CONVEYANCER & PROP. LAW. 365 (2008).

G. Douglas, J. Pearce & H. Woodward, *Money, Property, Cohabitation and Separation: Patterns and Indications*, *in* SHARING LIVES, DIVIDING ASSETS: AN INTERDISCIPLINARY STUDY (J. Miles & R. Probert eds, 2009).

G. Mohan & K. Stokke, *Participatory Development and Empowerment: The Dangers of Localism*, 21 THIRD WORLD Q. 247 (2000).

G. Thomas Kingsley et al., *Patterns of Section 8 Relocation in the HOPE VI Program*, 25 J. URB. AFF. 427 (2003).

G. Thomas Kingsley, *Appendix A: Scope and Status of the Hope VI Program*, *in* FROM DESPAIR TO HOPE: HOPE VI AND THE NEW PROMISE OF PUBLIC HOUSING IN AMERICAN CITIES 300 (Henry C. Cisneros & Lora Engdahl eds, 2009).

GENTRIFICATION, DISPLACEMENT, AND NEIGHBORHOOD REVITALIZATION (J. John Palen & Bruce London, eds, 1984).

Gerry Frug, *The City As a Legal Concept*, 93 HARV. L. REV. 1057 (1980).

Gerry Stoker, *New Localism, Progressive Politics and Democracy*, *in* RESTATING THE STATE? (A. Gamble & T. Wright eds, 2004).

Governor Edward M. Gramlich, Predatory Lending, Remarks at the Fair Housing Council of New York (Apr. 14, 2000), *available at* http://www.federalreserve.gov/boarddocs/speeches/2000/200004142.htm.

Governor Edward M. Gramlich, Subprime Lending, Predatory Lending, Remarks at the Federal Reserve Bank of Philadelphia (Dec. 6, 2000), *available at* http://www.federalreserve.gov/boarddocs/speeches/2000/20001206.htm.

Governor Edward M. Gramlich, Subprime Mortgage Lending: Benefits, Costs and Challenges, Remarks at the Financial Services Roundtable Annual Housing Policy Meeting (May 21, 2004), *available at* http://www.federalreserve.gov/boarddocs/speeches/2004/20040521/default.htm.

Guadalupe T. Luna, *Chicana/Chicano Land Tenure in the Agrarian Domain: On the Edge of a 'Naked Knife'*, 4 MICH. J. RACE & L. 39 (1998).

Guido Calabresi & Douglas Melamed, *Property Rules, Liability Rules, and Inalienability: One View of the Cathedral*, 85 HARV. L. REV. 1089 (1975).

H.L.A. Hart, *Positivism and the Separation of Law and Morals*, 71 HARV. L. REV. 593 (1958).

Hanoch Dagan & Michael A. Heller, *The Liberal Commons*, 110 YALE L. J. 549, 566 (2001).

Hayward, *Family Values in the Home:* Fowler v. Barron, 21 CHILD & FAM. L. Q. 242 (2009).

Henry A. Span, *How the Courts Should Fight Exclusionary Zoning*, 32 SETON HALL L. REV. 1 (2003).

HENRY CAMPBELL BLACK, BLACK'S LAW DICTIONARY (1991).

HENRY G. CISNEROS, LORA ENGDAHL & KURT L. SCHMOKE, FROM DESPAIR TO HOPE: HOPE VI AND THE NEW PROMISE OF PUBLIC HOUSING IN AMERICA'S CITIES (2009).

HERBERT J. GANS, THE WAR AGAINST THE POOR: THE UNDERCLASS AND ANTIPOVERTY POLICY (1995).

Herb Marsh, Jr & Robert Dinsmoor, *El Paso Courthouses: Past and Present*, 40 PASSWORD 80 (1995).

HM TREASURY & OFFICE OF THE DEPUTY PRIME MINISTER, THE GOVERNMENT'S RESPONSE TO KATE BARKER'S REVIEW OF HOUSING (2005).

HOMES & COMMUNITIES AGENCY, AFFORDABLE HOUSING CAPITAL FUNDING GUIDE, http://cfg.homesandcommunities.co.uk/nbhb-rents.

HOMES & COMMUNITIES AGENCY, COUNCIL OF MORTGAGE LENDERS AND NATIONAL HOUSING FEDERATION, SHARED OWNERSHIP: JOINT GUIDANCE FOR ENGLAND (2010).

HOMES & COMMUNITIES AGENCY, DATA COMPENDIUM: A COLLATION OF PUBLISHED DATA ABOUT THE INTERMEDIATE MARKET (2010), *available at* http://www.homesandcommunities.co.uk/public/documents/Data-Compendium-autumn2010.pdf.

HOMES & COMMUNITIES AGENCY, FIRSTBUY BUYERS' GUIDE (2011), http://www.homesandcommunities.co.uk/sites/default/files/our-work/firstbuy-buyers-guide-010711.pdf.

HOMES & COMMUNITIES AGENCY, FIRSTBUY PROSPECTUS (2011), http://www.homesandcommunities.co.uk/sites/default/files/our-work/firstbuy-prospectus_0.pdf.

HOMES & COMMUNITIES AGENCY, COUNCIL OF MORTGAGE LENDERS & NATIONAL HOUSING FEDERATION, SHARED OWNERSHIP: JOINT GUIDANCE FOR ENGLAND (2010), http://www.housing.org.uk/Uploads/File/Policy%20briefings/Research%20Futures/Shared%20Ownership%20guidance%202010.pdf.

HOUSING CORPORATION & CHARTERED INSTITUTE OF HOUSING, HOUSING ASPIRATIONS AND SHARED OWNERSHIP (2008), http://www.cih.org/publications/pftf/pdfs/Aspirations.pdf.

HOUSING CORPORATION (UK), A HOME OF MY OWN: THE REPORT OF THE GOVERNMENT'S LOW COST HOME OWNERSHIP TASK FORCE (2003).

Hua Hsu, *The End of White America?*, THE ATLANTIC, Jan–Feb. 2009 (*available at* http://www.theatlantic.com/magazine/archive/2009/01/the-end-of-white-america/7208/).

Ian Cole & David Robinson, *Owners Yet Tenants: The Position of Leaseholders in Flats in England and Wales*, 15 HOUSING STUD. 595 (2000).

Interview by Jo Ann Hovious with Aileen Hague Hill, April 10, Interview 79, Oral History Institution, University of Texas at El Paso (April 10, 1973).

Interview by Leon Metz and Robin Fuller with Mrs. Hugh White, Interview 48, transcript, at 11, Oral History Institute, University of Texas at El Paso (June 3, 1968).

J. Dewar, *Land, Law, and the Family Home*, *in* LAND LAW: THEMES AND PERSPECTIVES (S. Bright & J. Dewar eds, 1998).

J.J. BOWDEN, SPANISH AND MEXICAN LAND GRANTS IN THE CHIHUAHUAN ACQUISITION (1971).

J. Lawrence McConville, A History of Population in the El Paso-Ciudad Juárez Area (1966) (unpublished master's thesis, The University of New Mexico).

J. Mee, *Property Rights and Personal Relationships: Reflections on Reform*, 24 LEGAL STUD. 414 (2004).

J. Miles & R. Probert, *Sharing Lives, Dividing Assets: Legal Principles and Real Life*, *in* SHARING LIVES, DIVIDING ASSETS: AN INTERDISCIPLINARY STUDY (2009).

J. Miles, *Property Law v Family Law: Resolving the Problems of Family Property*, 23 LEGAL STUD. 624 (2003).

J. MORGAN BROADDUS, THE LEGAL HERITAGE OF EL PASO (1963).

J. Peter Byrne & Michael Diamond, *Affordable Housing, Land Tenure, and Urban Policy: The Matrix Revealed*, 34 FORDHAM URB. L.J. 527 (2007).

J. Peter Byrne, *Two Cheers for Gentrification*, 46 HOW. L.J. 405 (2003).

JAMES D. GWARTNEY, JOSHUA C. HALL & ROBERT LAWSON, ECONOMIC FREEDOM OF THE WORLD: 2010 ANNUAL REPORT (2010).

James E. Rosenbaum et al., *Can the Kerner Commission's Housing strategy Improve Employment, Education and Social Integration for Low-Income Blacks*, *in* RACE, POVERTY, AND AMERICAN CITIES 275 (John Charles Boger & Judith Welch Wegner eds, 1996).

James J. Kelly Jr, *Homes Affordable for Good: Covenants and Ground Leases as Long-Term Resale-Restriction Devices*, 29 ST. LOUIS U. PUB. L. REV. 9 (2009).

James J. Kelly, Jr, *Land Trusts that Conserve Communities*, 59 DEPAUL L. REV. 69 (2009).

JAMES W. ELY, JR, RAILROADS AND AMERICAN LAW (2001).

Jamison E. Colburn, *Localism's Ecology: Protecting and Restoring Habitat in the Suburban Nation*, 33 ECOLOGY L. Q. 945 (2006).

Jeff Bishop, *From Parish Plans to Localism in England: Straight Track or Long and Winding Road?*, 25 PLAN. PRAC. & RES. 611 (2010).

Jeffrey R. Kling, Jeffrey B. Liebman & Lawrence F. Katz, *Experimental Analysis of Neighborhood Effects*, 75 ECONOMETRICA 83 (2007).

JERRY J. SALAMA, MICHAEL H. SCHILL & JONATHAN D. SPRINGER, FURMAN CENTER FOR REAL ESTATE AND URBAN POLICY, REDUCING THE COST OF NEW HOUSING CONSTRUCTION IN NEW YORK CITY: 2005 UPDATE (2005).

JERRY YUDELSON, THE GREEN BUILDING REVOLUTION (2008).

JILL MORGAN, ASPECTS OF HOUSING LAW (2007).

Jill Sherman, *Super-Rich Barred as Kensington Keeps It in Family*, THE TIMES NEWSPAPER, November 14, 2005.

Jo Ann Platt Hovious, Social Change in Western Towns: El Paso, Texas, 1881–1889, 123 (1972) (unpublished master's thesis, University of Texas at El Paso).

JOEL BLAU, THE VISIBLE POOR: HOMELESSNESS IN THE UNITED STATES (1993).

John Alder, *Co-operative Housing Associations—An Alternative Tenure—Part 1*, CONV. & PROP. L. 187 (1988).

JOHN ALLEN, DOREEN MASSEY & ALAN COCHRANE, RETHINKING THE REGION (1988).

John Emmeus Davis, *Between Devolution and the Deep Blue Sea: What's a City or State to Do?*, *in* A RIGHT TO HOUSING: FOUNDATION FOR A NEW SOCIAL AGENDA (2006).

JOHN H. COATSWORTH, GROWTH AGAINST DEVELOPMENT: THE ECONOMIC IMPACT OF RAILROADS IN PORFIRIAN MEXICO (1981).

JOHN STUART MILL, CONSIDERATIONS ON REPRESENTATIVE DEMOCRACY (New York, Harper & Bros. 1862).

John. R. Nolon, *In Praise of Parochialism: The Advent of Local Environmental Law*, 26 HARV. ENVTL. L. REV. 366 (2002).

Joint Ctr. for Hous. Studies, Harvard University, About Us, http://www.jchs.harvard.edu/aboutus/index.html (last visited Nov. 6, 2011).

Jon Hanson & Kathleen Hanson, *The Blame Frame: Justifying (Racial) Injustice in America*, 41 HARV. C.R.-C.L. L. REV. 413 (2006).

Jon May, *Globalization and the Politics of Place: Place and Identity in an Inner London Neighbourhood*, 21 TRANSACTIONS OF THE INST. OF BRITISH GEOGRAPHERS 194 (1996).

JUDITH HUGGINS BALFE, PASSING IT ON: THE INHERITANCE AND USE OF SUMMER HOUSES (1999).

Julie MacLeavy, *(Re)Analysing Community Empowerment: Rationalities and Technologies of Government in Bristol's New Deal for Communities*, 46 URB. STUD. 849 (2009).

K.GRAY & S. GRAY, ELEMENTS OF LAND LAW (5th ed., 2009).

Keith L. Bryant, Jr, *Entering the Global Economy*, *in* THE OXFORD ENCYCLOPEDIA OF THE AMERICAN WEST (Clyde A. Milner, II, Carol O'Connor & Martha A. Sandweiss, eds, 1994).

KENNETH T. JACKSON, CRABGRASS FRONTIER: THE SUBURBANIZATION OF THE UNITED STATES (1985).

Kensington's Drive to Keep Out Outsiders, ESTATES GAZETTE, February 18, 2006.

Kim McKee, *Promoting Homeownership at the Margins: The Experience of Low-Cost Homeownership Purchasers in Regeneration Areas* 4 PEOPLE, PLACE & POL'Y ONLINE 38 (2010), *available at* http://extra.shu.ac.uk/ppp-online/issue_2_290710/documents/homeownership_margins_ lowcost_regen_areas.pdf.

L. FOX, CONCEPTUALISING HOME, THEORIES, LAWS AND POLICIES (2007).

L. Fox, *The Meaning of Home: A Chimerical Concept or a Legal Challenge*, 29 J.L. & Soc'y 580 (2002).

L. G. Sager, *Tight Little Islands: Exclusionary Zoning, Equal Protection, and the Indigent*, 21 Stan. L. Rev. 767 (1969).

Larry Buron et al., The Hope VI Resident Tracking Study (2002), *available at* http://www.urban.org/uploadedpdf/410591_HOPEVI_ResTrack.pdf.

Laura F. Edwards, *Status without Rights: African Americans and the Tangled History of Law and Governance in the Nineteenth-Century U.S. South*, 112 Am. Hist. Rev. 365 (2007).

Law Commission, Cohabitation: The Financial Consequences of Relationship Breakdown (Law Com No 307 Cm 7182, 2007), *available at* http://www.justice.gov.uk/lawcommission/docs/cp179_Cohabitation_Consultation_overview.pdf.

Law Commission, Report No. 297, 1 Renting Homes: The Final Report (2006), *available at* http://www.lawcom.gov.uk/docs/lc297_vol1.pdf.

Law Commission, Sharing Homes: A Discussion Paper (Law Com No. 278, 2002).

Lawrence Pratchett, *Local Autonomy, Local Democracy and the 'New' Localism*, 52 Pol. Stud. 358 (2004).

Lee Anne Fennell, *Homeownership 2.0*, 102 Nw. U.L. Rev. 1047 (2008).

Leo M. Jacques, *Have More Quick Money Than Mandarins: The Chinese in Sonora*, 17 J. Ariz. Hist. 201 (1976).

Liam Reynolds, Shelter Safe and Secure? The Private Rented Sector and Security of Tenure (2005), http://england.shelter.org.uk/__data/assets/pdf_file/0017/48041/Safe_and_Secure.pdf.

Liberal Democrat Manifesto (2010).

Lillian Hague Corcoran, *He Brought the Railroads to El Paso—the Story of Judge James P. Hague*, 1 Password 57 (1956).

Lord Neuberger, Chancery Bar Association Annual Lecture, The Conspirators, The Tax Man, The Bill of Rights and a Bit About the Lovers (Mar. 10 2008).

Loretta Lees, *A Reappraisal of Gentrification: Towards a 'Geography of Gentrification'*, 24 Prog. Hum. Geogr. 389 (2000).

Lorna Fox-O'Mahony, *Homeownership, Debt, and Default: The Affective Value of Home and the Challenge of Affordability*, *in* Affordable Housing and Public-Private Partnerships 169 (Nestor M. Davidson & Robin Paul Malloy eds, 2009).

Louise Tickle, *Here Come the Students—and There Goes the Neighbourhood*, Educ. Guardian, May 15, 2007.

Luis Torres, Chamizal National Memorial (1994).

Lydia Lum, *The Obama Era: A Post-racial Society?*, *in* 25 Diverse: Issues in Higher Education 14 (2009).

M. Dixon, *The Never-Ending Story—Co-ownership after* Stack v. Dowden, Conveyancer & Prop. Law. 456 (2007).

Making Sense of Localism (Jo Coles, Yvette Cooper & Nick Raynsford eds, 2004).

Mandara Meyers, *(Un)equal Protection for the Poor: Exclusionary Zoning and the Need for Stricter Scrutiny*, 6 U. Pa. J. Const. L. 349 (2004).

Manel Baucells & Steven A. Lippman, *Justice Delayed is Justice Denied: A Cooperative Game Theoretic Analysis of Hold-Up in Co-Ownership*, 22 Cardozo L. Rev. 1191 (2001).

Manuel Castells, The Information Age: Economy, Society and Culture, The Rise of the Network Society 1 (1996).

Marc Auge, Non-Place: Introduction to an Anthropology of Supermodernity (1995).

Margaret A. McKean, *Success on the Commons: A Comparative Examination of Institutions for Common Property Resource Management*, 4 J. Theoretical Pol. 247, 261 (1992).

Margaret F. Brinig, *The Family Franchise: Elderly Parents and Adult Siblings*, 1996 Utah L. Rev. 393 (1996).

Margaret Jane Radin, *Property and Personhood*, 34 Stan. L. Rev. 957, 959 (1982).

María E. Montoya, Translating Property: The Maxwell Land Grant and the Conflict over Land in the American West, 1840–1900 (2002).

Mario T. Garcia, Desert Immigrants: The Mexicans of El Paso, 1880–1920, 131 (1981).

Marjorie Austin Turner et al., Estimating the Public Costs and Benefits of HOPE VI Investments: Methodological Report (2007), *available at* http://www.urban.org/url.cfm?ID=411497.

Mark Edwin Miller, Forgotten Tribes: Unrecognized Indians and the Federal Acknowledgment Process (2004).

Mark Joseph, *Early Resident Experiences at a New Mixed-Income Development in Chicago*, 30 J. Urb. Aff. 229 (2008).

Mark L. Joseph et al., *The Theoretical Basis for Addressing Poverty Through Mixed Income Development*, 42 Urb. Aff. Rev. 369 (2007).

Mark L. Joseph, *Is Mixed-Income Development an Antidote to Urban Poverty*, 17 Housing Pol'y Debate 209 (2006).

Mark L. Joseph, Robert J. Chaskin & Henry S. Weber, *The Theoretical Basis for Addressing Poverty Through Mixed Income Development*, 42 Urb. Aff. Rev. 369 (2007).

Mark Purcell, *Urban Democracy and the Local Trap*, 43 Urb. Stud. 1921 (2006).

Martin Knox & David Alcock, Approaches to Community Governance: Models for Mixed Tenure Communities (2002).

Matthew A. Edwards, *The FTC and New Paternalism*, 60 Admin. L. Rev. 323 (2008).

Matthew A. Edwards, *The Law, Marketing and Behavioral Economics of Consumer Rebates*, 12 Stan. J. L. Bus. & Fin. 362 (2006–2007).

Matthew Hughes, Office of National Statistics, Social Trends No. 39 (2009).

Matthew J. Parlow, *Progressive Policy-making on the Local Level: Rethinking Traditional Notions of Federalism*, 17 Temp. Pol. & Civ. Rts. L. Rev. 371 (2008).

Melody L. Boyd et al., *The Durability of Gains from the Gautreaux Two Residential Mobility Program: A Qualitative Analysis of Who Stays and Who Moves from Low-Income Poverty Neighborhoods*, 20 HOUSING POL'Y DEBATE 119 (2010).

Mesilla Valley Independent, July 12, 1879.

MICHAEL B. KATZ, THE UNDESERVING POOR (1989).

Michael Diamond, *Affordable Housing and the Conflict of Competing Goods: A Policy Dilemma*, *in* AFFORDABLE HOUSING AND PUBLIC-PRIVATE PARTNERSHIPS 1 (Nestor M. Davidson & Robin Paul Malloy eds, 2009).

Michelle Wilde Anderson, *Mapped Out of Local Democracy*, 62 STAN. L. REV. 931 (2010).

MILO KEARNEY & ANTHONY KNOPP, BORDER CUATES: A HISTORY OF THE US-MEXICAN TWIN CITIES (1995).

Molly Thompson, *Relocating from the Distress of Chicago Public Housing to the Difficulties of the Private Market: How the Move Threatens to Push Families Away from Opportunity*, 1 NW. J.L. & SOC. POL'Y 267 (2006).

MORAG MCDERMONT, GOVERNING INDEPENDENCE AND EXPERTISE: THE BUSINESS OF HOUSING ASSOCIATIONS (2010).

Mortgage Bankers Ass'n, About MBA, http://www.mbaa.org/AboutMBA.

N Piska, *Intention, Fairness and the Presumption of Resulting Trust after* Stack v. Dowden, 71 MODERN L. REV. 114 (2008).

N. Glover & P. Todd, *The Myth of Common Intention*, 16 L. STUD. 325 (1996).

N. Hopkins, *Regulating Trusts of the Home: Private Law and Social Policy*, 125 L. Q. REV. 310 (2009).

N. Piska, *A Common Intention or a Rare Bird? Proprietary Interests, Personal Claims and Services Rendered by Lovers Post Acquisition*, 21 CHILD & FAM. L.Q. 104 (2009).

N. Piska, *Two Recent Reflections on the Resulting Trust*, CONVEYANCER & PROP. LAW. 441 (2008).

NANCY HAMILTON, BEN DOWELL: EL PASO'S FIRST MAYOR (1976).

NANCY LEE HAMMONS, A HISTORY OF EL PASO COUNTY TEXAS, TO 1900 (1983).

Nat'l Ass'n of Home Builders, Mission & Vision, http://www.nahb.org/page.aspx/generic/sectionID=88.

Nat'l Ass'n of Realtors, NAR's Mission and Vision, (April 5, 2011), http://www.realtor.org/realtororg.nsf/pages/narmission.

Nat'l Hous. Conference, NHC Mission & Goals, http://www.nhc.org/about/NHC-Mission-Goals.html.

Nat'l Low Income Hous. Coalition. Mission and Goals, http://www.nlihc.org/template/page.cfm?id=31.

Neil Smith, Toward a Theory of Gentrification: A Back to the City Movement by Capital, Not People, APA Journal.

Newspaper Tree, Judge Albert Armendariz Federal Courthouse "a fitting tribute to a hometown hero" (Sept. 9, 2010), http://newspapertree.com/news/4239-judge-albert-armendariz-federal-courthouse-a-fitting-tribute-to-a-hometown-hero.

Nicholas Benson, Note, *A Tale of Two Cities: Examining the Success of Inclusionary Zoning Ordinances in Montgomery County, Maryland and Boulder, Colorado*, 13 J. GENDER RACE & JUST. 753 (2010).

Nicholas Blomley, *Flowers in the Bathtub: Boundary Crossings at the Public-Private Divide*, 36 GEOFORUM 281 (2005).

Nicholas Hopkins & Emma Laurie, *Housing or Property? The Dynamics of Housing Policy and Property Principles in the Right to Buy*, 26 L. STUD. 65 (2006).

Nicholas P. Houser, The Ysleta Grant (to the Place of Beginning), *in* Ysleta Del Sur Pueblo Archives (2000).

Nick Clark, *In What Sense 'Spaces of Neoliberalism'? The New Localism, the New Politics of Scale, and Town Twinning*, 28 POL. GEOGRAPHY 496 (2009).

Nick Gallent & Phillip Bell, *Planning Exceptions in Rural England: Past, Present and Future*, 15 PLAN. PRACT. AND RES. 375 (2000).

Nick Gallent, Alan Mace & Mark Tewdwr-Jones, *Dispelling a Myth? Second Homes in Rural Wales*, 35 AREA 271 (2000).

Nikolas Rose, *The Death of the Social*, 25 ECON. AND SOC'Y 327 (1996).

Noel Castree, *Differential Geographies: Place, Indigenous Rights and 'Local' Resources*, 23 POL. GEOGRAPHY 133 (2004).

Norman McIntyre et al., *Home and Away: Revisiting 'Escape' in the Context of Second Homes*, *in* MULTIPLE DWELLING AND TOURISM: NEGOTIATING PLACE, HOME AND IDENTITY 114 (Norman McIntyre et al., eds, 2006).

Norman Williams & Tatyana Doughty, *Studies in Legal Realism: Belle Terre, Mount Laurel and Berman*, 29 RUTGERS L. REV. 73 (1976).

Norman Williams, *The Background and Significance of Mount Laurel II*, 26 WASH. U.J. URB. & CONTEMP. L. 3 (1984).

North Cornwall District Council, Affordable Housing Explained: A Guide for Parish Councils, *available at* http://www.cornwall.gov.uk/pdf/AffordableHousingParishPack.pdf.

Note, *Law, Race, and the Border: The El Paso Salt War of 1877*, 117 HARV. L. REV. 941 (2002).

Office of Management and Budget, A New Era of Responsibility: Renewing America's Promise (2009), *available at* http://www.gpoaccess.gov/usbudget/fy10/pdf/fy10-newera.pdf.

Office of the Deputy Mayor for Planning and Economic Development, New Communities, The District of Columbia, http://dmped.dc.gov/DC/DMPED/Projects/New+Communities.

OFFICE OF THE DEPUTY PRIME MINISTER, SUSTAINABLE COMMUNITIES: HOMES FOR ALL (2005).

Oliver A. Pollard, III, *Smart Growth: The Promise, Politics, and Potential Pitfalls of Emerging Growth Management Strategies*, 19 VA. ENVTL. L.J. 247 (2000).

Orlando E. Delogu, *Dilemma of Local Land Use Control: Power without Responsibility*, 33 ME. L. REV. 15 (1981).

OSCAR J. MARTINEZ, BORDER BOOM TOWN: CIUDAD JUAREZ SINCE 1848 (1978).

Pat Conaty, Johnston Birchall, Steve Bendle & Rosemary Foggitt, Common Ground —For Mutual Home Ownership (2003), http://www.neweconomics.org/sites/neweconomics.org/files/Common_Ground.pdf.

Patrick Allen, Shared Ownership: A Stepping Stone to Home Ownership: Survey of Local Authority Shared Ownership Schemes (1982).

Paul Cloke, Paul Milbourne & Chris Thomas, *Living Lives in Different Ways? Deprivation, Marginalization and Changing Lifestyles in Rural England*, 22 Transactions of the Inst. of British Geographers 210 (1997).

Paul Cool, Salt Warriors: Insurgency on the Rio Grande (2008).

Peter Dreier, *Federal Housing Subsidies: Who Benefits and Why?*, *in* A Right To Housing: Foundation For A New Social Agenda 111 (2006).

Peter Hetherington, *Tory Localism Isn't Totally Convincing*, Guardian Newspaper, March 31, 2010.

Peter King, Housing Policy Transformed: The Right to Buy and the Desire to Own (2010).

Peter Marcuse, *Housing Policy and the Myth of the Benevolent State*, *in* Critical Perspectives on Housing 255 (Rachel B. Bratt et al., eds, 1986).

Peter Medoff & Holly Sklar, Streets of Hope: The Fall and Rise of an Urban Neighborhood (1994).

Phyliss Craig-Taylor, *Through a Colored Looking Glass: A View of Judicial Partition, Family Land Loss, and Rule Setting*, 78 Wash. U. L.Q. 737, 753 (2000).

President Lyndon B. Johnson, Annual Message to the Congress on the State of the Union (Jan. 8, 1964).

Press Release, DCLG, Local Powers for Councils to Protect Communities and Improve Standards in the Private Rented Sector (Jan. 27, 2010).

Press Release, Federal Reserve Board, Board Issues Final Rule Amending Home Mortgage Provisions of Regulation Z (Truth in Lending) (July 14, 2008).

R. Arnott, *Time for Revisionism on Rent Control?*, 9 J. Econ. Pers. 99 (1995).

R. George, Stack v. Dowden—*Do as We Say and Not as We Do?*, 30 J. Soc. Welfare & Fam. L. 49 (2008).

R. Lee, Stack v. Dowden: *A Sequel*, 124 L. Q. R. 209 (2008).

R. Probert, *Cohabitants and Joint Ownership: The Implications of* Stack v. Dowden, 38 Fam. L. 924 (2007).

R. Probert, *Equality in the Family Home?* Stack v. Dowden, 15 Feminist L. Stud. 341 (2007).

R. Probert, *Family Law and Property Law: Competing Spheres in the Regulation of the Family Home*, *in* New Perspectives on Property Law, Human Rights and the Home (A. Hudson ed., 2003).

Rachel Bratt, Michael Stone & Chester Hartman, *Why a Right to Housing Is Needed and Makes Sense: Editors' Introduction*, *in* A Right To Housing: Foundation For A New Social Agenda 1 (2006).

Rachel Dwyer, *The Limits of the Deconcentration of Poverty: The Spatial Context of the Poor*, 11 City & Community (2012).

RAY FORREST, ALAN MURIE & PETER WILLIAMS, HOME OWNERSHIP: DIFFERENTIATION AND FRAGMENTATION (1990).

Ray Pahl, *Class and Community in English Commuter Villages*, 5 SOCIOLOGIA RURALIS 5 (1965).

Report of the Grand Jury, reprinted in El Paso Times, Nov. 24, 1885.

Republican National Committee, 2008 Republican National Platform (2008), *available at* http://www.gop.com/2008Platform/2008platform.pdf.

Research: Second-Home Market Snapshot, Realtor, May 2009, *available at* www.realtor.org/rmonews_and_commentary_secured/articles/2009/0905.

RESTATEMENT (SECOND) OF PROP.: LANDLORD & TENANT § 5.1 (1977).

Rex E. Gerald, *Aboriginal Use and Occupation by Tigua, Manso, and Suma Indians*, *in* APACHE INDIANS (David Agee Horr ed., 1974).

Richard Best & Mark Shucksmith, *Homes for Rural Communities*, *in* REP. OF THE JOSEPH ROWNTREE FOUND. RURAL HOUSING POL'Y F. 1 (2006).

Richard Briffault, *Home Rule and Local Political Innovation*, 22 J.L. & POL. 1 (2006).

Richard Briffault, *Home Rule for the Twenty-First Century*, 36 URB. LAW. 253 (2004).

Richard Briffault, *Localism and Regionalism*, 48 BUFF. L. REV. 1 (2000).

Richard Briffault, *Our Localism: Part I—The Structure of Local Government Law*, 90 COLUM. L. REV. 1 (1990).

Richard C. Schragger, *The Limits of Localism*, 100 MICH. L. REV. 371 (2002).

Richard C. Stedman, *Places of Escape: Second-home Meanings in Northern Wisconsin, USA*, *in* MULTIPLE DWELLING AND TOURISM: NEGOTIATING PLACE, HOME, AND IDENTITY 129 (Norman McIntyre et al., eds, 2006).

RICHARD GRISWOLD DEL CASTILLO, THE TREATY OF GUADALUPE HIDALGO: A LEGACY OF CONFLICT (1990).

Richard M. Alston, J.R. Kearl & Michael B. Vaughan, *Is There a Consensus Among Economists in the 1990s?*, 82 AM. ECON. REV. 203 (1992).

RICHARD WHITE, "IT'S YOUR MISFORTUNE AND NONE OF MY OWN:" A NEW HISTORY OF THE AMERICAN WEST (1991).

Richard Yarwood, *Parish Councils, Partnership and Governance: The Development of Exceptions' Housing in the Malvern Hills District, England*, 18 J. RURAL STUD. 275 (2002).

RICK HENDRICKS & W.H. TIMMONS, SAN ELIZARIO: SPANISH PRESIDIO TO TEXAS COUNTY SEAT (1998).

Rob Rosenthal & Maria Foscarinis, *Responses to Homelessness: Past Policies, Future Directions, and a Right to Housing*, *in* A RIGHT TO HOUSING: FOUNDATION FOR A NEW SOCIAL AGENDA 319 (2006).

ROBERT HALPERN, REBUILDING THE INNER CITY (1995).

Robert J. Chaskin & Mark L. Joseph, *Building "Community" in Mixed Income Developments: Assumptions, Approaches, and Early Experiences*, 45 URB. AFF. REV. 299 (2010).

Robert Pollack, *A Transaction Cost Approach to Families and Households*, 23 J. Econ. Literature 581 (1965).

Robert Reigel, The Story of the Western Railroads (1926).

Rosemary Hiscock, Ade Kearns, Sally MacIntyre & Anne Ellaway, *Ontological Security and Psycho-Social Benefits from the Home: Qualitative Evidence on Issues of Tenure*, 18 Housing, Theory & Soc'y 50 (2001).

S. Bridge, Jones v. Kernott*: Fairness in the Shared Home—the Forbidden Territory or the Promised Land?*, 74 Conveyancer & Prop. Law. 324 (2010).

San Diego Housing Commission, Choice Communities, http://sdhc.org/Rental-Assistance/Rental-Assistance-Participants/Request-to-Move/Choice-Communities/.

San Francisco Bulletin, Dec. 3, 1883.

Sarah Elwood, *Partnerships and Participation: Reconfiguring Urban Governance in Different State Context*, 25 Urb. Geography 755 (2004).

Sarah Monk & Christine Whitehead, *Conclusions*, *in* Making Housing More Affordable: The Role of Intermediate Tenures 261 (Sarah Monk & Christine Whitehead eds, 2010).

Sarah Monk & Christine Whitehead, *Introduction*, *in* Making Housing More Affordable: The Role of Intermediate Tenures 1 (Sarah Monk & Christine Whitehead eds, 2010).

Second Homes Biggest Threat, Western Morning News (Truro), Feb. 4, 2004.

Shared Ownership: Facts & Figures, Promoting Shared Ownership, http://www.shared-owner.co.uk/_media/static/SO-the_facts.pdf (last visited Feb. 8, 2011).

Sheldon B. Liss, A Century of Disagreement: The Chamizal Conflict, 1864–1964 (1965).

Sheryll Cashin, *Localism, Self-Interest, and the Tyranny of the Favored Quarter: Addressing the Barriers to New Regionalism*, 88 Geo. L.J. 1985 (2009).

Simon Graham, The Role of Shared Ownership in the Future Housing Market 10 (2010), http://www.shared-owner.co.uk/_media/static/May_2010-The_role_of_shared_ownership_in_the_future_housing_market-a_discussion_paper.pdf.

Simon Pinnegar, Vivienne Milligan, Dana Quintal, Bill Randolph, Peter Williams & Judith Yates, Innovative Financing for Home Ownership: The Potential for Shared Equity Initiatives, *in* Australia 34, Australian Housing and Urban Research Institute Position Paper No. 137 (2008), *available at* http://www.ahuri.edu.au/publications/projects/p70394.

Sir William Wade and Christopher Forsyth, Administrative Law (10th ed., 2009).

Stephanie M. Stern, *Residential Protectionism and the Legal Mythology of the Home*, 107 Mich. L. Rev. 132 (2009).

Stephen Steinberg, *The Myth of Concentrated Poverty*, *in* The Integration Debate: Competing Futures for American Cities 213 (Chester Hartman & Gregory Squires eds, 2010).

Steve Wilcox, UK Housing Review 2009/2010 (2010), *available at* http://www.york.ac.uk/res/ukhr/ukhr0910/tables&figures/pdf/09-020a-d.pdf.

Stuart J. Hollander, Saving the Family Cottage (2007).

Susan Bright & Nicholas Hopkins, *Home, Meaning and Identity: Learning from the English Model of Shared Ownership*, 28 Housing, Theory & Soc'y 377 (2011).

Susan Bright, Landlord and Tenant Law in Context (2007).

Susan Clampett-Lundquist, *Moving Over or Moving Up? Short-Term Gains and Losses for Relocated HOPE VI Families*, 7 Cityscape 57 (2004).

Susan J. Popkin et al., A Decade of HOPE VI: Research Findings and Policy Challenges (2004), http://www.urban.org/UploadedPDF/411002_HOPEVI.pdf.

Susan J. Popkin, *The HOPE VI Program: What has Happened to the Residents*, *in* Where are the Poor to Live: Transforming Public Housing Communities (Larry Bennett et al., eds, 2006).

Tenant Services Authority, Existing Tenants Survey 2008 (2008), *available at* http://www.tenantservicesauthority.org/upload/pdf/ETS_technical_report.pdf.

Terrance Sandalow, *The Limits of Municipal Power Under Home Rule- A Role for the Courts*, 48 Minn. L. Rev. 643 (1964).

The Declaration of Independence para. 1 (US 1776).

The El Paso Mission Trail, *available at* http://www.epcounty.com/history/missiontrail.htm.

The Laws of Texas, 1822–1897 (H.P.N. Gammel ed., 1898).

The Lone Star, April 8, 1882.

The Lone Star, Dec. 5, 1883.

The Lone Star, Feb. 1, 1882.

The Lone Star, March 4, 1882.

The Lone Star, Nov. 12, 1884.

The Lone Star, Nov. 7, 1883.

The Lone Star, Nov. 2, 1881.

The Lone Star, Oct. 29, 1881.

The Royal Borough of Kensington and Chelsea, *Affordable Home Ownership*, *available at* http://www.rbkc.gov.uk/housing/findingahome/affordablehomeownership.aspx (last visited Jan., 31 2011).

Thomas A. Green, *Folk History and Cultural Reorganization: A Tigua Example*, 89 J. Am. Folklore (1976).

Tim Cresswell, In Place/Out of Place: Geography, Ideology, and Transgression (1993).

Tim Iglesias, *Our Pluralist Housing Ethics and the Struggle for Affordability*, 42 Wake Forest L. Rev. 511 (2007).

Tim O'Riordan & Chris Church, *Synthesis and Context*, *in* Globalism, Localism & Identity (Tim O'Riordan ed., 2001).

Tony Crook & Christine Whitehead, *Intermediate Housing and the Planning System*, *in* Making Housing More Affordable: The Role of Intermediate Tenures 101 (Sarah Monk & Christine Whitehead eds, 2010).

TROWERS & HAMLINS LLP, SHARED OWNERSHIP TRUSTS: DELIVERING LOW COST HOME OWNERSHIP (2007), http://www.trowers.com/attachments/published/1615/Shared%20ownership%20trusts%20delivering%20low%20cost%20home%20ownership.pdf.

US Bureau of the Census, Report on the Population of the United States, Eleventh Census, 1890 (1895).

US CENSUS BUREAU, HOUSING CHARACTERISTICS: 2000 5 (2001).

US CENSUS BUREAU, U.S. CENSUS (2010).

US Department of Housing and Urban Development & US Department of Commerce, American Housing Survey for the United States: 2007 (2008).

US Department of Housing and Urban Development, HUD Strategic Plan FY 2010–2015 (2010), *available at* http://portal.hud.gov/hudportal/HUD?src=/program_offices/cfo/stratplan.

US Federal Housing Administration, Third Annual Report of the Federal Housing Administration (1937).

US Nat'l Advisory Comm'n on Civil Disorders, Report of the National Advisory Commission on Civil Disorders (1968).

Univ. Tex., Handbook of Texas Online, s.v. "James Price Hague," *available at* http://www.tsha.utexas.edu/handbook/ online/articles/HH/fhaff.html.

Universal Declaration of Human Rights, art. 25, § 1, G.A. Res. 217A, U.N. GAOR, 3d Sess., 1st plen. mtg., U.N. Doc. A/810 (Dec. 12, 1948).

Victoria Jenkins, *Local Government Reform and Sustainable Development in Wales and Ireland*, ENVT'L. L. REV. 21, 25 (2009).

Vivien Lowndes & Helen Sullivan, *How Low Can You Go? Rationales and Challenges for Neighbourhood Governance*, 86 PUB. ADMIN. 53 (2008).

W. Swadling, *The Common Intention Constructive Trust in the House of Lords: An Opportunity Missed*, 123 LAW Q. REV. 511 (2007).

W.H. TIMMONS, EL PASO: A BORDERLANDS HISTORY (1990).

WILLIAM CRONON, NATURE'S METROPOLIS: CHICAGO AND THE GREAT WEST (1994).

WILLIAM DEVERELL, WHITEWASHED ADOBE: THE RISE OF LOS ANGELES AND THE REMAKING OF ITS MEXICAN PAST (2005).

WILLIAM G. THOMAS, LAWYERING FOR THE RAILROAD: BUSINESS, LAW, AND POWER IN THE NEW SOUTH (1999).

WILLIAM JULIUS WILSON, MORE THAN JUST RACE: BEING BLACK AND POOR IN THE INNER CITY (2009).

WILLIAM JULIUS WILSON, THE TRULY DISADVANTAGED: THE INNER CITY, THE UNDERCLASS, AND PUBLIC POLICY (1987).

William M. Rohe & Michael A. Stegman, *The Effects of Homeownership on the Self-Esteem, Perceived Control and Life Satisfaction of Low-Income People*, 60 J. AM. PLAN. ASS'N 173 (1994).

Cases

Abbott v. Abbott, [2007] UKPC 53 (P.C.) at 4 (Baroness Hale).
Adekunle v. Richie, [2007] EW Misc 5.
Albrecht v. Clifford, 767 N.E.2d 42 (Mass. 2002).
Barnes v. Sheffield CC, [1995] 27 H.L.R. 719 (UK).
Berman v. Parker, 348 US 26 (1954).
Birmingham Corp. v. MHLG, [1964] 1 Q.B. 178; (1963) 3 All E.R. 688 (UK).
Burns v. Burns, [1984] Ch. 317 (C.A.).
Caceci v. Di Canio Const. Corp., 526 N.E.2d 266 (NY 1988).
Caradon v. Paton, [2001] 33 H.L.R. 34 [6] (UK).
Carlton v. Goodman, [2002] 2 FLR 259, ¶ 44 (Ward LJ).
Crossley v. Crossley, [2005] EWCA Civ. 1581, ¶ 5 (Sir Peter Gibson).
Drake v. Whipp, [1996] 1 FLR 826, 827 (Peter Gibson LJ).
Dyer v. Dyer, [1788] 2 Cox Eq Cas 92.
Entick v. Carrington, [1795]19 State Trials 1029.
Fowler v. Barron, [2008] EWCA Civ 377 (CA).
Frost (Inspector of Taxes) v. Feltham, [1981] 1 W.L.R. 452 (UK).
Gautreaux v. Chicago Housing Authority, 296 F. Supp. 907 (ND Ill. 1969).
Gissing v. Gissing, [1971] A.C. 886 (HL) (appeal taken from Eng.).
Goodman v. Gallant, [1986] Fam 106.
Grant v. Edwards, [1986] Ch. 638 (CA) 646 (Nourse LJ).
Hammond v. Mitchell, [1992] 2 All ER 109, 112 (Waite J).
Harwood v. Harwood, [1991] 2 FLR 274 (CA).
Hills v. Gautreaux, 425 US 284 (2006).
Hodgson v. Marks, [1971] 2 WLR 1263 (CA).
Holman v. Howes, [2007] EWCA (Civ) 877.
Huntingford v. Hobbs, [1993] 1 FLR 736 (CA).
James v. Thomas, [2007] EWCA (Civ) 1212 (CA).
Javins v. First National Realty Corp., 428 F.2d 1071 (D.C. Cir. 1970).
Jones v. Kernott, [2009] EWHC 1713.
Jones v. Kernott, [2010] EWCA (Civ) 578.
Laskar v. Laskar, [2008] EWCA (Civ) 347.
Le Foe v. Le Foe, [2001] 2 FLR 970.
Lipan Apache Tribe v. United States, 180 Ct. Cl. 487 (1967).
Lloyd's Bank v. Rosset, [1991] 1 A.C. 107 (HL)
Lyles v. State, 41 Tex. 172 (1874).
McDonald v. Mianecki, 398 A.2d 1283 (NJ 1979).
McKenzie v. McKenzie, [2003] All ER (D) 155.
Midland Bank v. Cooke, [1995] 2 FLR 915.
Midland Bank v. Cooke, [1995] 4 All ER 562 (CA).
Morris v. Morris, [2008] EWCA 257 (CA).
Oxley v. Hiscock, [2004] EWCA Civ. 546 (CA).
Pettitt v. Pettitt, [1970] A.C. 777 (HL) (appeal taken from Eng.).

R (on the application of Hossack) v. Kettering BC, [2003] 2 P & CR 34 (UK).
Rogers v. Islington LBC, [2000] 32 H.L.R. 138 (UK) (Per Nourse LJ).
Sec'y of State for Env't., Transp. and Regions v. Waltham Forest LBC, [2002] EWCA (Civ) 330 (Eng.).
Simmons v. Pizzey, [1979] A.C. 37 (UK).
Skerritts of Nottingham, Ltd. v. Sec'y of State, [2001] Q.B. 59 (Walker LJ) (UK).
Springette v. Defoe, [1992] 2 FLR 388 (CA).
Stack v. Dowden, [2005] EWCA (Civ) 857 (CA), ¶ 75 (Carnwath LJ).
Stack v. Dowden, [2007] UKHL 17 (HL).
Stevens v. Galveston, Harrisburg & San Antonio Ry. Co., 169 S.W. 644, 648 (1914 Tex. App.).
Thorner v. Major, [2009] UKHL 18 (HL).
UKPC 11 (PC) and Chartbrook Ltd v. Persimmon Homes Ltd., [2009] UKHL 38 (HL).
Vill. of Arlington Heights v. Metro. Hous. Dev. Corp., 429 US. 252 (1977).
Walker v. Hall, [1984] FLR 126 (CA).
Warth v. Seldin, 422 US 490 (1975).
Webster v. Webster, [2008] EWHC 31 (HC).
Yeoman Row v. Cobbe, [2008] UKHL 55 (HL).

Reports

[2008] Landlord & Tenant Reports 31 (Eng.).
Department of Environment, Food and Rural Affairs, Affordable Rural Housing Commission: Final Report (2006).
Conservative Party, *Control Shift Returning Power to Local Communities: Responsibility Agenda Policy*, Green Paper No. 9, 12 (2010).
DCLG, *Delivering Affordable Housing* [63] (2006).
DCLG, *Evidence Gathering—Housing in Multiple Occupation and Possible Planning Responses Final Report* (2008).
DCLG, *Formative Evaluation of the Take-Up and Implementation of the Well Being*
Power—Annual Report 2006 (2006).
DCLG, *Planning Policy Statement 3: Housing* (2010).
Matthew Taylor, Living Working Countryside: The Taylor Review of Rural Economy and Affordable Housing (2008).
NALC, *National Association of Local Councils, Annual Report 2009–2010* (2010).
ODPM, *Formative Evaluation of the Take-Up and Implementation of the Well Being Power, 2003–2006—Baseline Report* (2005).
The Law Commission Report No 181, Transfer of Land: Trusts of Land (1989).
US Counsel on Environmental Quality, *The Quiet Revolution in Land Use Control* (1971).

Statutes and Legislative Materials

12 U.S.C.A. § 1464(c) (West 2010).
12 U.S.C.A. § 1735(f)-(7) (West 2010).
12 U.S.C.A. § 1828 (West 2010).
12 U.S.C.A. § 1843 (West 2010).
12 U.S.C.A. § 371 (West 2010).
134 Cong. Rec. H4,468–02 (June 20, 1988).
140 Cong. Rec. S11,316–17 (April 11, 1994).
15 U.S.C.A. § 1602(aa) (West 2010).
15 U.S.C.A. § 1602(f) (West 2010).
15 U.S.C.A. § 1602(h) (West 2010).
15 U.S.C.A. § 1602(w) (West 2010).
15 U.S.C.A. § 1639(c)-(l) (West 2010).
15 U.S.C.A. § 45 (West 2010).
15 U.S.C.A. § 57a(f) (West 2010).
272 PARL. DEB., H.C. (6th ser.) (1996) 3–4W (UK).
42 U.S.C.A § 1437f (West 2010).
42 U.S.C.A § 1437v (West 2010).
42 U.S.C.A § 1441 (West 2010).
42 U.S.C.A §§ 3601–3619 (West 2010).
976 PARL. DEB., H.C. (6th ser.) (1980) 1445 (UK) (Michael Heseltine, Conservative Secretary of State for the Environment).
Administration of Justice Act, 1970, c.31, §36 (Eng.).
Civil Partnership Act 2004 sched.
Civil Partnership and Certain Rights and Obligations of Cohabitants (Ireland) Act 2010.
Council of Europe, *European Charter of Local Self-Government,* 1985, art. 4.3.
Cranston-Gonzalez National Affordable Housing Act, Pub. L. No. 101–625, § 102, 104 Stat. 4079 (1990).
D.C. Code Ann. § 6–226 (2011).
Demonstration Cities and Metropolitan Development Act of 1966, Pub. L. No. 89–754, 80 Stat. 1255 (1966).
Dodd-Frank Wall Street Reform and Consumer Protection Act, Pub. L. No. 111–203, § 1411 (2010).
Economic Opportunity Act of 1964, Pub. L. No. 88–452, § 202, 78 Stat. 508, 516 (1964).
Economic Opportunity Amendments of 1972, Pub. L. No. 92–424, § 712, 86 Stat. 688 (1972).
Family Law (Scotland) Act 2006.
Federal Trade Commission Act Amendments of 1994, Pub. L. No. 103–312, § 9, 108 Stat. 1691 (1994) (codified as amended at 15 U.S.C.A. § 45(n) (West 2010)).
Federal-Aid Highway Act of 1956, Pub. L. No. 84–627, 70 Stat. 374 (1956).

H.R. Rep. No. 102–330 (1991).
H.R. Rep. No. 103–652 (1994) (Conf. Rep.).
Home Equity Loan Consumer Protection Act of 1988, Pub. L. No. 100–709, §§ 2, 3 (1988).
House of Commons Standing Committee on Bills, Home Energy Conservation Bill, 2002, col. 106.
Housing (Right to Buy) (Limits on Discount) (Amendment) Order SI 2003/498.
Housing Act 1988 sched. 2
Housing Act, 1980, c. 51, (Eng.).
Housing Act, 1985, c. 68, § 156A (Eng.) (introduced by the Housing Act, 2004, c. 34 (Eng.).
Housing Act, 1988, c. 50, § 129 (Eng.).
Housing and Planning Act, 1986, c. 63 §2(2)(b) (Eng.).
Housing and Regeneration Act, 2008, c.17, §79(1).
Law Commission's Work Leading to the Trusts of Land and Appointment of Trustees Act, 1996, c. 47 (Eng.).
Law of Property Act 1925 § 53(1)(b).
Leasehold Reform Act, 1967, c. 88 sched. 4A, 4A (Eng.) (inserted by the Housing and Regeneration Act, 2008 c. 17) and the Housing (Right to Enfranchise) (Designated Protected Areas) (England) Order 2009/2098.
Localism Bill, 2010–11, H.C. Bill [126] cl. 149 (Eng.).
Matrimonial Causes Act 1973 Part II.
Montgomery County, Md., Code § 25A–1 (2006).
Moving to Opportunity for Fair Housing, Pub. L. No. 103–120, § 3, 107 Stat. 1148 (1993) (codified at 42 U.S.C. §§ 1437f (2006)).
Pub. L. No. 102–242, § 304, 105 Stat. 2354 (1991) (current version at 12 U.S.C.A. § 1828(o) (West 2010)).
Pub. L. No. 103–325, § 152, 108 Stat. 2160 (current version at 15 U.S.C.A. § 1639 (West 2010)).
Pub. L. No. 93–533, § 2–10, 88 Stat. 1724 (1974).
Pub. L. No. 94–205, § 7, 89 Stat. 1157 (1975).
Pub. L. No. 97–320, § 322, 96 Stat. 1469 (1982).
Pub. L. No. 97–320, § 403(a), 96 Stat. 1510 (1982).
Pub. L. No. 97–320, § 804, 96 Stat. 1469 (1982) (current version at 12 U.S.C.A. § 3803 (West 2010)).
Quality Housing and Work Responsibility Act of 1998, Pub L. No. 105–276, 112 Stat. 2461, 2473–74 (1998) (codified at 42 U.S.C. § 1437v (2006)).
S. Rep. No. 103–130 (1993).
S. Rep. No. 103–169 (1993).
S. Rep. No. 111–176 (2010).
S. Rep. No. 93–866 (1974).
S. Rep. No. 96–368 (1979).
S. Rep. No. 97–536 (1982).
S. Rep. No. 97–641 (1982) (Conf. Rep.).

Treaty of Guadalupe Hidalgo, Feb. 2, 1848, US-Mex., art. VIII, 9 Stat. 922.
Trusts of Land and Appointment of Trustees Act 1996.
United States Statutes at Large, 16:673–679 (1871).

Administrative and Executive Material

Interagency Guidance on Non-traditional Mortgage Product Risks, 71 Fed. Reg. 58,609 (Oct. 4, 2006) (final guidance).
Interagency Guidance on Non-traditional Mortgage Products, 70 Fed. Reg. 77,249 (Dec. 29, 2005) (proposed guidance).
Limitation on Loans to One Borrower, 48 Fed. Reg. 23,032 (May 23, 1983).
Office of the Deputy Prime Minister, Consultation Paper: HomeBuy—Expanding the Opportunity to Own (2005), *available at* http://www.communities.gov.uk/documents/housing/pdf/142115.pdf.
Office of the Deputy Prime Minister, Consultation Paper: HomeBuy—Expanding the Opportunity to Own: Final Regulatory Impact Assessment (2005), *available at* http://www.communities.gov.uk/documents/housing/pdf/142385.pdf.
Office of the Deputy Prime Minister, Sustainable Communities: Building for the Future (2003), *available at* http://www.communities.gov.uk/documents/communities/pdf/146289.pdf.
Office of Thrift Supervision, 61 Fed. Reg. 50,951 (Sept. 30, 1996).
Real Estate Lending by National Banks, 48 Fed. Reg. 40,698 (Sept. 9, 1983).
Statement on Subprime Lending, 72 Fed. Reg. 37,569 (July 10, 2007) (final guidance).
Truth in Lending, 66 Fed. Reg. 65,604 (Dec. 20, 2001).
Truth in Lending, 73 Fed. Reg. 1,672 (Jan. 9, 2008) (proposed rule).
Truth in Lending, 73 Fed. Reg. 44,522 (July 30, 2008).
Unfair or Deceptive Acts or Practices, 72 Fed. Reg. 43,570 (Aug. 6, 2007).

Index

For Product Safety Concerns and Information please contact our EU representative GPSR@taylorandfrancis.com
Taylor & Francis Verlag GmbH, Kaufingerstraße 24, 80331 München, Germany

www.ingramcontent.com/pod-product-compliance
Ingram Content Group UK Ltd.
Pitfield, Milton Keynes, MK11 3LW, UK
UKHW021301190926
475701UK00009B/498
9781138250215